EZEKIEL'S HIERARCHICAL WORLD

Society of Biblical Literature

Symposium Series

Christopher R. Matthews, Editor

Number 31

EZEKIEL'S HIERARCHICAL WORLD
Wrestling with a
Tiered Reality

edited by
Stephen L. Cook and Corrine L. Patton

EZEKIEL'S HIERARCHICAL WORLD
Wrestling with a Tiered Reality

edited by
Stephen L. Cook and Corrine L. Patton

Society of Biblical Literature
Atlanta

EZEKIEL'S HIERARCHICAL WORLD

Wrestling with a
Tiered Reality

Copyright © 2004 by the Society of Biblical Literature

All rights reserved. No part of this work may be reproduced or transmitted in any form or by any means, electronic or mechanical, including photocopying and recording, or by means of any information storage or retrieval system, except as may be expressly permitted by the 1976 Copyright Act or in writing from the publisher. Requests for permission should be addressed in writing to the Rights and Permissions Office, Society of Biblical Literature, 825 Houston Mill Road, Atlanta, GA 30333-0399, USA.

Cover photo of Pesher Habakkuk, Qumran, courtesy of the D. Samuel and Jeane H. Gottesman Center for Biblical Manuscripts, The Israel Museum, Jerusalem.

Library of Congress Cataloging-in-Publication Data

Ezekiel's hierarchical world: wrestling with a tiered reality / edited by Stephen L. Cook and Corrine L. Patton.
    p.   cm.—(Society of Biblical Literature symposium series ; no. 31)
  Includes bibliographical references and indexes.
  ISBN 1-58983-136-5 (paper binding : alk. paper)
  1. Bible. O.T. Ezekiel—Criticism, interpretation, etc. 2. Social stratification—Biblical teaching. 3. Hierarchies—Biblical teaching. 4. Priests, Jewish. I. Cook, Stephen L., 1962– II. Patton, Corrine, 1958– III. Series: Symposium series (Society of Biblical Literature) ; no. 31.
  BS1545.6.S59E94 2004b
  224'.406—dc22   2004020862

12 11 10 09 08 07 06 05 04   5 4 3 2 1

Printed in the United States of America on acid-free, recycled paper conforming to ANSI/NISO Z39.48-1992 (R1997) and ISO 9706:1994 standards for paper permanence.

Table of Contents

Preface vii

Contributors ix

Abbreviations xi

Introduction: Hierarchical Thinking and Theology in Ezekiel's Book
   Stephen L. Cook and Corrine L. Patton 1

Essays

Priesthood in Exile according to the Book of Ezekiel
   Friedrich Fechter 27

Putting Priests in Their Place: Ezekiel's Contribution to the History
of the Old Testament Priesthood
   Iain M. Duguid 43

A Priest Out of Place: Reconsidering Ezekiel's Role
in the History of the Israelite Priesthood
   Baruch J. Schwartz 61

Priest, Prophet, and Exile: Ezekiel as a Literary Construct
   Corrine L. Patton 73

God's Land and Mine: Creation as Property in the Book of Ezekiel
   Julie Galambush 91

From Harshness to Hope: The Implications for Earth
of Hierarchy in Ezekiel
   Keith Carley 109

The Silence of the Lands: The Ecojustice Implications
of Ezekiel's Judgment Oracles
Norman Habel 127

Ezekiel in Abu Ghraib: Rereading Ezekiel 16:37–39
in the Context of Imperial Conquest
Daniel L. Smith-Christopher 141

'With a Mighty Hand and an Outstretched Arm':
The Prophet and the Torah in Ezekiel 20
Risa Levitt Kohn 159

Creation and Hierarchy in Ezekiel:
Methodological Perspectives and Theological Prospects
David L. Petersen 169

Cosmos, *Kabod*, and Cherub:
Ontological and Epistemological Hierarchy in Ezekiel
Stephen L. Cook 179

Proverb Performance and Transgenerational Retribution in Ezekiel 18
Katheryn Pfisterer Darr 199

Responses

In Search of Theological Meaning:
Ezekiel Scholarship at the Turn of the Millennium
Daniel I. Block 227

Contemporary Studies of Ezekiel: A New Tide Rising
Steven Shawn Tuell 241

Selected Bibliography 255

Index of Modern Authors 261

Index of Primary Sources 267

Subject Index 283

Preface

This book bears witness to the current vitality of Ezekiel studies, particularly as evinced in the continuing work of the Seminar on Theological Perspectives on the Book of Ezekiel, which meets at each SBL Annual Meeting. Corrine L. Patton and Dexter E. Callender Jr. currently chair the seminar, which has continued to be a place of innovation and discovery, lively scholarly interchange, and warm collegiality since it arose out of the Ezekiel Consultation of the SBL chaired by Katheryn Pfisterer Darr from 1993 to 1995. The editors express their gratitude to the seminar for entrusting them with the honor and responsibility of preparing this volume.

This focus of the volume, Ezekiel's hierarchical thinking, almost forced itself upon us. Even as the chosen topics of our seminar shifted in recent sessions from creation, to priesthood, to land, a consistent, vocal concern has been Ezekiel's unusually pronounced hierarchical dimensions. Many contemporary readers experience these dimensions as oppressive, and some have suggested that Ezekiel no longer be read (presumably as a canonical book, authoritative for religious communities). The need is pressing, we realized through this repeat experience, to address the meaning and import of Ezekiel's hierarchical theology in a probing, wide-ranging, and balanced manner. This is the challenge that the editors posed to those we invited to contribute to this collection.

Twelve essayists and two respondents accepted the challenge of participating in this project. The considerable diversity of backgrounds, stances, methods, and perspectives they represent means that this volume has no single thesis or pointed argument. What it offers, rather, is a powerful contemporary sampling of energetic, skillful studies of Ezekiel that directly or indirectly illuminate the ancient and modern meanings and implications of hierarchy in that difficult and engrossing book of Scripture.

Many people provided us with assistance and support as we labored over several years to produce this volume. Chris Matthews, series editor, provided solid advice and feedback as we first conceived this collection and unstinting support as we forged it into a book. Bob Buller, Editorial Director at the SBL, worked tirelessly with us, shepherding the project through its multiple stages of production.

Stephen would like gratefully to acknowledge the support of his institution, Virginia Theological Seminary, and especially the help during his recent sabbatical of Karen Madigan, public services librarian at the school's Bishop Payne Library, Dr. Mitzi J. Budde, head librarian. Also, Kevin Seaver, M.Div., a former student of Stephen's and recent graduate of the seminary, assisted with the work of bibliographies and indexes.

Corrine would like to thank her institution, the University of St. Thomas, especially the Aquinas Foundation, which provided funding to her for a course release, and the department of information technology for all of its technical support. In addition, this volume would never have been a possibility without the hard work of the co-chairs and advisory board of the seminar under whose sponsorship many of these papers were first presented; special mention goes to John Strong, John Kutsko, and Maggie Odell, who provided their expert advice in the earliest stages of this project.

STEPHEN L. COOK, *Virginia Theological Seminary*
CORRINE L. PATTON, *University of St. Thomas*
EDITORS

Contributors

Daniel I. Block
John R. Sampey Professor of Old Testament Interpretation
Southern Baptist Theological Seminary
Louisville, Kentucky

Keith Carley
Lecturer in First Testament Studies
St. John's College
Auckland, New Zealand

Stephen L. Cook
Associate Professor of Old Testament
Virginia Theological Seminary
Alexandria, Virginia

Katheryn Pfisterer Darr
Associate Professor of Hebrew Bible
Boston University School of Theology
Boston, Massachusetts

Iain M. Duguid
Associate Professor of Old Testament
Westminster Theological Seminary
Escondido, California

Friedrich Fechter
Lecturer in Old Testament
Friedrich-Alexander Universität
Erlangen-Nürnberg, Germany

Julie Galambush
Associate Professor of Religious Studies
The College of William and Mary
Williamsburg, Virginia

Norman C. Habel
Professorial Fellow
Flinders University
Bellevue Heights, Australia

Risa Levitt Kohn
Associate Professor of Religious Studies
San Diego State University
San Diego, California

Corrine L. Patton
Associate Professor of Theology
University of St. Thomas
St. Paul, Minnesota

David L. Petersen
Professor of Old Testament
Candler School of Theology, Emory University
Atlanta, Georgia

Baruch J. Schwartz
Senior Lecturer of Bible
Hebrew University
Jerusalem, Israel

Daniel L. Smith-Christopher
Professor of Theological Studies
Loyola Marymount University
Los Angeles, California

Steven S. Tuell
Associate Professor and Chair of Religious Studies
Randolph-Macon College
Ashland, Virginia

Abbreviations

AB	Anchor Bible
ABD	*Anchor Bible Dictionary.* Edited by D. N. Freedman. 6 vols. New York, 1992
AJSL	*American Journal of Semitic Languages and Literatures*
AnBib	Analecta biblica
ANEP	*The Ancient Near East in Pictures Relating to the Old Testament.* Edited by J. B. Pritchard. Princeton, 1954
ANET	*Ancient Near Eastern Texts Relating to the Old Testament.* Edited by J. B. Pritchard. 3d ed. Princeton, 1969
ATD	Das Alte Testament Deutsch
BBB	Bonner biblische Beiträge
BETL	Bibliotheca ephemeridum theologicarum lovaniensium
BHT	Beiträge zur historischen Theologie
Bib	*Biblica*
BibInt	Biblical Interpretation
BibInt	*Biblical Interpretation*
BJRL	Bulletin of the John Rylands University Library of Manchester
BKAT	Biblischer Kommentar, Altes Testament. Edited by M. Noth and H. W. Wolff
BT	*The Bible Translator*
BZAW	Beihefte zur Zeitschrift für die alttestamentliche Wissenschaft
CBQ	*Catholic Biblical Quarterly*
CBQMS	Catholic Biblical Quarterly Monograph Series
Colloq	*Colloquium*
ConBOT	Coniectanea biblica: Old Testament Series
DDD	*Dictionary of Deities and Demons in the Bible.* Edited by K. van der Toorn, B. Becking, and P. W. van der Horst. Leiden, 1995
ETL	*Ephemerides theologicae lovanienses*
ExpTim	*Expository Times*
FAT	Forschungen zum Alten Testament
FB	Forschung zur Bibel
FCB	Feminist Companion to the Bible

FOTL	Forms of the Old Testament Literature
FRLANT	Forschungen zur Religion und Literatur des Alten und Neuen Testaments
HAR	*Hebrew Annual Review*
HeyJ	*Heythrop Journal*
HSM	Harvard Semitic Monographs
HSS	Harvard Semitic Studies
HUCA	*Hebrew Union College Annual*
IBC	Interpretation: A Bible Commentary for Teaching and Preaching
ICC	International Critical Commentary
IDBSup	*Interpreter's Dictionary of the Bible: Supplementary Volume.* Edited by K. Crim. Nashville, 1976
Int	*Interpretation*
IRT	Issues in Religion and Theology
ITC	International Theological Commentary
JANESCU	*Journal of the Ancient Near Eastern Society of Columbia University*
JBL	*Journal of Biblical Literature*
JFSR	*Journal of Feminist Studies in Religion*
JSOT	*Journal for the Study of the Old Testament*
JSOTSup	Journal for the Study of the Old Testament: Supplement Series
LD	Lectio divina
NCB	New Century Bible
NIB	*The New Interpreter's Bible*
NICOT	New International Commentary on the Old Testament
OBO	Orbis biblicus et orientalis
OBT	Overtures to Biblical Theology
Or	*Orientalia* (NS)
OTL	Old Testament Library
OtSt	*Oudtestamentische Studiën*
PAAJR	Proceedings of the American Academy of Jewish Research
RB	Revue biblique
SBL	Society of Biblical Literature
SBLDS	Society of Biblical Literature Dissertation Series
SBLSP	Society of Biblical Literature Seminar Papers
SBLSymS	Society of Biblical Literature Symposium Series
SBT	Studies in Biblical Theology
SHR	Studies in the History of Religions (supplement to *Numen*)
SO	Symbolae osloenses
TDOT	*Theological Dictionary of the Old Testament.* Edited by G. J. Botterweck and H. Ringgren. Translated by J. T. Willis, G. W. Bromiley, and D. E. Green. 8 vols. Grand Rapids, 1974–

TLOT	*Theological Lexicon of the Old Testament.* Edited by E. Jenni, with assistance from C. Westermann. Translated by M. E. Biddle. 3 vols. Peabody, Mass., 1997
TWOT	*Theological Wordbook of the Old Testament.* Edited by R. L. Harris and G. L. Archer Jr. 2 vols. Chicago, 1980
TynBul	*Tyndale Bulletin*
TZ	*Theologische Zeitschrift*
VT	*Vetus Testamentum*
VTSup	Supplements to Vetus Testamentum
WBC	Word Biblical Commentary
WW	*Word and World*
ZAW	*Zeitschrift für die alttestamentliche Wissenschaft*

Introduction: Hierarchical Thinking and Theology in Ezekiel's Book

Stephen L. Cook and Corrine L. Patton

I. Defining Hierarchical Thinking and Theology

The noun *hierarch* (ἱεράρχης) in Greek meant originally a "sacred" (ἱερός) "leader" (ἀρχός), a steward or president of sacred rites, for example, a high priest. From this noun derived the term *hierarchy* (Gk. ἱεραρχία), meaning the power or rule of a chief prelate or archbishop. Since such a leader ranks highest in an order of officials, hierarchy came to indicate not only a system with a central head but also one with divisions or levels of authority.

In accord with its Greek etymological roots involving "sacred" persons or leaders, the term hierarchy in the English language originally denoted ranks of angels or of church officials. In speculative writings on the nature of the divine realm, heavenly beings have long appeared organized in tiers, with seraphim at the top, cherubim under them, and then archangels and angels at lower levels of authority. Within the human realm, the term hierarchy has also long been associated with the tiered polity of organizations such as the Catholic Church, which assert clearly defined levels of sacred authority.[1]

These original usages of our term are relevant for this essay, as we shall see; Ezekiel asserts cosmic and natural-world hierarchies, but levels of sacred authority are predominant. The book understands both heavenly beings (the cherubim) and human priests (the Zadokites) to occupy special spheres of holiness and authority close to God's presence. They act as boundary-holders and mediums of God's holy presence to people located at farther and safer distances from the sacred center.

With time, the term hierarchy has shed its tight association with sacred realities. Now, in common usage, it refers to any organization or classification of people or things into orders or ranks, each constitutive of, or subordinate to, the one above

---

1. See, for example, *Lumen Gentium,* a document of Vatican Council II, 1964, ch. 3 (A. Flannery, ed., *Vatican Council II,* vol. 1, *The Conciliar and Postconciliar Documents* [Northport, N.Y.: Costello; Dublin: Dominican, 1998]).

2. The various levels of a hierarchy may relate to each other in a great variety of ways, including progressive generation, levels of organization, and lines of authority or spiritual communion.

it.² Metaphors such as concentric circles, the rungs of a stepladder, or Russian dolls packed inside one another help us picture the nature of hierarchies as series of nested and enfolded phenomena. Hierarchy may entail a line of command, and often this "line" is experienced as vertical, stretching from authorities who are "higher" to subordinates who are "lower." Social standing often involves a vertical hierarchy, based, however, more on lines of wealth and status than of political power. Another common type of hierarchy unfolds in terms of degrees of complexity or wholeness. In biology, the cell has a relationship to the body that is hierarchical and participatory without being based on domination. In church ecclesiology, the metaphor of the church as the "body" of Christ implies that elements within the church serve the needs of the whole organism.³ While the book of Ezekiel clearly contains images of divine and human hierarchy, the hermeneutical challenge remains: how do we appropriate those images within the contemporary debates over the meaning and function of hierarchy within church and synagogue?

From the time of Aristotle in the fourth century B.C.E., we have known that hierarchy is not merely an invention for organizing human spheres, such as politics and religion, but a foundational part of nature. Indeed, recent scientific and philosophical advances have shown hierarchy to be even more fundamental to existence than previously realized. Among others, Ken Wilber has recently noted how reality in all of its dimensions exhibits nested orders of being. "Virtually all growth processes, from matter to life to mind, occur via natural . . . orders of increasing holism and wholeness," he writes.⁴ These orders of increasing wholeness and inclusion inescapably involve rankings.

Cyril Stanley Smith has demonstrated the foundational role of structural hierarchy in areas of experience as diverse as science, art, and society. He writes, "Structure . . . has much of the character of a universal metaphor. A field of view comprising relatively clear interrelations between parts in the middle and progressively more indistinct but nevertheless essential interactions toward the fringes can be applied at almost any level in almost any medium."⁵

Despite its foundational presence in such areas as nature and art, many people nowadays view hierarchy suspiciously, or even negatively; at least this is true for sig-

---

3. For two recent discussions of different ways to understand ecclesiastical hierarchy, see Terence L. Nichols, *That All May Be One: Hierarchy and Participation in the Church* (Collegeville, Minn.: Liturgical Press, 1997), and J. Michael Byron, "*Communio* as the Context for Memory: On the Universal-Local Church Relationship," in *Revelation and the Church: Vatican II in the Twenty-first Century* (ed. R. A. Lucker and W. C. McDonough; Maryknoll, N.Y.: Orbis, 2003), 67–85.

4. Ken Wilber, *A Brief History of Everything* (Boston: Shambhala, 1996), 28. We are indebted to Keith Carley for suggesting this reference. Cf. Arthur Peacocke's statement: "The expansion of our scientific knowledge of the natural world has more and more shown it to consist of a hierarchy of systems in levels of organization, each successive member of which is a whole constituted of parts" (*Theology for a Scientific Age: Being and Becoming—Natural and Divine* [Oxford: Blackwell, 1990], 22).

5. Cyril Stanley Smith, *A Search for Structure: Selected Essays on Science, Art, and History* (Cambridge, Mass.: MIT Press, 1981), 389.

nificant liberal circles of our world's northern hemisphere. Feminist theologians often equate hierarchy with patriarchy because of women's experience of the unjust use of power often wielded by those who claimed a natural or divinely sanctioned right to subjugate women. Theologians influenced by Marxism hope for a world liberated from unjust human oppressions.[6] Currently, mention of hierarchy often brings to mind either a rigid system of control or the stifling domination of bosses and masters over underlings and slaves. It is commonly overlooked that hierarchies may equally involve relatively healthy and flexible structural groupings. Many of the tiered structures of our world facilitate the flow of communication and power both up and down the system, in a manner benefiting both the smaller parts and the larger aggregates.[7]

Clear historical precedents paved the way for the current, widely held presumption that hierarchy is an odious phenomenon. With the rise of modern times, the traditional, perduring hierarchies of Western society began to look increasingly obnoxious because they functioned to buttress manifestly arbitrary inequalities of power and wealth. By the seventeenth century, influential thinkers were rebelling against the wisdom of the past, including Aristotle's notion that natural, permanent differences separated human beings into various classes.[8] By the eighteenth and nineteenth centuries, powerful ideas of change and progress in history challenged the notion that static, authoritarian social orders were the permanent will of God. Fealty, order, and obedience were fading fast as people's paramount values.

Already in 1651, Thomas Hobbes in *Leviathan* characterized Aristotle's assertions about fixed tiers of human nature as baseless and prideful. Humanly enacted laws—not naturally occurring categories and tiers of human quality—are what bring about inequity between people, Hobbes countered. All people naturally hold

---

6. This stance is characteristic of many liberation theologians, including biblical scholars such as George E. Mendenhall and Norman K. Gottwald, for whom the ideal phase of Israelite society was the premonarchic period, which, they assert, shows little evidence of a hierarchical social structure.

7. Nichols distinguishes between what he calls a "command model" of hierarchy (where "power tends to be centralized, control is from the top down and is based on force or the threat of force") and a "participatory model" (where the goal is the good of the whole) (*That They All May Be One*, 7–9).

8. In book 1 of the *Politics*, e.g., Aristotle writes, "Hunting ought to be practiced—not only against wild animals, but also against human beings who are intended by nature to be ruled by others and refuse to obey that intention" (*The Politics of Aristotle* [ed. and trans. E. Barker; London: Oxford University Press, 1980], 21). Aristotle's basic error consisted in applying observations of naturally occurring hierarchies to his thinking about human nature. His database for this move was extremely weak; his low opinion of "barbarians," for example, was based only on observations of captured and enslaved foreigners. By the same token, he never observed women functioning in a society where they enjoyed an equal footing with men. Aristotle's predecessor Plato anticipated him in postulating the existence of tiered levels of human worth. Plato wrote that society's proper guardians were made of gold, whereas its warriors were of silver and its workers and peasants of base metals. Later thinkers were able to build on such ill-conceived suppositions to legitimate dominating systems of control. Obviously, this type of thinking easily breeds racism and sexism.

themselves to be the equal of others; even a weakling can find a way to kill the strongest person he knows.
Hobbes writes:

> The question who is the better man, has no place in the condition of meer Nature; where . . . all men are equall. The inequality that now is, has bin introduced by the Lawes civill. I know that Aristotle in the first booke of his Politiques, for a foundation of his doctrine, maketh men by Nature, some more worthy to Command . . . others to Serve . . . as if Master and Servant were not introduced by consent of men . . . which is not only against reason; but also against experience. . . . I put this, *That every man acknowledge other for his Equall by Nature*. The breach of the Precept is *Pride*.[9]

A century later, in 1762, Jean-Jacques Rousseau reiterated in the *Social Contract* that all people are born free and equal. They thus have a natural right to cast off any fetters that seem to bind them within fixed hierarchies of social control. No government enjoys a permanent and absolute claim to power, but retains legitimacy based only on the consent of the governed. In one of his most memorable lines, Rousseau states, "Man was/is born free, and everywhere he is in chains."[10]

II. Taking Responsibility for Our Own Context as Interpreters

As we explore and evaluate hierarchical theology in Ezekiel, it is helpful to remember our own social and intellectual context as interpreters. Of necessity, we react to Ezekiel from our own located situation. We now know, in a way that no ancient Near Easterner could have, that human beings need freedom from the bonds of absolute power and authority in order to develop our full human potentials. We have a new suspicion of hierarchies, having become aware that despots and dictators use such structures to concretize power and authority and constrict the full expression of their subjects' humanity. Such sinful behavior is not unique to those who wield political power; unjust use of status and authority are part of the human condition.

Ancient Near Easterners were certainly well aware of the evils of human oppressors and tyrants, as texts such as Mic 3:1–4 make painfully clear. One could even argue that the book of Ezekiel proffers the notion that human leaders are inherently

---

9. Thomas Hobbes, *Leviathan* (ed. C. B. Macpherson; Pelican Classics; Harmondsworth, U.K.: Penguin, 1968), 211. Hobbes does not claim that all people have the same abilities; he asserts, rather, that the differences between them are not so considerable that one can claim benefits that others have no hope of acquiring (*Leviathan*, 183). In large measure, we owe our modern belief in the equal rights of all people to an intellectual movement begun by Hobbes. For Hobbes, even a brilliant man, such as an Einstein, has no more rights by nature than an idiot.

10. Jean-Jacques Rousseau, *On the Social Contract: With Geneva Manuscript and Political Economy* (ed. R. D. Masters; trans. J. R. Masters; New York: St. Martin's, 1978), 46.

handicapped, incapable of doing what they know is right on their own. This hardly means, however, that the ancients shared our modern liberal value of human autonomy. Within the Hebrew Bible, even those strains of tradition most enamored of decentralized power and checks on the control of rulers hardly embrace a social policy of egalitarianism. And no biblical tradition advocates human liberation from the service and tutelage of God, a notion that stems from the Renaissance and the Enlightenment. Rather, a text such as 1 Sam 8, which laments the clear and inevitable evils of monarchic systems of power (vv. 10–18), can, in the same breath, lament God's loss of position as absolute ruler of the people (v. 7).

Since the work of Niccolò Machiavelli (1469–1527), people have developed a heightened sensitivity to the role of self-interest and hypocrisy in the exercise of human authority in society. With this sensitivity has come a loss of appreciation of leadership and authority as legitimate structures for organizing human relationships and fostering persons' human potential and growth.

Before Machiavelli, Western civilization expected its leaders to embody human virtues, to promote justice, and to benefit society. Hierarchical structures facilitated their efforts in these directions. Machiavelli introduced a new and different vision of an ideal leader, the legacy of which has been a deep-seated suspicion of the moral character of *any* human, top-down exercise of authority. Many people today believe that *all* wielders of power are ready, without a qualm, to stoop to scandal and vice if that is what most expediently secures their position.

In his best-known work, *The Prince*, Machiavelli advocated a highly pragmatic and amoral exercise of authority over society and its various levels. In a programmatic statement, he declares self-interest rather than ethics to be the proper concern of a ruler: "Any man who tries to be good all the time is bound to come to ruin among the great number who are not good. Hence a prince who wants to keep his post must learn how not to be good and use that knowledge, or refrain from using it, as necessity requires."[11] Moral qualities are vices or virtues only as they help or hinder the goal of efficient political functioning. Machiavelli writes, "If you look at matters carefully, you will see that something resembling virtue, if you follow it, may be your ruin, while something else resembling vice will lead, if you follow it, to your security and well-being."[12]

Hypocrisy and dishonesty are fine, Machiavelli advises, when employed as efficient tools of effective rule. Rather than dealing in honesty and truth, successful leaders should use artifice to control those around them. Machiavelli writes, "Those princes have accomplished most who paid little heed to keeping their promises, but who knew how craftily to manipulate the minds of men."[13]

---

11. Niccolò Machiavelli, *The Prince* (ed. and trans. R. M. Adams; Norton Critical Editions; New York and London: Norton, 1977), 44.
12. Ibid., 45.
13. Ibid., 49.

Rulers ought not to use the structures of power at their command to uplift their subjects, Machiavelli advised. Rather, the empowerment of others should be the last thing on a ruler's mind: "The man who makes another powerful ruins himself."[14] Successful rulers keep their subjects dependent and off balance to encourage their loyalty in times of crisis. "A wise prince will think of ways to keep his citizens of every sort and under every circumstance dependent on the state and on him; and then they will always be trustworthy."[15]

In full accord with Machiavelli's brutal portrait of an ideal prince's pragmatic exercise of authority, Thomas Hobbes later sketched a skeptical and pessimistic picture of the motivations and character of society's priests. Believing that most religion was pure superstition, he claimed that priests promote belief in invisible powers as a means of securing personal power. By getting people to fear the supernatural and to believe that he can influence it, the priest imposes his authority on others. Hobbes writes, "So easie are men to be drawn to believe any thing, from such men as have gotten credit with them; and can with gentlenesse, and dexterity, take hold of their fear, and ignorance."[16]

We should acknowledge that as heirs to Machiavelli's and Hobbes's thought, we have difficulty today accepting that the ancient authors of Ezekiel could have propounded their hierarchical assumptions and programs out of pure motives. Our cultural history predisposes us to interpret theological claims about proper structures, especially those of rulers and priests, as little more than mystifying appeals to tradition and divine right that aim at securing mundane power. Like Hobbes, we generally put little stake in "power invisible," at least not when we are engaged in discourse in the public arena.[17]

The original audience of the book of Ezekiel would have approached its claims about structures of reality differently than we do now, and would not have understood our resolutely skeptical stance. Though fully aware of the abuses of power that plague human life, they would not have automatically assumed, as many modern people do, that theological claims and visions are of necessity a cover for the worldly ambitions of their advocates. Theoretical atheism was unknown or extremely rare in Ezekiel's day, and although people in contexts of stress and despair did question God's proximity and care (e.g., Ezek 8:12; 9:9; 33:17; 37:11), they did not doubt the reality of the heavenly sphere and its supremacy over earth.

---

14. Ibid., 12.
15. Ibid., 31.
16. Hobbes, *Leviathan*, 177.
17. Hobbes defines "religion" as: "*Feare* of power invisible, feigned by the mind, or imagined from tales publiquely allowed" (ibid., 124).

III. Formulating a Balanced Appraisal of Hierarchies

Describing the hierarchical views of the authors of Ezekiel is a different task than analyzing hierarchy in a classic such as Aristotle, even if both bodies of literature have shaped contemporary culture. Hosts of modern religious believers acknowledge the book of Ezekiel to be revelatory, canonical, and authoritative. Does that mean its views on cosmic and anthropological hierarchy are all revealed, true, and binding? Responsible modern interpreters hesitate before answering. Ezekiel requires a critical, balanced appraisal of its hierarchical dimensions.

When a scriptural corpus such as Ezekiel advocates hierarchical systems, we must proceed with great caution in appropriation. We do not want the biblical text, as was the legacy of Aristotle's position, to become a tool of arbitrary social control or of discrimination against one or another cross section of humanity. That would cut against much of the witness of the Hebrew Bible as a whole. We are also now increasingly aware of the foolishness and arrogance of a dominating and exploitative attitude toward the earth, humanity's home. In pointing out the possible abuses of hierarchy, modern negative appraisals make a significant contribution to ecology, political science, philosophy, and theology.

It may be helpful to specify two general, related abuses to which hierarchies have long proven vulnerable. First, there is the type of abuse decried by Hobbes and Rousseau. It occurs when attitudes of superiority and pride arise within any particular element of a hierarchical system, accompanied by prejudice and discrimination against neighbor elements. The renegade element rejects the idea of its being an interlocking *part* of an authentic level of being and imagines itself as qualitatively superior. It may then go on to create a new, artificial hierarchy where none is necessary or productive. Critics rightly decry the "domination hierarchy" that emerges.[18] Physicians appropriately use chemotherapy on cancerous cells that attempt to dominate their surroundings; subjects justly revolt against a tyrant who constantly threatens their lives and liberty.

A second, related abuse entails a revolt at one level of a hierarchical system against upper levels and limits. The thrill of authority may create the allusion of infinitude, and a subordinate element may always be tempted to usurp a new, unnaturally high position. This is disastrous, because it places the usurping element in a role that it is inherently unable to fulfill. When Phaethon tried to drive his father's sun-chariot through the sky, he lost control and nearly burned up the earth. When the emperor Caligula threatened to install his favorite horse in the Roman senate, everyone understood the act as a hubristic and contemptuous claim to rule as a god.

Despite their clear potential for abuse, however, it is unwise to view all hierar-

---

18. For the term "domination hierarchy," see Riane Eisler, *The Chalice and the Blade: Our History, Our Future* (San Francisco: Harper & Row, 1987), 105.

chies as inherently obnoxious. Even if existence were possible without hierarchies, humans would likely choose to embrace them anyway. This is because hierarchical organization has demonstrable benefits, which at base level revolve around the advantages of *wholeness*. The creation of levels of greater embrace within reality allows for the realization of deeper, more valuable enterprises and potentials. Introducing hierarchy is the only way to take a "heap" and make it into a "whole." And we humans naturally value "wholes," which are greater than the sum of their parts.[19]

Take natural existence first. Here, hierarchical organization allows for the unfolding of high-level spheres in which individual worth and human rights are of value. As Wilber astutely observes, "Equal rights can *never* be achieved in the biosphere, where big fish eat little fish; but they can be achieved—or certainly aimed for—in the noosphere [the sphere of human consciousness]."[20]

Second, consider art and aesthetics. Smith, in his fascinating researches on the comparable nature of science and art, illumines how both realities heavily depend upon interpenetrating sequences of structural levels. He shows how patterns in the details of fine paintings support the aesthetic impact of larger sectors, whose structures, in turn, are essential to the overall power of the complete artworks. He concludes that in art "as more levels of hierarchy can be constructed from the simple initial components, the richer becomes the experience."[21]

Hierarchical organization also has benefits in the case of the political sphere, especially in groups that are highly complex or amorphous. Hierarchy provides a mechanism for unity of otherwise disparate parts. A republic such as the United States, for example, seems to work better than an absolutely pure democracy. This is because republics involve a system of representatives who have fixed terms of office and participate in deliberative bodies such as the Senate. In such a system, one can make hard decisions without suffering immediate political demise, and one can test and hone one's positions in a context of challenge and argument. If all U.S. citizens had an equal vote in every governmental decision, the country would quickly lose stability and direction.

Again, thinking of the example of the United States, there is clear value in placing the fifty states under the authority of a federal government. Without this hierarchical system, we would lose our ability to explore space, to catalog and collect all new books in the Library of Congress, to stabilize the economy through the Federal Reserve System, and to control communicable disease and test new drugs as well as we do.

If hierarchical structuring contributes basic strengths in the areas of nature, art, and politics, may it not also have something to contribute to theology? The essays

---

19. As Wilber argues, to say that a whole is greater than the sum of its parts means that it is at a "higher or deeper level of organization than its parts alone—and that's a hierarchy" (*Brief History of Everything*, 28).

20. Ibid., 262.

21. Smith, *Search for Structure*, 385.

of this volume test different stances on this question, and there is plenty of fascinating disagreement. If hierarchy does contribute something theologically valuable, it is likely due to its general ability to manage problems of characterization, boundary identification, and mechanisms of change.

As Friedrich Fechter notes in his essay, the exiles in Babylonia struggled to characterize God and humanity adequately, given their historical experience and the competing pantheon of their captors. The writers of Scripture needed a way to clarify the nature of a solitary, true God, separate from creation who at the same time cannot leave the world alone. Might hierarchical thinking have provided a necessary tool for sorting out such a theological problematic, and for explaining how God's saving power might reach out into creation to transform Israel and prevent the disasters of the past?

More specifically, hierarchical thinking may have provided a rare, logical explanation for the destruction of Israel's previous existence as well as desperately needed lessons on how to prevent a repeat experience. Daniel Smith-Christopher and other of our contributors note the profound existential urgency of this set of theological problems for the exiles. Prisoners of war, such as Ezekiel, may likely have turned to hierarchical thinking less to assert power and privilege than to find their way in an overturned world.

As Cyril Stanley Smith explains, in nature as well as culture, hierarchical environments are particularly subject to overthrow through the spread of "impurity."[22] A healthy tiered structure can manage both stability and change well, through successful communication and interaction across its scale of clumpings. The intricate connectivity and interpenetration of the structure, however, comes at the price of certain vulnerability. "Impurity" and "rebellion" easily render such a superstructure metastable, when new nuclei of power form at the periphery and grow via an interface of high disorder or chaos. Such a revolution soon overthrows the center of the structure, and fundamentally alters its overall phase.

If there are indeed good and bad hierarchies in reality, how might we distinguish between those that are healthy and those that are arbitrary and obnoxious? One useful criterion may be that of *inclusion*. We may say that a hierarchical system is relatively healthy if it creates a greater whole out of various fragments, while fully embracing the worth of each part. This greater whole, if it is truly inclusive, should link its parts together to their common benefit, so that they are better off in some way than they would have been by remaining mere fragments.

Another test of whether a given hierarchy is healthy or not may turn on the vitality of the interaction between structural levels. The center should allow for appropriate (i.e., non-impure, noncancerous) freedom and growth at the periphery through active sensitivity to a flow of communication and responsibility up and

---

22. Ibid., 380–82.

down the scale of clumpings. Ideally, there should be a two-way flow of benefits and empowerment within the system.

IV. Ezekiel's Unique Hierarchical Emphases

As argued above, the modern philosophical suspicion of hierarchy first began to gather steam with seventeenth-century thought, with the critique of Aristotle's politics. If this is so, one might justly anticipate finding hierarchical thinking imbedded deeply in almost all discourse and writing before modern times, especially in the ancient world with its city-states, kingdoms, and empires. Why should we single out the book of Ezekiel for a critique and appraisal of hierarchical theology in the Hebrew Scriptures?

Perusal of the contributions to this volume soon reveals that hierarchical thinking in Ezekiel is particularly rich and developed, even over against other Scriptures and the general ancient Near Eastern environment. Friedrich Fechter, in his essay, lays out some of the priestly, Zadokite thinking of Ezekiel's group that is particularly "pyramidal." Julie Galambush discusses in a clear manner how Ezekiel prioritizes *settled* land and *ordered* society, and how he does so in a way that really differs from other biblical traditions. Keith Carley and Norman Habel argue for a radical subjugation of land and earth in Ezekiel, which contrasts with more eco-friendly Scriptures. Stephen Cook's essay describes the uniquely storied cosmos envisioned by Ezekiel, and then goes farther to argue that Ezekiel also has a hierarchically ordered understanding of human knowing.

A common literary device in the book of Ezekiel is the reuse and expansion of earlier themes and traditions. For example, the vision of God's presence enthroned atop the cosmos in the first chapter expands the prophetic call imagery found in Isa 6. Similarly, the descriptions of Jerusalem as God's wife in Ezek 16 and 23 pursue images found in earlier prophets to an almost grotesque point. This literary characteristic elaborates and intensifies images and issues of hierarchy that are already present in other biblical texts. It makes the book a uniquely appropriate testing ground for studying hierarchical thinking in the Hebrew Bible.

Perhaps the clearest example of the way Ezekiel's configuration focuses attention on questions of hierarchy and power can be found in its ordering of Israelite society. In any system, a basic building block in the creation of boundaries and hierarchies is the device of distinctions and contrasts. While other biblical texts may differentiate between simple dyads, such as priests and laity, or Israelites and foreigners, the social distinctions in Ezekiel merely start there. The book's elaborate differentiations and polarities construct especially articulate hierarchies.[23]

---

23. Ezekiel's three-part, or "triadic," distinctions are particularly noteworthy, because, as Saul Olyan argues, "If binary oppositions are a rhetorical strategy to differentiate, triadic constructions provide a context to do so to a greater extent, articulating hierarchy in more detail" (*Rites and Rank: Hierarchy in*

Sacerdotal rank in Ezekiel, for example, entails a complex classification scheme with nuanced regulations. The scheme creates a key hierarchy of the book, initially dividing society into three strata: the priests, the Levites, and other Israelites. Only priests may enter the temple's inner court and the sanctuary proper in Ezekiel's system. Only they may offer sacrifices (Ezek 44:15–16). The Levites have no part in these duties, but are restricted to the role of temple guards and gatekeepers, and they perform the temple's chores (Ezek 44:11). Other Israelites may worship in the outer court under the Levites' guidance, but are prohibited from slaughtering their own offerings (Ezek 44:11)—a hierarchical stricture unknown in other priestly Scriptures (e.g., Lev 1:5, 11).[24]

Ezekiel's strict priestly hierarchy is foreign to other biblical understandings, which present differing views of how the priestly lineages of Levi, Aaron, and Zadok should relate to one another. Deuteronomy 18:1–8 speaks of the whole tribe of Levi as priests, all of whom have a right to attend before God (v. 7; cf. Jer 33:18, 21, 22; contrast Ezek 40:46; 44:15).[25] Malachi 2:1–9 holds both Aaronide priests and Levites accountable to a single priestly covenant between God and Levi, not two separate sets of rules. For its part, the Priestly Torah (PT) source of the Pentateuch does not elaborate on the functional distinction between priests and Levites. If its authors had specific opinions about the role of the Levites at the temple, they did not express them in the document as it has come down to us.[26] Compared to the Priestly Torah, Ezekiel is uniquely hierarchical.

Ezekiel may even recognize an additional sacerdotal polarity, beyond the book's distinction between priests and Levites. The priesthood itself may have two ranks:

Biblical Representations of Cult [Princeton: Princeton University Press, 2000], 7). Strictly speaking, for Olyan, a "triadic construction" involves the explicit mention of all three members of a three-part distinction in one scriptural passage. We are being less precise in the present context, contenting ourselves with noting more general evidence from the whole biblical book of Ezekiel that its authors made both two-part and three-part distinctions in dividing and classifying reality.

24. Ezekiel imposes other strictures on temple service and the functions of priests and Levites not recorded elsewhere in Scripture. For examples, see Moshe Greenberg, "The Design and Themes of Ezekiel's Program of Restoration," *Int* 38 (1984): 196 nn. 31 and 32.

25. Olyan states: "No secondary class of 'Levites' who are inferior functionaries exists for Deuteronomy and related materials" (*Rites and Rank,* 19; cf., e.g., John Emerton, "Priests and Levites in Deuteronomy," *VT* 12 [1962]: 138). Steven Shawn Tuell affirms this assessment, but notes evidence of some differentiations within the Levitical priesthood of Deuteronomy and the Deuteronomistic History (*The Law of the Temple in Ezekiel 40–48* [HSM 49; Atlanta: Scholars Press, 1992], 124–31, 138–39).

26. See Israel Knohl, *The Sanctuary of Silence: The Priestly Torah and the Holiness School* (Minneapolis: Fortress, 1995), 66, 85, 192, 209–12; contrast Olyan, *Rites and Rank,* 19. In contrast to PT, the HS source develops a clear hierarchical ranking between priests and Levites (e.g., Num 16:5, 7; 18). On the relatively new scholarly distinction between the PT and HS sources within the priestly strand of the Pentateuch, see Jacob Milgrom, *Leviticus 1–16: A New Translation with Introduction and Commentary* (AB 3; New York: Doubleday, 1991), 1–2, 13–42, 48; Knohl, *Sanctuary of Silence.* More recently, Baruch J. Schwartz advances this new understanding in *The Holiness Legislation: Studies in the Priestly Code* (Jerusalem: Magnes, 1999), in Hebrew. See further, Israel Knohl, *The Divine Symphony: The Bible's Many Voices* (Philadelphia: Jewish Publication Society, 2003).

altar priests and temple priests. Ezekiel 40:44–46 in particular describes two groups of priests, both with access to the restricted inner court of the temple. One set of priests, the sons of Zadok, "have charge of the altar." The other priests merely "have charge of the temple." The passage is often understood as a sort of way station on a path of development leading to the sharp distinction between Zadokites and Levites in later redactional levels, such as that of Ezek 44:9–16.[27] Such a diachronic reading is, of course, possible. It is also possible, however, to understand Ezek 40:44–46 as having nothing to do with the Levites, but rather as distinguishing between two lines of Aaronide priests—the line of Eleazar/Zadok and the line of Ithamar.[28]

Such a distinction is known from the Holiness School corpus (HS), which elevates the line of Eleazar, the ancestor of Zadok, over that of Ithamar.[29] The Priestly Torah corpus, in contrast, contains no such polarity, but identifies Israel's official priests as *all* the living descendents of Aaron. This includes full priestly rights for the line of Ithamar (Exod 28:1; Lev 10:12, both PT; cf. 1 Chr 5:27–34 [Eng. 6:1–8]).

Ezekiel, along with the Holiness School, understands the laity to occupy spheres of society distinctly less holy than the sphere of the Levites and that of the priests.[30] Other Israelite traditions disagreed, as is clear from the obvious polemics of texts such as Ezek 44:13 and Num 16:3 (HS). These passages betray anti-hierarchical perspectives on holiness within Israel, which, arguing that "all the congregation are holy, every one of them," pressed for a more open access to God's presence in the temple than Ezekiel's book allows.[31] Such perspectives appear within

---

27. See Hartmut Gese, *Der Verfassungsentwurf des Ezechiel* (BHT 25; Tübingen: Mohr Siebeck, 1957), 64–67, 121–22; Walther Zimmerli, *Ezekiel: A Commentary on the Book of the Prophet Ezekiel* (2 vols.; Hermeneia; Philadelphia: Fortress, 1979, 1983), 2:458; Tuell, *Law of the Temple*, 32–33, 72, 132. In favor of this interpretation, note the common language used of both the lower-tier "priests" of Ezek 40:45 and the "Levites" of Ezek 44:14. Both are assigned to "keep charge" (שׁמר) of the "service of the house/temple" (משמרת הבית), as Gese aptly notes (*Der Verfassungsentwurf des Ezechiel*, 65). Personnel of varying status and rank, however, could easily have shared responsibility for a common set of sacral responsibilities, probably with one group as supervisors.

28. According to the Pentateuch, both Eleazar and Ithamar were sons of Aaron. Note that Steven Tuell hints at something similar to the interpretation suggested here (*Law of the Temple*, 32 n. 37, 134, 139).

29. HS does not deny Ithamar's existence, but is at pains to subordinate him to his brother Eleazar, the ancestor of Zadok. HS places Ithamar in charge of Levites with lesser duties, while it has Eleazar direct the Levites responsible for the most important items of the tabernacle (Num 3–4, HS). At Num 3:32, HS even calls Eleazar the "chief over the leaders of the Levites." Num 25:10–13 (HS) goes farther, narrating God's grant of a covenant of perpetual priesthood specifically to Eleazar's son, Phinehas.

30. For Ezekiel and HS, holiness remains only an aspiration of lay Israelites, who should pursue it as part of an ongoing process of sanctification (e.g., Lev 21:8; 22:32). The priesthood, in contrast, possesses a distinct, permanent holiness, since priests interact directly with God's glory atop a pyramidal structure of holiness (Ezek 44:15–16; Num 18:7).

31. Over against the arguments of Olyan, Knohl is doubtless correct to assign the non-J material in Num 16 to HS rather than PT (see Knohl, *Sanctuary of Silence*, 73–82; Olyan, *Rites and Rank*, 136 n. 63). Against Olyan, Num 16 does not restrict holiness in general to the priesthood, as PT would, but only the highest gradation or stratum of holiness associated with sacrificial rites, as HS does. See, e.g.,

the Hebrew Bible not only as foils for the Holiness School and Ezekiel but also as scripturally authoritative tenets of belief in such texts as Exod 19:6 (E/D) and Deut 14:2 (cf. Deut 7:6; 14:21; 26:19; 28:9).[32]

The uniquely hierarchical theology of Ezekiel's book is nowhere clearer than in the design of the restored temple and land in Ezek 40–48. These chapters create an unmistakably unique world, quite different from that of other Scriptures. The stress on spatial order, separation, and gradation, which borders on hyperbole, unfolds a new "failsafe" reality in Israel that ensures the permanent dwelling of God's glory (Ezek 43:7; 44:2) and the safe diffusion of God's holiness throughout the land (Ezek 47:1–48:35).

Ezekiel's temple complex contains six or seven core zones of graded holiness, whereas the Priestly tabernacle and the temple of Solomon have only three. While there continues to be a sanctuary building with two (or three) main sections, the courtyard of Ezekiel's temple contains multiple new zones with defined entry restrictions. Its walled inner court and altar area is restricted to priestly use, barred to Levites and laity alike (Ezek 42:14; 44:19; 46:3). Intermediate zones between the temple's inner and outer courtyards are constituted by three gate buildings (Ezek 40:28–37). In particular, the northern and eastern buildings have vestibule areas reserved respectively for ritual activities of the Levites and of the political ruler (Ezek 40:38–43; 46:2).

The outer court has its own new, unique zones (cf. Ezek 44:1–3), and a new series of three gatehouses. As noted above, Levites and laity have use of the temple's outer court, but no one uncircumcised, profane, or foreign has access (Ezek 42:20; 44:9). The temple's outer gates lead forth into a newly conceived "holy district" of land (the תרומה, Ezek 45:1–8) with two distinct parts. This district surrounds and protects the temple complex, and its two parts provide dwelling space for the priests, the Levites, and their families.

The primary zones of both the desert tabernacle and Solomon's temple, in contrast, were merely threefold: the inner section of the sanctuary, its outer section (with porch, in the temple's case), and a surrounding courtyard (e.g., Exod 26:33; 27:9–19, both PT; Num 4:4; 3:28; 4:26, all HS).[33] The yard area in particular is relatively undifferentiated (at least physically), specifically lacking Ezekiel's inner court barred to nonpriests. (Note, though, that some biblical texts do suggest two courts of some

---

Num 16:8–10, which distinguishes three spheres of nearness to God: that of the congregation, that of the Levites, and that of the priests.

32. As Patrick Miller states, in Deuteronomy "there is no particular reference to priests and a special sphere of holiness that they inhabited" (*The Religion of Ancient Israel* [Library of Ancient Israel; Louisville: Westminster John Knox, 2000], 159). Cf. Norbert Lohfink, "Opfer und Säkularisierung im Deuteronomium," in *Studien zu Opfer und Kult im Alten Testament* (ed. A. Schenker; Tübingen: Mohr Siebeck, 1992), 15–43.

33. See Philip Peter Jenson, *Graded Holiness: A Key to the Priestly Conception of the World* (JSOTSup

sort around the preexilic temple.) In Ps 26:6, the psalmist speaks of full lay access to the temple's courtyard, including all sides of the sacred altar.

Several pronounced—even exaggerated—physical features further distinguish Ezekiel's new temple from other temples of the Hebrew Bible. The character of the outer gate buildings is a case in point (Ezek 40:5–16; cf. 43:1–5; 44:1–3). They are simply colossal in size, and their importance is signaled by the intricate detail with which they are described. Moshe Greenberg writes, "The massive size of the gatehouses verges on caricature: their dimensions (25 x 50 cubits) exceed those of the main hall of the Temple (20 x 40 cubits); their length is half that of the inner court (100 cubits)!"[34]

A series of terraces and successively narrowing entrances further define and demarcate the intricate tiers of holiness within the complex. Rising stages of courts and platforms—so that height demarcates gradations of holiness—is clear from Ezek 40:22, 26, 31; and 41:8. A narrowing of successive entrances is apparent in the description of the sanctuary proper (Ezek 40:48; 41:2, 3). These devices signal increasing holiness as one enters farther up and into the temple. Like the hierarchy of sacerdotal roles, this detailed spatial hierarchy guards the temple's sanctity, and it allows the Israelite congregation a safe, tempered exposure to the burning, sanctifying power of God.[35]

To reiterate, Ezekiel's complex system of boundaries and differentiations within the temple complex are foreign to descriptions of the preexilic temple of Solomon and the Priestly tabernacle. As Greenberg summarizes, "Ezekiel introduces rigor into the separation and gradation of areas in the sanctuary precincts; moreover, his requirements are more stringent than those of the Pentateuch."[36] Here again, a variety of evidence requires us to reckon with unusually hierarchical dimensions in Ezekiel's thinking and theology compared with other biblical texts and traditions.

V. Ideological Considerations and the Political Aims of Ezekiel's Group

How do we account for the particularly strong showing of hierarchical thinking in the book of Ezekiel, even in comparison to the general suppositions of its age? The rubrics of *propaganda* and *ideology* may immediately spring to mind. In the cur-

---

106; Sheffield: JSOT Press, 1992), 89–93; Miller, *Religion of Ancient Israel*, 147; Olyan, *Rites and Rank*, 24–25.

34. Greenberg, "Design and Themes," 193.

35. Cf. Patrick Miller's statement: "That such effecting and safeguarding [the temple system of sacred spheres] had a self-serving dimension does not diminish the degree to which the Israelite community really found in this interaction of spheres the effecting of a realm that seemed to enhance the openness of the community to the divine and, certainly in the Priestly tradition, the preservation of the community in the face of the danger of the encounter with the holy God" (*Religion of Ancient Israel*, 143).

36. Greenberg, "Design and Themes," 203.

rent practice of biblical scholarship, employment of such rubrics is widespread, to some extent justified, and worth the effort to clarify and explicate.

Human beings never do theology in a vacuum, but always with a particular mind-set and from a definite social location. Presuppositions and vested interests inevitably form a part of the located context where theology gets done. The hierarchical theology of Ezekiel is no exception, and interpreters have a valid interest in exploring its interrelationship with the social roles and political and economic aims of Ezekiel's group. Whether they were conscious of it or not, group assumptions, concerns, and agenda could not help but shape and color Ezekiel's prophetic writings.[37]

To give a more obvious example, to a modern reader, it immediately seems too convenient that Ezekiel's priestly group has received from God an ideal vision of the cosmos that reserves a central place for ritual officials and temple duties. Does not this vision strain to conceal its nature as a literary artifice or stratagem for advancing Ezekiel's inner circle and pacifying outsiders? Living in the wake of Machiavelli's work, most of us find ourselves barely capable of taking Ezekiel's proposals about the cosmos at face value and giving them a nonpolitical hearing.

Several objections, however, confront our attempts to read Ezekiel's prophecy in any straightforward way as a Machiavellian artifice. First, Ezekiel's vision for the future introduces significant qualifications when it assigns the Zadokites a leading role in an ideal new Israel. Such qualifications appear gratuitous and counterintuitive under the hypothesis that Ezekiel's book is pure propaganda. The restoration of the Zadokites to leadership comes only after participating in Israel's face-to-face judgment by God, which entails the purging of all rebels and transgressors from the returnee group (Ezek 20:33–38). Those who eventually do return to the homeland will have to leave their old "hearts of stone" behind in Babylonia, and come with new, divinely engrafted hearts and spirits (Ezek 36:26). They will be incapable of repeating the corruptions of the past that led to the exile, since God will "hardwire" them for obedience (Ezek 36:27–28). It is hard to imagine a sane politician making such campaign promises involving miraculously and permanently transformed leadership!

Second, the Zadokites whom God restores to temple service in Ezekiel know they will face frightful, unenviable danger. In the restored cult they will have to risk their lives in approaching God's blazing presence to offer sacrifices at God's altar (Ezek 44:15–16; cf. 1:28; 3:23). Failure in their duties will expose them to the lethal quality of God's holiness, with fatal effect (cf. Num 18:1–7 [HS]). Unless they held their sacred traditions, especially those of the Holiness School, about this dangerous

---

37. Richard and Kendall Soulen understand "ideology" as follows: "An ideology is a set of attitudes and ideas, consciously or unconsciously held, that reflects or shapes understandings (and misunderstandings) of the social and political world, and that serves to justify collective action aimed at preserving or changing it." See Richard N. Soulen and R. Kendall Soulen, "Ideological Criticism," in *Handbook of Biblical Criticism* (3d ed.; Louisville: Westminster John Knox, 2001), 84.

role in the temple to be fundamentally mistaken, would they have actively campaigned to take the role up?

Third, the same Holiness School traditions that Ezekiel's school treasured glaringly clash with Machiavellian ethics. The Holiness School corpus possesses an overriding *moral* dimension, which would have been the source of considerable anxiety for any of its Ezekielian tradents attracted to an amoral political program. Its texts not only command righteousness and social justice (e.g., Lev 19:9–18, 33–36; 23:22; 24:17–22) but also envision an ideal society promoting the humanity and economic independence of its members (e.g., Lev 25:10, 23–24, 42). It is no coincidence that, relying on the Holiness School, Ezekiel's blueprint for the future denies princes the power to evict subjects from their family homesteads (Ezek 45:8–9; 46:18; cf. 22:27).[38]

On the theme of human dignity, Holiness School texts have a distinctively modern ring. They stress that God values the worth and holiness of all of God's people, the whole congregation of the children of Israel (see esp. Lev 19:2). Ezekiel is indebted to this theology, as texts such as Ezek 20:12; 37:28; and 43:9 make fully clear. Significantly, so is our modern ideal of the value of all individual persons. Modern critics sometimes forget that the Hebrew Bible, especially a text such as Lev 19:2 (HS), was a primary impetus behind the modern convictions about personal dignity of John Locke and Thomas Jefferson. Based on such texts, Locke and Jefferson asserted the legal equality and intrinsic rights of all individuals. This is not at all to claim that Ezekiel's book, and the Holiness School traditions behind it, contain a modern, democratic understanding of individual "freedom." It is to assert, however, that the hierarchical thinking in these Scriptures does not aim to enslave the parts/members of the system that lie at the periphery.[39] To the contrary, it aims to embrace their worth, promote their independence, and secure their sanctification. Locke and Jefferson were not wrong to treasure Lev 19.

The above considerations suggest that the type of ideology at issue in Ezekiel is less likely to be a conscious and "voluntaristic" sort as it is to be unintentional—that is, a tacit and relatively unrecognized ideology.[40] Ideological factors are always at play in the production of literature, but in Ezekiel's case, they are no deliberate tactic of

---

38. Cf. the arguments of Jon D. Levenson, *Theology of the Program of Restoration of Ezekiel 40–48* (HSM 10; Missoula, Mont.: Scholars Press, 1976), 116–25.

39. Susan Niditch writes that in the new world of Ezek 40–48, "All is ordered, well-oiled, God-given, and God-blessed. . . . Ezekiel leaves social structure very much intact. But social institutions are to work well; the cosmos with its structure is ideally ordered" ("Ezekiel 40–48 in a Visionary Context," *CBQ* 48 [1986]: 220).

40. Jacques Berlinerblau has suggested that biblical critics should pay more attention to ideology in this sense—as an unexamined cultural subtext, as a set of assumptions that a group of writers' social world imparts to them and their texts. He recommends Pierre Bourdieu's notion of "doxa" as an appropriate term for what he has in mind. This essay is interested in a somewhat narrower circle of shared assumptions, however, than what doxa encompasses. See Berlinerblau, "Ideology, Pierre Bourdieu's *Doxa*, and the Hebrew

mystification that aimed to secure authority and territory for one privileged group. Rather, they represent an indirect and largely unconscious reflection of the authors' historical and social location. Unthought assumptions buttress, shape, and color the Ezekielians' hierarchical theology, assumptions that went without saying in their lives.

Because Ezekiel's authors were Zadokite priests and a central elite, we may expect the terms in which they express their theology to be almost unavoidably educated, cosmopolitan, male, and ritualistic. It is easy for a sensitive modern reader, from a distance of more than two thousand years, to see how Ezekiel's authors unintentionally skewed the book's prophecies in ways insensitive to women (cf. Ezek 36:17; 44:22). It is not hard to imagine, as Julie Galambush reveals, how the authors' burning desire to regain stable control over their homeland unconsciously led them to denigrate almost everything wild and untamed in their writings. Or again, it is fairly apparent to observant critics, as Keith Carley shows, how Ezekiel's anthropocentric preoccupation with proper *human* ritual and purity led him to neglect any love of nature for nature's sake.

VI. When Ideology Adheres to Theology

The experience of the world as an interplay of power differentials permeates the theological assertions of Ezekiel's book. God is clearly depicted as the quintessential "hierarch" as experienced by those lower in the cosmic order. In parallel, human ethical behavior is defined in terms of the maintenance of the power differential: it is good for those in power to maintain control over other humans, animals, and nature. For contemporary readers of the text who view the exercise of such human power as sinful, or who find the notion of an autocratic deity offensive, the question remains: can one reject this particular construal of hierarchy without rejecting the text as revelatory of the God that it proclaims? If not, does the book ask contemporary readers to rethink their views of hierarchy and to accept that not only is God "above" humans but also that the whole cosmos, including ideal human society, is tiered?

The essays in this volume grapple with these questions in a variety of ways. Some use more traditional modes of biblical interpretation in order to unpack the text's rhetoric within its historical context. Others focus on the effect of the text on contemporary readers. The topics of each paper differ as well. Some focus on human hierarchy, especially through the lens of the priesthood. Others look at cosmic ordering, while still others ask about the function of a tiered system. Nor do all the papers reach the same conclusion about the merits of Ezekiel's presentation. Some view the

---

Bible," *Semeia* 87 (1999): 193–214 (issue edited by R. A. Simkins and S. L. Cook, with the theme of "The Social World of the Hebrew Bible: Twenty-five Years of the Social Sciences in the Academy").

hierarchy in the text as an essential element in the book's theology. Others recommend a rejection of what appear to them to be tiered systems of abuse.

Our volume begins with four essays focusing on the role of priesthood in the book. In the first of these essays, Friedrich Fechter ("Priesthood in Exile according to the Book of Ezekiel") traces redactional layers within the texts of Ezekiel referring to priests. In the authentic prophecies of Ezekiel, there is no distinction between priests and nonpriests with respect to culpability for Judah's destruction. However, in exile priests found that they needed to maintain group identity, and did so by focusing on genealogies. This eventuality is reflected in the oldest editorial stratum of Ezek 40–48. The next layer of these chapters differentiates between altar servants and temple servants without assigning each a distinct status. Finally, status differentiation further demarcates Zadokites and Levites. Fechter concludes that these distinctions were not primarily the result of feuding political factions, but were natural developments that accompanied a growing monotheistic theology. Just as God is both part of the world and separate from it, so the priest is both part of the people and distinct from them. The primary function of the priest is to mediate a divine presence that otherwise might be too remote.

Iain Duguid ("Putting Priests in Their Place: Ezekiel's Contribution to the History of the Old Testament Priesthood") also focuses on the theological motivation for Ezekiel's understanding of the priesthood. Duguid expressly rejects the idea that Ezekiel's hierarchical positions are mere political propaganda. Rather, they are a means to encourage lives of obedience to God, to strengthen the wall dividing the holy and the profane, and to protect the sanctuary's integrity, preventing another exile. After a brief review of the history of the priesthood, Duguid highlights the portrayal of Ezekiel as a priest in exile. This portrayal sets up Ezekiel as the model of faithfulness. Similarly, the Zadokites in chapters 40–48 are depicted as the only group in exile not guilty of sin. The centrality of the Zadokites, like the centrality of Ezekiel, is a reward for faithfulness, while the marginalization of Levites and laity results from their past sins. Yet, in the final analysis, Ezekiel's new future restores everything and everyone to the way they always ought to have been. In that new future, God becomes accessible to all the people through the service and mediation of a faithful priesthood, and blessings flow like a stream down a hierarchical interface to the entire community.

Baruch Schwartz ("A Priest Out of Place: Reconsidering Ezekiel's Role in the History of the Israelite Priesthood") offers a very different assessment of how the book, written in exile, addresses the question of priesthood. Arguing that there is no such thing as a "priesthood" without a temple, Schwartz probes the function of the text as idealization and its portrayal of Ezekiel as one that identifies him as a prophet. Ezekiel the prophet, Schwartz contends, has totally abandoned the priestly role. The description of the temple in Ezek 40–48 is a prophetic vision, not priestly legislation. Ezekiel's speeches are prophetic oracles, not priestly divinations. Priesthood is no longer a functioning social category, and all references to priests in the book serve to highlight their deserved end. Even the blueprint of an ideal cult at the book's end is furnished, not to regulate the temple's reconstruction, but only to shame those who should better recognize their culpability. Ezekiel represents the priesthood only insofar as he is no longer a priest. While this essay does not explicitly address questions of hierarchy, the social collapse that the author sees reflected in the text would leave little option for any future human hierarchy.

Corrine Patton ("Priest, Prophet, and Exile: Ezekiel as a Literary Construct") also looks to the characterization of Ezekiel as central to the book's themes. Focusing on a rhetorical analysis of the book's final form, she argues that its initial notice of Ezekiel's priestly lineage and social status serves as a lens through which the remainder of its texts are read. Patton rejects the easy demarcation of priests and prophets evident in many sociological and anthropological approaches to Israelite priesthood, instead advocating an approach that lets the texts speak for themselves. When this is done, several insights emerge. Texts about priests as well as the portrayal of Ezekiel himself reinscribe multiple hierarchies in the book. The rhetoric of these hierarchies, however, does not simply promote one group over others, but problematizes all notions of hierarchy in light of a divine sovereign. Human hierarchy in Ezekiel is an outgrowth, not of political concern, but of the book's own insistence on the otherness of God.

The next three essays look at a more problematic element in the text of Ezekiel: the relationships among God, humans, and the realm of nature. Julie Galambush ("God's Land and Mine: Creation as Property in the Book of Ezekiel") reveals how Ezekiel's hierarchical thinking prioritizes land that is settled and animals that are owned and incorporated into the ordered world. In contrast to perspectives seen in Jeremiah, Job, and other Scriptures, land in Ezekiel is profoundly "human space," "space-for-me." This privileging of tamed over wild, settled over barren, is not surprising. The book of Ezekiel is written from the perspective of those who have lost their land, who control no property, and their texts mirror their anxiety and sense of violation over their fate. Galambush explores the way the authors' images of "wildness" express a cognitive dissonance between the de facto loss of land-possession and the assertion that, de jure, the land is theirs. The focus on Yahweh's hierarchical control over nature expresses the exiles' desire once again to control the land.

In one of the more negative assessments of the book of Ezekiel's hierarchical thinking, Keith Carley ("From Harshness to Hope: The Implications for Earth of Hierarchy in Ezekiel") demonstrates the disregard for Earth in the book of Ezekiel. In Ezekiel, he states in his essay, "Earth is the passive object of horrifying maltreatment meted out by God in the process of punishing human misdeeds." Carley notes that there are different models for understanding hierarchy, but among these models, God's actions in Ezekiel clearly reflect a "dominator hierarchy." This hierarchy of domination reflects the political agenda of the exilic author who does not identify with those closer to the land. Ezekiel himself "stood to benefit from the dominator hierarchy that his text created." Any element of hope in the book is focused on social reconstruction, but not on any renewal or restoration for the earth. The danger, in Carley's view, is that this rhetoric is couched in language about God. God's domination of the natural world, he pleads, should not be considered "determinative" for contemporary theology.

Norman Habel ("The Silence of the Lands: The Ecojustice Implications of Ezekiel's Judgment Oracles") also reads the book of Ezekiel from the perspective of Earth, and the prophecies do not fare well under his scrutiny. Beyond Ezekiel's "anthropocentric" bias, the prophet's perspective also emerges as that of an urbanite whose center is Jerusalem; areas outside of the city and its cultivated lands are wild, dangerous, and chaotic.[41] The desolation of Earth in Ezekiel shows that it has no intrinsic value, nor does it have a voice even in the face of undeserved destruction at the hands of an egotistical God. As Habel states, "There is a hierarchy of values from the sacred center to the dangerous wilds on the fringe of the cosmos." For him, this hierarchy derives from a human political agenda.

According to Daniel Smith-Christopher ("Ezekiel in Abu Ghraib: Rereading Ezekiel 16:37-39 in the Context of Imperial Conquest"), scholars who imagine Ezekiel's texts to be the writings of a dominator class misapprehend the actual situation from which they stem. Emphasizing the Ezekielians as a privileged cosmopolitan elite, scholars have too often overlooked the group's fate as humiliated refugees and prisoners. Smith-Christopher argues that the refugee status of the Ezekielians may far better account for their book's extreme, sometimes tortured images than their status as typical patriarchal power holders. As Ezekiel and his colleagues are first and foremost prisoners of war, subsisting amid the neo-Babylonian imperial conquests of Palestine and the collapse of the only world they knew, their rhetoric is the language of suffering, not the normal, everyday language of an elite group at ease. In their various metaphors, they probably do not identify with God or other wielders of power but with those who suffer judgment and disgrace. Particularly in their metaphors of stripped and humiliated adulteresses, it may well be the women and their awful ordeals that mirror their experience and self-image, not the irate husbands or the gawking onlookers.

Among the Hebrew prophetic books, Ezekiel marks a watershed point in the scribal appreciation and textual preservation of sacred tradition. In her essay, Risa Levitt Kohn (" 'With a Mighty Hand and an Outstretched Arm': The Prophet and the Torah in Ezekiel 20") demonstrates Ezekiel's thorough indebtedness to preexisting Scriptures, especially the extent of Ezekiel's enmeshment in Israel's major pentateuchal traditions. On the one hand, Ezekiel's blending of legal elements found

---

41. Habel's claim in his essay, however, that "Ezekiel's valued world apparently begins and ends with the city" probably needs to be qualified, at least over against the theology of Ezek 40–48. If Levenson is correct, Ezekiel's restoration program models ideal Israel on its prestate form, intentionally retreating from the people's later entrenchment in city life (*Theology of the Program*, 122).

in both D and P suggests that the compilation of the Pentateuch may have its beginnings in the early exile. But, on the other hand, Ezekiel does not consider himself bound to these legal traditions. As both a priest and prophet, he is free to offer his own new legislation. He manipulates traditions as one with authority, that is, as a new Moses. Ezekiel was no mere scribe, but an inspired interpreter of tradition for his times and, in the later parts of the book, a prophetic channel of a fresh divine word for the future.

The last three papers cover a variety of ways that hierarchy is manifested in Ezekiel's book. David Petersen ("Creation and Hierarchy in Ezekiel: Methodological Perspectives and Theological Prospects") argues that although the author of Ezekiel is aware of Israelite creation traditions, they are not important for his book's theological argument. Far from wanting to defend the goodness of creation, Ezekiel holds that humanity as originally created is defective and in need of a new heart and new spirit. Ezekiel's vision for the future does not entail restoring the old creation, but a new divinely revealed Torah, whose plan derives from principles of spatial and social hierarchies. For Petersen, "Hierarchies in Ezekiel's restoration vision reflect primarily the impact of the sacral world." Hierarchy thus derives from theology.

Stephen Cook ("Cosmos, *Kabod*, and Cherub: Ontological and Epistemological Hierarchy in Ezekiel") uses Ezekiel's texts about cherubim to illuminate the theological power of hierarchical thinking in the prophet's book. These texts reveal a cosmos with a graded infrastructure of holiness, which plays the positive role of allowing God to abide unusually near humanity and to reach out to sanctify the willing. Encamped so closely around the deity, the congregation can emulate the holiness in their midst. The cherubim in Ezekiel's system mediate the divide between God and the people, while participating in the dangerous quality of the numinous. The four faces of the cherubim looking out into the four cardinal directions illustrate the fact that, for the prophet, God on high has profound "horizontal" interests in the people of Israel and the world. Taking an epistemological cue from Karl Rahner, Cook further argues that Ezekiel's cherub symbolism betrays a hierarchy of levels of human knowledge of God. The cherubim's "archetypal" and "transcendental" form, revealed through an examination of archaeological, mythological, and psychological evidence, gives their symbolism special power in Ezekiel to communicate theological truth to foreign peoples, who have no access to Israel's intimate, covenantal knowledge of God.

In the book's final essay, Katheryn Pfisterer Darr ("Proverb Performance and Transgenerational Retribution in Ezekiel 18") provides a thorough analysis of the rhetoric of Ezek 18. This rhetorical analysis is firmly grounded in both the text's historical-cultural context (its performance) as well as in linguistic and comparative analysis. This analysis examines anew the issues of authority, and thus hierarchy, that lie beneath the surface of the text. Proverbs work insofar as they are perceived as "universal knowledge." Within a given society, appeals to this type of universal knowledge levels the playing field among participants who may come from various strata of a social organization. Darr discusses four elements that contribute to a proverb's authority: its form (it "sounds right"), its theme (which includes the way it may draw on cultural traditions), the context in which it is performed, and the identity of the speaker or performer. Leaving aside the question of whether chapter 18 preserves an actual proverb performance, Darr demonstrates how God's role in the text, speaking through the prophet, serves to trump an earlier "authoritative" proverb.

Our text concludes with the contributions of two respondents, Daniel Block ("In Search of Theological Meaning: Ezekiel Scholarship at the Turn of the Millennium") and Steven Tuell ("Contemporary Studies of Ezekiel: A New Tide Rising"). Not only are both authors published experts on the book of Ezekiel, but both have also been regular participants in the seminars that produced many of these essays. As Block notes, these seminars have provided Ezekiel scholars a collegial locale within which to explore various aspects of the book. As the careful responses demonstrate, these conversations neither expect uniformity of opinion nor hostile response. Both scholars offer different critiques of the works presented here, but both note the ways contemporary Ezekiel scholarship utilizes older methods of biblical interpretation as well as newer approaches to the book. Both authors admire approaches that combine questions of the historical context of the book with awareness of contemporary meaning. What strikes us most, however, is that both authors advocate a method of interpretation that allows the text its own unique voice. Tuell uses the image of a dialog, which needs not only the voice of the interpreter but also the voice of the text. In a sense, then, both authors advocate allocating the biblical text an important role in the hierarchy of interpretation.

The structure of this collection allows for multiple approaches to the book of Ezekiel to become apparent. What is presented is not a monograph that uncovers one source for the hierarchical images in the book (whether that be politics, theology, ontology, etc.), but rather complicates the analysis of hierarchy by pointing to its various sources, causes, and results. While every author attests to the pervasiveness of hierarchical images in Ezekiel, each author has his or her own analysis of the significance of this fact.

VII. Conclusion

We have tried to present a multilayered volume with competing voices on the issue of hierarchy in Ezekiel. The essays by our respondents offer layers of complexity that deepen appreciation of the problem. We hope that this structure captures the level of engagement over this issue that has manifested itself in our annual seminars. We invite the reader into our discussion in order to ponder the fundamental questions posed by these essays. Can the hierarchical thinking in the text be reduced to simply a matter of human ideology or politics? Does hierarchical thinking always encode oppression? Can hierarchical images ever have a positive function? Perhaps the questions raised here boil down to this: do contemporary views of hierarchy problematize the text of Ezekiel, or does this puzzling scriptural book problematize our contemporary assumptions about hierarchy?

ESSAYS

Priesthood in Exile according to the Book of Ezekiel

Friedrich Fechter

I. Textual Basis

The expression "priest" occurs only three times in Ezek 1–39, specifically in 1:3; 7:26; and 22:26, but in the *Verfassungsentwurf* (the "constitution project" of chs. 40–48) twenty-two times. Statistical results show that priests play hardly any role in the prophet's announcements of disaster, while they play a central role in the utopian outline of the future shrine and new city called "Yhwh is here" (48:35).

If we ask what we can learn from the book of Ezekiel about the role and status of the priesthood during the exile, we inevitably come to a barrier. For, as the statistical results already show, none of the texts addresses this question; the passages from Ezek 1–39 concern priests in the time before 587 B.C.E., while the constitution project takes the time of the new construction programmatically into view.

There is, nevertheless, a connection between the two periods, even if such a connection is not directly obvious in the texts. This connection consists in the authors of the texts. As I will show, these authors are closely related to each other and to the prophet. At the same time, it will also be demonstrated that the small number of texts possibly stemming from Ezekiel actually originated instead from later tradents who developed their program of the new temple and the new city under his name.

II. Examination of the Results

A. Ezekiel 1–39

There are two passages dealing with priests within Ezek 1–39, and both of them are announcements of disaster. They represent the prophet's preaching before 587 B.C.E. Ezekiel 7:26 describes a forthcoming situation in which one disaster follows another, and one piece of bad news is only followed by more bad news. In situations like these, one would ordinarily consult the responsible institutions: priests, prophets, and elders. The announcement of disaster, however, insists that now none of these institutions will be able to work as expected. The prophet will not have any vision, the priest will not give torah, and the elders will not know any counsel (7:26). Obviously, priests were expected to provide torah, that is, instruction.

On the other hand, Ezek 22:26 reproaches the priests:

> Their priests have done violence to my teaching and have profaned my shrines; they do not distinguish between sacred and common, neither have they taught the difference between impure[1] and pure. Before my Sabbaths they veil their eyes—so that I am profaned in their midst.

This reproach notes that the tasks of priests have consisted in the following: to give instruction, to protect the shrine from being violated, to make decisions concerning the distinction between the sacred and profane, pure and impure, and to observe the Sabbath. It seems astonishing that there is no mention of the sacrificial cult at all.

Here priests are referred to in the context of a *Ständepredigt*, that is, at the second position immediately after the prince (נשׂיא).[2] He is accused of reigning violently, killing people, and arbitrarily appropriating property. The reproaches against prince and priests are followed by reproaches against the institutions of government (שׂרים) and the prophets. None of them acts in an appropriate fashion. Finally, the "people of the land" (עם הארץ) are also accused, because they oppressed the powerless. No one in the entire society has proven to be an exception; everyone is guilty. Yhwh, in fact, did not have any choice: he had to punish this behavior. Ezekiel 22:24–31 must be considered a retrospective explanation of the catastrophe of 587. There is no future perspective.

To sum up: Both Ezek 7:26 and 22:26 demonstrate what priests should have done if they had only done their job in the correct manner; but they did not act in this way. In this context, they are blemished, having caused the destruction of Jerusalem together with all of Yhwh's people. There is no difference between priests and laity in this respect.

B. The Constitution Project: Ezekiel 40–48

Overview. While little is said about priests in Ezek 1–39, the situation is completely different in the last nine chapters of the book: beside the prince and the "people of the land," priests and Levites play a central role in this portion of the text. Primarily, Ezek 43:18–27 and 44:4–31 carry much weight. Therefore, these two texts shall be analyzed literarily in what follows. No literary analysis will be conducted on the other references to priests in these chapters, however,[3] though some reference will be made to these texts in order to strengthen the argument.

---

1. The article on ובין־הטמא seems to be an addition.
2. The text must be corrected at Ezek 22:25 in line with the Septuagint. On the status of the priests in Ezekiel, see the discussion of Steven S. Tuell, *The Law of the Temple in Ezekiel 40–48* (HSM 49; Atlanta: Scholars Press, 1992), 105–12.
3. See Ezek 40:45–46; 42:13–14; 45:1–8, 18–25; 46:19–24; 48:6–15.

The consecration of the new altar: Ezek 43:18–27. In a striking passage,[4] "Ezekiel" himself is summoned to consecrate the new altar (vv. 19–21).[5] He should act as follows: he should give a bull to the priest for a sin offering (v. 19). With the blood of this bull, "Ezekiel" alone should decontaminate the altar and make expiation for it (v. 20). After that, Ezekiel should take that bull, and "someone" should burn the bull at a certain place outside the sanctuary, yet still inside the temple area.[6] Verse 21bβ has a third-masculine-singular subject; the subject might be understood as an impersonal "one," expressing that the addressed "Ezekiel" should not act on his own. It remains totally unclear who that "someone" is—except for the fact that "Ezekiel" himself could never be that "someone," otherwise the change of subject in v. 21b would be inexplicable. Verse 22b, however, makes for real difficulties. Suddenly we hear about the action of several persons, whose activity is compared with other actions already performed by these same persons. Especially vv. 22b, 24b, 25b–27bα are astonishing in this respect.

Be that as it may, it seems clear that the instruction about the Day of Atonement in Lev 16 must be seen in the background of the text of Ezek 43. It is determined in Lev 16:27–28 that somebody should go outside the camp in order to burn the young bull and the goat from the sin offering. The one who is burning the animals should fulfill some purification rites before he is allowed to return into the camp. If we take this text into consideration, we have to recognize that the ritual instruction of Ezek 43 contains two different rites: the blood rite at the altar and, after that, the burnt offering outside the sanctuary.

In spite of that, v. 22b says: "and *they* have to decontaminate the altar as *they had decontaminated* it with the bull." With certainty, this means that the priests *must* have been involved in the ritual of decontamination previously. This ritual, however, consists of two elements, as has been shown above. This means that the priests took part in the second expiation ritual and had to execute the blood rite as well.

Of course, we should question whether this contradiction might be the consequence of literary expansion. Indeed, v. 22 could be omitted without any break in the literary structure of the passage. But if this is the case, then we would not be able to answer the question why this verse should have ever been inserted here after the passage had already been formulated. It seems rather impossible that v. 22 could be a later addition.

There is another problem in the text, namely, v. 25. The change of subject here

---

4. With one exception, there seems to be no reason for text-critical emendations in this text. Verse 21 in the MT reads ולקחת את הפר החטאת and, therefore, the article before פר seems to be wrong. It is possible to understand the text as follows, however: "and you shall take the bull as the sin offering." This rendering of the passage seems to make sense, and allows us to maintain the text's present form.

5. The Septuagint tries to alter the text in order to avoid this difficulty; even papyrus 967, which often follows the MT against the LXX, does so. But MT makes sense and has the benefit of being the *lectio difficilior*.

6. This assignment reminds one of the phrase "outside the camp" in Lev 4:12, 21; 8:17; 9:11; 16:27.

is more striking than in v. 22. Verses 23–24 seem to form a classic closing, especially with the use of the verb כלה (v. 23). Obviously, the purification and expiation of the altar were considered to be finished by the offering of the bull and the goat. This is also attested by the ritual of the Day of Atonement in Lev 16:18–19, in which expiation of the altar on יום הכפרים ("the Day of Atonement") had to ensue with the blood of a bull and a goat. If we look at Ezek 43:24, we find that the offering of a bull and a ram with the participation of the priests is clearly separated from the ritual of consecration. Rather, the priestly offerings open the series of regular offerings on this altar from that moment onward. Verses 25–27 must be an addition, because of their return to the theme "consecration of the altar." The change of subject in v. 25 results from the attempt to combine the instructions directly addressed to "Ezekiel" in vv. 18–24 with the plural instructions of vv. 25–27. These verses are formed in the style of ritual legislation, which is commonly in the third-person plural.

The addition lengthens the period of consecration of the altar to one full week.[7] "Ezekiel" offers a goat, and the priests offer a bull and ram. In vv. 25–27, the ritual is changed relative to vv. 18–24. The offering of a bull in v. 25 cannot be the same as the bull of the sin offering in vv. 19–21. The bull of the burnt offering is rather the same as the concluding offering from vv. 23–24. The one who added vv. 25–27 also added this sacrificial bull to the ritual of expiation. The series of regular offerings begins with this consecration ritual lasting one week. In addition, vv. 25–27 differ from vv. 18–24, because the beginning of regular offerings, according to vv. 25–27, starts on the eighth day, whereas this offering (according to vv. 23–24) takes place with the second or perhaps the third day after starting the expiation ritual. Finally, yet importantly, we have to take into consideration that there are plain terminological differences between the two parts of the text.[8]

The concluding v. 27 has a somewhat parenetic character because of its address in the second person, masculine plural. This is the first time in the whole of the passage that an outside perspective comes into play in regard to its function as an offering. After all, the interests of the community in offerings aim at calming the deity, assuring his shelter, welfare, as well as his assistance and help. Exactly these elements can be found in the concluding promise in the second part of v. 27, including the cult-legal term רצא ("accept"). Ezekiel himself probably never used this verb; elsewhere in the book, it is only found in 20:40–41, in the context of an announcement of salvation, which seems to be an expansion of one of the additional layers in Ezek 20.[9]

---

7. It is possible that there is a connection with Lev 8:33, 35.

8. In vv. 18–24, we find the verbs עלה ("sacrifice"), זרק ("splash"), נתן (here, "put on"), כפר (Piel, "to make atonement for"), שרף ("burn"), קרב (Hiphil, "offer"), and שלך (Hiphil, "throw"). In vv. 25–27, the verbs עשה ("prepare") and טהר (Piel, "cleanse") appear. Only כפר (Piel, "expiate") is used without difference, though this use is not significant because of the theme of expiation.

9. Stefan Ohnesorge has found quite a few different layers in Ezek 20 (*Jahwe gestaltet sein Volk neu: Zur Sicht der Zukunft Israels nach Ezechiel 11:14–21, 20:1–44, 36:16–38, 37:1–14, 15–28* [FB 64; Würzburg:

Altogether this passage strongly recalls the ordination ritual,[10] which is instructed in Exod 29:1–37 and executed in Lev 8:15–34. In this text, Moses functions as the initiator. After the ordination of the priests, Moses expiates and consecrates the altar and then executes the first offerings, especially the עיל־המלעים ("consecration ram").[11] This seems to be some kind of prophylactic offering for the newly ordained priests. There is nothing comparable in Ezek 43:18–27.[12] There is a simple reason for this lack of ritual: the priests in Ezek 43 already are considered ordained priests.

In sum, Ezek 43 is a priestly legislation text that draws on distinctive features of the book of Ezekiel but lacks signs of the book's prophetic character.[13]

Higher and lower clergy: Ezek 44:4–31. The introduction of the complex represents the beginning of a new visionary guided tour (*Führungsvision*) following 44:1–3.[14] But Ezek 44:6–46:18 shows no sign of that form.[15] Instead, we find within the background of accusations several regulations used to denounce a former behavior. The guided tour does not find its explicit continuation before 46:19–47:12. From these observations it follows that the section 44:6–31 might be a part of an expansion layer.[16]

Ezekiel 44:6–9aα is arranged in the structure of a *begründete Unheilsankündigung* (i.e., a "substantiated disaster announcement"). The first part of it opens with a summons to speak and a messenger formula, and then turns in reproach directly

---

Echter, 1991], 96–101). His arguments are not convincing in every case, but overall he seems to be right. First there are some double readings and tensions, which question the literary unity of Ezek 20:32–44. Especially v. 40bα and 41aα are not a unity at all. (Thomas Krüger has overlooked this [*Geschichtskonzepte im Ezechielbuch* (BZAW 180; Berlin and New York: de Gruyter, 1989), 271–72].) The change of person between v. 40bα and v. 40bβ is not motivated from third masculine plural to second masculine plural. Beyond that, the theme of v. 40a, bα differs from that in v. 40bβ, 41aα. Probably v. 40bα once concluded the passage with v. 40. In this way, it expresses the idea that Yhwh accepts Israel's offerings on this mountain. On the other hand, it is said in v. 40bβ and following that Yhwh accepts them gracefully, because they bring their offerings, as soon as they will be gathered from their Diaspora. By these words, vv. 40bβ, 41, 42 express a postexilic, temple-offering, cultic perspective, whereas v. 40a, bα lacks this perspective.

10. Cf. Leslie C. Allen, *Ezekiel 20–48* (WBC 29; Dallas: Word, 1990), 251.

11. Cf. Erhard Gerstenberger, who renders the Hebrew as "Einsetzungswidder" ("consecration ram") (*Das dritte Buch Mose: Leviticus* [ATD 6; Göttingen: Vandenhoeck & Ruprecht, 1993], 6, 89; Eng. trans., *Leviticus: A Commentary* [trans. D. W. Stott; OTL; Louisville: Westminster John Knox, 1996]).

12. The anointing of the altar is missing in Ezek 43, but this will not be discussed.

13. The term "regulations of the altar" often is paralleled with "regulations of torah" in Num 19, or with the superscription of the Passover instruction in Exod 12:43. These parallels cannot be discussed here.

14. For a detailed text-critical analysis of the passage, see Friedrich Fechter, "Priesthood in Exile according to the Book of Ezekiel," *SBL Seminar Papers 2000* (SBLSP 39; Atlanta: Society of Biblical Literature, 2000), 679–81.

15. Cf. Ernst Vogt, *Untersuchungen zum Buch Ezechiel* (AnBib 95; Rome: Biblical Institute Press, 1981), 161, 175.

16. See similarly Krüger, *Geschichtskonzepte im Ezechielbuch,* 311–12, with different layers.

to the addressees, who are accused of serious offenses. Classically, a second messenger formula (v. 9) then follows, which opens the announcement part. The announcement proper is found in here, too, but the structure of the announcement differs clearly from those examples that can be traced back to the prophet himself. While in other texts Yhwh's intrusion into history is announced, the introduction of a new cult order is carried out here (vv. 9–16). Certainly, this announcement of a new cultic order likewise contains punishment, but this is not referred to as Yhwh's interruption of history. The result of the punishment is a lasting demotion in status of part of the cult staff. In addition, there is a change from direct address (vv. 6b–8) to a speech in the third person (vv. 9–16). Embedded in this passage we can find another part of a *begründete Unheilsankündigung*. This one opens with the expression, typical of Ezekiel, יען אשר ("because," v. 12). But there is no לכן ("therefore") at the beginning of the announcement portion; instead, על־כן ("therefore") is used. This shows an imitating style. It is thoroughly unusual to find in an announcement of punishment, here in the form of status reduction for a part of the cult staff, an announcement of a reward suddenly proffered for a different part of the cult staff. Like the announcement of punishment before it, this announcement of reward is grounded in the behavior of part of the cult staff. Nowhere else in the book of Ezekiel does Yhwh act in favor of human beings on account of their behavior. Yhwh's saving acts are elsewhere justified in the divine free will alone.

Elements of Ezekielian language are picked up (e.g., "house of rebellion," formulas, structure of *begründete Unheilsankündigung*), but there are more than a few ideas and terms that are completely unusual to Ezekiel the prophet as well as to the early expansion layers. One example is circumcision. Not to be circumcised seems to be characteristic of foreign peoples (28:10; 31:18; 32:19–32) in later additions.[17] Similarly, the rejection of the stranger (vv. 7–9) is very atypical for the prophet himself. Such a rejection stems from assumptions about the ethnic and religious identity of the people of Yhwh, a typically postexilic topic. In these times, circumcision becomes a religiously founded distinction of the people of Yhwh, contrasting them with the foreign nations. This distinctive mark must have gained so much weight during the Second Temple period that it gained entrance in legislation, particularly because the stranger now lived amid Israel. This rejection of all strangers is in clear contradiction to 3:6, which implies that Yhwh could have sent Ezekiel to any nation.

The distinction of the cult staff separated into two castes also cannot be explained by exilic circumstances. There is a significant parallel in Num 18, but without the strong polemics against the Levites found here.[18] A somewhat compa-

---

17. Cf. the discussion in Risto Nurmela, *The Levites: Their Emergence as a Second-Class Priesthood* (South Florida Studies in the History of Judaism 193; Atlanta: Scholars Press, 1998), 92–95.

18. There are no hints that Num 18 might be the older conception, as Allen suggests (*Ezekiel 20–48*, 261, referring to Michael Fishbane, *Biblical Interpretation in Ancient Israel* [Oxford: Clarendon, 1985], 138–43).

rable situation can only be detected in the so-called Korah-revision (*Korach-Bearbeitung*) of Num 16, also stemming from postexilic times.[19]

The phrase "when Israel/the Israelites went astray" occurs two times in the text. Presupposed is a phase of the history that is now thought to be completed and that is to be followed by a new phase, presently under way. Such a view is nearly impossible for exilic times.

Verses 17–31, which give instructions regarding the behavior of the priests in the new order, can be distinguished from the hierarchy of the cult staff in the prior section, which had been formed in prophetic style. The origin of these determinations should be subtly differentiated. Though the form of the regulations corresponds to the priestly torah, the composition reminds one of a Decalogue. The regulations herein come from ten (different) taboo areas. An exception is the regulation in vv. 17–19 concerning the dresses for inside and outside. This regulation occurs in similar form in 42:14.[20] On the one hand, it emphasizes the distinction between sacred and common areas, while, on the other hand, asserting the peculiar position of the priest as mediator between the sphere of holiness and the people. Verse 18 interrupts this dress code for inside and outside the sanctuary, adding the general rule that service at the shrine has to be carried out exclusively in linen clothes.[21] Therefore, v. 18 may originally have been connected with the following instructions. This composition, however, does not seem to be unified either. For example, the regulations concerning the cleaning of the priest after having contact with a deceased person seems to be a later addition. This can be demonstrated first by comparison with Lev 21:1–4, which has the same theme, and, second, with the fact that vv. 25–26 suddenly talk about the priest in singular form. Beyond that, Ezek 44:26–27 may mirror Num 19:11 concerning the instruction about the seven-day period of purification.

Further inconsistencies can be found in Yhwh's "I," which appears suddenly in vv. 23–24 and 28, as well as in the direct address (which had not come into view in

---

19. Ludwig Schmidt has shown that this layer in Num 16 is a revised edition of the story of the 250 men, which has been composed by the authors of the Priestly Document (*Studien zur Priesterschrift* [BZAW 214; New York: de Gruyter, 1993], 135–46). Like Ezek 44, the Korah-revision has as its theme the opposition of Levites and priests. While Korah and Aaron are the representatives of their opposing groups in Num 16, only Zadok is mentioned in Ezek 44. He, however, is not an actor but an identifying figure. On the other hand, there is no figure on the side of the Levites in Ezek 44 who might be compared with Korah in Num 16. There also is a difference in regard to the distinction between both of the cult staff groups in the two texts. Both texts speak in common of seduction. In Num 16, however, this motif has come into the text because of the secondary revision of the older story about the 250 men. Thus, it does not figure significantly in comparing Ezek 44 and Num 16.

20. See Lev 6:4, where the priest has to remove his linen clothes when leaving the sanctuary.

21. See also Exod 29:39, 42–43; 39:27–29; Lev 6:3. It seems interesting that woolen clothing is strictly forbidden "while they do service within the gates of the inner court and in the house." Walther Zimmerli suggests that sweating might not necessarily be the only reason for this instruction (*Ezechiel II* [BKAT 13; Neukirchen-Vluyn: Neukirchener, 1969], 1134).

vv. 9–27) in v. 28b and 30. In addition, v. 30bα mentions the priest in the singular and v. 30bβ changes to the second-person singular. The parenetic character of vv. 28b and 30a leads to the inference that we find here the continuation of the framework-address delivered earlier to the "house of rebellion" in vv. 6–8. Verse 30 seems to have been placed here because it addresses the question of the supply of priests, which is regulated in v. 29.

The following picture arises from the text: the determinations concerning the priestly caste, with its distinctions between upper and lower classes of clergy, may have formed the core of the text. It was completed by regulations concerning inner and outer spaces in vv. 17 and 19. This complex may have been expanded on thematic grounds by the priestly torah of vv. 18, 20–22, 25, 29, and 31, so that v. 18 became part of the inner/outer space regulations. Those passages containing Yhwh's "I" also seem to be expansions. Without exception, these deal with the relation between the priests and the people. The priests are pictured instructing the people to distinguish between pure and impure, sacred and profane (v. 23),[22] acting as judges (v. 25a), supervising the feasts (v. 25b), and, finally, receiving a settlement in regard to a נחלה ("inheritance," v. 28a). Verse 28b is striking because of its use of אחזה ("holding") instead of נחלה, and its address in the second masculine plural. This addition might date to the final redactor of the chapter, the same one who formed the framework addressing the "house of rebellion." He is responsible for imbedding and revising the text in vv. 6–8, 28b, 30a. The addition in v. 30bα probably dates to the time of Nehemiah; v. 30bβ is of even later origin.

In conclusion, the text can under no circumstances date from Ezekiel. Indeed, it seems with very high probability to be of postexilic origin. Although space does not allow for a full discussion of Num 18, it should be taken into account that Num 18 seems to be some kind of counterpart to Ezek 44. It contains the same combination of priestly order and priestly supply as Ezek 44.

III. Conclusions for the Question of the Investigation

A. The Statements of the Texts

Ezekiel and Moses. The question whether Ezekiel himself could have been a priest or merely the son of the priest Buzi arises from Ezek 1:3. The precise reference to which הכהן ("the priest") refers cannot be recognized definitively. Now we can answer this question with a greater degree of certainty, however, from the viewpoint of the authors of Ezek 43:18–27. Ezekiel has indeed been a priest. He initiates the postexilic sacrifice in the temple. By that act, Ezekiel is equated with Moses, who inaugurated cultic service in Israel. This is also theologically interesting, for it means that, in the eyes of the author, Ezekiel repaired the broken relation between God and the people, since this relation is obviously mediated by the sacrificial cult. It is deci-

---

22. Note the reference back to Ezek 22:26.

sive that this reparation does not start out from humankind, but rather depends on a free initiative of Yhwh. The prophetic scheme of rhetoric is wrapped around the priestly ritual legislation, and thus shows that no one brings service, not even a priestly person, but Yhwh himself causes, ordains, and organizes it as a means of salvation for humankind.

Before the altar can be used for sacrifice, it must be cleansed of sin. Sin is regarded as something like a *substantia*, which must be removed from the altar. We must draw the conclusion that humans can only progress toward salvation after sin has been removed.

The priests are not characterized as mediators but as executors. The first time the altar is used, it must be Ezekiel-Moses who acts to consecrate the new altar. Ordinary priests do not suffice here. Ezekiel-Moses is only responsible for the initiation, though; the priests then are to follow in his succession.

Status difference. According to Ezek 40:45–46, there are two groups of priests in the service of the visionary temple: temple servants and altar servants.[23] The groups are hierarchically ordered, although Zimmerli does not share that view.[24] The two are to reside in opposite places. As the later addition shows, the origin of the two priestly groups is the criterion that distinguishes their service: the Zadokites alone are allowed to come close to Yhwh.

On the other hand, 42:13–14 might represent an older stage, because the distinguishing of priests found in 40:45–46 is missing. Also, in this passage two rooms are mentioned, but these are used by all of the priests without reference to rank.

In comparing the two texts, one sees the beginning of an important development. At first, only one distinction is made, namely, the one between priests and non-priests. The regular whereabouts of the priests is in the immediate proximity of the place of sacrifice. Everything that comes into contact with the sacrifice is withdrawn from normal use. The criterion of this distinction is holiness. Later, a differentiation takes place within the priesthood.

This differentiation is central in Ezek 44:10–16. Such a differentiation had not existed in older times, according to the author's opinion.[25] The text of v. 13 says: "they are not allowed to come close to me in order to serve as priests for me and to

---

23. As Zimmerli (*Ezechiel II*, 1035–36) has shown, 40:38–46 interrupts the logic of the visionary guided tour in 40:1–37, 47–49; 41:1–4. In particular, the dramatic address to the guided visionary in 41:4 is destroyed, if there is some interpreting word before it. At the redactional level, however, there is a specific relation between 40:45–46 and 41:4. The former mentions those who are allowed to come close to Yhwh, the latter explains the place of the abode of Yhwh. In any case, 40:44–46 relies on 40:38–43. Verse 46b seems to be a later addition, which might have been inserted here in order to identify the altar priests with the Zadokites.

24. Ibid., 1028.

25. This seems to correlate with the literary-historical development of the book of Ezekiel. Cf. Ellen F. Davis, *Swallowing the Scroll: Textuality and the Dynamics of Discourse in Ezekiel's Prophecy* (JSOTSup 78; Sheffield: Almond, 1989), 163 n. 44.

approach all my holy things, to the holy of holies." This can only mean that they had been permitted to do a priestly service in former times. This permission now is abrogated, because the Levites had left YHWH (v. 10: רחק ["went far"]) as Israel "went astray" (v. 10: תעה). One can recognize that the author is in so great a temporal distance from the event that he virtually works out of an epochal structure of history: time of going astray, time of purification, time of new beginnings. The latter is the author's time. In regard to the Levites, it is characterized as a time when they must bear the negative results of their sinful behavior. There is no temporal limitation on this punishment. Indeed this means status reduction; the Levites are no longer called כהן ("priest"), a title they must have possessed in former times. Moreover, 40:45, 46a[26] distinguishes between the two priestly groups, as has been shown above. One group's members were servants of the house, the other one's members, servants of the altar. Yet there seems to be no status difference in 40:45, 46a. On the other hand, Ezek 44 knows of status reduction of those who must carry out the service of the house. In principle, such a status reduction can only take place if there had been a higher status before. This higher status was valid apparently up to the time of the preaching of the new order and, therefore, until the author's time. It becomes recognizable, then, that Ezek 44 represents an expansion of the basic layer of the constitution project. However, this expansion has inserted a further element besides the status reduction of a part of the priesthood, and this is the distinction between Levites and Zadokites.

Two principles become clearer with this:

1. Priesthood was exercised in former times by two groups. Both of them traced their genealogies back to Levi. They differed only in respect to the areas of their responsibility.
2. Originally, both had access to the sacrificial service of YHWH.

Ezekiel 44 undertakes all efforts to strengthen the already existing role differentiation by adding the factor of status reduction. The major reasons for the reduction are mentioned with regard to the group whose status is devalued. Although the reproach mentioned is massive—the Levites are accused of having practiced foreign cults—one cannot easily harmonize that reproach with the actual activities of the Levites. The text does not say anything about the details of their preexilic apostasy. In regard to this point, we can conclude that the author must be a member of the Zadokites. He uses linguistic and traditio-historical elements of Ezekiel's own texts and is, therefore, probably a member of Ezekiel's circle. This circle, then, seems to be composed chiefly, if not exclusively, of Levite-Zadokite priests. It is highly improbable that Ezekiel himself was not a priest (see above, "Ezekiel and Moses"). Quite obviously, he never performed his ministry in the Jerusalem temple, as most

---

26. Note that v. 46b is a later insertion.

of his closer, intimate friends had not. But this responsibility for the temple without doubt stamped the circle's conception of themselves as priests.

The other texts (Ezek 45:1–8;[27] 46:19–24; 48:8–15) also strongly devalue the Levites in favor of the Zadokite priesthood. Several times in these texts the theme of the distribution of land comes into play. A specific area in the middle of the land plays an important role, which is called a תרומה ("portion," "offering"). Its measurements are 25,000-by-20,000 cubits. It is remarkable that everywhere the number 20,000 (עשרים) occurs in the text with respect to the distribution of land it has been changed into 10,000 (עשרה).[28] The one who changed the text wanted to assert that the holy תרומה only existed in an area measuring 25,000-by-10,000 cubits. This area is the piece of land designated for the servants of the shrine, but not for the Levites. The Levites should not live on holy ground. This was not the intention, of course, in the original text, but it shows the trend moving in the direction of 44:10–16 that gradually gained authority.

B. The Problem of the Exilic Priesthood: Role and Status

It is striking that all of the actions regarding the ordination of priests, which are ordered in Exod 29 and carried out in Lev 8, are missing in Ezek 43. We can draw the conclusion that there must have been a regular succession of priests during exilic times. According to the opinion of the members of the Ezekielian circle, the priesthood remained valid in exile without practicing the sacrificial cult. Such a conception of one's own social group presupposes a collective process, which is flanked by delimiting measures against others who do not belong to the group. The members of the Ezekielian circle had to dissociate themselves clearly from all other groups in the *Gola* to be able to keep this profile. They must have been able to maintain the basic principles of priestly regulations that had constituted the priesthood before 597/587. Quite likely, a number of the regulations may have first been designed, if not literally fixed, in exilic times, based on the delimiting efforts of the Zadokite priestly group against all others. For the sake of these efforts, the internal priestly distinctions that are evident in texts such as Num 16, 18, or Ezek 44 may also have been carried out. But what could have triggered this internal effort to make a Levitical distinction? Was it conflict that had become virulent first in the

---

27. According to the context, it seems clear that 45:1–8 must be regarded as a secondary insertion (Allen, *Ezekiel 20–48*, 255; Tuell, in contrast, speaks of an early foreshadowing of the connection between "prince" and priests [*Law of the Temple*, 174]). It might have been added because of the expression תרומה (44:30; 45:1, 6, 7). This text tries to explain the tension between the prohibition of possessing land in 44:28 and the distribution of land in 48:10–12. Therefore, Ezek 45:1–8 had to be added exactly in this place. This text was probably composed for its present location in the book. Verse 8 connects this text with the admonition of the princes in v. 9. An even later addition seems to be v. 2, because there is a clear relation between v. 1 and v. 3. In addition, the use of הקדש ("the sanctuary") in v. 2 is unique in the book of Ezekiel, as is the idea of an uncultivated green area around the sanctuary.

28. E.g., Ezek 45:1, where the LXX has "20,000" whereas the MT has "10,000." Cf. Ezek 48:9.

Gola? Or was it conflict that in principle had already existed in preexilic times, whose social consequences, however, first appeared only in the exile?[29]

There is simply no textual evidence for the former possibility. We do not know what might have happened in the *Gola* in this respect. Although it is wrong to conclude from this that there had not been such conflicts between the different groups, we simply know nothing about this.[30]

C. The Lineage of Zadok[31]

Zadok seems to be the one who was the most suitable figure in Israel's past on whom to base the ideal of legitimate priesthood as developed during the exile by the Ezekielian circle.

Zadok had been the one who, according to 2 Sam 8:17, had been priest under David's rule, together with Abiathar. He functioned as a negotiator between the citizens of Jerusalem and David in the rebellion of Absalom (2 Sam 15:24–29). This leads to the opinion that Zadok and Abiathar might have already been Jebusite priests in pre-Davidic times. Beyond that, we have to recognize that Zadok's lineage seems to have been traced back to the Elide priests of Shiloh via the figure of Ahitub. This Ahitub is said to have been Zadok's father (2 Sam 8:17). The name Ahitub (originally, perhaps another figure) also appears in 1 Sam 14:3 as a grandson of Eli.[32] If we take this into account, Zadok might have been regarded as the first Yhwh-priest at Jerusalem, who also served at the tabernacle of Yhwh (cf. 2 Sam 15:24–25).

There is yet another genealogical tradition according to the Chronicler. There, Zadok belongs to the lineage of Aaron's son Eleazar (1 Chr 5:29–34; 6:35–38; 24:1–4). This lineage does not contain the name of Eli, the former priest of Shiloh. So it can be assumed that Eli might have belonged to the line of Ithamar, Aaron's other son.[33] Because of the guilt of Eli's sons, Eli's line should be extinguished (1 Sam 2:27–36). Ithamar's lineage obviously was regarded as the lower one,[34] because Ithamar had to control the Levites (Exod 38:21; Num 4:28, 33). Zadok, who did not belong to Ithamar's and Eli's descendants, thus became the appropriate ancestor of the Jerusalem priesthood.

D. The New Exilic Emphasis on Priestly Lineage

The tendency of differentiating two castes of priests with different statuses permits certain conclusions about the development of the priesthood in the exile. The

---

29. "Exile" has to be understood in two ways: temporally and locally.

30. For remarks on Levitical and priestly history within Israelite religion, see my excurses in Fechter, "Priesthood in Exile," 690–94.

31. Cf. Nurmela, *Levites*, 19–21.

32. Of course, both persons might be identified as the same figure. But we must leave this question open. The genealogical connections are unclear. See 1 Sam 22:20: Ahitub–Ahimelech–Abiathar, and 2 Sam 8:17: Ahitub–Zadok and Abiathar–Ahimelech.

33. Nadab and Abihu died in the wilderness without sons, according to Lev 10:1–3; 1 Chr 24:2.

34. This seems to be mirrored by the lower number of priests from Ithamar's lineage in 1 Chr 24:4.

question "Who is a priest?" took on increasingly greater significance, apparently in view of the absence of the practice of sacrifice during that time. The genealogical connection with one common ancestor apparently became the decisive criterion. The innovative moment was that Levi no longer took part in the sacrificial cult. But the relation of priests to Levi was irreversible, and could not be eliminated. This genealogical connection must have already been a fixed part of priestly identity in preexilic times. But it was possible to distinguish between the Levites of one category and those of another. This distinction was first executed by Ezek 44:10–16. It was based on genealogical reasons as well. A very narrowly defined connection with the Jerusalem sanctuary was combined with this distinction. Some members of the Levitical lineage were not able to claim this connection. These are mentioned as "Levites" in Ezek 45:5, whereas the others are "the priests"; the expression "Levitical priests," as in 44:15, is now avoided. Ezekiel 45:1–8 obviously shows the next stage of development in status differentiation: priests and Levites are set in opposition to one another.

In addition, Ezek 45:1–8 says that the Levites possess an אחזה ("a holding"). By this the Levites are taken out of the regulations concerning priests in Ezek 44:28, because they no longer can be considered to have only Yhwh for an אחזה.[35] The distinction between priests and Levites is thus sharpened.[36]

To sum up: the delimitation of the priesthood seems to be closely tied to the question of succession. The idea of lineage-control fixed the boundaries between the groups and formed the rules of identification.

IV. Further Conclusions

Priesthood in exile according to the book of Ezekiel seems to be determined by three factors:

1. The representation of their own identity by the complete succession or descent of their group from the common ancestor Zadok; one can see how this factor arises (compare 44:10–16 against the older 40:45–46) and disappears (48:9–14; 46:19–24).
2. Combined with the first factor, the sharp delineation from the former non-Jerusalem priesthood, who are called "the Levites."
3. The conscious separation of both groups as clergy in opposition to all other members of society.

---

35. The term "holding" is avoided for the Zadokites in 44:28, 45:4, and 48:12, but it is used for the Levites' land in 45:5.
36. Ezekiel 46:19–24 seems to be of still later origin. Priests and "Levites" are totally different in this passage. The term "Levites" is even completely avoided; the text only speaks of house servants. There are some connections with Lev 17:3–9, which wants to withdraw the liberalization that allowed for profane slaughtering (Deut 12:15).

These three factors do not rely on cultic service, which seems to be very important. We have to note that neither circumcision nor observance of the Sabbath played any role. None of these elements, which played such an important role for the community of postexilic Judah, is of any interest in this respect. Ezekiel 44:17–31 probably contains those elements that were decisive in order to distinguish between those who were clergy and all of the others. A determination that regulates the sharp distinction of the clothing for use inside and outside the sanctuary—or, should we say, in contact with Yhwh and in contact with ordinary people—is placed at the top of these regulations. There is a sharp distinction between sacred and common, pure and impure, priest and non-priest. The ability to make this distinction might be the point for which the caste of priests trained during exile. This took place in the circle around the prophet Ezekiel. He may have been a central integrating figure of the exiled priests. Yhwh had called him to be a watchman against the people of Judah. Ezekiel, though part of this people, had to take a place outside of them. There was a sharp distinction between Yhwh and the prophet, on the one hand, but also between Yhwh's prophet and the people, on the other. The Ezekielian circle took over this distinction for all members belonging to it.

In later times, the men of the Ezekielian circle started projecting the design of the new town and the new sanctuary. They created a utopian model,[37] concentric in style with its center being the altar of Yhwh. The beginning of the cult was connected with the ancestor of their ideas (Ezekiel), and the definition of the cultic personnel was connected with the ancestor of their lineage (Zadok), the first Jerusalem priest, who came from the line of Eleazar. In this fashion, they formed a pyramidal picture of the new order.

The architects were not able to execute their project. Other groups insisted on Aaron as the legitimating ancestor. Jerusalem could not be designed in the way that the city "Yhwh is Here" had been projected. Yhwh's cult had to struggle against others (Isa 57:3–10). And the limitation against strangers did not work as intended (Isa 56:1–8). But some of the ideas developed in the *Gola* asserted themselves, first of all the differentiation between priests and Levites. The Ezekielian priests were very successful: the lists of people returning home from Mesopotamia in Ezra and Nehemiah show a great number of priests, but only a few Levites. The priestly propaganda had done its job.

Why did they do so? There is still another aspect that has not been mentioned yet, but it seems in my opinion to be the most important one. Let us take a last glance at the texts. With Ezek 48:8–15 an additional aspect comes into view. There

---

37. Recently, John F. Kutsko has interpreted Ezek 36–37 as caused by "appropriating standard Mesopotamian language of re-creation and repatriation of cult statues, inverting the whole system by applying it to [the prophet's] description of the revivification and restoration of Israel" (*Between Heaven and Earth: Divine Presence and Absence in the Book of Ezekiel* [Biblical and Judaic Studies from the University of California, San Diego 7; Winona Lake, Ind.: Eisenbrauns, 2000], 147). If Kutsko is right, it might be possible to combine this hypothesis with the question of the concept of Ezek 40–48 as well.

is a hierarchical picture in regard to the distribution of land. Sacred and common areas are strictly separated from each other. But they are not only separated, they are at the same time indivisibly related to one another. This seems to reflect the self-understanding of the priests more adequately. Priests are those who are separated from all the others and exempted from service, but who nevertheless live in the midst of the land among all of the citizens. They are not allowed to bring together sacred and common areas, but at the same time they have to be mediators between both.

This seems to be the result of a monotheistic picture of God. Only if God is completely separate from the world and at the same time turns to the world can God be described as the only deity. If there is no severe distinction between God and the world, one cannot deny that God is—at least in part—dependent upon the world. If there is no turning to the world, the question of the *absentia Dei* causes a problem for salvation. So the concept of the constitution project in Ezek 40–48 tells us about the effects of these dialectics on the picture of priesthood. There must have been an intense discussion among the exiled priests[38] concerning other religions. Under the pressures of the Babylonian pantheon, they had to confront a world that had not even been created by one single god, and even worse, was not governed by only one. If there is one single God alone, this deity can only be thought of as a deity completely identical with the world or totally separate from it. Israel's faith traditions show, from earliest times onward, that there has never been an option for the first. In the exile in Babylonia, the priests started a process of clarification of the picture of God as the only one, who must be both totally separate from the world yet who also cannot leave it alone. The abode of the priests according to Ezek 48:8–15 reflects well this picture of God. The priests became, then, the necessary mediators between God, the Holy One, and the people. Priestly sacrificial service, thus, became the only saving path (*Heilsweg*) to God.

---

38. See Lester Grabbe, *Priests, Prophets, Diviners, Sages: A Socio-Historical Study of Religious Specialists in Ancient Israel* (Valley Forge, Pa.: Trinity Press International, 1995), 47.

Putting Priests in Their Place: Ezekiel's Contribution to the History of the Old Testament Priesthood

Iain M. Duguid

From the time of Julius Wellhausen onward, Ezekiel has been widely regarded as a pivotal figure in the downgrading of a particular group of priests from full priestly status to the role of temple servants.[1] On this understanding, the main goal of Ezek 44 was the provision of an ethical justification for this downgrading.[2] More recent scholarship has also often seen a tendentious political agenda behind Ezekiel's program, with Ezekiel fabricating charges of idolatry against the Levites in pursuit of the political agenda of the dominant Zadokites.[3] The prophet's goal is thus understood to be putting the various priestly groups in their proper place.

In this essay, I want to suggest that Ezekiel's intent was indeed to put priests in their proper place, but in a rather different way than has often been supposed. Ezekiel's contribution was not single-handedly to reshape the history of the priesthood, but rather to reflect the figure of a faithful priest in exile. His own faithfulness to the place he had been assigned, and his depiction of rewards for others who had likewise been faithful to their places of service and of judgment on those who had been unfaithful, was intended to encourage and challenge people to similar lives of obedience.

In order to establish this thesis, it is necessary first to lay out in broad terms the place and task of the priesthood in preexilic society. Then we shall examine the impact that the exile itself would have had on the status and role of the priestly class. Third, we shall consider the place and task of the priesthood in the immediate post-

---

1. I would like to thank Corrine Patton and Stephen Cook for reading this essay carefully and suggesting many improvements.
2. In Wellhausen's often-quoted phrase, Ezekiel "drapes the logic of facts with a mantle of morality" (*Prolegomena to the History of Ancient Israel* [trans. J. S. Black and A. Menzies; Edinburgh: Black, 1885], 124; trans. of *Prolegomena zur Geschichte Israels* [2nd ed.; Berlin: Reimer, 1883], 128).
3. For the accusation in its strongest terms, see Paul D. Hanson, *The People Called: The Growth of Community in the Bible* (San Francisco: Harper & Row, 1986), 268.

exilic period. Finally, with that as a backdrop, we shall consider how Ezekiel's priestly prophecy fits into and contributes to that picture.

I. PRIESTHOOD PRIOR TO THE EXILE

The role of the priest in Israel is laid out in Deut 33:8–10.[4] According to this passage, the priests consist of a restricted group, linked together by a shared ancestor, namely, Levi. They had the responsibility of consulting God by means of the Urim and Thummim, of teaching Yahweh's ordinances and laws, and of altar ministry, offering incense and whole burnt offerings.

The use of the Urim and Thummim to determine God's will was an essential part of the priestly task in the early days of the priesthood.[5] This kind of priestly divination is undertaken by Ahijah for Saul (1 Sam 14:18–19) and, later, by Abiathar for David (1 Sam 23:6, 9–12; 30:7–8). However, after David ascended to the throne, the giving of priestly oracles apparently rapidly decreased in significance. This seems to have been related to, though not necessarily caused by, the corresponding rise in the prophetic movement. Thus it is striking that the implied question regarding the temple in 2 Sam 7 is addressed to Nathan the prophet, not to a priest (2 Sam 7:2–3). Thereafter, the kings of Israel and Judah consistently sought Yahweh's will through the mediation of prophets.

We are further told that after the return from the exile there was no priest able to handle the Urim and Thummim (Ezra 2:63).[6] From that point on, if not already earlier, the oracular function of the priesthood effectively ceased, superseded by their second task (according to Deut 33:10), teaching Israel God's ordinances and laws. This task, however, is by no means a new task after the exile. It is already assigned

---

4. The discussion of any aspect of ancient history must assume a certain perspective on the date and historical reliability of the ancient texts, over which there may be considerable disagreement among scholars. In particular, any attempt to construct a full history of the Old Testament priesthood would require the assigning of a date to the so-called Priestly source of the Pentateuch. My own conviction is that the writings of this source are early and comprise an accurate historical reflection. Nonetheless, the picture I shall seek to sketch out here of the priestly office immediately prior to the exile is not, in my opinion, particularly controversial among mainstream scholarship. In broad terms, it summarizes the positions laid out by, e.g., Aelred Cody, *A History of the Old Testament Priesthood* (AnBib 35; Rome: Pontifical Biblical Institute, 1969), and Lester L. Grabbe, *Priests, Prophets, Diviners, Sages. A Socio-historical Study of Religious Specialists in Ancient Israel* (Valley Forge, Pa.: Trinity Press International, 1995).

5. The exact nature of the Urim and Thummim continues to provoke scholarly debate. For two possible views, compare Edward Robertson, "The Urim and Tummim: What Were They?" *VT* 14 (1964): 67–74, and Cornelis van Dam, *The Urim and Thummim: A Means of Revelation in Ancient Israel* (Winona Lake, Ind.: Eisenbrauns, 1997).

6. Note that the point of Ezra 2:63 is not the absence or loss of the Urim and Thummim themselves but the absence of a priest able to utilize them. Thus *b. Yoma* 21b, which states that the Urim and Thummim "were present but did not function." See van Dam, *Urim and Thummim*, 220.

to the priests in Lev 10:11 and Deut 24:8, where it is highlighted as one of the chief priestly tasks.[7]

Of especial importance in these texts is the task of drawing the boundary lines of ritual cleanliness, separating between clean and unclean. The priests are responsible to teach the law of Moses, and the people are to be careful to heed their words. "Teaching the law" can even be considered the definitive contribution of the priests to society in the time leading up to the exile, as central to the priestly role as "giving wisdom" is to the function of the wise and "giving the word" is to the task of the prophet (Jer 18:18). The related role of acting as judges in disputes, especially those requiring a divine decision, seems a natural outgrowth of this priestly expertise in torah.[8]

As well as drawing the lines between the spheres of clean and unclean, the priests were also uniquely qualified to cross the lines between the area of the sacred and that of the profane.[9] They alone were able to offer incense before Yahweh and to manipulate the blood from the sacrifices on the altar. This required that the priests themselves had to be ritually clean; hence, the lengthy list of restrictions on the priests' behavior in Lev 21. This reasoning is explicit in Lev 21:6: "[The priests] shall be holy to their God, and not profane the name of their God." If they were to approach God, they had to be perfectly clean and without defect, like the sacrificial animals that they offered.

This setting-apart as "holy men" in a unique sense meant that priests would necessarily have served as attendants and overseers of the sanctuary. Indeed, the very existence of a sanctuary, as opposed to an open-air altar, presupposes the need for an organized group of people dedicated to taking care of it, guarding it, and preventing the intrusion of the profane onto holy ground. It is therefore no surprise that we encounter a depiction of a regular, organized priesthood in Israel for the first time in conjunction with the creation of the first permanent (though mobile) sanctuary, the tabernacle.

The priests' societal standing and significance would have risen or fallen with the prestige of their sanctuary. In a simple sanctuary, such as that at Shiloh in Samuel's time, a single priestly family was apparently sufficient to carry out all of the duties. After the building of the Jerusalem temple, however, and especially after the centralization of worship there, the complexity of the task and the numbers of priests required at the central sanctuary would have increased dramatically. With the centralization of worship at a single sanctuary would also have come the concentration of the economic benefits associated with the priesthood.[10] By the time of the

---

7. Jacob Milgrom, *Leviticus 1–16* (AB 3; New York: Doubleday, 1991), 617. Also see n. 27 below.
8. See Deut 17:8–13; 21:5. So Cody, *History of the Old Testament Priesthood*, 71–72.
9. Richard D. Nelson, *Raising Up a Faithful Priest: Community and Priesthood in Biblical Theology* (Louisville: Westminster John Knox, 1993), 83.
10. On the economic benefits associated with priesthood, see Jon L. Berquist, *Judaism in Persia's Shadow: A Social and Historical Approach* (Minneapolis: Fortress, 1995), 150–53.

exile, the priests at the central sanctuary comprised a substantial and powerful grouping within Judean society.

The priests who controlled the central sanctuary at Jerusalem also became influential civil servants. From the beginning, priests had served as royal advisors (2 Sam 20:26; 1 Kgs 4:2, 5); later, they seem to have functioned as tax collectors and assessors, as well as bankers.[11] Although they were eminent in society, however, prior to the exile the priests were not preeminent in the corridors of power. Even in the running of the temple, the priests were constantly subject to the will, and even the whims, of the king.[12] Both reforms and abuses in temple worship generally stemmed from the initiative of the ruling king, not the high priest.

There is also evidence that at various times conflicts emerged between different priestly families over priestly rights. This is most visible in the texts describing the rise of the house of David to replace the house of Saul, which is accompanied by a corresponding rise on the part of the house of Zadok to take the place of the house of Eli. For a while, during David's reign, Zadok and Abiathar, the Elide priest, existed side by side. The definitive break came when they took opposite sides in the struggle to succeed David (1 Kgs 1:7–8). Zadok, who supported Solomon, subsequently emerged as the sole claimant to the title of "the priest," with Abiathar sent home in disgrace (1 Kgs 2:26, 35).[13] From then on, the Zadokites seem to have held effective sway in the priesthood in Jerusalem, although this never seems to have been elevated into an exclusive claim to priestly office.[14]

In addition to the socially upper-class role of priest, there was also much menial work to be done in the temple. This included the various tasks of supply, storage, cleaning, repair, and security, as well as the responsibilities of singing and playing musical instruments to accompany the worship.[15] This work is generally depicted in the texts as the proper responsibility of the Levites, especially in the Priestly source

---

11. Nelson, *Raising Up a Faithful Priest*, 47.

12. This may be seen in the erection of a new altar in the temple by Uriah in 2 Kgs 16:10–16. This altar was made at the bidding of, and according to the design of King Ahaz, whom Uriah obeys without complaint or comment. One notable exception, however, is Jehoiada's key involvement in the coup against Queen Athaliah (2 Kgs 11).

13. This outcome, however, is depicted in the biblical record not merely as the vicissitudes of fate. The Deuteronomistic History as a whole has little interest in such priestly struggles. Rather, this is recorded as the precise fulfillment of an earlier oracle against the house of Eli, for their unfaithfulness during the early years of Samuel (1 Kgs 2:27; see 1 Sam 2:27–36), a much more central concern for the author (see Richard D. Nelson, "The Role of the Priesthood in the Deuteronomistic History," in *Congress Volume: Leuven 1989* [ed. J. A. Emerton; VTSup 43; Leiden: Brill, 1991], 137–41).

14. Jeremiah, for example, came from a priestly family in Anathoth, the ancestral home of the family of Eli (Jer 1:1; see 1 Kgs 2:26). As part of Josiah's reforms it appears that many rural Yahwistic priests were relocated to Jerusalem to prevent any resurgence of non-central sacrifice (2 Kgs 23:8). Those who had not participated in the worship of the high places were apparently incorporated into the temple clergy. Those who had participated in the unauthorized worship were provided with food, but not permitted to minister (2 Kgs 23:9; see Nelson, "Priesthood in the Deuteronomistic History," 142–43).

15. Grabbe, *Priests, Prophets, Diviners, Sages*, 64.

and the book of Chronicles, although the same basic depiction is present in other books.[16] However, it is also clear that at some times in Israel's history other groups filled at least some of these positions. Thus Josh 9:27 speaks of the Gibeonites being made hewers of wood and drawers of water for the sanctuary, while 2 Kgs 11:4–19 attests the practice of employing foreign temple guards. The latter was a natural choice, given the strategic significance of the temple as a royal chapel, adjoining the palace.

II. Priesthood during the Exile

After capturing the city of Jerusalem in 586 B.C.E., Nebuchadnezzar burned the temple along with the rest of the city (2 Kgs 25:9). This clearly would have affected both the status and function of the priests, since in the absence of the temple in which all of the legitimate worship had been centralized, there was nowhere to offer sacrifices or to bring offerings. The leading priests of the day were shortly thereafter taken out and put to death (2 Kgs 25:18–21). The majority of the remainder of the priests, as men of high social standing, would have been included in the subsequent mass deportation to Babylon (2 Kgs 25:11). There they would have found many of their relatives, deported already by Nebuchadnezzar in 597 B.C.E. Ezekiel himself was removed from his homeland in that deportation (Ezek 1:2–3), presumably one among many of the priestly class who suffered that fate.

The priests must have made up a significant proportion of those exiled from Judah.[17] Since the Babylonian policy of exile was to take the best and the brightest, naturally almost all the priests would have been taken, but perhaps relatively few of the more menial class of Levites.[18] Since the deportation would likely have focused on the capital, it would certainly have been natural for Zadokites to form the dominant party among the exilic priests.

In exile in Babylon, there was neither sanctuary nor sacrifice. However, they could still continue to perform other priestly tasks, even while at a distance from Jerusalem. As was the case before the exile, the priestly task of divining Yahweh's will

---

16. Nelson, "Priesthood in the Deuteronomistic History," 134.

17. On the basis of the figures in 2 Kgs 24:14–16, Elias Auerbach estimated that priests made up about one-seventh of those exiled at the time of Jehoiachin (around 1,500 of the total of 10,000; see "Der Aufstieg der Priesterschaft zur Macht im Alten Israel,"in *Congress Volume: Bonn 1962* [ed. G. W. Anderson, P. A. H. De Boer, and G. R. Castellino; VTSup 9; Leiden: Brill, 1963], 240). A broadly similar figure is gained from the proportion of the returnees in the time of Zerubbabel that were priests: they numbered 4,289 out of a total figure of 42,360 returnees, or slightly more than 10 percent of the total (Ezra 2:36–39). The number of Levites who returned, in comparison, is a mere 74 (Ezra 2:40). It is routinely assumed that this small number of Levitical returnees was due to a reluctance among the Levites to go back to the lower office of temple servants. However, although this may have been a factor, the low number may also simply be due to that fact that fewer Levites were taken into exile in the first place.

18. Cody, *History of the Old Testament Priesthood*, 144–45; Hugh G. M. Williamson, *Ezra, Nehemiah* (WBC 16; Waco, Tex.: Word, 1985), 35.

had been superseded by the activity of prophets. Thus Jeremiah attests the activity of false prophets at work in Babylon (Jer 29:8, 15), while in the book of Ezekiel the elders come to Ezekiel as a prophet, not as a priest, to seek a word from Yahweh (Ezek 8:1; 14:1; 20:1).

On the other hand, the task of teaching God's law seems to have taken up an increasing amount of their time during the exile, to the point that Ezra's chief qualification, apart from a good priestly pedigree, was his familiarity with the law of Moses (Ezra 7:6). Ezra shows us the classic picture of the faithful priest in exile, devoting himself to the study and teaching of torah (Ezra 7:10).

The rationale for this increased attention to teaching on the part of the priests is not hard to seek. On the one hand, in the absence of a temple, their sole claim to value and authority within the community lay in their ability to transmit and mediate the authoritative traditions and texts of the community. On the other hand, there was a conviction among many in the exilic community that one major factor that had led up to the exile was the defilement of the land.[19] Since it was the priests' task to teach the people to distinguish between clean and unclean (Lev 10:10–11), then if such defilement were to be avoided in the future there had to be renewed vigilance in this area of proper societal ordering according to God's design; otherwise, the whole woeful cycle would simply recur (Ezek 44:23).[20]

The status of the priestly class in exile is also not clear. Berquist has pointed out that there were two different destinations for exiles, depending on their usefulness to the imperial system: some went to the capital, while others went to rural locations.[21] He suggests that those who possessed civil-service skills and the priests would have been taken to Babylon itself, to serve the various needs of the palace and temple, while the rest (landowners, merchants, and military officials) would have been assigned to the land, to raise crops.[22] It is likely, however, that the assignment process was not as straightforward as that. Had there been an effort to assimilate the Judean priests into the worship of the Babylonian gods, it seems likely that at least some of the priests would have had conscientious objections, and that those who did not would have been the target of prophetic rebuke. At the same time, it should be noted that the only person from a priestly family among the exiles in Babylon whose location there we can identify with certainty, Ezekiel, was located not in Babylon but

---

19. The stress on purification and atonement during this period of Israel's history is a reflection of that perception. See Peter R. Ackroyd, *Exile and Restoration* (Philadelphia: Westminster, 1968), 101.

20. Note, e.g., the fact that failure to observe the Sabbath is seen as a crucial element leading up to the exile in both Ezek 20:12, 13, 16, 20–21, 24; 22:26 and 2 Chr 36:20–21. Circumcision was another aspect of distinction between God's people and the nations, a distinction that received renewed emphasis during the exile (see Samuel Pagán, "Sociology, Theology, and Hope: The Priestly Case in Exile," *BT* 39 [1988]: 323).

21. *Judaism in Persia's Shadow*, 15.

22. Ibid., 16.

among the rural exiles (Ezek 1:1–3). So the evidence for priests as a class being co-opted into Babylonian temple worship is slender, to say the least.

On the other hand, that is not to say that some of the priests were not employed within the Babylonian civil service. Their level of education and literacy would have made them potentially useful to the empire for a variety of nonreligious tasks. The later example of Ezra, who was a priest living at the center of the Persian Empire, may provide an analogy. He seems to have served in some administrative capacity in the government, thereby attracting the favorable attention of King Artaxerxes.[23] This kind of administrative service seems a far more likely use of the skills of the Judean priests than a widespread assimilation into the service of pagan cults.

III. Priesthood after the Exile

In 538 B.C.E., there was a momentous change in the fortunes of the Jewish people. The Persian king Cyrus issued a decree permitting them to return home from exile and to reestablish worship at their temple in Jerusalem. In the first instance, however, the returned exiles began with a much more limited task, that of renewing the altar of the temple, so that sacrifices could again be made (Ezra 3:2). In this way, the priestly income could be restored, as well as their social standing, and the requisite sacrifices of purification offered. As tradents of the official tradition, the priests would have been responsible for seeing that these sacrifices were performed properly, in compliance with the law of Moses.

Shortly thereafter, work on the foundations of the temple itself was begun.[24] This work was supervised by the Levites and inaugurated with a praise service, led by priestly trumpets and Levitical praise in music and song, just as had been the practice prior to the exile (Ezra 3:10). Although few Levites had returned, there seems no obvious shortage of Levites for service. This may reinforce the perception that many of the Levites had remained in Judah during the period of the exile.

In the immediate aftermath of the exile, as before, the prophets were more prominent than the priests in the task of discerning God's will.[25] The guidance concerning the pressing need to rebuild the temple came through Haggai and Zechariah, not through Joshua the high priest. In addition to their renewed sacrificial tasks, the focus of the priestly work immediately subsequent to the exile was on

---

23. The title assigned to Ezra by Artaxerxes in Ezra 7:12, "the scribe of the law of the God of heaven," has been regarded as an official Persian title, perhaps even a "minister/secretary of state for Jewish affairs." See Williamson, *Ezra, Nehemiah*, 100.

24. The exact date of the beginning of rebuilding work on the temple itself is debated. See the discussions in Frank Charles Fensham, *The Books of Ezra and Nehemiah* (NICOT; Grand Rapids: Eerdmans, 1982), 61–62, and Williamson, *Ezra, Nehemiah*, 43–45.

25. This distinction should not be pressed into an opposition between the two offices. Zechariah was a priest as well as a prophet, as was Ezekiel. Yet when an inquiry was made to the priests and prophets in Jerusalem regarding fasting, Zechariah responded in the prophetic mode with a "word" from the Lord, rather than by means of a priestly "torah" (Zech 7).

the teaching of the law. Thus, as we have noted above, Ezra is described as one who "had set his heart to study the law of the LORD, and to do it, and to teach the statutes and ordinances in Israel" (Ezra 7:10). A similar description of the faithful priest of the postexilic era, personified (somewhat anachronistically) in the person of Levi, is found in Mal 2:6–7:

> True instruction was in his mouth, and no wrong was found on his lips. He walked with me in integrity and uprightness, and he turned many from iniquity. For the lips of a priest should guard knowledge, and people should seek instruction from his mouth, for he is the messenger of the LORD of hosts.

In fact, Malachi gives us a clear picture of this postexilic twofold focus of the priestly task on teaching the torah and sacrifice, since it is precisely the failures of the priests in these two areas that form the center of his attentions (Mal 1:6–2:9). More specifically, in the language of the books of Deuteronomy and Leviticus, the priests of his day have not distinguished between the clean and the unclean: they have allowed defective animals to be offered as sacrifices, thereby rendering the whole sacrificial system worthless (Mal 1:7–10).

This confusion of priestly categories lies at the heart of another major concern in the postexilic period, namely, the intermarriage of Jews with the surrounding peoples. This lack of separation involved priests and Levites themselves, as well as other leaders in the community (Ezra 9:1; Neh 13:28–29). Both Ezra and Nehemiah acted in their own ways to eliminate this problem (Ezra 9–10; Neh 13:23–28).

Priests clearly held a central position in the restoration community. They were naturally central to the rebuilding of the altar (Ezra 3:2) and the temple (Ezra 3:8). In the book of Nehemiah, they were an important power to be reckoned with: they were the first of three authority groups listed in Neh 2:16, while they head the list of those who contributed to the building of the wall (Neh 3:1). Priests appear alongside the civil authorities on almost every occasion of significance in the postexilic period. Much of the concern of the latter chapters of the book of Nehemiah lies in making proper provision for the maintenance and support of the priests and Levites, even though it is clear that not all of the priests were supporters of Nehemiah's reforms (Neh 13:4–8).

The question of the priests' right of access into God's presence became a serious issue after the exile. Did not the sojourn of the priests in an unclean land disqualify them from access into the presence of the Holy One? This is the concern behind Zech 3, with its vision of the high priest, Joshua, dressed in soiled clothing. The answer comes in a dramatic reclothing of the high priest, which is followed by a charge in which the legitimacy of the postexilic Jerusalem priesthood is affirmed and they are granted administrative power within the temple and judicial authority, along with access into the presence of God (Zech 3:7).

This affirmation seems to represent a significant increase in their powers in the community, compared to the preexilic setting. Before the exile, as we have seen above, both in the administration of the temple and in the judiciary they would have been subject to the overriding authority of the king. After the exile, priest and civil leader appear side by side: even though the two offices are not equal, it is envisioned that they will share power in new and significant ways.

Perhaps surprisingly, in light of the relatively small number of Levites who returned from Babylon, the Levites were an important part of the postexilic community from the outset. They were assigned the task of overseeing the work of rebuilding the temple (Ezra 3:8) and leading the musical praise of God (Ezra 3:10). Their presence was a necessity in Ezra's mind for his return; when none was initially found among his party, he sent envoys to recruit a party of Levites to join him (Ezra 8:15–20). Their unfaithfulness in the matter of intermarriage with foreigners, along with that of the priests, was a matter of great concern to Ezra (Ezra 9:1; 10:5). Likewise, Nehemiah was concerned not merely to provide sustenance for the priests but also for the Levites, in accordance with the requirements of the law (Neh 12:44). However, the Levites regularly appear in the postexilic writings as subordinate to the priests, working harmoniously alongside them in the ministry of the house of God.[26]

IV. Ezekiel's Contribution to the History of the Priesthood

The preceding discussion forms a necessary backdrop against which we can evaluate Ezekiel's contribution to the development of the Old Testament priesthood. I would suggest that it is a failure to discern this backdrop that has led to some of the more extreme evaluations of Ezekiel's agenda and his impact. Against this backdrop, many of Ezekiel's priestly concerns become clearer and his agenda more discernible. At the same time, aspects of his teaching that have sometimes been regarded as idiosyncratic and novel turn out to be merely in line with contemporary thought. Although he certainly had his visionary dreams for the future, those dreams are by no means as bizarre and innovative as is sometimes thought.

A. Drawing Lines

As we have seen, a central concern of the priesthood by the time of the exile was the teaching of the law (torah). The connection between the priest and the law was sufficiently self-evident to have become proverbial, as may be seen from Ezek 7:26 and Jer 18:18, which suggests that it was certainly not a new development during the exile.[27] Failure in this regard forms the sole basis for Ezekiel's critique of the

---

26. The book of Malachi does not focus on distinctions between priest and Levite, but addresses them as a unified group of temple officiants. This does not demonstrate that such distinctions were unknown; rather, all classes of temple officiants were equally implicated in the prophet's sweeping rebuke. On this issue, see Julia M. O'Brien, *Priest and Levite in Malachi* (SBLDS 121; Atlanta: Scholars Press, 1990).

27. See Hos 4:6; Mic 3:11.

priests of his own day (Ezek 22:26).[28] Given the central nature of this responsibility to the priestly task, especially in exile, where there could be no sacrifice, we would anticipate finding its marks on Ezekiel's own ministry. If the primary task of the priest is to distinguish between clean and unclean, then as a priest Ezekiel himself ought to be engaged in that task. How do we see this concern coming to the fore in his oracles?

The first place where such priestly concerns emerge is in the prophet's call to be a watchman (Ezek 3:16–21). Here he is engaged to pronounce "life" and "death" to the righteous and the wicked on the basis of their actions. The priestly background of this language has long been recognized.[29] Yet Ezekiel scholarship has been surprisingly unwilling to allow it priestly overtones in this context, insisting that it serves rather as Ezekiel's induction specifically into the office of prophet.[30] To be sure, there are clear prophetic aspects to Ezekiel's calling to be a watchman. The calling itself is transmitted in a "word of Yahweh" (3:16), while all the available biblical evidence points to prophets as the ones who pronounced upon specific individuals the sentences of life and death.[31] Yet one wonders if the priestly aspects of this calling have not been undervalued.[32] Ezekiel's calling as a watchman is to be a prophet-priest, who declares torah to the house of Israel, thereby distinguishing between righteous and wicked. Those who are righteous shall live, while those who are wicked and disobey the torah shall die.

What such a prophetic-priestly activity as a watchman looks like in practice is surely evident in a related passage in Ezek 18. There Ezekiel proclaims a priestly torah to the people to refute the claim that the people's punishment is unjust (Ezek 18:2–3). In this chapter, Ezekiel draws extensively on the old sacral-law code, found especially in Lev 18–20, to teach the people their own unrighteousness and to encourage people to turn and live. It is not simply that Ezekiel's priestly background has in some general sense influenced his form of expression; rather, he is here acting as a priest, drawing the lines between clean and unclean.

In the same way, just as the priests were responsible for some judicial functions prior to the exile, Ezekiel is commissioned by God to act as judge of the elders of his people (Ezek 20:4), of the bloody city of Jerusalem (Ezek 22:2), and of the two sis-

---

28. As I have argued at length elsewhere, the priests are not held accountable by Ezekiel for the abuses in temple worship cataloged in Ezek 8–11. See my *Ezekiel and the Leaders of Israel* (VTSup 56; Leiden: Brill, 1994), 68–72.

29. Walther Zimmerli, "'Leben' und 'Tod' im Buche des Propheten Ezechiel," *TZ* 13 (1957): 494–508; Daniel I. Block, *The Book of Ezekiel*, vol. 1, *Chapters 1–24* (NICOT; Grand Rapids: Eerdmans, 1997), 142–43.

30. Block, *Ezekiel 1–24*, 143. The path in this direction seems to have been set by Henning G. Reventlow's study, *Wächter über Israel: Ezechiel und seine Tradition* (BZAW 82; Berlin: Töpelmann, 1962), 110–11.

31. Moshe Greenberg, *Ezekiel 1–20* (AB 22A; New York: Doubleday, 1983), 94.

32. For a more positive evaluation, see Margaret Odell, "You Are What You Eat: Ezekiel and the Scroll," *JBL* 117 (1998): 240–41.

ters in the parable, Oholah and Oholibah (Ezek 23:36). This commission to act as judge is unique among the prophets, which has led some commentators to translate the verb התשפט as "Will you arraign?" rather than "Will you judge?"[33] Yet as priest it is entirely appropriate that Ezekiel should act as judge in a case involving "abominations" (תועבת; Ezek 20:4; 22:2; 23:36), and declare not only the charges that are alleged but also the sentence which will be imposed on the guilty party in each case.

A similar priestly concern to draw clearly the lines between clean and unclean and between holy and profane is evident throughout the vision of the restored temple and land in Ezek 40–48. The temple, with its thick walls and dominant gateways to prevent unauthorized access, loudly proclaims the separation of the holy from the profane, in order to protect the sanctity of the holy. The entire temple area is surrounded by a wall, whose purpose is explicitly to divide between the holy and the profane (Ezek 42:20). Close attention is paid to regulations that are designed to prevent the involuntary transmission of holiness from the sacred area to areas of lesser sanctity. Thus, the priests who minister in the sanctuary are required to eat their portions of the most holy offerings in a special set of chambers in between the inner and outer courts (Ezek 42:13). These liminal rooms also provide an area where the priests can change from the garments in which they have ministered, which have thereby contracted holiness, into other clothing (Ezek 42:14). Kitchens are provided in the corners of the inner court so that the sacrificial offerings may be cooked within the sacred sphere, rather than risk contact between holy and profane (Ezek 46:20).

Specific past breaches in the wall of separation between holy and profane are also addressed. The preexilic arrangement in which the temple was the next-door neighbor of the royal palace would be discontinued. No longer would God's threshold be next to that of the earthly king, nor would there be any more memorial stele[34] erected in honor of monarchs within the temple grounds (Ezek 43:7–8). These defile the sanctity of the place that is dedicated to the name of the divine king (Ezek 43:7). Therefore, even the lands assigned to the נשיא ("prince") are distinct and separate from the sacred portion containing the temple (45:7 and 48:21–22).

Another breach in the separation between holy and profane lay in the introduction of foreigners, who were uncircumcised in heart and flesh into the sanctuary itself, thereby profaning it (Ezek 44:6–8). The historical referent of this accusation has been variously evaluated, but most probably it at least includes the well-attested practice of employing foreign temple guards (2 Kgs 11:4–19).[35] This fits best with

---

33. So Greenberg, *Ezekiel 1–20*, 363. Block comments that Ezekiel is "hardly in a position to sit in judgment over Israel" (*Ezekiel 1–24*, 619).

34. On the פגרי מלכיהם, see the discussion in Theodore J. Lewis, *Cults of the Dead in Ancient Israel and Ugarit* (HSM 39; Atlanta: Scholars Press, 1989), 141.

35. See Duguid, *Ezekiel and the Leaders of Israel*, 76.

the context in which the solution to the problem is seen as reassigning the Levites to "keep charge of the temple, to do all its chores, and all that is to be done in it" (Ezek 44:14). "Keeping charge of the temple" is equivalent to control of the entrances and exits of the temple, a central focus of the temple vision (Ezek 43:11; 44:5).[36]

The task assigned to the Levites also includes a broad range of temple ministry, interfacing between the people and the Zadokite priests. That these tasks are not seen as being an entirely new development may be seen from the description of the former situation as a breach of covenant (Ezek 44:7). If using uncircumcised foreigners rather than Levites as temple guards and servants is a breach of covenant, then some legislation assigning the latter group that task, such as Num 18:3–4, is presupposed.[37] Nevertheless, the ministry of the Levites is extended when compared with the preexilic situation. Now they must slaughter the burnt offerings and sacrifices on behalf of the people (Ezek 44:11), something the people had previously done for themselves.

Ezekiel's purpose in these regulations is not grounded in political propaganda against the Levites. Rather, his concern here is, as elsewhere in the temple vision, a priestly desire to heighten and strengthen the wall dividing the holy and profane. In pursuit of that goal, he utilizes and further develops old legislation to depict in visionary form a new future that restores things to the way they ought to have been in the past. The priests and the Levites are to be put back in their proper places.

Similar concerns dominate the division of the land in Ezek 45:1–8 and 47:13–48:29. If the design for the new temple expresses theological concepts through the mediums of architecture and of legislation, the division of the land expresses theology through geography.[38] The assignment has little to do with historical or political realities and a great deal to do with the principle of separation between the sacred and the profane. In both formats, the concepts of space, access, and position relative to the temple are crucial.[39] The sacred portion of the land receives the lion's share of the description and provides a means of surrounding the temple area with buffer zones of diminishing sanctity. The temple complex is surrounded by an open space (Ezek 45:2; 48:17), which in turn is succeeded by priestly lands (Ezek 45:3–4; 48:10–12). Next to them come the lands assigned to the Levites (45:5; 48:13–14).

---

36. Jacob Milgrom has argued that שמר משמרת is cultic terminology that refers to guard duty (*Studies in Levitical Terminology, I: The Encroacher and the Levite; the Term 'Aboda* [Berkeley and Los Angeles: University of California Press, 1970], 8–10).

37. See Raymond Abba, "Priests and Levites in Ezekiel," *VT* 28 (1978): 6; Albin van Hoonacker, "Les Prêtres et les Lévites dans le Livre d'Ezéchiël," *RB* 8 (1899): 183. On the Levitical responsibilities prior to the exile, see Timothy Polk, "The Levites in the Davidic-Solomonic Empire," *Studia Biblica et Theologica* 9 (1979): 11–15.

38. Leslie C. Allen, *Ezekiel 20–48* (WBC 29; Dallas: Word, 1990), 285.

39. Kalinda R. Stevenson, *The Vision of Transformation: The Territorial Rhetoric of Ezekiel 40–48* (SBLDS 154; Atlanta: Scholars Press, 1996), 151.

The lands assigned to the נשׂיא ("prince") and the various tribes are thereby kept at a distance from the realm of the sacred.

This theme of separation between sacred and profane is underlined in other ways in the land division. Each of the twelve tribes is assigned an equal portion of the land (Ezek 47:14), in the form of a strip running from east to west. This orients the entire land along the sacred east-west axis of the temple. At the same time, the tribal strips themselves are left dimensionally undefined; the borders between the tribes are not marked by any geographic indicators, nor are their dimensions given. Only the central sacred portion has dimensions that are minutely recorded. This contrasts dramatically with the division of the land in Josh 13–21, whose roots are in historical rather than theological geography, where the boundaries between the different tribes are clearly defined. However, it corresponds exactly with the trend within the temple complex itself to define precisely the areas within the most holy zone, while leaving the outer areas less completely defined.[40] Holy space is important: it must be completely defined; profane space is less significant and may therefore have blurred edges. The difference between the two is clearly being taught by the priest-prophet Ezekiel, thereby fulfilling his priestly calling.

B. Crossing Lines

We mentioned above the fact that access into the presence of God was one of the principal privileges of the priesthood. They were uniquely qualified to cross the lines between the realm of the sacred and that of the profane. In order to do so, however, they had to maintain a special state of ritual purity. This combination of concerns over purity and access are also central to Ezekiel's interests.

In the first place, Ezekiel is concerned to maintain his own purity, which is necessary to his own functioning as a priest. Thus, in a unique outburst, the otherwise entirely submissive prophet protests Yahweh's instruction to him to eat defiled food (Ezek 4:14).[41] In return, he is granted the concession of preparing his food over a fire of animal dung rather than human excrement, thereby apparently avoiding the taint of uncleanness.[42] That the focus is particularly on the issue of cultic cleanliness may be seen from the absence of any protest from the prophet when he is instructed immediately afterward to shave his head (Ezek 5:1), a procedure forbidden for priests in Lev 21:5 and Ezek 44:20. Presumably the difference between the two actions lies in this: being shaved might render Ezekiel temporarily unclean, but his hair would grow back; however, eating defiled food would apparently have had a permanently defiling effect.

In a stimulating article, Margaret Odell has argued that Ezek 1–5 records an

---

40. Ibid., 39–40.
41. Margaret Odell notes, "[H]is objection to eating food cooked over dung is his only expression of personal will or desire in the entire book" ("You Are What You Eat," 239).
42. Walther Zimmerli, *Ezekiel: A Commentary on the Book of the Prophet Ezekiel* (2 vols.; Hermeneia; Philadelphia: Fortress, 1979), 1:171.

initiation rite that transforms Ezekiel from a priest into a prophet.[43] In support of her thesis, she has marshaled an impressive array of parallels between Ezek 1–5 and priestly initiation rites. There are certainly priestly dimensions to Ezekiel's actions in these chapters, which support our contention that he appears as a faithful priest in exile.[44] This priestly status of Ezekiel is perhaps most obvious during his tour of the visionary temple (Ezek 40–42). There he is permitted to accompany the angel even into the inner court (Ezek 40:28–41:26), a place whose access is explicitly restricted only to the priests (Ezek 44:15–16).[45] Similarly, Ezekiel plays a central role in the consecration of the new altar in Ezek 43:18–27. He personally participates both in the sacrificial ritual and in the blood rites associated with the cleansing of the altar, while the Zadokite priests act as his assistants. Given Ezekiel's strong concerns to tighten the restrictions on the offering of sacrifices, it is unthinkable that he should envisage such actions at the altar of the inner court being performed by someone who was not a priest.[46]

Indeed, the cosmogonic process of creating and rightly ordering the new world of Ezek 40–48, in which Ezekiel participates, is a task that resonates with priestly overtones. The process of division and subdivision, of border-marking and hierarchical definition has much in common with the cosmogonic, ordering, and categorizing emphases of Gen 1–11, which are widely recognized to be a priestly interest.[47]

Ezekiel's priestly access to the inner world of the new temple is a fitting reward for his personal faithfulness and purity. Such qualities are also a necessary prerequisite for access, even in visionary form, to the inner world of the new temple. But Ezekiel is not the only one whose purity must be affirmed. If the Zadokites are to

---

43. "You Are What You Eat," esp. pp. 234–47.

44. Odell notes the significance of the enigmatic "thirtieth year," seeing it as a reference to the normal age of priestly initiation. Other signals of priesthood include Ezekiel's actions in not eating unclean food, while being willing to eat the scroll, just as priests would ingest the sin offering on behalf of the people; Ezekiel's calling as a watchman; and his binding as a sign act. Perhaps because she sees priests as inextricably linked with temples, Odell does not recognize Ezekiel's exilic ministry as in any fruitful sense a priestly one. Yet it is not at all clear to me that at the end of the process of initiation in Ezek 1–5, Ezekiel is less of a priest than he was at the beginning. To be sure, he is separated from the Jerusalem temple and so cannot participate in the full range of priestly activities. Yet he nonetheless remains a priest throughout his ministry.

45. That the usual temple rules of access are not suspended during Ezekiel's visit is evident from the fact that he does *not* accompany the angel inside the most holy place (Ezek 41:3–4). This space is so holy that it is perpetually off-limits to all, even Ezekiel himself. See Duguid, *Ezekiel and the Leaders of Israel*, 82.

46. J. Gordon McConville, "Priests and Levites in Ezekiel: A Crux in the Interpretation of Israel's History," *TynBul* 34 (1983): 28. To be sure, the closest parallel for his actions here is the role of Moses in the dedication of the altar of the tabernacle in Exod 29, rather than that of Aaron, for this is a cult-foundational event rather than a regular sacrifice.

47. On these parallels, see Susan Niditch, "Ezekiel 40–48 in a Visionary Context," *CBQ* 48 (1986): 216–17.

be granted access to the inner court to minister, they too must be found to be ritually pure, just as was the high priest Joshua in Zech 3. Ezekiel, however, envisages no necessity for such a cleansing transformation on the part of the Zadokite priests as a whole. On the contrary, it is their past faithfulness during a time of general unfaithfulness that fits them for the priestly task (Ezek 44:15–16). Faithfulness is rewarded by a central place in the new kingdom.

To be sure, as I have argued elsewhere, this faithfulness on the part of the Zadokites is relative, not absolute.[48] The writer of Ezek 44 is hardly unaware of Ezek 22:26, in which the priests are charged with failing to distinguish between holy and common, and between clean and unclean. He makes explicit reference to that fact in v. 23, in which he asserts that in the future the priests *will* teach the difference between holy and common and how to distinguish between clean and unclean.[49] Nonetheless, Ezekiel insists that the Zadokites as a class have faithfully kept the charge of the sanctuary at a time when the rest of the Israelites went astray (Ezek 44:15). It is this past faithfulness that fits them for the privilege of access to the inner court and service in that sphere. In contrast, the Levites, who served the people in their idolatry (Ezek 44:12), are assigned a lesser (although still privileged) degree of access. The access granted to the נשיא ("prince") is likewise privileged but restricted, while the people as a whole are kept most strongly at a distance. They too are being put in their place.

The sanctity of the priests is not simply an affirmation, it is also a requirement in Ezekiel's vision. Greater access into the realm of the holy carries with it greater responsibilities and limitations, ranging from dress, to marriage, and cultic cleanliness requirements (Ezek 44:17–27). Once again, the concern to protect the holiness of the sanctuary is central, for it was failure in this area that resulted in the exile in the first place. Never again will this holiness be compromised as it was in the past.

C. Sacrifice

The important place held by sacrifice in Ezekiel's vision of the temple is evident in the prominence it ascribes to the altar of burnt offering (Ezek 43:13–27). The altar's importance is underlined not so much by its physical dimensions, which are comparable to those of the Solomonic temple (2 Chr 4:1), but rather by its location at the geometric center of the temple complex. In addition, it is the only piece of cultic furniture described in any detail. Since these two features (precision of description and geometric location) are the two primary means of emphasizing importance in the temple vision, it is safe to assert that the altar ministry is highly valued, especially as a means of purifying the temple grounds from any accumulated

---

48. See *Ezekiel and the Leaders of Israel*, 80–83. So also the access that they are granted is relative, not absolute. No one receives access to the holy of holies in Ezek 40–48, but the priests receive the greatest access on the grounds that they demonstrated the greatest fidelity.

49. My emphasis here is on volition; see Bruce K. Waltke and Michael O'Connor, *An Introduction to Biblical Hebrew Syntax* (Winona Lake, Ind.: Eisenbrauns, 1990), sec. 31.5c.

impurity.⁵⁰ The consecratory rites are also described in detail, for they are the necessary prerequisite for the restoration of the proper sacrificial worship of Yahweh.

Ezekiel goes on to describe the regular offerings in some detail (Ezek 45–46). The priestly role comes to the fore in the description of the ritual for the first day of the first and seventh months (Ezek. 45:18–25). There the priest is instructed to take a young bull as a sin offering and apply its blood to the doorposts of the temple, the corners of the altar and the gateposts of the inner court. Its purpose is explicitly stated as "to cleanse the sanctuary," in keeping with the general emphasis of these chapters on purification.

Ezekiel's stress on sacrifice, especially sacrifices of purification, is entirely consonant with the similar focus in the postexilic writings, as we noted above. Like the returning exiles in the book of Ezra, Ezekiel recognizes that the restoration of the sacrificial service on the altar of burnt offering lies at the heart of the restoration of the worship of the temple itself (Ezra 3:1–6). Like Malachi, he knows that unless the sacrificial system is pure and acceptable to God, it is a worthless ritual (Mal 1:7–10).

V. Conclusions

The picture that emerges from a study of Ezekiel's ministry as a priest in exile is that he fits comfortably within the profile one would expect. The text itself highlights his priestly heritage and calling, and that calling shapes his concerns in significant ways, even though his ministry is necessarily restricted in some ways because of his presence in an unclean land far away from home. Ezekiel shares the central concerns of the priesthood of his time to teach the people torah, thereby enabling them to distinguish between clean and unclean, and to remind them of the importance of sacrifice.⁵¹

Both of these elements are present in the vision of Ezek 40–48. The strong stress on the lines that must be drawn between holy and profane and on the utter exclusion of all profane elements from the visionary temple has a teaching purpose. A close study of the design of the temple, especially the entrances and exits by which access to the holy is controlled and limited, is intended to convict Ezekiel's hearers of their sin (Ezek 43:11). They are thereby to become ashamed of their iniquities, which by rights would place them utterly on the outside, separated from all access to God. It is this broader priestly responsibility and agenda, not political propaganda, that motivates the line-drawing between Zadokite priests and the Levites in Ezek 44. Those who are faithful, such as Ezekiel himself, are assigned a place of

---

50. Stevenson, *Vision of Transformation*, 160.

51. The absence of the concern over intermarriage with the surrounding nations—indeed, the total lack of interest in relationships with surrounding nations—reinforces the impression of a date during, rather than after, the exile.

honor in the new world order. Those who have been unfaithful are assigned a place in the margins of society. All are to be put in their place.

Yet at the same time as the temple design convicts the people of their sin and failure, paradoxically it also preaches to them God's grace and accessibility. The pure visionary temple provides assurance that the presence of God will never again be driven from the midst of the people as it was at the time of the exile. Putting the priests in their place is necessary for God to return to the temple. The sacrificial system will provide effective purification for the temple complex, removing the defilement of the people. The healing stream that flows out of the temple bridges the gap between the presence of the holy God and the unholy people, transforming everything it touches from death to life.[52] When God is once more in the temple or, to use the prophet-priest's own words, יהוה שמה ("Yahweh is there," Ezek 48:35), then blessing will flow to all, whatever their place in the renewed society.

---

52. For an exposition of these themes, see Iain Duguid, *Ezekiel* (NIV Application Commentary; Grand Rapids: Zondervan, 1999).

A Priest Out of Place:
Reconsidering Ezekiel's Role
in the History of the Israelite Priesthood

Baruch J. Schwartz

The fact of Ezekiel's priestly birth, background, and heritage is not in question. Even if it were not reported to us explicitly by the anonymous interpolator of Ezek 1:2–3a,[1] and even if we did not have Ezekiel's account of his response to YHWH's appalling demand that he partake of bread baked on cakes of excrement (Ezek 4:14),[2] and even if we dismiss the fanciful medieval suggestion that Ezekiel was led "round about" the valley of the dry bones (Ezek 37:2) but did not actually enter it in order to avoid corpse-contamination,[3] we would still be in no doubt as to his

---

1. On vv. 2–3 as a divine "interruption" in the prophet's words, see Rashi ad 1:1: "The Prophet obscured his words, since he did not explain who he is and did not clarify from which event he dated. Therefore the Holy Spirit interrupted his words by the following two verses to identify the prophet and (to give) the basis of his chronology." The verses were acknowledged to be a scribal interpolation by Eliezer of Beaugency (comm. ad 1:1): "The verses are not Ezekiel's words. He had not even identified himself . . . the scribe who edited all his teachings added these two verses with the intent to explain what he left obscure." See Robert A. Harris, "Awareness of Biblical Redaction among Rabbinic Exegetes of Northern France," *Shenaton* 12 (2000): 289–310, esp. 293–94 [Hebrew]; idem, "Biblical Interpretation, Medieval French," *The Encyclopaedia of Judaism* (ed. J. Neusner et al.; Leiden: Brill, 2004), 5:2051–55 (the translations are those of Willem Arie VanGemeren, "The Exegesis of Ezekiel's 'Chariot' Chapters in Twelfth-Century Hebrew Commentaries" [Ph.D. diss., University of Wisconsin, Madison, 1974], 21, 118). In light of the LXX ἐπ' ἐμέ (= עלי) in place of MT עליו in 1:3 (see *BHS*), it is preferable to confine the interpolation to vv. 2–3a; for discussion, see, e.g., George R. Berry, "The Title of Ezekiel (1:1–3)," *JBL* 51 (1932): 54–57; Julius A. Bewer, "The Text of Ezekiel 1:1–3," *AJSL* 50 (1933/4): 96–101; G. A. Cooke, *A Critical and Exegetical Commentary on the Book of Ezekiel* (ICC; Edinburgh: T. & T. Clark, 1936), 3; Walther Zimmerli, *Ezekiel: A Commentary on the Book of the Prophet Ezekiel* (2 vols.; Hermeneia; Philadelphia: Fortress, 1979), 1:100–101.

2. See below for the discussion of how these verses are correctly to be understood in light of Ezekiel's priestly lineage.

3. See Rashi ad Ezek 37:2; his view was rejected by Menahem Ben Shimon of Posquières and David Kimhi (see their commentaries ad loc. in *Miqra'ot Gedolot "Haketer," Ezekiel* [ed. Menahem Cohen; Ramat Gan, Israel: Bar-Ilan University, 2000], 242–43). Only priests are commanded to avoid contracting corpse-contamination (Lev 21:1–4, 11); lay Israelites are merely expected to cleanse themselves of it once they have contracted it (Num 19:10b–22).

priestly pedigree. This is so because everything the prophet says is determined by it. He explains what went wrong, depicts the results of what went wrong, and predicts the eventual rectification of everything that went wrong, from a thoroughly priestly standpoint.[4] The issue in question is: what is the significance of this fact? Is stating the fact that Ezekiel was a *priest* in exile the same as asserting that there was an exilic priest*hood*? My view is that it is not, and that the priestly influences on Ezekiel have nothing at all to do with any exilic priestly activity.

According to the classic, Wellhausenian approach, Ezekiel was believed to mark a watershed in the historical development of the Israelite priesthood. His prophetic activity, especially his vision of the future temple and its cult, was held to have had a decisive influence on the "theocratic" Judaism of postexilic times, and his view of the priesthood was thought not merely to have anticipated later developments but indeed to have had a major role in shaping them. Further, the literary work in which these developments are believed to be reflected (P) was thought to be not only subsequent to his prophetic teaching but also in large measure the product of it.[5] Yet, as correctly argued by later scholars, most recently Iain Duguid, Ezekiel's visionary predictions of the rebuilt temple and his futuristic descriptions of the purified cult of restored Israel are evidence of his concerns and theology but not of what actually came to pass—much less of anything that Ezekiel can be credited with inventing or instituting.[6] Moshe Greenberg, following Yehezkel Kaufmann, reminds us that nothing of what Ezekiel reports having been told was ever put into practice.[7] Even the lines that Ezekiel draws between the Zadokites and the Levites in 44:10–27 reflect not his partisan agenda or any actual power struggle between rival priestly classes but only the prophet's theological standpoint.[8]

---

4. I deal with this topic in my essay "When a Priest Becomes a Prophet" (forthcoming); for the present, see Yehezkel Kaufmann, *The Religion of Israel: From Its Beginnings to the Babylonian Exile* (trans. and abridged by M. Greenberg; Chicago: University of Chicago Press, 1960), 426–46, esp. 435–36. On Ezekiel's familiarity with, and reliance on, the priestly writings, see, most recently, Risa Levitt Kohn, *A New Heart and a New Soul: Ezekiel, the Exile, and the Torah* (JSOTSup 358; Sheffield: Sheffield Academic Press, 2002), 30–85.

5. Julius Wellhausen, *Prolegomena to the History of Ancient Israel* (Gloucester, Mass.: Peter Smith, 1885), 121–67. See the studies in the present volume; cf. Marvin A. Sweeney, "Ezekiel: Zadokite Priest and Visionary Prophet of the Exile," *SBL Seminar Papers, 2000* (SBLSP 39; Atlanta: Society of Biblical Literature, 2000), 728–51, esp. 728–31, and most recently Levitt Kohn, *New Heart*, 6–13.

6. See, in the present volume, Iain M. Duguid, "Putting Priests in Their Place: Ezekiel's Contribution to the History of the Old Testament Priesthood," and the extensive literature cited; Jon D. Levenson, *Theology of the Program of Restoration of Ezekiel 40–48* (HSM 10; Atlanta: Scholars Press, 1986), esp. 129–58.

7. Moshe Greenberg, "The Design and Themes of Ezekiel's Program of Restoration," *Int* 38 (1984): 181–208; idem, *Ezekiel 1–20* (AB 22; Garden City, N.Y.: Doubleday, 1983), 15, citing Y. Kaufmann, *Religion of Israel*, 443.

8. See Rodney K. Duke, "Punishment or Restoration? Another Look at the Levites of Ezekiel 44.6–16," *JSOT* 40 (1988): 61–81; for a different view, see Steven S. Tuell, *The Law of the Temple in Ezekiel 40–48* (HSM 49; Atlanta: Scholars Press, 1992), 139–52.

Ezekiel is a visionary, not a legislator. A *prophet's* report of what he says he was instructed in a vision is not legislation for the future—indeed, nowhere does the Hebrew Bible acknowledge the existence of legislation attributed to anyone but Moses.[9] Rather, it is part and parcel of his condemnation of the past and present, of his agony and sorrow at what has taken place, expressed, as prophetic passion so often is, in the form of a vision of what should be. And so it is one thing simply to say that Ezekiel's prophecies, in the form that they are preserved in the book bearing his name and the distinctive mark of his personality, are permeated throughout by priestly tradition both practical and literary, by priestly theology and by priestly concerns. It is quite another to assert that this amounts to a turning point, or even a stage, in the history of the priesthood. Especially once it is recognized that priestly thought and language, and the priestly literature in which they are expressed and preserved (P), are preexilic,[10] it becomes apparent that they, rather than some form of exilic priestly activity, are the components of Ezekiel's education and heritage, and this is the reasonable and sufficient explanation for the priestly character of his prophetic teaching. What is more, although Ezekiel's training to think, speak, and write as a priest took place in his pre-deportation days, there is no evidence that he ever actually functioned as a priest before his deportation from Jerusalem. While it is obvious that he was steeped in priestly learning and thought, it is possible that, due either to his young age[11] or to the unstable situation in the Jerusalem temple up to and following 597 B.C.E. (or both), Ezekiel never had the opportunity to perform any priestly duties himself. The biblical text is silent on this, and it is best to avoid the automatic assumption that Ezekiel arrived in Babylonia with a personal history of active service in the temple.

---

9. The anomalous case of 1 Sam 30:25 is the exception that proves the rule. As for Ezekiel's so-called law code, care should be exercised in treating it as actual legislation. The form employed, and the literary heritage from which the prophecy derives (see Menahem Haran, "The Law-Code of Ezekiel XL–XLVIII and Its Relation to the Priestly School," *HUCA* 50 [1979]: 45–71) notwithstanding, the prophet reports a vision, not a set of commands to be conveyed and put into practice; see below.

10. The scholarly literature supporting the preexilic provenance of P is far too extensive to list here; for the present context, it will suffice to refer to Levitt Kohn, *New Heart*, 6–13.

11. As can be deduced from Ezek 29:17, the prophet was still prophesying in 572–571 B.C.E. Since no information exists regarding how long after this he lived, there are no grounds for positing that in 572–571 he had attained old age; thus, he may have been as young as a teenager when he was deported in 597. The interpretation of "the thirtieth year" in Ezek 1:1 as a reference to the prophet's age in 597, advanced by Origen (*Homiliae in Ezechielem* 1, 4: "Ezechiel cum triginta esset annorum"; see Marcel Borret, trans. and ed., *Origène: Homélies sur Ézéchiel* [Paris: Cerf, 1989], 58) and followed in the modern period by Karl Budde ("Zum Eingang des Buches Ezechiel," *JBL* 50 [1931]: 20–41, esp. 28–31) and, more recently, James E. Miller ("The Thirtieth Year of Ezekiel 1:1," *RB* 99 [1992]: 499–503) and, among other commentators, Daniel I. Block (*The Book of Ezekiel*, vol. 1, *Chapters 1–24* [NICOT; Grand Rapids: Eerdmans, 1997], 80–82), was rightly rejected in the twelfth century by R. Menahem ben Shimon of Posquières (see his commentary ad loc. in Menahem Cohen, *Miqra'ot Gedolot "Haketer," Ezekiel*, 3); see also Greenberg, *Ezekiel 1–20*, 39–40, where this suggestion is correctly placed among "ancient and modern guesses" and deemed not convincing.

A final caution: even if we were to find that Ezekiel himself continued to function in some sense as a priest after deportation to Babylonia, would we then be justified in speaking of an exilic priest*hood*? Probably we would not, for we would still only have evidence of *a* priest in exile, not an exilic priest*hood*. A single priest does not a priesthood make; there is no evidence that other priests conducted themselves in Babylonia as Ezekiel did.

It goes without saying that the chief role of the priests, that of performing the altar and sanctuary rituals associated with the worship of YHWH, rituals which were their responsibility alone, ceased to exist when the temple was destroyed. Worship in Israel, largely even before the Josianic reform of 622 B.C.E., and certainly thereafter, was inextricably connected with the idea of the divine abode.[12] With the abolition of local shrines and the eradication of the provincial priesthood by Josiah, this meant that YHWH could only be worshiped in the single remaining divine abode—the Jerusalem temple. When this, the last earthly resting place of the divine presence, was destroyed, the worship of YHWH became impossible. Not only did the primary, defining role of the priest simply become extinct, for all intents and purposes, the priests themselves were no longer priests. They were simply former priests, and their descendants were merely people of priestly lineage—a fact that was later to be of considerable importance, but which was of no significance whatsoever the moment the temple went up in flames.

It must be recalled that for those who witnessed the events of 597 and 586, whether deported to Babylonia or not, the catastrophe was final. There is no indication that it was perceived initially as something temporary, and there is no basis for positing that the Israelite priesthood had any sense that its sacrificial functions were simply to be held in abeyance for a time, later to be restored. For those who witnessed and survived them, the events culminating in the fall of Jerusalem in 586 were cataclysmic: they marked what was surely understood to be the end of Israel's existence as YHWH's people and certainly the end of the worship of YHWH (see Ezek 8:12; 9:9; and especially 33:10; 37:11; cf. Lam 3:18, 54). Continued cultic service by priests was utterly unthinkable without the temple, and was unimaginable in Babylonia—as evidenced by the total lack of any mention of it in the Hebrew Bible.[13]

---

12. See Menahem Haran, *Temples and Temple-Service in Ancient Israel* (Oxford: Clarendon, 1978; repr., Winona Lake, Ind.: Eisenbrauns, 1985), 13–25 and passim; idem, "Priesthood, Temple, Divine Service: Some Observations on Institutions and Practices of Worship," *HAR* 7 (1983): 121–35, esp. 122–27.

13. Subsequent developments in Judea and in Elephantine notwithstanding, the deportees to Babylonia seem to have taken this as self-evident. They are reported to have planned once and for all to end their relationship with YHWH by worshiping *other* deities, derogatively called by Ezekiel "wood and stone" (Ezek 20:32), but there is no evidence that they ever contemplated worshiping YHWH there. The imaginative suggestion that the elders approached Ezekiel (20:1) with a plan to erect an altar to YHWH in Babylonia, first put forward by M. Ish Shalom [= Friedmann] in 1888 and later accepted by several scholars, has rightly been rejected; for details see Greenberg, *Ezekiel 1–20*, 387–88.

Nothing reported of Ezekiel's prophetic activity corresponds in any way to the cultic function of the priest, nor could it. Neither through his preaching of the indispensability of sacrifice nor by predicting its eventual restoration does Ezekiel preserve in his own actions any vestige of the priest's cultic role. There is no evidence that he, or anyone else, viewed his repeated preaching of the determined conviction that YHWH's worship *must* be restored (20:40–41; 37:26–28; chs. 40–48) as anything other than that. The notion that *speaking of* the required sacrifices and rituals, and hoping for—or even predicting—their renewal, might be tantamount to performing them, though it ultimately became central to Jewish worship, would be a long time in coming.[14] There can be no suggestion that anything in Ezekiel's deeds or words served, or was perceived by his fellow exiles, either as a form of worship or as a replacement or substitute for it.[15]

But are there other aspects of Ezekiel's prophetic activity in exile that might be said to constitute a continuation of, or even an extension of, the role of the priest in preexilic times, whether actually performed by Ezekiel before his deportation to Babylonia or not? The answer depends in large measure upon the image of the preexilic priesthood one adopts. The standard portraits of the ancient Israelite priesthood, assembled from evidence carefully culled from biblical texts held to be of preexilic authorship or at least to reflect preexilic times, and supplemented by evidence gathered from texts that admittedly reflect the postexilic priesthood but may be presumed to shed some reliable light on earlier times as well,[16] generally attribute to the priests two further roles in addition to their primary, cultic functions: that of divining YHWH's will, and that of imparting the laws, texts, and traditions of Israel to the people. Both are associated with the Hiphil of the verb ירה "instruct" and the noun תורה "instruction," which the texts in question employ when referring to nonritual priestly activity.

To be sure, even if this picture of the ancient Israelite priesthood were to be accepted, it would remain questionable whether Ezekiel's activity as a prophet corresponded in any real sense to the types of תורה purportedly provided by priests, that is, determining the divine will and disseminating the divine word. Regarding the former type, the resemblance would appear to be quite superficial; the prophetic word is quite unlike priestly divination.

Torah (תורה), in the sense of oracular divination, as performed by priests, entails the manipulation of the Urim and Thummim or other devices. It is occa-

---

14. The classic expression of this belief is the midrashic exegesis of Hos 14:3 (Eng. 14:2), read by the rabbis to mean, "instead of bulls we will pay with our lips"; see, e.g., *b. Yoma* 86b.

15. Contra Duguid, "Putting Priests in Their Place," 47–48.

16. See Aelred Cody, *A History of the Old Testament Priesthood* (AnBib 35; Rome: Pontifical Biblical Institute, 1969); Julia M. O'Brien, *Priest and Levite in Malachi* (SBLDS 121; Atlanta: Scholars Press, 1990), 1–23; Lester L. Grabbe, *Priests, Prophets, Diviners, Sages: A Socio-historical Study of Religious Specialists in Ancient Israel* (Valley Forge, Pa.: Trinity Press International, 1995); cf. Tuell, *Law of the Temple*, 121–52.

sioned by an inquiry initiated by someone other than the priest, and it is aimed at discerning a particular piece of information, known to exist but not accessible (or at least not readily accessible) by the means available to mortals. This might include a person's guilt or innocence of a crime or the identity of a culprit—that is, knowledge that the deity would otherwise not be inclined to communicate.[17] Prophecy on the other hand consists of rebuke, arraignment, threat, and condemnation. Insofar as it includes prediction of the future, whether distant or near, blessed or doomed, it is intertwined with the judgment of the past and present. Interaction with the people is initiated by the prophet, who is convinced that the deity has something to say to them—something that, in Ezekiel's case at least, is conveyed to him by the overpowering force of YHWH's hand, not by any means that he can activate.

Not unexpectedly, Ezekiel has couched many of his prophecies in legal-sounding language—a natural expression of his priestly heritage. One good example is the watchman prophecy (Ezek 3:17–21; 33:7–20). But although the passage is shaped by a form reminiscent of laws and commandments,[18] it is not torah in the sense of priestly oracle. Nor does it assign to Ezekiel the task of pronouncing torah—oracular verdicts.[19] The watchman figure is a metaphor, a rhetorical symbol—*of the role of the prophet*. The figure itself is not priestly; rather, it is drawn from prophetic tradition.[20] The passage does not assign to Ezekiel any task other than the prophetic one itself: to announce (symbolized in the figure by sounding the horn) to the Israelite people (symbolized in the figure by the townspeople) that YHWH (implicitly symbolized in the figure by the approaching enemy) is coming to destroy them.

Some have interpreted the long speeches in chapters 20, 22, and 23, in which the prophet is explicitly ordered to pronounce judgment, as instances of this type of priestly torah.[21] But התשפט ("judge") in these prophecies (20:4; 22:2; 23:36) means "arraign, indict," not determine a verdict or pronounce a sentence. As for pronouncing *divine* sentences of death, even on individuals, that is exclusively the role of prophets, never priests.[22]

---

17. See Cornelis Van Dam, *The Urim and Thummim: A Means of Revelation in Ancient Israel* (Winona Lake, Ind.: Eisenbrauns, 1997); on oracular justice specifically, see Bernard M. Levinson, *Deuteronomy and the Hermeneutics of Legal Innovation* (New York: Oxford University Press, 1997), 112–16.

18. See Walther Zimmerli, "The Special Form- and Traditio-Historical Character of Ezekiel's Prophecy," *VT* 15 (1965): 524; Moshe Greenberg, "The Meaning and Location of the 'Lookout' Passage in Ezek 3:16–21," *PAAJR* 46–47 (1978–79): 265–80, esp. 275–77; Paul Joyce, *Divine Initiative and Human Response in Ezekiel* (JSOTSup 51; Sheffield: JSOT Press, 1989), 58.

19. Greenberg, *Ezekiel 1–20*, 94–95. Duguid's assertion that the oracular role of priests had largely ceased even prior to the exile ("the priestly task of divining Yahweh's will had been superseded by the activity of prophets") seems to me questionable ("Putting Priests in Their Place").

20. The image of the watchman is present in Hos 9:8 (see Frances I. Andersen and David N. Freedman, *Hosea* [AB 24; Garden City, N.Y.: Doubleday, 1980], 533); see also 5:8 and 8:1. It is most explicit in Jer 6:17.

21. See Duguid, "Putting Priests in Their Place," 52–53.

22. Greenberg, *Ezekiel 1–20*, 363. As noted by Duguid, "all the available biblical evidence points to prophets as the ones who pronounced upon specific individuals the sentences of life and death" ("Putting Priests in Their Place," 52).

As for the second type of priestly torah postulated by scholars, consisting of "teaching Yahweh's ordinances and laws," "transmitting and mediating the authoritative traditions and texts of the community,"[23] it too bears little resemblance to Ezekiel's prophetic activity. Ezekiel's prophetic diatribe is indeed *based on* authoritative texts and traditions—though not of "the community" but of the priesthood—but it in no way consists of transmitting them. In fact, nothing that Ezekiel (or any other prophet for that matter) says can be characterized as תורה ("instruction") in this sense. The mere fact that the prophet is imparting something he believes to be the divine word does not make his words תורה. Torah (תורה) is normative: it tells what to do in order to be in accord with existing law and how to do it. Prophecy, even when it is exhortative and corrective, is not תורה. It threatens and promises, cajoles and condemns, but it does not instruct.[24]

This is especially so for Ezekiel. His prophetic tirade consists entirely of the reflective, accusatory, reprobational theodicy of the past and present, and the dire prediction of an unalterable future. In his teaching, the only steps that can and must be taken to rectify the present catastrophe will be taken *by YHWH himself*.[25] Even with regard to sacrifice: true, "Ezekiel recognizes that the restoration of the sacrificial service . . . lies at the heart of the restoration of the worship of the temple" and that "unless the sacrificial system is pure and acceptable to God, it is a worthless ritual (Mal 1:7–10)."[26] But while Malachi clearly exhorts the priesthood to live up to these standards, Ezekiel does not: he merely states that they *will* do so, once YHWH has stepped in and taken control of things.

Ezekiel does not rehearse the laws of worship, nor does he exhort his listeners to do so. Similarly, though he speaks about the Sabbath—in chapter 20, in the context of Israel's ancient sin, and in 22:26 in the context of the sins that brought about the current exile—he does not instruct his listeners on how to observe it or even exhort them to do so; his intent is to cast blame. For Ezekiel, the renewed sanctifi-

---

23. "Putting Priests in Their Place," 48.
24. See Yehezkel Kaufmann, *Toledot HaEmuna HaYisre'elit* 1/3 (Jerusalem: Mosad Bialik, 1967; repr., Tel Aviv: Dvir, 1972), 715–20. The role of Moses is no exception. To be sure, in the Elohistic-Deuteronomic tradition, at least, the figure of Moses is portrayed in a way somewhat analogous to prophecy. But prophecy per se arrived on the scene at an entirely different stage in Israelite history. This depiction is thus anachronistic, and indeed the resemblance is only formal. Moses' giving of the law qualifies "technically" as prophecy in that it consists of the relaying of a message from the deity to the people, but phenomenologically it is worlds apart from prophetic activity as the latter eventually materialized historically. On close examination, it becomes evident that even in E and D, although the giving of the law is somewhat analogous to prophecy, "torah" per se is not a prophetic activity. Moreover, the image of Moses found in J and P is thoroughly nonprophetic, and even in E and D Moses' prophet-like activity is kept distinct from that of the "real" prophets that followed (Num 12:6–8; Deut 18:15–22; 34:10–12).
25. I have explored this theme in Baruch J. Schwartz, "Ezekiel's Dim View of Israel's Restoration," in *The Book of Ezekiel: Theological and Anthropological Perspectives* (ed. M. S. Odell and J. T. Strong; SBLSymS 9; Atlanta: Society of Biblical Literature, 2000), 43–67, esp. 48–49, 58–64.
26. Duguid, "Putting Priests in Their Place," 58.

cation of the Sabbaths and the restoration of the Sabbath offerings will be brought about by Yhwh, not by the Israelites—and not yet. This sort of divine word is anything but תורה, even in the broad sense attributed to the term in scholarly descriptions of Israelite priestly instruction.

But the real question is: is the scholarly description of this second type of priestly instruction, that of disseminating the already-existing divine word, correct? Priests, after all, were not rabbis or sages, nor were they local or itinerant teacher-preachers. To say that the priests were responsible for teaching the law of Moses[27] implies not only that their role was educational in the absolute sense—that is, that they were charged with imparting a body of knowledge to the populace for its edification and indoctrination—but also that the "law of Moses" existed in some teachable, priestly form in preexilic times. And indeed, this is how rabbinic midrash and medieval commentary often understood "torah" in such passages as Lev 10:11; Deut 24:8 and 33:10; Jer 18:18; Ezek 7:26; and even Mal 1–2.[28] But taken on their own terms and in context, all these passages and others show that this exegesis is thoroughly anachronistic.[29] The priest's task of תורה in the sense of *instruction* was not an independent undertaking, separate from his cultic duties. It was completely ancillary to, and dependent upon, his role as cultic practitioner and specialist, and it consisted of informing the worshiper which ritual needed to be performed and how to do so, of supervising its proper performance, and of ruling and responding on matters requiring expert determinations, as posed by the worshiper or as necessitated by circumstances.[30] Is this person or object pure or impure? Do I have צרעת

---

27. Ibid.; see also Corrine Patton, "Priest, Prophet, and Exile: Ezekiel as a Literary Construct," *SBL Seminar Papers, 2000* (SBLSP 39; Atlanta: Society of Biblical Literature, 2000), 722–23, a revised form of which appears in this volume.

28. E.g., *Sipra, Shemini* 1:9 (ET: J. Neusner, *Sifra: An Analytical Translation*, vol. 2 [BJS 139; Atlanta: Scholars Press, 1988], 142); *b. Keritot* 13b; *b. Berachot* 5a; cf. Rashi, ad Exod 32:32 and esp. Kimhi, ad Jer 18:18; Mal 2:7.

29. See also Michael Fishbane, "*tôrâ*," *Encyclopædia Biblica* (9 vols.; Jerusalem: Mosad Byalik, 1950–1988), 8:469–83 [Hebrew]; Moshe Weinfeld, *Deuteronomy 1–11* (AB 5; New York: Doubleday, 1991), 17–18.

30. For a more precise understanding of priestly תורה, see, in addition to the studies of Fishbane and Weinfeld mentioned in the previous note, e.g., S. Wagner, "yarâ III," *TDOT* 6:343–44. Hosea 4:6 and Mic 3:11 reflect not a teaching role but rather the priests' responsibility for providing specific legal-ritual rulings as needed (contra Hans W. Wolff, *Hosea* [Hermeneia; Philadelphia; Fortress, 1974], 79). To be sure, the requisite priestly expertise is believed to derive ultimately from commands received from the deity; this is the assumption underlying Lev 10:10–11 (P), and it is stated explicitly in Deut 24:8 (D)—and it is for this reason priestly תורה is called "*Your* laws/*Your* instruction" (Deut 33:10), "the instruction *of your God*" (Hos 4:6) or "*My* instruction" (Ezek 22:26), but this in no wise suggests that the priests were entrusted with any written law (nor is this implied by Hos 8:12), much less that they were charged with disseminating it. In fact, the only real instance of priestly teaching of the law is the septennial reading of the torah-book envisaged by D (Deut 31:10–13). There is no evidence that this unique, ceremonial event ever actually took place; in any case, it is quite different from the sort of regular educational activity on the part of priests posited by scholars. Haran's description of the priest's role as "teacher" is worthy of quo-

or some other skin disease? Is this animal unacceptably blemished or may it be sacrificed? Has my offering been accepted or not? Is today a holy day or will that be tomorrow? Ancient Israelite priesthood was not a ministry to the people; it was a ministry on behalf of the people to the deity. It existed in order to facilitate worship, which may be defined as the constant offering of tribute to the deity, and to maintain the purity and sanctity of the deity's earthly abode in order to insure that his presence did not depart. All of the instruction that priests provided was for these purposes only. It may be noted in passing that P, of all the pentateuchal sources, does not even speak of a written torah, nor does it mention any ongoing method of teaching or transmitting the laws (which it records in full and which, it relates, were given to Moses orally) to the people, by priests or anyone else.[31]

The idea that priests were "teachers" thus anachronistically interprets biblical passages employing the word תורה according to the word's postexilic and postbiblical meaning. When preexilic priests are chastised for not performing their task, the point is to castigate them for failing to instruct the people as to the proper performance of their cultic duties, thus bringing about desecration of the sacred and contamination of the pure—not for failing to teach them the texts and traditions of Israel. The anachronistic understanding of priestly instruction also relies heavily on the assumption that the image of the sage and teacher presented by the figure of Ezra (especially in postbiblical literature) is a true reflection of the priest qua priest. But no priestly figure *other than* Ezra is ever said to have been a teacher, and this is because it is not part of the priestly role. Ezra *was* a priest, by lineage, and his *learning* was surely a result of this heritage. But teaching—publishing, translating, interpreting, promulgating, and transmitting law codes and texts—is not. It is something new and unprecedented, for which, we are explicitly told, Ezra was qualified by virtue of his being a סֹפֵר מָהִיר (Ezra 7:6)—not a priest.

One particularly telling example of Ezekiel's total abandonment of the priestly role is his radically new teaching regarding the maintenance of purity. Trained as he was in the teachings of the priesthood, Ezekiel viewed the destruction of the temple as the result of the contamination of the divine abode, ultimately forcing the deity to depart.[32]

---

tation: "The Priests also served as teachers of '*torah*' to the people. This function is mentioned as early as the blessing of Moses (Deut 33:10). The priests' instruction of the people did not exist as a special institution but was generally a by-product of their other activities. Thus, *torah* followed from the legal discussions held before the priests (Deut 17:11; 33:10). *Torah* was also taught by way of guidance given by the priests to the people in matters of impurities and diseases (Deut 24:8; Haggai 2:11ff.). Indeed, the various types of laws of impurity were called torah (Lev 11:46; 13:59; *et al.*)" (Menahem Haran, "Priests and Priesthood," *EncJud* 13:1080).

31. Baruch J. Schwartz, "The Priestly Account of the Theophany and Lawgiving at Sinai," in *Texts, Temples, and Traditions: A Tribute to Menahem Haran* (ed. M. V. Fox et al.; Winona Lake, Ind.: Eisenbrauns, 1996), 103–34, esp. 132.

32. This is dealt with in my forthcoming essay ("When a Priest Becomes a Prophet"); for the present, see John F. Kutsko, *Between Heaven and Earth: Divine Presence and Absence in the Book of Ezekiel* (Biblical and Judaic Studies 7; Winona Lake, Ind.: Eisenbrauns, 2000), esp. 77–93.

This contamination resulted from many factors, one of which was the Israelites' lack of diligence with regard to physical impurities. Ezekiel explicitly blames the preexilic priests for allowing this to happen (22:26), failing at their task of keeping the Israelites on guard against the accumulation of defilement (see Lev 15:31), and he insists that in the Israel of the future there will be no such failure. But he does not place any of the responsibility for bringing about this improved state of affairs upon the priests, nor does he engage in the task of providing any such instruction. For Ezekiel, it is too late for priestly teaching to rectify the problem—YHWH alone, not the Israelites, will perform the purification of the future. The past negligence of the priesthood signals its *end*, just as the sinfulness of Israel as a whole signals *its* end, and no teaching or preaching, no human efforts, can bring about the restoration: in Ezekiel's teaching Israel's rehabilitation is entirely YHWH's affair.[33]

Nothing Ezekiel says about purity and impurity constitutes torah. He speaks about the past in terms of the ultimately terminal process of the contamination of the temple and its consequences, and of the future in terms of YHWH's determination ultimately to purify the restored Israel. And yet, while Ezekiel's prophetic utterances in this area are not torah, they are completely consistent with priestly thought. In priestly thought, clean and unclean have no meaning outside of the dynamic of the temple and its defilement. The reason Israelites must be on guard against impurity (not only the priests are charged with this; their task is to oversee) is so that the divine abode not become contaminated and YHWH's presence not be forced to depart. Once this has already happened, however, there is no real validity to purity and impurity; in exile, they are meaningless categories. This, along with the fact that we have no intimation that Ezekiel ever expected to serve as a priest in the future, explains why Ezekiel made no real efforts to maintain his own priestly purity. The temple was no more; one need not maintain ritual purity in order to enter a *visionary* temple (nor does one need even to be a priest—see Isa 6) or to participate in the consecration of its altar.

The express purpose of communicating to Ezekiel these visions of the future temple is not to legislate, nor to reward "his personal faithfulness and purity,"[34] but to shame the exiles (Ezek 43:10).[35] The concern is with preventing the desecration of the holy realm, and this will be accomplished, in the future, by YHWH alone.

Ezekiel's horrified response when YHWH instructs him to bake bread on human dung fires in order to signal the siege of Jerusalem (Ezek 4:9–17) may be para-

---

33. See above, n. 25.
34. Duguid, "Putting Priests in Their Place," 56.
35. Indeed, as Duguid reminds us: "A close study of the design of the temple, especially the entrances and exits by which access to the holy is controlled and limited, is intended to convict Ezekiel's hearers of their sin (Ezek 43:11). They are thereby to become ashamed of their iniquities" ("Putting Priests in Their Place," 58).

phrased as follows: "I, being a priest, have never eaten carrion or torn flesh (which, in P, priests may not eat but lay Israelites may),[36] neither have I ever eaten anything defiling (which priests may do, but Ezekiel says he has so far taken care not to do); how can you expect me, being of so delicate a constitution, to eat *this* (which admittedly isn't defiling, but is still disgusting)?" (Ezek 4:14). YHWH's reply is indicative of Ezekiel's own sad realization: such delicateness of habit is a thing of the past; all your priestly customs are obsolete.

Following the lead of Jeremiah (Jer 18:18), Ezekiel expressly distinguishes the role of the prophet from that of the priest (Ezek 7:26): "instruction" is the task of priests; the task of the prophet is "vision" or "word." In light of this, it is unlikely that he would have allowed this intrinsic, essential difference to become blurred in his own mission. Indeed, it would appear that he did not. Not once does he use the word תורה to refer to his own prophetic teaching; even in the temple vision, where the word does appear (43:11–12; 44:5), it refers to laws that will be promulgated in the future when the visionary temple is built and the divine presence takes up its residence there. Prophetic appropriation of the word תורה does not make the priest-turned-prophet a lawgiver. Ezekiel *predicts* תורה, telling of a future time in which it will be imparted, but he himself does not impart it, and his communication of the temple vision is not legislation per se.

There is thus no evidence that Ezekiel viewed the prophetic task he was performing as that of a priest. Ezekiel never even says he is a priest—only the interpolator tells us this. I am not suggesting that this information is incorrect; but it is significant that the first-person narrative and the prophetic words recorded make no explicit mention of it. To me, this is yet another indication that he has knowingly left the priestly *role* behind. Of course, he has not left behind his priestly heritage; he has taken it with him into a comprehensive program of vocational retraining. As emphasized above, everything he says is thoroughly influenced by it. The fact of Ezekiel's priesthood is thus of enormous importance, but not for the purpose of reconstructing the priestly role during the exile—for there was none. Its importance lies rather in the indispensable aid it provides those who undertake to comprehend the theological, historical, and literary foundations of his message. Instead of asking "What can Ezekiel teach us about the priesthood," the question to pose is "What can the priesthood teach us about Ezekiel?"[37]

---

36. For discussion, see Baruch J. Schwartz, "The Prohibitions Concerning the 'Eating' of Blood in Leviticus 17," in *Priesthood and Cult in Ancient Israel* (ed. G. A. Anderson and S. M. Olyan; JSOTSup 125; Sheffield: JSOT Press, 1991), 34–66, esp. 64–66, and the bibliography cited there; later corrected by idem, " 'Profane' Slaughter and the Integrity of the Priestly Code," *HUCA* 67 (1996): 29 n. 33.

37. It is a pleasure to express my gratitude for the expert assistance I received from Mr. Guy Darsan in the preparation of this essay.

PRIEST, PROPHET, AND EXILE:
EZEKIEL AS A LITERARY CONSTRUCT

Corrine L. Patton

At the beginning of the book of Ezekiel, both the prophet and the narrator identify Ezekiel as a priest of the first deportation.[1] The audience "reads" the rest of the book through the lens of this particular social setting (elite priest). In addition, the reader of the final form of the text should also recognize that the author and Ezekiel are not identical: Ezekiel is a character within the prophetic narrative, through whom the reader experiences the exile.[2] Recent studies of the book have begun to take the narrative elements seriously,[3] including the characterization of Ezekiel. However, more studies have focused on his function as a prophet than on his characterization as a priest.[4] Since the restoration of the priesthood is so important at the end of the book, how the character of Ezekiel functions as priest contributes to a

---

1. Walther Zimmerli defines the event as less of a deportation than a taking of official hostages. See his discussion in *Ezekiel: A Commentary on the Book of the Prophet Ezekiel* (2 vols.; Hermeneia; Philadelphia: Fortress, 1979), 1:364–65, 507.

2. For a fuller treatment of the role of characterization within prophetic texts, see Pauline Viviano, "Characterizing Jeremiah," *WW* 22 (2002): 361–68; Kathleen M. O'Connor, "Jeremiah and the Formation of the Moral Character of the Community" (paper presented at the annual meeting of the Catholic Biblical Association, August 2003); and Corrine Patton, "Layers of Meaning: Priesthood in Jeremiah MT," in *The Priests in the Prophets: The Portrayal of Priests, Prophets, and Other Religious Specialists in the Latter Prophets* (ed. L. L. Grabbe and A. O. Bellis; JSOTSup; London and New York: T. & T. Clark, forthcoming, 2004).

3. See especially the studies by Moshe Greenberg, *Ezekiel 1–20* (AB 22; New York: Doubleday, 1983) and *Ezekiel 21–37* (AB 22A; New York: Doubleday, 1997); Ellen F. Davis, *Swallowing the Scroll: Textuality and the Dynamics of Discourse in Ezekiel's Prophecy* (JSOTSup 78; Bible and Literature 21; Sheffield: Almond, 1989); Kalinda R. Stevenson, *The Vision of Transformation: The Territorial Rhetoric of Ezekiel 40–48* (SBLDS 154; Atlanta: Scholars Press, 1996); Margaret S. Odell, "You Are What You Eat: Ezekiel and the Scroll," *JBL* 117 (1998): 229–48; Kelvin G. Friebel, *Jeremiah's and Ezekiel's Sign-Acts: Rhetorical Nonverbal Communication* (JSOTSup 283; Sheffield: Sheffield Academic Press, 1999); and Thomas Renz, *The Rhetorical Function of the Book of Ezekiel* (VTSup 76; Leiden: Brill, 1999).

4. Odell explores the interconnection of the priestly and prophetic roles of the character, although the focus is on the first five chapters as an extended prophetic initiation ("You Are What You Eat"). Andrew Mein's recent study of Ezekiel's priesthood is very close to this one, although he focuses on how it serves the exiles to maintain group identity in the Diaspora ("Ezekiel as a Priest in Exile," in *The Elusive Prophet: The Prophet as a Historical Person, Literary Character, and Anonymous Artist* [ed. J. C. de Moor; OtSt 45;

fuller understanding of the book's projection of the ideal priesthood. As a first-person sympathetic narrator,[5] Ezekiel is an idealized figure in the book; the reader experiences all speech, all action, through this figure.[6]

I presume that the book projects an idealization of priesthood, not only in its vision of the restored priesthood in Ezek 44, but also in its condemnations of Jerusalemite priests, and in its portrayal of the character of Ezekiel. This idealization may never have been the historical reality of what it meant to be a priest, nor is it a transparent window through which we glimpse the historical priests of the preexilic temple. Rather this is an idealization that comes out of the experience of the fall of the city, the destruction of the temple, and the functional cessation of all priestly activity.

The storytelling in the book is so artful that it draws the reader into assuming that what it says about Ezekiel reflects a historical person's real experience.[7] This study proceeds from the assumption that the text is controlled more by ideological struggles than by historical facts. It will examine the ideology of priesthood in relation to four areas: the priesthood's role and function especially in relation to prophecy, the social and moral hierarchy projected or assumed in the text, the characterization of Ezekiel as a priest, and, lastly, how this characterization informs the analysis of the Zadokite material in the final vision.

I. PRIESTS, PROPHETS, AND RELIGIOUS PERSONNEL

Before commencing with an analysis of the way priesthood functions in the book, the thorny problem of how a reader distinguishes priestly and prophetic activity comes to the fore.[8] There is a growing trend in studies on Israelite religion to

---

Leiden: Brill, 2001], 199–213). See also Menahem Haran, "The Law-Code of Ezekiel XL–XLVIII and Its Relation to the Priestly School," *HUCA* 50 (1979): 45–71.

5. On narration in the Hebrew Bible, see Adele Berlin, *Poetics and Interpretation of Biblical Narrative* (Bible and Literature 9; Sheffield: Almond, 1983), esp. pp. 43–59. See also Tremper Longman III, *Literary Approaches to Biblical Interpretation* (Foundations of Contemporary Interpretation 3; Grand Rapids: Zondervan, 1987), 85–87, and David M. Gunn, "Reading Right: Reliable and Omniscient Narrator, Omniscient God, and Foolproof Composition in the Hebrew Bible," in *The Bible in Three Dimensions: Essays in Celebration of Forty Years of Biblical Studies in the University of Sheffield* (ed. D. J. A. Clines, S. E. Fowl, and S. E. Porter; JSOTSup 87; Sheffield: Sheffield Academic Press, 1990), 53–64. On Ezekiel as narrator, see Renz, *Rhetorical Function*, 132–37.

6. At this point I am speaking about the implied or ideal reader, rather than the actual reader; see Davis, *Swallowing the Scroll*, 73–77.

7. For a fuller discussion of the literary qualities of the narrator, see the original form of this paper, "Priest, Prophet, and Exile: Ezekiel as a Literary Construct," *SBL Seminar Papers, 2000* (SBLSP 39; Atlanta: Society of Biblical Literature, 2000), 700–727.

8. This issue is examined in various ways in the forthcoming volume edited by Grabbe and Bellis, *Priests in the Prophets*. Recent studies have shown that much early writing on this topic was biased by prejudice either against Catholic religiosity, or against Jewish faith. Too often, the priest was viewed as negative, conservative, preserving traditions at all costs, and keeping religious expression tied to its ear-

recognize that the categories of priest and prophet are more interdependent than once thought. Anthropological studies of Israelite priesthood concede that there is a distinction between priesthood and prophecy, yet no one agrees on the exact articulation of that distinction. While it is generally agreed that a prophet is an intermediary while a priest is a ritual specialist, both are religious functionaries who mediate God's presence and can work within a cultic context. The book of Ezekiel focuses more on Ezekiel's prophetic activity than it does on his designation as priest. Yet, because the author assumes that the two social categories are distinct, it is first important that the book itself be allowed to define these two categories.

Ezekiel's interactions with God are associated with both visionary experience and oral communication. Ezekiel is charged to deliver both oral and visual revelations accurately (e.g., 3:10–11; 43:10–12; 44:5). Prophets are expected to discern whether a prophetic message is true.[9] While chapters 13 and 22 condemn prophets for delivering false oracles, both 13:23 and 22:28 note that these false oracles are the result of false visions that the prophets have actually received.[10] These prophets speak their oracles in the name of the Lord (13:7 and 22:28), although the text does not identify the source of their false visions. Presumably, they are condemned for their inability to discern between a true and false vision. The gravity of their sin is reinforced by the punishment announced in 13:9, namely, their permanent removal from Israelite society.[11] Ezekiel as the true prophet not only delivers prophetic messages accurately but also has successfully discerned that the messages are true.

Ezekiel's characterization as a prophet is part of a larger movement in the book to appropriate a wide range of traditions. Within the prophetic tradition, Ezekiel acts like an ecstatic prophet, while his revelations play on earlier oracles, such as Isa 6 and Hos 1–3.[12] The author of Ezekiel was a highly literate scribe, familiar with a

---

lier magical roots. I do not need to rehearse the criticism of this approach here; the point has been clearly made by other scholars.

One aspect of prophetic activity usually ignored in these articles is that of the prophetic "state," whether that is called frenzy, ecstasy, or possession; see, e.g., Mircea Eliade, *Shamanism: Archaic Techniques of Ecstasy* (Bollingen Series 76; Princeton: Princeton University Press, 1964); Leopold Sabourin, *Priesthood: A Comparative Study* (SHR 25; Leiden: Brill, 1973); and Robert R. Wilson, *Prophecy and Society in Ancient Israel* (Philadelphia: Fortress, 1980), esp. pp. 21–88. While this state is occasionally attributed to prophets in the Bible (e.g., 1 Sam 10:5–6; 1 Kgs 22:15–23, and, perhaps, Num 23:5, 12, 16; Isa 28:7–10), it is never noted as a component of priesthood.

9. For a similar discussion of the book's view of prophets, see Iain M. Duguid, *Ezekiel and the Leaders of Israel* (VTSup 56; Leiden: Brill, 1994), 91–103.

10. For a recent study of the condemnation of the female prophets, see Nancy R. Bowen, "The Daughters of Your People: Female Prophets in Ezekiel 13:17–23," *JBL* 118 (1999): 417–33. She concludes that the condemnation is part of the book's larger attempt to solidify power under one priestly group. See also Duguid, *Ezekiel and the Leaders*, 95–98.

11. The reference in 13:9 is not to exile, but to removal from a written roll of Israelites. This wording casts no aspersions on those who had been deported in 597.

12. For a full study of the book's use of earlier prophetic traditions, see Keith W. Carley, *Ezekiel among the Prophets* (SBT 31; Naperville, Ill.: SCM, 1974).

wide range of stories and traditions, which he uses to portray Ezekiel. Ezekiel, then, appropriates various prophetic traditions to become the quintessential prophet.

This does not mean that Ezekiel's function as prophet monopolizes the book. The author's ironic use of the prophetic epithet illustrates the text's complex attitude toward the prophetic office. The book most often utilizes the epithet "son of man," "mortal," "human one" (בן אדם) in divine speeches introduced by the prophetic formula, "The word of the Lord came to me." It is generally agreed that the language stresses Ezekiel's humble status, especially in relationship to God. In the Deuteronomistic History (Dtr), in contrast, the prophet is often referred to as the "person of God"[13] or "divine one" (איש אלוהים). This title appears most often in the earliest strata of the History, and, therefore, would reasonably have been a tradition known to the author of Ezekiel. The book's incessant replacement of this prophetic title ("person of God") with "child of a human" or "human one" serves a rhetorical function: all prophets other than Ezekiel are condemned to banishment from the Israelite community, while the only prophet left, Ezekiel, is not an איש אלוהים, but only a בן אדם.

Is Ezekiel's characterization as priest any less ambiguous? Although there are relatively few cross-cultural studies on the nature and function of Israelite priesthood,[14] many anthropologists agree on a range of functions associated with the priest, such as the maintenance of sacred space, and the care of the cult object.[15] The priest oversees the rituals in and around a sacred place, rituals that are usually in the form of sacrifice. The priest also mediates the divine resident's presence, often by reading

---

13. The traditional, gender-specific translations are "man of God" and "son of man"; these phrases have entered into scholarship as almost technical terms. The multiple meanings of each term in these titles undercut any claim to render an exact translation. However, since prophecy was not a gender-specific activity, gender-specific language should be avoided.

14. It is surprising to me the number of studies of temple ritual and priestly theology that never address the role and function of the priest. E.g., John G. Gammie (*Holiness in Israel* [OBT; Minneapolis: Fortress, 1989]), Frank H. Gorman (*Ideology of Ritual: Space, Time, and Status in the Priestly Theology* [JSOTSup 91; Sheffield: Sheffield Academic Press, 1991]), Philip P. Jenson (*Graded Holiness: A Key to the Priestly Conception of the World* [JSOTSup 106; Sheffield: JSOT Press, 1992]), and Saul M. Olyan (*Rites and Rank: Hierarchy in Biblical Representations of Cult* [Princeton: Princeton University Press, 2000]) discuss priestly holiness as an aspect of ritual, but not as a social force in and of itself. Even Catherine M. Bell (*Ritual Theory, Ritual Practice* [New York: Oxford University Press, 1992] and *Ritual: Perspectives and Dimensions* [New York: Oxford University Press, 1997]) pays only scant attention to the social function of the personnel responsible for ritual.

15. More general studies of the nature of priesthood can be found in Max Weber, esp. *Ancient Judaism* (trans. and ed. H. H. Gerth and D. Martindale; New York: Free Press, 1952), 364–67; Robert H. Pfeiffer, *Religion in the Old Testament: The History of a Spiritual Triumph* (New York: Harper, 1961), 77–82; Aelred Cody, "Priesthood in the Old Testament," in *Priesthood and Prophecy in Christianity and Other Religions* (Studia Missionalia 22; Rome: Gregorian University Press, 1973), 309–29; Sabourin, *Priesthood: A Comparative Study*; and Mary Beard and John North, eds., *Pagan Priests: Religion and Power in the Ancient World* (Ithaca, N.Y.: Cornell University Press, 1990).

oracles.¹⁶ All of the studies agree that the priest holds an elevated position, although it is often subordinated to political powers. This priestly office is part of a larger program of social maintenance associated with the temple; as a result, priesthood is often characterized as traditional, static, and opposed to innovation.¹⁷ Some of the cross-cultural categories resonate with the biblical witness to ancient Israelite priesthood.¹⁸ In addition to the priest's responsibility for ritual and social maintenance mentioned above, however, Israelite prophets stress the priest's role as teacher, presumably referring to ritual instruction.¹⁹

How does the book of Ezekiel define priesthood? The book provides a rather full view of priests in both its condemnations and vision of restoration. First, priests are servants of God (מְשָׁרְתִים; Ezek 44:11), with a duty to tend to the sanctuary. The priest is the expert in sacrificial preparation: selection of edible materials of suf-

---

16. On the problem of distinguishing between prophetic oracular activity and that of the priest in the ancient Near East, see the articles in Beard and North, *Pagan Priests*, esp. Amélie Kuhrt, "Nabonidus and the Babylonian Priesthood," 119–55; Herbert B. Huffmon, "A Company of Prophets: Mari, Assyria, Israel," in *Prophecy in Its Ancient Near Eastern Context: Mesopotamian, Biblical, and Arabian Perspectives* (ed. M. Nissinen; SBLSymS 13; Atlanta: Society of Biblical Literature, 2000), 47–70; and Daniel E. Fleming, "Prophets and Temple Personnel in the Mari Archives," in Grabbe and Bellis, *Priests in the Prophets*.

17. See, e.g., Paula M. McNutt, *Reconstructing the Society of Ancient Israel* (Library of Ancient Israel; Louisville: Westminster John Knox, 1999), 176–81.

18. Much of what follows is dependent on studies of Israelite priesthood, such as Aelred Cody, *A History of Old Testament Priesthood* (AnBib 35; Rome: Pontifical Biblical Institute, 1969); Richard Nelson, "The Role of the Priesthood in the Deuteronomistic History," in *Congress Volume: Leuven, 1989* (ed. John A. Emerton; VTSup 43; Leiden: Brill, 1991), 132–47; Victor H. Matthews and Don C. Benjamin, *Social World of Ancient Israel: 1200–587 BCE* (Peabody, Mass.: Hendrickson, 1993), 187–98; Richard D. Nelson, *Raising Up a Faithful Priest: Community and Priesthood in Biblical Theology* (Louisville: Westminster John Knox, 1993); Lester L. Grabbe, *Priests, Prophets, Diviners, Sages: A Socio-historical Study of Religious Specialists in Ancient Israel* (Valley Forge, Pa: Trinity Press International, 1995); Joseph Blenkinsopp, *Sage, Priest, Prophet: Religious and Intellectual Leadership in Ancient Israel* (Library of Ancient Israel; Louisville: Westminster John Knox, 1995), 66–114, and *A History of Prophecy in Israel* (rev. ed.; Louisville: Westminster John Knox, 1996); Michael S. Moore, "Role Pre-emption in the Israelite Priesthood," *VT* 46 (1996): 316–29; Deborah W. Rooke, "Kingship as Priesthood: The Relationship between the High Priesthood and the Monarchy," in *King and Messiah in Israel and the Ancient Near East: Proceedings of the Oxford Old Testament Seminar* (ed. John Day; JSOTSup 270; Sheffield: Sheffield Academic Press, 1998), 187–208; Peter J. Leithart, "Attendants of Yahweh's House: Priesthood in the Old Testament," *JSOT* 85 (1999): 3–24; and McNutt, *Reconstructing the Society of Ancient Israel*, 176–81. See also recent studies of the priesthood in the Second Temple period, such as Michael E. Stone, "Ideal Figures and Social Context: Priest and Sage in the Early Second Temple Period," in *Ancient Israelite Religion: Essays in Honor of Frank Moore Cross* (ed. P. D. Miller, P. D. Hanson, and S. D. McBride; Philadelphia: Fortress, 1987), 575–86; Stephen L. Cook, *Prophecy and Apocalypticism: The Postexilic Social Setting* (Minneapolis: Fortress, 1995); Joseph Blenkinsopp, "The Judaean Priesthood during the Neo-Babylonian and Achaemenid Periods: A Hypothetical Reconstruction," *CBQ* 60 (1998): 25–43; and Gary N. Knoppers, "Hierodules, Priests, or Janitors? The Levites in Chronicles and the History of the Israelite Priesthood," *JBL* 118 (1999): 49–72.

19. The priests are condemned in the book for not carrying out their duty of instruction (7:26). For similar condemnations, see Jer 14:18; 18:18; Hos 4; Mic 3:11; and Ezra 10:10.

ficient quality (determined by ritual categories), the preparation and proper handling of both raw and cooked food products, for animal sacrifices the slaughter, butchering, and cooking of the meat with similar preparation for grain and wine offerings, and the distribution and disposal of prepared foods. They enacted the sacrifices of communal atonement. The priests alone handled the blood, guarded entrances and exits, and instructed the people. They maintained the calendar and the system of weights and measures and served as judges.[20] Ezekiel's Zadokite priests maintain higher levels of ritual purity than do priests in other Scriptures, including practicing exclusions on marriage and restrictions on contact with the dead. Their residence is limited; Zadokites reside on, but do not own, land adjacent to the temple (45:3–4 and 48:10–12), while Levites own land adjacent to that of the Zadokites (45:5 and 48:13–14).

Finally, in a few Israelite texts outside of Ezekiel, visionary experience was attributed to the priest. While visions are more often associated with prophets, Exod 24:9–10 describes a vision of God directed to the elders mediated by Aaron and his sons, much like those of Isaiah and Ezekiel. The priests are the first to "see" God's glory in the temple (1 Kgs 8:10–11), and in Isa 28:7 both priests and prophets err in vision. Like the call of Isaiah, which also takes place in the temple, the book of Ezekiel stresses this visionary component of his religious mediation experiences. In chapter 44, the final vision is to be "taught" like priestly torah (43:11–12 and 44:5).

Priesthood is literally a pivotal role,[21] and it is in this central position that questions of the intersection of priest and prophet arise. In some sense, the priest mediates the divine presence to the community, but this mediation is of a different character than the mediation of the prophet. Prophetic mediation consists in the mediation of some type of divine communication. There is a message, or substantive issue, that is tied to a particular historical situation. Priests, on the other hand, mediate a god's presence, acting as a buffer zone between God and the people. Priesthood's involvement with regulating purity issues is an integral part of this mediation. Mediation of divine presence is an ever-present communal need, rather than a situation-specific manifestation.

Too often, however, modern studies of priesthood have focused either on the social-maintenance function of the priest, or on functions dealing with negative aspects of God. While priesthood in Ezekiel was responsible for controlling dangerous contact with God, I would maintain that this was not the priests' primary function. Even more prominently, they were to maintain regular worship. In the final vision of chapters 40–48, high holy days, festivals, thank offerings, and the rest were not instituted primarily as a political-social move to control and distribute

---

20. See Moshe Greenberg, "The Design and Themes of Ezekiel's Program of Restoration," *Int* 38 (1984): 196–97. There is no evidence that Ezekiel's priests read oracles.

21. I avoid the use of the term "liminal" because of its association with rites of passage. The priest's role was not a temporary one. Instead, he is a "janus-figure" between God and the people. Nelson uses the term "boundary crosser(s)" (*Raising Up a Faithful Priest*, 83–110).

excess wealth, but they were a communal theological expression of the community's recognition of who God is. Ezekiel's interactions with God throughout the book portray the theological motivations for many priestly acts, while the vision makes the theological focus of the ritual more explicit.

II. Inscribing Multiple Hierarchies

One of the most common claims leveled against priests as a social category is that they are a "conserving" social group that reinforces hierarchical structures within a society.[22] Within the book of Ezekiel, however, priesthood both reinforces a human anthropology that is hierarchically arranged, and it becomes a vehicle that rearranges the monarchic social hierarchy. The status of the prophet does not serve as the linchpin to realign social structure in chapters 40–48; rather, the differentiated priestly groups inaugurate the realignment of the royalty, the city, and the nation. Social hierarchy begins at the "top" with the priestly groups.

The book of Ezekiel exhibits great concern for the various forms of leadership in Judah. It refers to the royal leader (king or prince), the priests, the prophets, and the elders. Although few historical leaders are actually named in the text, people in every leadership role are judged for their sins, including both the priests and the prophets. The final form of the vision of restoration in chapters 40–48 implies that the ideal reconstruction of the nation will include adjustments to social categories, such as the demotion of the king to a נשיא,[23] and the hierarchical differentiation of Zadokites and Levites in the temple.

The book defines social hierarchy in relation to three different phenomena: politics, economics, and ritual. Kings are responsible for international politics (17:11–21) and protection of the weak (34:4), prophets for responsible communication of divinely revealed oracles (3:17–21; 13:3–16; and 33:2–7), and priests for "instruction" on legal and ritual issues (7:26 and 22:26), and for maintaining proper levels of purity (spelled out in various laws for the priests in the final vision). Leaders are criticized for failure in their duties, while the moral responsibility of citizens is mitigated by the degree to which the leaders have failed to fulfill their own responsibilities. The long sentinel discourses (3:17–21 and 33:2–7) on the corporate

---

22. See, e.g., Carol L. Meyers, "David as Temple Builder," in Miller, Hanson, and McBride, *Ancient Israelite Religion*; Olyan, *Rites and Rank*, esp. 15–37.

23. The literature on Ezekiel's representation of the נשיא is abundant. See the study of this figure in Duguid, *Ezekiel and the Leaders*, 10–57. See also Levenson, *Theology of the Program*, 55–107; Charles R. Biggs, "The Role of the Nasi in the Programme for Restoration in Ezekiel 40–48," *Colloq* 16 (1983): 46–57; Stephen S. Tuell, *The Law of the Temple in Ezekiel 40–48* (HSM 49; Atlanta: Scholars Press, 1992), 103–20; Thilo Alexander Rudnig, *Heilig und Profan: Redaktionskritische Stuien zu Ez 40–48* (BZAW 287; Berlin: de Gruyter, 2000), 137–64; Daniel Bodi, "Le prophète critique la monarchie: Le terme *nāśîʾ* chez Ézéchiel," in *Prophètes et rois: Bible et Proche-Orient* (ed. André Lemaire; LD; Paris: Cerf, 2001), 249–57.

responsibility of the prophet serve as a model of leadership based, not on privilege, but on responsibility.

The author has little to say about economic hierarchy. In passages such as 7:11, 20, the author mentions loss of wealth for those being exiled, but as distinct from prophets such as Amos and Micah, he does not focus on an unjust distribution of wealth.[24] Instead, land is the primary source of economic status. In the final vision of restoration, land division is "equitable." The political leader has more land than any other individual does, but the purpose of this excess land is to provide for the sacrifices on the high holy days. The temple has the central parcel of land, presumably as a symbol of the centrality of the sacrificial services.[25]

Land distribution in these visions, however, reflects ritual hierarchy more than economic equity.[26] From the perspective of ritual, the tribes are *not* equal, but arranged hierarchically, with the most important being closest to the temple. In Ezekiel, while ritual hierarchy is most clearly in play in chapters 40–48, where the author explicitly limits access to sacred space, this element of the text is in continuity with the earlier sections of the book. The repeated stress on Judah's sins as abominations that lead to defilement assumes that there have been past violations of approach; this may be behind the explicit condemnation of the royalty in Ezek 43:8, and the condemnation of the Levites in 44:9–10. The fact that this defilement leads to God's abandonment of the temple suggests that these include violations of access. In Ezek 8:16, the people in the inner court are not called "priests" or even "Levites"; they are simply "men," suggesting that their sin includes their very presence in the inner court of the temple.

Within this ritual hierarchy, the book depicts the priests as having the top rung of the ladder. Priests control access to the temple precinct, and they alone have access to the area around the altar (40:46; 42:13; 44:15–16; and 48:11–12). In the final vision, hierarchy is projected, portrayed, and maintained by questions of access and approach. The king may have political and economic power. He may be able to conduct war, initiate treaties, and control trade, but all of this is ultimately insignificant if he cannot burn the whole burnt offering (44:3; 45:7–8, 16; 46:1–12; and 48:21–22). Since it is God's presence that determines ritual hierarchy, the "hierarchy of hierarchies" is ritual hierarchy.

How does the portrayal of Ezekiel address these various hierarchies? By the book's end, he has usurped the function and status of every leadership position. The most obvious usurpation has to do with royal power. Although in the ancient Near East, the ones responsible for temple building were the kings, Ezekiel is portrayed as usurping this royal role. God works with him to plan the new temple. The final

---

24. The reference to the shepherds eating fat in 34:2–3 may be an exception.
25. Stevenson (*Vision of Transformation*) focuses on this theological function of land in the final vision.
26. Menahem Haran call this the "hierarchy of approach" in "The Priestly Image of the Tabernacle," *HUCA* 36 (1965): 191–226.

vision also endows Ezekiel with royal power by having him receive a set of laws, a function either of the king or of a Mosaic prophet.[27] The elders, who consult Ezekiel in 8:1, 14:1, and 20:1, are also subordinated to the role and power of Ezekiel. This usurpation of political roles by the main character serves to elevate his political status over all other leaders.

Ezekiel's economic status must be inferred. As an exile, the reader may presume he has lost access to all wealth. If he were from the priestly family that had at one time controlled the temple of Jerusalem, the land to which he would have lost access would have been temple land. This makes the focus on the restoration of temple property at the end of the book expected: his own access to wealth would have been through that temple and its income. Similarly, the restoration of the sacrificial system would result in the restoration of his own economic status. In addition, the lack of a critique for the treatment of the poor may also reflect his inherently privileged status. He represents the concern for the restoration of the privileged group, not the effects of the siege and fall on the poor.

The primary way Ezekiel's status is asserted, however, is through ritual hierarchy. The powerful opening vision unquestionably establishes Ezekiel as the one who has fullest access to God's presence. Although Ezekiel is not, in fact, the high priest, the text portrays him as a priest who usurps the hierarchy of approach from the high priest, and even surpasses it. Even though Ezekiel never enters the holy of holies (41:3–4), he has access to God's presence that resides there, even when he is, in fact, not physically in Jerusalem. Within the narrative time frame, he sees God more clearly than the priests who remain in Jerusalem do.

Subtle notices about Ezekiel's purity also serve to elevate him to the pinnacle of the priestly group. Although the opening vision expands a similar vision from Isa 6, it does not portray Ezekiel as worried about the inherent danger of his own uncleanness. In fact, he asserts his own pure state when God commands him to eat food cooked on human dung (4:14). Other portions of the book portray God as the one who actively purifies Israel both at its establishment (chs. 16 and 23), and in visions of restoration (36:25, 33). Not once does the character of Ezekiel undergo a purification ritual, however, in spite of his direct contact with God. This portrayal then projects Ezekiel as essentially unlike any other character in the book, hierarchically better, more pure, and, therefore, more qualified to approach God than any other previous Israelite figure. This is especially striking in a book so focused on purity and defilement.

---

27. On Ezekiel as a "new Moses," see, e.g., Wilson, *Prophecy and Society*, 282–86; Bruce Vawter and Leslie J. Hoppe, *A New Heart: A Commentary on the Book of Ezekiel* (ITC; Grand Rapids: Eerdmans, 1991), 197; Corrine Patton, "'I Myself Gave Them Laws That Were Not Good': Ezekiel 20 and the Exodus Traditions," *JSOT* 69 (1996): 73–90; and Duguid, *Ezekiel and the Leaders*, 105–8. However, it must be noted that he is not a reluctant prophet in the style of Jeremiah, so the use of Mosaic traditions is ambiguous.

A more subtle hierarchy also pervades the book: moral hierarchy.[28] The discourse of sin and righteousness also serves to elevate Ezekiel over every other social group. While nowhere in the book does it seem that the author regards anyone as worthy of God's regard, Ezekiel as a character is reserved from this judgment of sin. Ezekiel maintains he has never been in a state of ritual impurity (4:14), which, given the intimate connection between cultic and ethical violations presumed in this book, means he has committed no sin. As a literary character, the reader is meant to take Ezekiel's self-portrait literally. Within Israelite literature, there are parallels with two other perfectly righteous men who experience disaster: Noah and Job. It can be argued whether references in Ezekiel to Noah and Job in 14:14 and 20 are references to the literary texts we have or references to the traditions in other forms,[29] but in this instance it does not seem to matter. What is important is that these are such fitting references in a book whose own hero is a perfectly righteous man suffering a horrible fate. The parallels to Job are particularly poignant: like Job, Ezekiel's sufferings include loss of wealth, status, and family. Like Job, he suffers a disease that limits his interaction with society. Like Job, he has to eat his bread in a defiling place. Similarly, like Noah, he cannot save his own sinful community. Like Noah, the plan for the restoration of civilization is mediated through him. Wisdom, righteousness, and unfair suffering are integral parts of all of these stories.

This portrayal of Ezekiel plays out a debate over who is responsible for the exile. Chapter 18 stresses that responsibility for sin is not multigenerational; each generation is punished for its own sin.[30] Ezekiel is among those who themselves were deported; he is not someone born in exile. Given the book's stress that punishment is meted out to the sinner, it would seem that Ezekiel too must logically assume that those, including himself, who had been deported were sinners. How does the book distance Ezekiel from the sin attributed to the rest of his generation?

---

28. On the moral vision of the book of Ezekiel, see esp. Gordon H. Matties, *Ezekiel 18 and the Rhetoric of Moral Discourse* (SBLDS 126; Atlanta: Scholars Press, 1990); Baruch Halpern, "Jerusalem and the Lineages in the Seventh Century BCE: Kinship and the Rise of Individual Moral Liability," in *Law and Ideology in Monarchic Israel* (ed. B. Halpern and D. W. Hobson; JSOTSup 124; Sheffield: JSOT Press, 1991), 14–27; Benjamin Uffenheimer, "Theodicy and Ethics in the Prophecy of Ezekiel," in *Justice and Righteousness: Biblical Themes and Their Influence* (ed. H. G. Reventlow and Y. Hoffman; JSOTSup 137; Sheffield: JSOT Press, 1992), 200–227; Jacqueline E. Lapsley, *Can These Bones Live? The Problem of the Moral Self in the Book of Ezekiel* (BZAW 301; Berlin: de Gruyter, 2000), and "Shame and Self-Knowledge: The Positive Role of Shame in Ezekiel's View of the Moral Self," in *The Book of Ezekiel: Theological and Anthropological Perspectives* (ed. M. S. Odell and J. T. Strong; SBLSymS 9; Atlanta: Society of Biblical Literature, 2000), 143–74; John F. Kutsko, "Ezekiel's Anthropology and Its Ethical Implications," in Odell and Strong, *Book of Ezekiel*, 119–42; and Andrew Mein, *Ezekiel and the Ethics of Exile* (Oxford Theological Monographs; Oxford: Oxford University Press, 2001).

29. While this passage deals with the question of intercession (see, e.g., Blenkinsopp, *History of Prophecy in Israel*, 173), this does not negate the fact that what these figures have in common is their remarkable righteousness in the context of unjust suffering.

30. As Paul Joyce points out, this is not identical with the notion of individual responsibility (*Divine Initiative and Human Response in Ezekiel* [JSOTSup 51; Sheffield: JSOT Press, 1989], esp. 33–77).

The reader recognizes that the repeated pattern in the book is not sin-punishment-repentance-restoration, but sin-punishment-restoration-repentance.[31] Those in the land are still on the first step of this pattern; not yet punished, they continue to sin. The deportees have reached the second stage, but Ezekiel in his visions has alone completed the pattern. By the end of the book, he has seen the restoration with all of its theological and anthropological implications clearly shown. The reader participates in this narrator's knowledge. While the book promises the real exiled audience that they will soon participate in this vision and understand God, within the narration this pattern leaves Ezekiel in a unique position. He is the one who does not sin, yet suffers punishment. Within the time frame of the narrative, he is the only one who fully understands the onerous demands of a God such as Yahweh. By the end of the book, he is also the only one who has returned, albeit in a vision. He experiences how seeing the restoration leads to a clearer understanding of God, with its requisite demands on humanity. The other characters are promised a future when they can be like Ezekiel. Therefore, with respect to moral hierarchy, Ezekiel functions not to personify some group whom the author addresses, but rather as a symbol of hope for the whole exiled audience after the fall of the city.

Ezekiel's righteousness is attributed to his role as priest rather than that as prophet. His righteousness is defined in terms of his purity status and is further reinscribed by God's visionary revelations to him, revelations that at the end of the book leave Ezekiel literally standing in the place of an elite priest. As a prophet, on the other hand, he had been rendered mute as soon as he was given the message to prophesy;[32] even toward the end of the book, his prophetic role is still not recognized (33:30–33). The book cuts against the power of the prophet in one final way: there is no explicit place for prophets in the restoration. This suggests that for the author prophecy is only a necessary phenomenon in times of crisis, and not a stable element of Israelite society. In the future, the priest will channel all divine mediation.

Berquist notes that in the Persian period the temple serves to demarcate social boundaries,[33] but with the destruction of the temple, social categories are up for grabs. The characterization of Ezekiel as a priest is part of a larger program in the book to reconfigure social hierarchies. In this program, Ezekiel embodies an ideal, the one at the top of the social ladder. This social view maintains an inherently hierarchical structure within society. Placement within the hierarchy includes economic and political rights, such as land ownership, authority, power, and wealth, but

---

31. For a discussion of this in ch. 20, see Joseph Blenkinsopp, *Ezekiel* (IBC; Louisville: John Knox, 1990), 86–91.

32. Davis also highlights the ways in which Ezekiel's prophetic power is severely limited. She identifies this as a transformation in the social role of the prophet, and not as an element in the interplay between priest and prophet; see esp. *Swallowing the Scroll*, 133–40.

33. Jon L. Berquist, *Judaism in Persia's Shadow: A Social and Historical Approach* (Minneapolis: Fortress, 1995), 147–54.

within these leadership roles, the author has made clear that the most essential hierarchy is that of approach or access to God's presence. Ezekiel the priest, by being the one closest to God, models the perfect leader. As perfect leader, though, the author reminds the audience that the model of leadership is one of responsibility, not privilege. The stress on Ezekiel's debased human status (son of man), the symbols of his own impediments to function as a leader (mute and confined to his own house), as well as the dire warnings to Ezekiel if he fails highlight the irony of leadership in this system: it may be a gift you really would rather not have.

III. The Rhetoric of Characterization

At the beginning of the book in its final form (1:2–3), the author breaks the frame to inform the reader that the profession of the first-person voice of the book is that of a priest. While this notice is probably secondary, it does not contradict the portrayal of Ezekiel in the rest of the book; in fact, it merely makes obvious what the rest of the book implies about his social context. One cannot simply remove the few references to priesthood in the text and have some sort of classical prophet. Clearly, the designation of Ezekiel as a priest is fully in line with the concerns and ideology of the book. Ezekiel's title of priest seems to play itself out throughout the book in a variety of ways. The obvious affinity with H and P so often noted is one way that the priestly office is reinforced, but I would argue not the most significant way. These parallels seem to attach more to the author and the ideology of the book as a whole than they do to Ezekiel; in fact, you could say that God sounds more like P than Ezekiel does.

The characterization of Ezekiel as a priest is reinforced in other ways in the text.[34] First, his protest about defiling his own purity suggests his priestly status (4:14). Only a priest of some rank would have kept such strict purity observation. Second, the significance of the reaction of Ezekiel to the death of his wife takes on added meaning in light of the fact that priestly wives had a certain prescribed status (44:22). His failure to mourn her would be publicly noticeable. Third, his own knowledge of ritual forms, temple architecture, and issues of defilement depict him as someone specially trained in these areas. He is consulted by elders: these consultations closely parallel the elders' consultation of Moses in Exod 18:15. Although it is unclear in this text whether Moses is portrayed as priestly or prophetic, he is advised in this matter by a priest, Jethro.[35] Lastly, the reference to the "thirtieth year"

---

34. Mein also notes that Ezekiel's priestly role is evidenced by this practice of purity, by the way he uses purity categories to designate sin, and by the content of the final vision ("Ezekiel as a Priest"). Blenkinsopp's proposal of an elite priestly, ultimately Zadokite redactor stems from similar observations (*History of Prophecy in Israel*, esp. 167–70).

35. For a similar conclusion, see Cody, *History of Old Testament Priesthood*, 144–48.

at the beginning of the book may in fact be a reference to the age of Ezekiel's ordination, with the last date corresponding to the age of priestly retirement.[36]

Although he does not do much to serve God, Ezekiel does many of the priestly activities related to the community. He bears the punishment of the people, a function of the priest as the one who atones for the sins of the people (4:4–8).[37] He prays, albeit unsuccessfully, for the people (9:8). He is called to judge the people (22:1–2 and 23:36), and he is commanded to write down items for future instruction (24:2; 37:16 [bis]; 37:20; 43:11–12). Ezekiel also raises several laments, a job in Mesopotamia often associated with priests (2:10; 19:1 and 14; 21:6–7; 27:1; 28:11; 32:2; and 32:18). The ritual nature of the lament is seen in contrast to the prohibition to mourn for the death of his wife (24:18–24), an individual rather than communal action.

In the final form of the book, the characterization of Ezekiel as priest serves as the background to the more overt texts reflecting priestly hierarchy in chapters 40–48. Without the explicit statements of Zadokite prerogative, it might be possible to conclude that Ezekiel's characterization arises from his co-opting all leadership functions within the book. However, the emphasis on the hierarchical distinction between priests and all other Israelites, first, and then between Zadokites and Levites, opens up a layer of polemic, which further shapes the rhetorical function of Ezekiel as a literary figure. Whether or not this Zadokite layer is original to the book or a secondary addition,[38] the rhetorical effect remains.

Chapters 44–48 use space and ritual privilege to establish a hierarchical order between two priestly groups.[39] In this Ezekiel is not unlike many other biblical tra-

---

36. This view is argued most thoroughly by James E. Miller, "The Thirtieth Year of Ezekiel 1:1," *RB* 99 (1992): 499–503, although the idea is much older than this: it even appears in Jerome's commentary on Ezekiel (*Comm. Ezech.*, I.1.a). For other ways in which the book reflects cultic institutions, see L. Monloubou, "La signification du culte selon Ézéchiel," in *Ezekiel and His Book: Textual and Literary Criticism and Their Interrelation* (ed. J. Lust; BETL 74; Louvain: Louvain University Press/Peeters, 1986), 7–20.

37. For a similar view of priestly atonement, see Marvin A. Sweeney, "Ezekiel: Zadokite Priest and Visionary Prophet of the Exile," in *SBL Seminar Papers, 2000* (SBLSP 39; Atlanta: Society of Biblical Literature, 2000), 732–33 (see further pp. 739–43 on chs. 8–19 as a purification ritual). This view contrasts with the more limited view of this priestly function in Odell, "You Are What You Eat," 239.

38. On the term, see Hartmut Gese, *Der Verfassungsentwurf des Ezechiel (Kap. 40–48): Traditionsgeschichtlich Untersucht* (BHT 25; Tübingen: Mohr Siebeck, 1957). Most scholars see the material as secondary, since the rivalry among priestly groups is not expressly stated in any other part of the book. However, even if secondary, I am among those who would still date it to the exilic period, since it does not seem to reflect the issues over priesthood seen in Persian Period literature.

39. The literature on the way the view of priesthood in Ezek 40–48 fits into the whole history of Israelite priesthood is myriad. All of the commentaries, e.g., deal with the question in one way or another. For specialized studies of Ezekiel, see, e.g., Cody, *History Of Old Testament Priesthood*, 166–68; Levenson, *Theology of the Program*, 129–51; Raymond Abba, "Priests and Levites in Ezekiel," *VT* 28 (1978): 1–9; J. Gordon McConville, "Priests and Levites in Ezekiel: A Crux in the Interpretation of Israel's History," *TynBul* 34 (1983): 3–31; Tuell, *Law of the Temple*, 121–52; Duguid, *Ezekiel and the Leaders,*

ditions that note the subordination or limitation of Levitical service. In Ezek 40–48, the Levites are always inferior to and more limited in the scope of their service, and they are explicitly condemned for past sin or failure. The only ambiguity is whether the text envisions a new inferior status for the Levites, or if it simply maintains their preexilic status.[40]

Ezekiel's own elevated status as ritually pure, morally innocent, and near to God implies that Ezekiel represents a Zadokite priest.[41] The only way this priesthood remains blameless for the sins of chapter 8 is if the priests who control activity in the inner court are not Zadokites, but Levites. Many scholars have noted the connections among the three vision pericopes of chapters 1, 8–11, and 40–48.[42] I suggest

---

58–90; Stephen L. Cook, "Innerbiblical Interpretation in Ezekiel 44 and the History of Israel's Priesthood," *JBL* 114 (1995): 193–208. For studies of the distinction between Levites and other priestly groups throughout Israelite literature, see Antonius H. J. Gunneweg, *Leviten und Priester: Hauptlinien der Traditionsbildung und Geschichte des israelitisch-jüdischen Kultpersonals* (FRLANT 89; Göttingen: Vandenhoeck & Ruprecht, 1965); Nigel Allan, "The Identity of the Jerusalem Priesthood during the Exile," *HeyJ* 23 (1982): 259–69; Julie M. O'Brien, *Priest and Levite in Malachi* (SBLDS 121; Atlanta: Scholars Press, 1990); Blenkinsopp, "Judaean Priesthood," 25–43; Risto Nurmela, *The Levites: Their Emergence as a Second-Class Priesthood* (South Florida Studies in the History of Judaism 193; Atlanta: Scholars Press, 1998), esp. 85–104; Joachim Schaper, *Priester und Leviten im achämenidischen Juda: Studien zur Kult- und Sozialgeschichte Israels in persischer Zeit* (FAT 31; Tübingen: Mohr Siebeck, 2000); and William R. Millar, *Priesthood in Ancient Israel* (Understanding Biblical Themes; St. Louis: Chalice, 2001).

40. There is a great deal of discussion on the assessment of the condemnation attached to the oracle establishing Levitical duties in ch. 44. Rodney K. Duke ("Punishment or Restoration? Another Look at the Levites of Ezekiel 44.6–16," *JSOT* 40 [1988]: 61–81) has been very influential, arguing that the Levites are not demoted in Ezek 44. Stevenson, following Duke, argues that the Levites merely take on the sin of the people; they are not themselves guilty of sin (*Vision of Transformation*, 66–78). These views are found in many recent commentaries, such as Daniel I. Block (*The Book of Ezekiel*, vol. 2, *Chapters 25–48* [NICOT; Grand Rapids: Eerdmans, 1998], 626–32) and Katheryn Pfisterer Darr ("The Book of Ezekiel: Introduction, Commentary, and Reflections," *NIB* 6:1575–77). However, since I agree that the visions of chs. 8–11 do not reflect historical fact, but serve the rhetoric of the book, I argue that the final form of the book affects how the reader interprets ch. 44. Even if the priests did not yet limit access to the inner court in the premonarchic period, they certainly had some say over what went on there ritually. The sins of chs. 8–11 implicate the priesthood, even (or especially!) if they are absent from that temple scene. There are only two priestly groups named in the whole book, so the rhetorical effect is that the blame can only fall on the Levites.

41. For the identification of Ezekiel's followers with the Zadokites, see, e.g., Paul D. Hanson, *The Dawn of Apocalyptic: The Historical and Sociological Roots of Jewish Apocalyptic Eschatology* (rev. ed.; Philadelphia: Fortress, 1979), 225–40, and idem, "Israelite Religion in the Early Postexilic Period," in Miller, Hanson, and McBride, *Ancient Israelite Religion*, 486–88; Blenkinsopp, *History of Prophecy in Israel*, 169–70; Stephen L. Cook, *Prophecy and Apocalypticism*, 97–98 and 105–9. Rainer Albertz, however, argues that the historical Ezekiel was distinct from the anti-Babylonian Zadokite priests (*A History of Israelite Religion in the Old Testament Period*, vol. 1: *From the Beginnings to the End of the Monarchy* [OTL; Louisville: Westminster John Knox, 1994], 238), while Rudnig does not identify his priestly author (*Heilig und Profan*, esp. 354–64).

42. Most recently, Odell examines the Assyrian background of these visions ("Ezekiel Saw What He Said He Saw: Genres, Forms, and the Vision of Ezekiel 1," in *The Changing Face of Form Criticism for the Twenty-first Century* (ed. M. A. Sweeney and E. Ben Zvi; Grand Rapids: Eerdmans, 2003), 162–76.

that priesthood is one more linking element often overlooked in these passages. The inaugural vision established Ezekiel as the representation of the legitimate but exiled priest, with full access to God's presence in the temple, even though he is impossibly removed in exile. Chapters 8–11 depict sins that occur in the temple prior to the city's fall; to some degree these sins must have been ultimately the fault of the priesthood that controlled the temple before the final fall of the city.[43] Although chapter 44 when read in isolation may not blame the Levites for these sins, the force of the book as a whole implicates whatever priesthood had the duty to control activity in the temple. Because of the relative ritual status of Levites and Zadokites in the final vision, the only priesthood this could be would be the Levites. An additionally obvious, though unstated conclusion is that Ezekiel was a Zadokite, not a Levite. Both the characterization of Ezekiel and the visions that structure the book serve the interests of the Zadokite priesthood over any other group with a priestly claim.[44]

This dual function of Ezekiel and the Zadokites is reinforced in Ezekiel's recommissioning in 44:4–5. Before God sends him to establish the visionary distinction of the two groups, the text recapitulates the scene that opened the book: Ezekiel sees God's glory and prostrates himself (1:28b–2:5). God tells him to pay attention, this time to what he sees, and to report it to the rebellious people. These two commissions form an *inclusio* to the book. Once again in chapter 44, Ezekiel stands in the place of the high priest, so it is not surprising that the first thing the subsequent statutes address is the identity of the priestly group who will be elevated within the subsequent vision of ritual hierarchy.

The characterization of Ezekiel as a prophet begins to fade with this second commissioning. As the laws progress the reader barely notices that there are no provisions for prophets in the vision of restoration, no laws governing their behavior or insuring that they no longer deliver false oracles. Ezekiel, no longer associated with that social group, is increasingly aligned with the priests as he tours the temple and walks through the life-giving river, where even he fades from the scene. In fact, Ezekiel does not even appear in the last chapter of the book. Instead, the vision itself takes over, with the Zadokites firmly entrenched in the most holy land (48:10–12).

IV. A Final Implication: Priesthood and Theology

In spite of the restoration of priesthood at the end of the book and the command to Ezekiel to teach the law of the temple in the future (43:11–12), nowhere does the character of Ezekiel do anything one would consider particularly priestly. He does not sacrifice, maintain a ritual calendar, nor make decisions of purity or cleanness for his community. He is not depicted as performing the rituals that could

---

43. See, e.g., Greenberg, "Design and Themes," 183, and Duguid, *Ezekiel and the Leaders*, 58–90.

44. While Renz concludes that the purpose of chapters 40–48 is to give a vision to the people as a whole (*Rhetorical Function*, 243–45), they still do so by elevating one group over all others.

have been conducted in exile, such as circumcision, observation of the Sabbath or Passover. He does not condemn those remaining in Jerusalem for continuing the sacrificial system, nor does he contend that those in charge of the temple are illegitimate for this service.

Certainly many of these negations occur because the book is written when no temple exists. Yet, in light of this, the book's insistence that the role and function of the priest not only continues to exist but also is a vital component for mediating a vision of restoration is significant. These voids point away from those aspects of the priesthood having to do with public performance and, in their place, invite the reader to think more clearly about the function of priesthood in its relationship to both God and the people.[45] Priesthood in Ezekiel, while it does serve to realign human hierarchies, ultimately serves to remind the reader of the great gulf between humanity and divinity.

Ezekiel as priest functions as a transparent figure: the audience inside the text, as well as the reader of the text, sees God through him. Ezekiel is the ultra-servant of God; even though he does not perform sacrifices or rituals, he does everything God asks, mediates God's presence, and controls access to God. As a sign, he is a model of responsiveness to God; with only one exception (4:14), he always fulfills God's commands.[46] As a priest, he is a conduit for true teaching. This priestly role is especially emphasized in the final vision. He is the one who will preserve the torah of this temple vision and clarify the obligations incumbent upon the community, but in his dialogues with God he remains utterly human, mortal, debased even. Ezekiel as priest does not represent God nor does he attain anything approaching divine status. He crosses the boundaries set up within the human geography, but not the boundary between heaven and earth.

Ultimately, Ezekiel's priesthood is depicted as wholly dependent on the nature of God. God has created the office of the priest to maintain the divinely decreed order of the world, and to preserve the realization that God is not like us. God is wholly other, something/someone to be feared, mediated, obeyed, worshiped, served. Restoration is only possible with a purified priesthood that maintains service to both God and the community. Only with the priesthood can God reside in the temple, sacrifice and ritual be reinstated, atonement be effectual, and lamentations turn to praise. Ezekiel personifies this pivotal function: he both serves as a link to God and a reminder of human subordination to God.

When one looks at some of the more general definitions of the priest offered by cross-cultural studies, Ezekiel clearly violates many of these. He is no mere conservator of ancient traditions. He is repeatedly depicted as one who innovates and

---

45. Davis investigates the transformation of the prophetic role (*Swallowing the Scroll*, 133–40). I see this as a similar program in the book. Stevenson (*Vision of Transformation*) mentions more than once that human geography ultimately addresses the question "Where is God?" but she does not explore how the location of the priest within this geography answers that question.

46. Renz, *Rhetorical Function*, 150–60.

willingly transgresses older traditions. He is shown to be a clever "parable maker," as well as a lawgiver. He willingly rewrites history and envisions a new Israel whose whole land is changed. He also does not appear to be one focused solely on getting ritual "right" in a sort of postmagical retention of ritual. Again, when it comes to ritual matters, he understands that violations around the cult do not simply insult a god who has arbitrarily assigned these rituals, nor do they ruin some magical sequence. Rather, the rituals, along with everything else around the temple, are prescribed to protect the community from committing abominations, violations of approach that will lead to social upheaval and the abandonment of that community by God. Correct rituals must be maintained, because they are simply expressions of the world order created by their God.

The characterization of Ezekiel as priest achieves several ideological ends. First, the status of Ezekiel asserts the importance of the Zadokite priesthood over any other social group. Second, Ezekiel's moral rectitude maintains the possibility of a righteous remnant among the old Jerusalem priesthood, without which the restoration to their prior social status is impossible. The portrait also asserts the priesthood over prophecy. Ezekiel is a better mediator of God's presence to Israel than prophets are, representing a permanent social vehicle for this mediation, in contrast to the obliteration of prophecy. As mediator, Ezekiel has no false visions, and the message he delivers is always clear.

The book plays with irony in its exploration of the absurd condition of the exile. Ezekiel cannot speak, but he "out-communicates" the prophets. He cannot sacrifice, but he ends up in the place of the high priest. He is no "man of God," but as a lowly "son of man," he is a sign for the people. And even as an exile, he is a righteous sufferer. The greatest irony in the book is that Israel's hope for a future comes, not through the international politics of Zedekiah, but through this exiled "singer of love songs."

God's Land and Mine:
Creation as Property in the Book of Ezekiel

Julie Galambush

It is a commonplace that ancient Near Eastern cultures saw in creation stories the struggle of the god or gods to assert order over chaos.[1] This "order" included not only the natural order, but also a divinely appointed social order, which tended to be identified with the social order of the society in which the creation story was produced.[2] Divine control was embodied within established political, religious, and social structures, including rituals, personnel, and monuments. A certain circularity obtains here: cosmogonies reinforced existing power structures by presenting them as derived from the divine order asserted by the cosmogony. Divine and human orders are thus mutually reinforcing.

The book of Ezekiel does not contain a cosmogony as such. On the contrary, the text's narrative world assumes both a long-established created realm and a divinely appointed social order. Nonetheless, the plot of Ezekiel revolves around a form of *Chaoskampf*: the exile of the leadership (from a sociopolitical perspective), caused by the apostasy of Judah's leaders (from a theological perspective), has disrupted the established social order. As a result, over the course of the narrative YHWH must struggle to reassert divine authority and to reimpose the order that manifests heavenly sovereignty. The vision of YHWH's victory and enthronement in chapters 40–48 employs symbols of creation to assert the renewal of divine order.[3] Ezekiel is not concerned with how the world came into existence, but with re-forming a world gone awry. In this essay I shall focus on how the depictions of YHWH's *Chaoskampf* within the already-created world are an attempt to reassert the order—both divine

---

1. This paper is a revision of "Castles in the Air: Creation as Property in Ezekiel," previously published in *SBL Seminar Papers, 1999* (SBLSP 38; Atlanta: Scholars Press, 1999), 147–72.

2. See discussions in Bernard W. Anderson, "Introduction," in *Creation in the Old Testament* (ed. B. W. Anderson; IRT 6; Philadelphia: Fortress; London: SPCK, 1984), 1–24; Richard J. Clifford and John J. Collins, "Introduction," in *Creation in the Biblical Traditions* (ed. R. J. Clifford and J. J. Collins; CBQMS 24; Washington, D.C.: Catholic Biblical Association of America, 1992), 1–15.

3. See, e.g., Jon D. Levenson, *Theology of the Program of Restoration of Ezekiel 40–48* (HSM 10; Atlanta: Scholars Press, 1986), 29; Richard J. Clifford, *The Cosmic Mountain in Canaan and the Old Testament* (HSM 4; Cambridge: Harvard University Press, 1972), 158–60.

and social—that has been disrupted by the experience of exile. I shall focus on the status of what modern people would call the natural world. This essay concerns the nature of nature in Ezekiel.

In *The Land Is Mine: Six Biblical Land Ideologies*, Norman Habel explores the ideological significance of the land as a social construct in the Hebrew Bible.[4] The current study will include not only the land, but other "natural" categories as well—plants, animals, and even weather—as ideological constructs that fulfill specific functions within a social system.[5] After surveying representations of the natural world in Ezekiel, I shall address the question of how such symbols function socially, expressing the needs, desires, and assumptions of the people for whom the writing attributed to Ezekiel carried authority in its earliest settings. I shall assume that a representative of the Jerusalem priesthood wrote some form or substantial precursor of the current book in sixth-century Babylonia. As Stephen Cook has demonstrated, however, the concerns reflected by the book's narrator are consistent with those of both a sixth-century prophet-priest and a later priestly hierarchy.[6]

I. Animals

Animals function as surprisingly complex signifiers within the text of Ezekiel. "Wild" animals (either specific species, such as jackals, or simply חיה, understood as "beasts") play a variety of roles, both positive and negative. The term חיה is used both of wild animals and of the "living beings" identified as cherubim (Ezek 1 and 10). That is, the category may include denizens of either the divine or the human realms. Both "wild animals" (חיה רעה) as a group and specific examples of wild animals pose a threat to settled human life. Thus, the uninhabitable condition of the war-ravaged land is symbolized by its takeover by "evil" animals (חיה רעה; 5:17; 14:15, 21; 34:25). Human enemies are likewise metaphorically depicted as wild animals (34:5, 8). The category "wild animal" thus signifies a presence inimical to the socially ordered world. The wild animal, like the wilderness with which it is associated, is the polar opposite of both the people and the livestock of the settled realm. As a force of (hostile) nature, wild animals may be "sent" by Yhwh as punishment (5:16–17) along with pestilence, famine, fire, and the sword. Literally, famine and

---

4. Norman C. Habel, *The Land Is Mine: Six Biblical Land Ideologies* (OBT; Minneapolis: Fortress, 1995).

5. For discussion of nature as a system symbolizing social norms and tensions, see Mary Douglas, *Natural Symbols: Explorations in Cosmology* (New York: Pantheon, 1970), and Frederic Jameson, *The Political Unconscious: Narrative as a Socially Symbolic Act* (Ithaca, N.Y.: Cornell University Press, 1981), 111–12.

6. Stephen L. Cook, *Prophecy and Apocalypticism: The Postexilic Social Setting* (Minneapolis: Fortress, 1995), 85–121. Two recent studies, Iain Duguid, *Ezekiel and the Leaders of Israel* (VTSup 56; Leiden: Brill, 1994), and Kalinda R. Stevenson, *The Vision of Transformation: The Territorial Rhetoric of Ezekiel 40–48* (SBLDS 154; Atlanta: Scholars Press, 1996), demonstrate from different perspectives a plausible congruence between the narrator's social agenda and an exilic setting.

disease are frequent effects of war, and ruined houses and towns may well become homes to scavenger animals. Symbolically, the stock images of military destruction—fire, pestilence, wild animals, famine, the sword (5:16–17; cf. Lev 26:14–22)—evoke a picture of the destruction of order and the takeover of chaos. If wild animals inhabit houses then the "natural" order, in which people inhabit the houses and wild beasts the wilderness, has been inverted.

The image of the wild animal serves an additional metaphorical function in Ezekiel, as a figure for hostile humans. Predatory and unscrupulous humans—both foreign and Israelite—are represented by the figure of the wild animal. The soldier who invades the land is as much of a wild animal as the jackal that comes afterward to scavenge the ruined countryside. Pharaoh is a sea monster (29:3–9 and 32:1–16), and the Edomites make plans to devour Israel (35:12), images that play on the connection between the suspect otherness of the foreigner and the perception of wild beasts as outside of and hostile to the settled world. Even Israel's own leaders, when corrupt, may be depicted as human-eating lions (22:25), jackals (13:4), and wolves (22:27). These political and religious authorities prey on the people (cf. the images of sheep in ch. 34) and are accordingly identified through the metaphor as hostile to the social order. They are elements working from within that order, which nonetheless function as agents for the "outside," as forces inimical to settled life. Destructive Israelite officials are "wild beasts" because the effect of their actions on the social order mimics those of marauding outsiders. Indeed, the damage done by the wild beasts within renders the community vulnerable to attack, first by hostile foreign armies and finally by roaming scavengers of the field. This identification between "wild beast" and "hostile force" is so strong that at times, as in 34:28, the distinction between human and animal invader disappears entirely.

The topos of the wild animal functions as a wide-ranging symbol applicable to any force perceived as a hostile and predatory other. Wild animals, variously referred to as חיה, חית הארץ, חית השדה, and חיה רעה, are defined almost exclusively as predators and scavengers. (Only in the references to the cherubim, and in 31:6, 13; 38:20, and 47:9, do they carry a neutral connotation.)[7] Perhaps the most telling aspect of the signifier "wild animal" is the opposition created between the categories "wild animal" (חיה) and "livestock" (בהמה). The latter term, which usually can designate wild or even all animals (cf. Prov 30:30, in which the lion is the mightiest בהמה), is limited in Ezekiel to animals domesticated for human use. Livestock are paired with humans as a unit (אדם ובהמה), and as such are opposed by the wild beasts (14:13–16). Wild and domestic animals represent chaos and order respectively, animals of the wilderness versus animals of the settled land.

Like other embodiments of chaos in the Hebrew Bible, however, wild animals are perceived as hostile to Yhwh's purposes only when they are outside of divine

---

7. I am leaving aside the question of Ezek 7:13, which has textual difficulties.

control.[8] Like foreign armies, they are an embodiment of chaos that may be co-opted to perform Yhwh's (avenging) will. Yhwh may use wild animals to punish Israel; they are "sent" against the inhabited land, which is then "given" over to them as their domain (e.g., 5:17; 14:21; and 33:27). The wild animals are even dignified to play a ritual role as they feast upon the sacrificed bodies of Yhwh's enemies (39:17). Here, wild animals are assigned a place within an inverted ritual system in which they play a role analogous to Israel's priests. Like priests, whose special sanctity allows them to consume food offerings in the Jerusalem temple, here wild animals appear as anti-priests, agents whose diametrical opposition to the realm of purity and order specially qualifies them to partake of the unclean sacrifice.

Like the foreign nations, however, the wild beasts serve only temporarily as divine agents. Yhwh commands the forces of chaos but does not become their permanent ally. Ultimately, even as the invading foreigners are "punished" for their zeal in the very role Yhwh has assigned them, so also the wild beasts must be cleared away in favor of domestic animals and settled land. Thus, when Yhwh establishes the covenant of peace with Israel in 34:25–29, God first banishes wild beasts from the land, thereby both protecting the order of the settled world and also extending it, allowing *the Israelites* to live "in the wild and sleep in the woods" (34:25). Israel for its part is Yhwh's "flock," those animals that are good by virtue of being owned and thus incorporated into the ordered world. Strikingly, under Yhwh's "covenant of peace" no wild animals at all remain in the land. Rather than assigning wild things to the wild places and orderly things to the ordered, the divine covenant is made solely with and for Israel. Yhwh makes peace with the animals only by eliminating them; the wild places will be appropriated by Israel, God's metaphorical flock, and by Israel's own, literal livestock.

Ezekiel's strong identification of wild beasts with hostile and chaotic forces is only partially reflected in the rest of the Hebrew Bible. Only Lev 26:6 shares the trope of "evil beasts" as something to be either banished from or sent into the land according to Israel's obedience or disobedience respectively.[9] In Gen 2:19 the term חית השדה covers all land animals, as members of creation and even as potential "partners" for the lonely human. Psalm 148:10 calls on the wild animals (חיה) together with the cattle to praise Yhwh and in Hos 2:20 (Eng. 2:18), a verse that probably underlies Ezekiel's covenant of chapter 34, Yhwh creates peace, not by cutting off wild animals, but by cutting a covenant *with* them. Hosea's new covenant does not abolish the wild animals, but assigns them their proper place within Yhwh's ordered world. While images of wild beasts as agents of destruction or as signs of devastation do occur outside Ezekiel (e.g., Jer 12:9), only in Ezekiel does the wild beast persistently signify a hostile and threatening other to be excluded from Israel, a land of domesticated animals and obedient citizens. Ezekiel expands the

---

8. Cf. Leviathan in Job 41, who is depicted as virtually a pet to Yhwh.
9. Cf. Gen 37:20, 33 and 2 Kgs 17:25.

"otherness" of non-domesticated animals into a signifier of otherness itself. Wild animals may be human or beast, Israelite or foreign, but their sole function is to threaten the integrity of the social order and the settled land.

II. Plants

The representation of plants follows a trajectory related but not identical to that of animals in Ezekiel: domesticated plants symbolize order and moral good; weeds stand for forces hostile to Israel or to the prophet himself; domesticated plants that have "gone wild" represent rebellion against Yhwh. At first glance, this schema seems analogous to that underlying the representation of animals: domesticated equals good, wild equals bad. On closer examination, however, one sees that plants play a different role from animals in the book's symbolic world. In the first place, in contrast to representations of animals, relatively few references are made to "bad" or wild plants (weeds) in Ezekiel. Only twice does Ezekiel refer to enemies as "briars and thorns" (2:6; 28:24), an image straightforwardly depicting hostile humans in terms of noisome plants.

Far more prominent in Ezekiel is the image of the unnatural plant, desirable in itself, but whose luxurious growth symbolizes overarching ambition or pride. Israel is a straying vine (ch. 17) or a towering one (19:10–14), a plant properly domesticated that has run wild. Here wildness represents not the inherent and threatening otherness embodied by the wild animals, but rebellion by something or someone properly set under authority. Although both Isa 5:1–2 and Jer 2:21 employ the conceit of Israel as a vineyard (rather than as a vine) whose produce is disappointing to Yhwh, Ezekiel focuses on the vine as luxuriant, but rebellious (cf. the thriving but rebellious woman of ch. 16). While the personified plant is not threatening in and of itself, its self-assertion warrants its destruction. In a parallel image, powerful foreign nations are depicted as mighty trees. As such, they give shelter to many but are subject to the vice of pride.[10] Both Egypt and Assyria (ch. 31), which presume to rival Yhwh, are threatening in their attitude—a refusal to know their place. Yhwh, of course, will not tolerate such affronts to divine sovereignty and will therefore destroy these haughty trees.

The offending vines and trees differ from the wild animals considered above in that they are not properly wild but have merely "run wild." This distinction yields important differences. First, the overly luxuriant vines and trees do not threaten the order of the settled realm. Unlike the presence of human-eating lions, wolves, or scorpions, no devastation of land or people is implied in the unbridled growth of plants. These vines and trees neither choke out the crops nor invade homes. On the contrary, the tree of Assyria is beneficial to wild birds and animals, and "beautiful in

---

10. Ironically, Israel is ridiculed in ch. 15 as a vine that fancies itself a tree. Not so, says Yhwh. If you were a tree, I could at least get some use out of your wood after cutting you down!

its greatness" (31:7). Yhwh claims to have created Assyria's beauty, a beauty unrivaled even by "the cedars in the garden of God" (31:8). Trees and vines have an implicitly positive rather than a negative connotation. Yhwh created Assyria's beauty, but Assyria grew proud and Yhwh accordingly had the unruly tree cut down. Israel the vine has stretched out recklessly toward one monarch after another, heedless of Yhwh's covenant, and must therefore be destroyed.

The trees and vines of these metaphors represent the rulers of the nations and as such are the proper subjects of divine sponsorship. Foreign kings are not Yhwh's rivals in these passages, but God's servants. The disobedience of favored servants represents a very different kind of threat than that posed by invading armies or wild beasts. Yhwh is still concerned with managing chaos, but now disorder takes the form of a challenge to divine honor. Yhwh will therefore both destroy the offending vines and trees, and also plant new growth. After Israel the vine has been uprooted, it will be replanted as a great tree. "I myself," emphasizes Yhwh (twice in 17:22), "will plant it on a high and lofty mountain." The resulting tree will be "noble" and fruitful. Yhwh will not be denied the traditional "garden of God," but neither will its trees be allowed to compete with God in glory. When God's own tree has been planted, says Yhwh, "All the trees of the field shall know that I am the Lord. I bring low the high tree, I make high the low tree; I dry up the green tree and make the dry tree flourish" (17:24). The vines and trees exist as markers valorizing Yhwh's potency. Trees, if they are to be high, must by their very height point toward Yhwh as source and owner of their glory. Other trees, "all the trees of the field," supply a validating gaze, admiring the trees belonging to a higher authority. Trees and vines in Ezekiel serve as status markers. They may be defective (or "disobedient") in this role and require correction or elimination, but they are properly positive signifiers revealing the potency of Yhwh.

The role of trees and vines as signs of Yhwh's sovereignty, implicit in the descriptions of the unruly plants, becomes fully articulated in the image of the miraculous trees of Ezek 47:1–12. After Yhwh has established the temple on the high mountain of Ezekiel's vision, a stream begins to flow from beneath its threshold. The background of the stream as a symbol of renewed fertility under the rule of the divine monarch has been well documented.[11] The stream of Ezek 47 recalls that of Gen 2:10–14 as it supports the growth of fruitful trees. Together, trees and stream form a garden. The garden appears as the special holding of monarchs and divine beings in various ancient Near Eastern cultures.[12] The god is the insurer of earth's fertility and the king is the god's regent. The growth of trees in Ezek 47 forms a recognizable trope indicating Yhwh's power to restore fertility to the land. The

---

11. See, e.g., Clifford, *Cosmic Mountain*, 100–102, 158–60; Steven S. Tuell, *The Law of the Temple in Ezekiel 40–48* (HSM 49; Atlanta: Scholars Press, 1992), 69–71.
12. See Howard N. Wallace, "Garden of God," *ABD* 2:906–7.

trees' supernatural ability to produce fruit and medicinal leaves in all seasons underscores the power of Yhwh, whose presence in the temple generates such abundance.

Ezekiel's emphasis on trees as signifiers indicating acceptance of or rebellion against divine authority stands in striking contrast to the symbolism of trees elsewhere in the Hebrew Bible. While it is outside the scope of this essay to undertake a thorough discussion of the symbolic function of trees in the Bible, it will be sufficient to observe that nowhere else is the image of the tree invested with overtones suggesting a tendency toward pride and rebellion against divine authority.[13] On the contrary, trees frequently evoke images of human rootedness in divine law: just as the well-nourished tree produces abundant fruit, so the disciplined and obedient person is both prosperous and productive (Ps 1:1–3; Jer 17:7–8). Alternatively, divine wisdom is depicted as a tree, an object that is strong and sustaining (Prov 3:18). While the literal use of trees for idolatrous worship (either as Asherah poles or as lumber for image-making) might seem to open the way for negative personification of trees as agents in Israel's infidelity, no such negative personification takes place. Rather, trees form part of the land that may be either blessed or blighted, depending on the conduct of its inhabitants (as in Jer 7:20).

Curiously, Ezekiel seems to share the perspective of other prophets and of the Deuteronomistic editors in regard to the role of actual trees in non-Yahwistic ritual: the worship of "wood and stone" is a temptation to which Israel was ever vulnerable, but the trees themselves are objects devoid of moral significance (Ezek 20:32; cf. Deut 12:3; 16:21). It is in his personification of trees that Ezekiel seemingly departs from literary tradition, creating a unique trope of the tree as a properly domesticated plant that willfully grows out of control and must be subdued. Compare this perspective with, for example, images from Ps 96:12 and Isa 44:23; 55:12, in which personified trees sing for joy and clap their hands in celebration of Yhwh's sovereignty. In Ps 148:9 the trees are called on to praise Yhwh. What is more, the trees are grouped together with heavens, earth, sea, and field, or with mountains and hills as examples of nature resounding with Yhwh's praise. When the trees join with hills and fields to sing, clap, and give praise to Yhwh, they do so specifically to exemplify the response of the natural world to its divine sovereign. The trees that clap their hands function metonymically for the created world, all of which is understood to reflect the glory of Yhwh. Here, of course, nature reflects the divine presence in an active rather than a passive way; personified hills and trees are sentient beings whose recognition of Yhwh's power is manifested as joy. This personification of the trees as united with Yhwh's purposes and perspective forms a stark contrast to Ezekiel's persistent trope of the rebellious tree.[14]

---

13. The closest equivalent would seem to be the boasting bush of 2 Kgs 14 (cf. Jotham's fable in Judg 9:8–15, in which virtuous trees refuse to let pride sway them from their appointed stations).

14. The prohibition against cutting down fruit trees during siege warfare (Deut 20:19–20) provides an interesting mix of perspectives, first countermanding the destruction of fruit trees on the grounds that trees are not humans to be laid siege to, but then giving permission to use as timber any trees that do not

In Ezekiel trees and vines are personified specifically as servants, metaphoric representations of human beings (e.g., the king of Assyria or of Judah). The personification of trees as representations of specific individuals or communities precludes their consideration as "natural" items. Trees serve as object lessons exhibiting qualities either of obedience or, more frequently, of disobedience. Ezekiel's representation of trees and vines draws directly on human agricultural experience: the cultivation of plants may yield either satisfaction or frustration. Appearing only as metaphorical objects of Yhwh's satisfaction or frustration with the human community, and not as objects in their own right, trees and vines lose the potential to represent any aspect of wild nature, except to reinforce the preference for domesticated nature over wild.[15]

III. The Land

Elements of weather, such as wind and storm, light and darkness, are seen in Ezekiel as thoroughly under Yhwh's control and serve as tools of punishment to be used against either Israel or its enemies, depending on the direction of the divine wrath (e.g., 19:12; 38:22). The dichotomies between wild and domesticated that obtained in the depiction of animals, or between obedient and rebellious that typified depictions of plant life, do not appear here. Unlike plants and animals, the weather is not personified, nor is it ever depicted as outside Yhwh's control. This unambiguous view of the weather as a tool of Yhwh may reflect ancient traditions of Yhwh as a storm god, but may equally well derive from the human experience that while both plants and animals are only partially susceptible to human control, the weather is entirely and unambiguously beyond human coercion.

Such a deep cultural certainty about the "otherness" of weather may serve to anchor it firmly in the human imagination as belonging to the divine realm. The tantalizing partialness of human control over the plant and animal realms renders these more susceptible to personification and to depiction within moral categories. Wild animals are unlike "our" animals, and their otherness is projected as hostility. This projection of human fear onto the wild animal (which is then fantasized as evil and threatening) is sympathized with, if not shared outright, by the deity, who promises to "banish wild beasts" from the land. The human struggle to cultivate good plants (crops) while limiting the growth of bad (weeds) is likewise projected onto Yhwh. Yhwh tends to crops, which in turn either fulfill or frustrate God's intent. The human community's struggle to control plants and animals is extended

---

yield fruit. What at first seems to assert the independent right of a tree to its life turns out to reflect a concern that extends only to those trees needed to sustain human life.

15. The prophecy of 21:1–5 (Eng. 20:45–49) against the forest of the south forms an interesting problem. Yhwh announces to the forest that a fire will be lit to consume it, both the green trees and the dry. No explanation is given for this action; no trespass is charged to the forest, nor does the text provide any hint as to whom the forest might represent.

into the divine realm through metaphors in which YHWH too struggles for control. The elements themselves, however, as objects outside of human control, are seen as *uniquely* under divine direction and thus excluded from the realm of perceived struggle. Thunder and lightning, wind and rain function exclusively as tools by means of which YHWH may bless or curse the people.

The role played by the earth itself receives little notice in Ezekiel. Instead, concern focuses on the land of Israel. Ezekiel makes constant reference to the condition of the "land" (ארץ), a term whose semantic range in Ezekiel encompasses both the political and the geographical territory of Israel. In addition, Ezekiel frequently employs the phrase אדמת ישראל ("the land of Israel"), an elocution unique to Ezekiel that seems to designate Israel as "homeland."[16] The term אדמה, which elsewhere in the Hebrew Bible covers everything from soil to dry land, in Ezekiel refers exclusively to the land of Israel. This extraordinary usage focuses on land as *land belonging to Israel,* an emphasis with strident political overtones, given both Babylonian domination of the land and the predominance of (former) landowners among the exiles.

For the most part the land of Israel figures in Ezekiel as a site of military destruction (e.g., 7:2; 21:7–8 [Eng. 21:2–3]); as such, the land symbolically represents its inhabitants as they undergo the devastation resulting from Israel's sin. As Elaine Scarry has argued, injury in warfare serves distinct symbolic purposes. Injury is both a means of establishing military victory and a literal display of power—visual evidence of harm inflicted by the victor.[17] The condition of the human body during and after war represents the condition—physical, political, and perhaps most importantly, ideological—of the body politic.[18] In Ezekiel's representation of the conflict between YHWH and the people, the site of injury is not primarily the individual body, but the land itself. Destruction is visited upon the land through the depletion of its inhabitants, the burning of its towns, and the harm done to its ecology. Damage wrought through both military activity and ecological disaster serves as a kind of war wound, a visible injury testifying to the power of the victor (in this case, YHWH) and to the consequent extension of this power over the lives of the conquered people. The desolation of the mountains depicted in chapter 6 and of the land in chapter 7 serve notice to the sinful people ("then they will know" [6:14; 7:9]) of YHWH's authority over them. Drought is likewise an anthropocentric phenomenon that exists to display YHWH's anger over human wrongs.

Images of the land as the site of destruction predominate in Ezek 1–24, that section of the book reflecting the buildup of tension before the destruction of Jerusalem. The land is repeatedly depicted as "sinful" or "bloody" and thus deserving of

---

16. See the discussion in J. G. Plöger, "אדמה," *TDOT* 1:88–98.
17. Elaine Scarry, *The Body in Pain: The Making and Unmaking of the World* (New York: Oxford University Press, 1985), 116.
18. See ibid., 114.

divine punishment. The "sinful" land metonymously represents its sinful inhabitants, as is clearly shown in passages such as chapter 7, an oracle directed against the land of Israel (אדמת ישראל). After an opening in which the personified land (ארץ) is informed that YHWH judges its ways, the oracle tells the addressee that the punishment has arrived in force. By v. 7, however, the figure who has thus far functioned as the implied audience of the oracle is identified, not as the land, but as the "*inhabitant* of the land" (יושב הארץ), a reference to the people as a whole. The personification of the mountains in chapter 6 is similarly transient. What begins as an oracle announcing to the mountains the end of their idolatrous altars quickly transmutes into an oracle against the idolaters themselves ("I will scatter your bones around your altars" [v. 5]). The oracle of 14:12–23 describing the fate of a land that "acts faithlessly" (v. 12) is particularly telling in this regard. Here, as in 7:3, the land itself is said to have sinned, and punishments are accordingly visited against it: famine rages while humans and domestic animals are "cut off" (v. 13). Wild animals are sent to ravage the land "so that it is made desolate, and no one may pass through because of the animals" (vv. 15, 21). Both sin and punishment are depicted in terms specific to the land; it is the land that has sinned and the land that will undergo devastation.

This view, that the land is culpable for the sins of its inhabitants and then suffers the consequences of their actions, shares, in part, the perspective of Lev 18:25, 28, in which the land, unable to bear the pollution caused by its inhabitants, reacts by vomiting them out. A related dynamic is also at work in Jeremiah, in which the personified land undergoes torment as it is ravaged by divinely sent drought and depopulation (e.g., Jer 4:23–28; 12:4, 11). As Habel has demonstrated, the imagery of Leviticus and Jeremiah reflects ideologies in which the land is understood to have rights that are defended by YHWH.[19] The innocent land demands or receives restitution because of injury inflicted by its inhabitants.

In Ezekiel, however, the tables are turned. The land is not a victim, but a party to its inhabitants' actions; it is guilty and suffers for its own sins. The personae of land and people are fused at every level, to the extent that the land's welfare is defined exclusively in terms of human needs and desires. The land is struck, not by "drought," but by "famine"; the true disaster is not environmental but social. Humans and domestic animals are cut off from the land and, as punishment, *wild* animals are allowed to roam there (14:12–15). Rather than the perspective seen in Leviticus and Jeremiah, in which the land stands apart from or even opposed to the human project, here the land is conceived as profoundly human space, as space-for-me, which is "violated" to the degree that it is rendered unfit for human habitation.

Ezekiel's depiction of the land's devastated reversion to nature obscures the alternative perspective, namely, that a land where "no one may pass through because of the animals" (14:15, 21) might be a land "liberated" from human occupation.

---

19. Habel, *The Land Is Mine*, 75–114.

Nor is the idea of the land benefiting from such "devastation" merely a retrojection of modern biophilia. In Lev 26:14–39 the land is made "desolate," with people removed and cities destroyed, but the same land whose condition "appalls" the neighbors as unfit for human settlement is in fact enjoying (רצה, v. 34) a well-deserved rest (cf. 2 Chr 36:21). The "destroyed" land is not ruined but unencumbered, freed from the burden of human habitation.

Ezekiel's land is not granted the same subject status that it has in both Leviticus and Jeremiah. Rather than existing, as in Leviticus and Jeremiah, as an independent entity that reacts (as it turns out, in protest) to the actions of its inhabitants, in Ezekiel the land is metonymous for its inhabitants (see, e.g., 7:2–4); their actions are its actions and its punishment is their punishment. It is precisely this identification between the moral status of land and people in Ezekiel that allows the land to serve as the "site of injury" in the conflict between Yhwh and the people. In Jeremiah the land is a victim whose injury Yhwh will avenge. In Ezekiel the land, representing the body politic, is the sinful body whose injury displays Yhwh's power.[20]

In the second half of Ezekiel, namely, chapters 25–48, the land appears primarily as an object of restoration. As the beneficiary of Yhwh's restoration, the land is "rehabilitated" following its punishment, and so reintegrated into the ordered cosmos as the settled realm. Like the domestic animals and plants, the land is sutured back into the cultural landscape of human and divine control. The once-devastated land blooms with new fertility, waste places are planted, ruined towns rebuilt (see, e.g., 36:8–12, 22–38). As indicated by the pairing of wasteland and ruined town, both of which will be "restored" by Yhwh, "land" is understood to be coterminous with sown and settled land. Ezekiel's privileging of the settled over the wild is extended to the point that the land is "promised" not only fertility but also urban development! The personified land finds itself equally blessed by both trees and towns.

The growth of fruit trees and the growth of cities are all but indistinguishable as indications of the land's welfare. Whereas earlier the land was personified as the embodiment of its inhabitants and punished for its sinfulness, in the restored land, cities, flocks, and people serve equally as markers of divine possession and control. Yhwh simultaneously restores the land's fertility, its security from invasion, and its human population. In the "covenant of peace" of 34:25 wild animals are removed and domestic animals multiplied. The fact that the metaphor blurs the distinction between Israel as flock and Israel as flock-owner or between wild beasts as human or as animal predators, is fully appropriate. Yhwh's "showers of blessings" on the land

---

20. An apparent exception to this pattern is 36:8–15, in which God addresses promises of restoration to the personified land. These promises, however, do not portray the land as a victim, but as the *perpetrator* of past offenses. The land will now be both reformed and forgiven: "You will no longer devour people" (36:14).

serve to benefit Israel as a settled territory and to eliminate all threats of reversion to wilderness. Yhwh is depicted through the traditional image of the shepherd of the people, but also as a returned exile—Yhwh will both rebuild the towns and replant the fields of Israel (36:36).

The restored land's goodness is certified by its desirability. The narrator posits the valorizing gaze of an anonymous onlooker. In 36:34–36 "those who pass by" are reported to say, "This land that was desolate has become like the garden of Eden; and the waste and desolate and ruined towns are now inhabited and fortified." Desolate land is replaced by its perceived opposite: tilled land, fertile as the garden of God. Desolate cities are similarly replaced by their opposite: populous, walled cities. It is striking that this miraculous renewal is not imagined as an unprecedented paradise, but rather as restoration per se; that is, the reestablishment of life in Israel before the exile. The land, while abundantly fertile, is still "worked" land requiring human effort for the yield of its produce. The towns are fortified towns, and though their safety is established by the divine removal of enemies, they are maintained by the more conventional means of strong walls.[21] The restoration of the desolate land is thus equated with restoration of the entire matrix of a mixed urban-agrarian economy. The land will be "blessed" by a return to the *status quo ante*.

IV. God's Land and Mine:
Creation as Property in the Book of Ezekiel

The nature of nature in Ezekiel is fraught with ambiguity, from Ezekiel's opening vision by the נהר Chebar—the "river" that is in fact a canal, an artifact—to his concluding vision in which the Dead Sea is changed from a natural wasteland into a supernatural venue for the fishing industry. Ezekiel's privileging of inhabited over barren land and of domestic over wild animals is consistent with ancient Near Eastern norms. In a world where the founding of a great city could be represented as the goal of all creation, the relative value of walled cities over open countryside would have been obvious.[22] To the extent that Ezekiel's outlook is merely indicative of a widespread cultural preference for the realm of human activity over wild nature, the book, while providing an excellent example of this ideological stance, is unremarkable. Ezekiel's lack of a mode by which to apprehend wild nature in anything like its own right may be read as simply an expression of a symbolic system according to which perceived order is good and perceived disorder, bad. But Ezekiel's symbolic landscape is neither an inevitable nor an insignificant extension of the wider cultural

---

21. Although the land is depicted as a land of "unwalled villages" in 38:11 (perhaps as a dramatic device indicating its vulnerability?), in chs. 40–48, the restored city is again protected by walls (48:30–35).

22. For a helpful discussion and bibliography regarding the valorization of wild nature in the Hebrew Bible, see Gene M. Tucker, "Rain on a Land Where No One Lives: The Hebrew Bible on the Environment," *JBL* 116 (1997): 3–17.

standard; the role played (or rather, not played) by wild nature in Ezekiel is distinctive, perhaps even diagnostic as an expression of the author's social location. A brief sampling of depictions of nature in Jeremiah and Deutero-Isaiah, two rough contemporaries of the historical Ezekiel, will serve to set Ezekiel's perspective in relief.

The usage of nature imagery in Jeremiah shows considerable overlap with that in Ezekiel. Faithless people are punished by the attack of wild animals (Jer 5:6) or are themselves depicted as such (Jer 12:8–9). Israel is planted as YHWH's vineyard but defies God by growing wild (literally "foreign," נכר; Jer 2:21). Drought is sent as divine punishment against the people (Jer 14:1–6). Jeremiah exhibits the same practical preference for fruitful land over desert and for tame animals over wild as does Ezekiel, but with important differences. While Jeremiah freely employs images drawn from nature to embody forces that threaten human welfare, this anthropocentrism is balanced by depictions of wild animals and of the land itself as having value apart from their utility in the settled realm. The snows of Lebanon and the mountain streams, for example, are cited as models of constancy (Jer 18:14). The earth, languishing under conditions of drought and warfare, is not bearing a well-deserved punishment as in Ezekiel, but is a victim of human crimes. The land mourns (Jer 4:28; cf. 12:4, 11) and either God (so MT) or the prophet (LXX) will mourn on its behalf (9:9 [Eng. 9:10]). The land is a precious possession of YHWH, injured by human abuse, rather than an object of divine wrath.

Like Ezekiel, Deutero-Isaiah expresses a utilitarian sensibility according to which nature's goodness is demonstrated by its contribution to human welfare. Thus, YHWH's gift of water flowing from the bare heights to the valleys and on into the wilderness (41:17–20) is wonderful because it responds to the needs of "the poor and needy." But in Deutero-Isaiah this divine gift of water is a blessing, not only to humans or their livestock, but to the wild animals as well. "The wild animals," says YHWH, "will honor me, the jackals and ostriches; for I give water in the wilderness" (43:20). This acknowledgment of an independent and positive relationship between YHWH and wild nature is not so fully developed as that reflected in Job, with its reminder that rain is sent on the land where no one lives (38:25–27), nor yet as that of Ps 104, with its catalog of creatures who look to YHWH for their sustenance. Still, both Jeremiah and Deutero-Isaiah, writing in the context of the Babylonian exile, include positive images of wild nature as such. Conversely, neither Jeremiah nor Deutero-Isaiah projects a sinful land made to suffer for its wicked excesses. Ezekiel is not distinctive among biblical texts in its utilitarian and anthropocentric strains; Ezekiel is distinctive only in admitting no other view.

The strongest potential exception to the rule of Ezekiel's exclusion of wild nature would seem to be the miraculous stream of chapter 47. The stream, as discussed above, derives from the restored temple. On its banks, it sustains miraculous trees, and the combination of abundant water with abundant fertility marks the renewed landscape (as was predicted in 36:35) as Eden, the garden of God.[23] The

---

23. On Eden imagery in Ezek 47, see Clifford, *Cosmic Mountain*, 100–102, and Levenson, *Theology of the Program*, 25–36.

trees are remarkable both for their growth and for their utility, their ability to bear fruit in all seasons while simultaneously producing medicinal leaves. The stream, in addition to sustaining the life of the trees, extends across the land to flow into the Dead Sea. Here the supernaturally fresh water demonstrates its own medicinal properties; it "heals" (רפא; cf. 2 Kgs 2:22) the Dead Sea waters, rendering them fresh. The newly healed waters promptly exhibit fertility of their own: "Wherever the river goes, every living creature that swarms will live, and there will be very many fish" (v. 9).[24] Indeed, the Dead Sea coastline will become a series of fishing ports, with variety equal to that of the "Great Sea," the Mediterranean (v. 10). The enlivening water transforms the barren landscape into one of superabundant fertility.

This passage may come as close as one gets to a validation of wild nature in Ezekiel; nonetheless, the wonder of the miraculous stream is tied explicitly to its extraordinary utility. The stream does the impossible: not only does it make salt water fresh but it also thereby creates a thriving fishing industry on the Dead Sea. The supernatural trees likewise respond directly to human need, eliminating with their monthly crops the *natural* cycles of plenty and want. Most telling in this vision of utopian fulfillment is the fate of the marshes bordering the Dead Sea. Following the description of the newly "healed" waters and their variety of freshwater fish the author adds an aside: "But its swamps and marshes will not become fresh; they are to be left for salt" (v. 11). This is a miracle firmly bounded by social and economic considerations. The re-creation of fresh water and fisheries stops miraculously short of interfering with already established routines of human commerce. The renewal of nature preserves just those bits of the old and salty world that suit human purpose.[25] Yhwh's powerful indwelling in the world yields a land of roses without thorns.

In terms of Ezekiel's ideological program, the renewing stream of 47:1–12 performs the same function as the property allotments that immediately follow. Both map out a new and perfected Israel. The path that is cut across the land by the healing river is neither more nor less "natural" than are the boundary lines laid out in 47:13–48:35. Streambed and property lines equally manifest the divine will. Ordered nature and ordered society are inscribed onto a landscape whose contours signify possession. To exist outside the realm of possession—and here divine and human possession are coterminous—means existing in opposition to the divine will. Wildness, whether the wildness of plant, animal, or human, signifies opposition to Yhwh. As such, it will cease to exist altogether.

Ezekiel's plotline whereby the land is successively reinscribed as an object of

---

24. Remarkably, כל־נפש חיה אשר־ישרץ will inhabit the ideal realm. Although clearly the "swarming" creatures serve no utilitarian purpose, it may be that they are included precisely to evoke the creation imagery of Gen 1.

25. Although some have seen the making of salt as fulfilling cultic needs, the amount of salt needed for the sacrifices of a single temple would be negligible, and would not require entire saline "swamps and marshes" for its production.

divine possession is of course an ironic one. The text's historical context, namely, the fact that the land is decidedly not an object of possession, but of desire, forms the unacknowledged backdrop to the rhetoric of divine ownership. The text was written in exile; its narrator, the exiled priest of a ruined temple, was a leader of a disenfranchised elite and representative of a dispossessed God. The inability of Ezekiel or his social group to assert control over the land of Israel may be understood as the *non-dit,* the suppressed contradiction underlying the plot of Ezekiel. The land placed so assiduously under *divine* control is a cipher for its diametric opposite—the land as the unobtainable object of *human* desire. It is as an object of frustrated desire that the land is labeled "other," untamed and (from the exiles' perspective) unowned. The creation, which should—by means of walled cities, fixed boundaries, and established leadership—stand as a visible monument to the divine will, has instead "gone wild." Ezekiel's battery of negative personifications—wild animals aggressively threatening the settled realm, cultivated trees growing wildly out of control, the land itself rebelling against divine authority—expresses outrage and anxiety over the exiles' loss of control. The conflict between the narrative demarcation of the land as divine and human property and the political reality of the land as the embodiment of the exiles' lack creates an irresolvable tension within the ideological structure of the book. The continually expressed tension between domesticated and wild, obedient and rebellious, owned and estranged mirrors the tension between the exiles' presumed right to hegemonic status and their current, excluded status.

The community in exile, which Ezekiel identifies as "the house of Israel," comprised those who would ordinarily have secure claim to social and political control. Given this contradiction between the exiles' assumed and actual power, the book's distinctive concern with control over the land comes into clearer focus. The exiles' own desire to repossess the land finds expression through constant reference to the divine perspective, a perspective that affirms the exiles as the rightful human owners of the land.

At the same time that the desire for land tenure is projected as the goal of divine order, the exiles' anxiety is projected onto those still in Jerusalem as a predatory desire to gain title to the privileged classes' land. The narrator fantasizes about the inhabitants' perception of the exiles: "They have gone far from the Lord; to us this land is given for a possession" (11:15). This projection of the exiles' anxiety as the homelanders' opportunism is quickly sutured over by divine reassurance: "I will gather you from the peoples, and assemble you out of the countries where you have been scattered, and I will give you the land of Israel" (11:17). The remaining inhabitants of Jerusalem, on the other hand, are designated by Yhwh as "those whose heart goes after their detestable things," and who will suffer divine judgment (11:21). In 33:24, Ezekiel returns to imagining the survivors' thoughts: "Abraham was only one man, yet he got possession of the land; but we are many; the land is surely given us to possess." This apparently reasonable argument (divine judgment did, after all, leave the remnant holding the land) is again met with Yhwh's withering response: "As I live, surely those who are in the waste places shall fall by the sword; and those who are in the open field I will give to the wild animals to be devoured" (33:27). The projected voice of Yhwh intervenes to pronounce a judgment consistent with the exiles' interests. The exiles' anxiety over their dispossessed status is removed even before it can be voiced. The homelanders, not they, inhabit the "waste places." The land, as the object of frustrated desire, floats below the surface of the text as a kind of phantom topic, continually driving the plot, while simultaneously it is denied.

Ezekiel's extreme preference for the ordered world—to the point of wild nature's exclusion—seems, in context, to reflect the sociopolitical tensions of the exile. In Ezekiel's sociohistorical context those with traditional claim to the land, including those who like himself represent the deity and whom he identifies as "the *whole* house of Israel" (11:15), are dispossessed, while the inhabitants of "the waste places" (33:27) have taken control. Divine outrage over unruly vines and wild animals mirrors the exiles' sense of violated ownership and authority. From the narrative perspective, the land has reverted to "wildness," effectively, to chaos. The hostile "other" has turned the land to "wildness": the custodians of divine order no longer control it. From this ideological stance, it is immaterial whether the land has literally been "devastated." Although widespread destruction, particularly of urban centers, had clearly occurred, the reduced and relatively impoverished population might well have been enjoying the new opportunities for land ownership and social reorganization. Ezekiel's "myth of the devastated land" parallels what Robert Carroll has called the "myth of the empty land," a narrative program that presents the land as "empty" and therefore awaiting the exiles' return.[26] To posit a land that is "devastated," "empty," or both is to posit both need and warrant for the return of the ruling classes and the displacement of those whose control is defined as chaos.

V. Conclusion: Castles in the Air

Walter Benn Michaels's work on Hawthorne's *The House of the Seven Gables* provides a provocative analysis of the role played by literary texts in expressing and resolving anxiety over land tenure.[27] According to Michaels, disputed real estate often appears in literature[28] as an expression of social conflict. In particular, Michaels points to a conflict between "legitimation of property by labor" and the claim of the aristocracy as a "claim to land that is unimpaired by the inability to

---

26. R. P. Carroll, "The Myth of the Empty Land," *Semeia* 59 (1992): 79–93.

27. Walter B. Michaels, *The Gold Standard and the Logic of Naturalism: American Literature at the Turn of the Century* (New Historicism 2; Berkeley and Los Angeles: University of California Press, 1987).

28. Michaels is concerned with the dynamics of "romance" literature. This is not the literature of romantic love, but wish-fulfillment literature, in which good triumphs over evil. For definitions and discussion of the genre, see Northrop Frye, *The Anatomy of Criticism: Four Essays* (Princeton: Princeton University Press, 1957), 37, 186–205; Jameson, *The Political Unconscious*, 110–12.

enforce that claim."²⁹ This irresolvable paradox of a dispossessed aristocracy is resolved through wish-fulfillment literature, which provides a "text of clear and unobstructed title."³⁰ The book of Ezekiel follows the pattern of realizing a "clear and unobstructed title" by purely literary means. As Hawthorne commented on *The House of the Seven Gables*, although the book concerns the accumulation of real estate, he constructed it "by laying out a street that infringes upon nobody's rights, and appropriating a lot of land which had no visible owner." He built the House of the Seven Gables, in short, "of materials long in use for constructing castles in the air."³¹ In Ezekiel, of course, the disputed land is real, not fictive; it is only the land's return to its divine-rightful owner that is fictional.

Political and theological tensions have long been seen to underlie the program of restoration in Ezek 40–48;³² it is possible, however, to read the book as a whole as articulating the desired historical "plot" of a specific social group. Such a plotting would accord with Fredric Jameson's description of the aesthetic as "an ideological act in its own right, with the function of inventing imaginary or formal 'solutions' to unresolvable social contradictions."³³ That the composition of the book of Ezekiel was "an ideological act in its own right" seems self-evident. In Ezekiel's case, the "unresolvable social contradictions" are those engendered by the circumstances of exile, contradictions centering on (from the exiles' perspective) the alienated status of the land. The land, in Ezekiel, is properly that realm whose ownership should display the authority and control of Yhwh, an authority most tangibly expressed through the hegemonic presence of Yhwh's designated representatives. In reality, Ezekiel faces the awkward situation of having authority without agency. Ezekiel possesses detailed knowledge of which land is "properly" owned by which social group within Israel, but it turns out that the land is quite perversely occupied by . . . well, by *others*.

The exiles' frustrated claims to the land are projected onto Yhwh as a frustration of divine power. So Yhwh also, despite a quite indisputable claim to the land, experiences embarrassing land poverty. In light of this fundamental contradiction within Ezekiel's social and theological worlds, the category of the natural world, the world as it is related to its divine master, becomes problematic indeed. The supreme creator God has no toehold in the land—indeed in *any* land. Like Abraham bargaining with the Hittites, Yhwh must maneuver from a position of weakness (however well disguised) in order to possess the land. In Yhwh's case, the problem is not so much to establish legitimate claim (God's claim is nothing if not legitimate) but to establish a claim that is credible under the historical circumstances of exile. As an

---

29. Michaels, *Gold Standard*, 92–93.
30. Ibid., 89.
31. Preface to *The House of the Seven Gables*, quoted in Michaels, *Gold Standard*, 88–89.
32. Duguid, *Ezekiel and the Leaders*, and Stevenson, *Vision of Transformation*, provide helpful readings of the ideological agenda represented by Ezekiel's vision.
33. Jameson, *The Political Unconscious*, 79.

ideological act, the book of Ezekiel enacts the hegemonic return of Yhwh and, by extension, of a *status quo ante* in which the exiles exert social and political control.[34] The exiles' need for return is, as Carroll has argued, specifically a need for hegemonic return,[35] a return to control that becomes projected in Ezekiel as a need for the reenthronement of divine authority. By defending God's own inalienable right to the land, Yhwh simultaneously secures the land for the dispossessed community of the elite. The exiles' separation from the land is depicted as Yhwh's own. And Yhwh's struggle to conform nature to the divine will and to assert overlordship symbolically fulfills the community's desires for hegemony.

Within the narrator's sociopolitical horizon, the land of Israel has become "wild," outside control and given over to elements whose presence is perceived as threatening to the ordered world. Yhwh's dilemma of possessing unlimited rights but uncertain power over creation fuels a dynamic in which the natural world is constantly dichotomized according to whether it is perceived as within or without the control of Yhwh. "Idolatrous" mountains are cursed; faithful mountains are blessed; animals are either "evil beasts" or domestic flocks. Trees under Yhwh's control bear miraculous fruit and eminently useful leaves; trees that defy Yhwh's authority must be destroyed. In the exiles' political context, where power and place have been disrupted, the natural world emerges as above all contested property. The profound land anxiety of the narrator and his fellow exiles is expressed through its exact opposite: an assertion of absolute divine right soon to be manifested through Yhwh's reestablishment of that divine "social order" of which they themselves are the guardians.

---

34. This conclusion is not intended to contradict that drawn by Duguid, who elucidates reforms anticipated in the new social order (*Ezekiel and the Leaders*, 140). These reforms, while real, represent a reshuffling of power *within* the ruling classes that serves to re-legitimate their control over temple and land.

35. Carroll, "Myth of the Empty Land," 81, 89.

FROM HARSHNESS TO HOPE:
THE IMPLICATIONS FOR EARTH OF HIERARCHY IN EZEKIEL

Keith Carley

I. INTRODUCTION

This article was originally written for a Society of Biblical Literature symposium in which contributors to a new series, The Earth Bible, focused on the theme of land in the book of Ezekiel.[1] Contributors to The Earth Bible read Scripture according to ecojustice principles, acknowledging Earth's vital role in the living cosmos and critiquing attitudes toward Earth expressed in the canon.[2] I had previously written about the harsh treatment God deals out to Earth according to the formula found frequently in Ezekiel: "I will make the land a desolation, and they will know that I am the LORD."[3] For the most part, in the book of Ezekiel Earth is the passive object of horrifying maltreatment meted out by God in the process of punishing human misdeeds. I wanted to explore the possibility of finding hope in the midst of such harsh justice. Recasting the essay under the rubric of *Ezekiel's Hierarchical World: Wrestling with a Tiered Reality* first requires some explanation of how hierarchy may be viewed.

"Hierarchy today has a very bad reputation, mostly because people confuse dominator hierarchies with natural hierarchies," writes Wilber.[4] Clarifying the distinction,

---

1. The annual meeting of the Society of Biblical Literature, Denver, November 2001.
2. The Earth Bible, vols. 1–5, ed. Norman C. Habel et al. (Sheffield: Sheffield Academic Press; Cleveland: Pilgrim, 2000–2002). For the "Guiding Ecojustice Principles" of the series, see Norman C. Habel, ed., *Readings from the Perspective of Earth* (Earth Bible 1; Sheffield: Sheffield Academic Press; Cleveland: Pilgrim, 2000), 38–53.
3. Variations on the synonymous verbal roots שמם and חרב are used to convey the desolation. For details see Keith Carley, "Ezekiel's Formula of Desolation: Harsh Justice for the Land/Earth," in *The Earth Story in the Psalms and the Prophets* (ed. N. C. Habel; Earth Bible 4; Sheffield: Sheffield Academic Press; Cleveland: Pilgrim, 2001), 143–57.
4. Ken Wilber, *A Brief History of Everything* (Boston: Shambhala, 1996), 27–28. Riane Eisler notes that the distinction between the two types of hierarchy is not made in conventional usage (*The Chalice and the Blade: Our History, Our Future* [San Francisco: HarperSanFrancisco, 1987], 105). Wilber's point that "hierarchy today has a very bad reputation" can be illustrated from Erhard S. Gerstenberger's recent

he notes that natural or normal hierarchies represent an order of increasing wholeness and integrative capacity. When it is said "the whole is greater than the sum of its parts," the "greater" implies "hierarchy." It does not indicate domination but integration, as for example when particles, atoms, cells, and organisms, or letters, words, sentences, and paragraphs, progress toward increasingly complex levels of function.[5]

Dominator or pathological hierarchies, on the other hand, inhibit the natural development of higher functions. They are systems of ranking "based on force or the implied threat of force, which are characteristic of the human rank orderings in male-dominant societies."[6] Such hierarchies, in Eisler's words,

> result in social systems in which the lowest (basest) human qualities are reinforced and humanity's higher aspirations (traits such as compassion and empathy as well as the striving for truth and justice) are systematically suppressed.[7]

It is the contention of this article that the relationship of God to Earth as portrayed in the book of Ezekiel is that of a dominator hierarchy. Awareness of that encourages us to find a voice for the silent Earth for the sake of its liberation and for God's, for dominator hierarchies distort open communication[8] and, as Eisler says, systematically suppress compassion and justice.

Dempsey's recent study of the Latter Prophets from a liberation-critical perspective includes Ezekiel in a group that has "as one of their central concerns justice for those who suffer profound injustice at the hands of others whose inordinate need for power and control has caused unnecessary oppression."[9] The first in this cluster of prophets is Amos, of whom Dempsey concludes:

> God's powerful deeds of chastisement were often themselves violent and destructive. In addition, God is portrayed as one who dominated the natural world to try to win back the cherished but wayward Israelites.[10]

Dempsey anticipates the point in her study when "the paradigm (will shift) fully from power over to empowerment, from violent injustice to peace-filled justice, from oppressive hierarchy to liberating reciprocity."[11]

---

statements: "the hierarchical explanation of the world no longer applies"; "ideally there is no hierarchical structure" (*Theologies in the Old Testament* [trans. J. Bowden; Minneapolis: Fortress, 2002], 285, 290).

5. Ken Wilber, *Sex, Ecology, Spirituality: The Spirit of Evolution* (Boston: Shambhala, 1995), 15–18. See also Arthur R. Peacocke, *Theology for a Scientific Age: Being and Becoming—Natural and Divine* (Oxford: Blackwell, 1990), 22, 37–40.

6. Eisler, *Chalice and the Blade*, 205 n. 5.

7. Ibid.

8. Wilber, *Sex, Ecology, Spirituality*, 22, with reference to Jürgen Habermas's social-critical theory.

9. Carol J. Dempsey, *The Prophets: A Liberation-Critical Reading* (Minneapolis: Fortress, 2000), 5.

10. Ibid., 21.

11. Ibid.

That point is scarcely reached in the book of Ezekiel. God is portrayed in the prophecy predominantly as vengeful and lacking in love.

II. The Vengeful and Loveless God

It has already been mentioned that a major theme in Ezekiel is the desolation Earth is about to suffer as divine punishment for human shortcomings. It may be the land of Israel, on account of its inhabitants' idolatry, as in Ezek 6:14—"I will stretch out my hand against them, and make the land desolate and waste, throughout all their settlements, from the wilderness to Riblah"—or foreign lands such as Egypt, for proving to be a disloyal ally to Israel, as in Ezek 29:9—"the land of Egypt shall be a desolation and a waste."[12]

The theme of retribution is prominent in the book of Ezekiel,[13] and the prophet assumes that God is justified—if not required, as a covenant guarantor—to punish wrongdoers.[14] But where is justice for Earth in such an assumption?

Beyond the destruction of land as a punishment for people's misdeeds, Ezek 21:8 (Eng. 21:3) calls in question even God's protection of the righteous:

> Thus says the Lord, "I am against you and I will draw my sword from its scabbard and hew down both righteous and wicked within you."[15]

Zimmerli confirmed the astonishing implications of this passage:

> Yahweh himself strikes unmercifully. . . . The formulation appears to be in flat contradiction to the statements (about saving one's life by righteous living in Ezek 18) and also to know nothing of the preservation of a remnant, as Ezek 9 leads us to expect.[16]

Furthermore, reflecting on the passage in which God claims, "I even gave them

---

12. Biblical quotations are from the New Revised Standard Version (NRSV) unless otherwise indicated.

13. Various scholars' attempts to deny that Ezekiel portrays God as vengeful are dealt with in Carley, "Ezekiel's Formula of Desolation," 150–52.

14. Ka Leung Wong, *The Idea of Retribution in the Book of Ezekiel* (VTSup 87; Leiden: Brill, 2001), 246–53.

15. "Righteous and wicked": both the Greek Septuagint and the Aramaic Targum adopt alternative readings at this point. The former renders the equivalent of "unrighteous and lawless," the latter "I will exile your righteous from you, in order to destroy your wicked"; see Daniel I. Block, *The Book of Ezekiel*, vol. 1, *Chapters 1–24* (NICOT; Grand Rapids: Eerdmans, 1997), 665 n. 41. "[W]ithin you": in my translation of this verse I have adopted one of the basic meanings of the preposition מִן in M. E. J. Richardson, *The Hebrew and Aramaic Lexicon of the Old Testament: The New Koehler-Baumgartner in English* (Leiden: Brill, 1995), 2:597.

16. Walther Zimmerli, *Ezekiel: A Commentary on the Book of the Prophet Ezekiel* (2 vols.; Hermeneia; Philadelphia: Fortress, 1979), 1:424.

laws that were not good and observances by which they could never live" (Ezek 20:25 JB), Miles writes:

> [T]he demonic strand in (God's) character, though never finally dominant, can never be excised from it. The Book of Ezekiel raises, though it does not develop, the possibility that the historical sufferings of Israel are the crime of God. The writer is willing to imagine, however fleetingly, that God seduced Israel into the very sins that he then punished—all to prove "that I am Yahweh," which is to say, to reveal his character, to put himself on display.[17]

Miles devotes a chapter of his book *God: A Biography* to the question "Does God love?" He observes: "It is no exaggeration to say that, to judge from the entire text of the Bible from Genesis 1 through Isaiah 39, the Lord does not know what love is."[18] Moreover, apart from rare exceptions (Gen 8:21; Deut 28:63; 1 Kgs 3:10), God takes no pleasure in anything or anybody. There is an almost total silence about divine joy, happiness, or pleasure. The LORD is endlessly angry and displeased,

> (like) many a power-hungry warlord who portrayed himself as without pity, beyond need, and above passion, intimidating in his unpredictable anger, and imperious for no discernible motive.[19]

Miles should not have limited his observation to "Genesis 1 through Isaiah 39," for what he says is certainly also true of the book of Ezekiel. Gowan comments that Ezekiel "never uses *'āhab* 'love,' *ḥesed* 'steadfast love,' or *ḥānan* 'have mercy,' and *raḥam* 'have compassion' appears only in 39:25."[20]

Not until Second Isaiah does Miles note a change in the face of God which "brings him from his condition of fierce and protracted affective latency to the lyric ardour that bursts upon us" in such passages as Isa 54:4, 7–8:

> Fear not, for you will not be ashamed [בוש];
> be not confounded [כלם], for you will not be put to shame [חפר];
> for you will forget the shame [בוש] of your youth, . . .

---

17. Jack Miles, *God: A Biography* (New York: Knopf, 1995), 333. In like vein, Andrew Davies comments on "the dubious morality of Yahweh" in the book of Isaiah (*Double Standards in Isaiah: Re-evaluating Prophetic Ethics and Divine Justice* [Biblical Interpretation 46; Leiden: Brill, 2000], 187).

18. Miles, *God: A Biography*, 238.

19. Ibid., 242. Daniel Smith-Christopher quotes Amelie Kuhrt's description of Assyrian reliefs depicting kings whose "royal power to inspire fear was visualized as a shining radiance . . . fearsome to behold, and it could strike his enemies down" ("Ezekiel on Fanon's Couch: A Postcolonialist Dialogue with David Halperin's *Seeking Ezekiel*," in *Peace and Justice Shall Embrace: Power and Theopolitics in the Bible* [ed. T. Grimsrud and L. L. Johns; Telford, Pa.: Pandora; Scottdale, Pa.: Herald, 1999], 108–44).

20. Donald E. Gowan, *Theology of the Prophetic Books: The Death and Resurrection of Israel* (Louisville: Westminster John Knox, 1998), 134.

> For a brief moment I forsook you,
>   but with great compassion I will gather you.
> In overflowing wrath for a moment
>   I hid my face from you,
> but with everlasting love I will have compassion on you
>   says the LORD, your Redeemer.[21]

But such was not yet the case with God as portrayed in Ezekiel. In the Ezekiel tradition, no end to shame is envisaged. On the contrary, in the new and everlasting covenant anticipated in Ezek 16:59–63, God's wife—Jerusalem—will remember her former ways and be ashamed (כלם Niphal, v. 61), never speaking another word because of her shame (both בוש and כלם are used) when God forgives her (v. 63).

> I will establish my covenant with you, and you shall know that I am the LORD, in order that you may remember and be confounded, and never open your mouth again because of your shame, when I forgive you all that you have done, says the Lord GOD. (Ezek 16:62–63)

A parallel outside the marriage metaphor reinforces the point. The passage in which it occurs is the one to which Gowan drew attention on account of its single reference to רחם in the book of Ezekiel (39:25–29). While God may "have mercy" on the house of Israel, they shall nonetheless bear[22] their shame (כלם, 39:26).

The theme is further reinforced in three other passages of Ezekiel in which the term קוט Niphal, indicating self-loathing and disgust, is used:

> [T]hen you shall remember your evil ways, and your dealings that were not good; and you shall loathe yourselves for your iniquities and your abominable deeds. (36:31; cf. 6:9; 20:43)

The positive intent of such remembering is, as Zimmerli says, that "any human boasting is done away with."[23] There is no forgetting the past and assuming that survival has been the result of one's own merits.

---

21. Miles, *God: A Biography*, 242–43. I have added the Hebrew roots to the quotation.

22. So with the Masoretic Text. "All the comparative material argues against the emendation of the Masoretic Text to read with the versions 'forget (their shame)'" (Zimmerli, *Ezekiel*, 2:295).

23. Zimmerli, *Ezekiel*, 1:470. Jacqueline E. Lapsley argues that "this sense of worthlessness, at least for Ezekiel if not in the view of modern psychology, can lead to the creation of a new self based on a more accurate self-understanding" ("Shame and Self-Knowledge: The Positive Role of Shame in Ezekiel's View of the Moral Self," in *The Book of Ezekiel: Theological and Anthropological Perspectives* [ed. M. S. Odell and J. T. Strong; SBLSymS 9; Atlanta: Society of Biblical Literature, 2000], 153). Lapsley's article, like those of Odell, Stiebert, and Bechtel following, refers to the considerable range of recent research on honor and shame in the biblical traditions; see also Johanna Stiebert, *The Construction of Shame in the Hebrew Bible: The Prophetic Contribution* (JSOTSup 346; Sheffield: Sheffield Academic Press, 2002).

Yet, understandable as that motive may be, one cannot help but query the effect of such persistent self-loathing, which may result in destructive behavior. Nathanson gives examples of such behavior, including crime and civil disobedience, and self-destruction is not uncommon.[24] However, he also warns against assuming that we understand precisely what the experience of shame is, for our contemporaries, let alone for people of other eras.[25]

Bechtel draws from the Psalms examples of how shaming "was often used by the upper class to dominate the middle class and to keep them in their place."[26] And, if we may assume some merging of horizons between Ezekiel's context and our own, there are contemporary insights that can help us understand shaming as a means of social control. A professional psychotherapist comments: "Shame is about power and if I feel shame I am putting the person I project the shame onto into a position of power. Shame keeps (dominator) hierarchies in place."[27] And an academic specialist in pastoral psychology identifies shame as one of the basic threats to hope. Donald Capps thinks shaming others reduces the possibility that we will be the objects of shame. It may also promote perfectionism that is bound in the end to fail. And shame, if it becomes chronic, is a threat to hope because it undermines what we believe it is possible for us to achieve.[28]

The survivors of Judah's demise under Babylon needed "a drastically different emotional basis"[29] than the rehearsal of shame and self-loathing if their restoration was going to achieve anything at all positive. Rather than meeting that need, Ezekiel's loveless overlord imposed self-reproach on the new occupants of the land, a measure unlikely to make them considerate of Earth and their environment.

It seems appropriate to conclude that in Ezek 16:63, with its conjunction of shame and forgiveness, and in the several passages anticipating self-loathing on the part of the survivors (6:9; 20:43; 36:31), we have an example of cognitive dissonance.[30] It arises on the one hand from the difficulty of ever satisfying the ethical

---

24. Donald L. Nathanson, *Shame and Pride: Affect, Sex, and the Birth of the Self* (New York: Norton, 1992), 472. Leonard J. Coppes comments that the emotional reaction may be so deep that the subject longs for his or her own extinction ("קוט," *TWOT* 2:792); in his suffering Job loathes his life (10:1).

25. Nathanson, *Shame and Pride*, 433. For that reason it seems unwise to make such categorical distinctions as "shame has little to do with an internal experience of unworthiness" (Margaret S. Odell, "The Inversion of Shame and Forgiveness in Ezekiel 16:59–63," *JSOT* 56 [1992]: 103). Johanna Stiebert sagely observes: "In practice, however, . . . shame-guilt distinctions are difficult to maintain" ("Shame and Prophecy: Approaches Past and Present," *BibInt* 8 [2000]: 257).

26. Lyn M. Bechtel, "The Perception of Shame within the Divine-Human Relationship in Biblical Israel," in *Uncovering Ancient Stones: Essays in Memory of H. Neil Richardson* (ed. L. M. Hopfe; Winona Lake, Ind.: Eisenbrauns, 1994), 85.

27. The Rev. Jeremy Younger, Auckland, New Zealand, in personal discussion.

28. Donald Capps, *Agents of Hope: A Pastoral Psychology* (Minneapolis: Fortress, 1995), 129–31.

29. Miles, *God: A Biography,* 244.

30. Odell appeals to Ps 22 for an example of "shame in the absence of guilt." She concludes that "shame is tied to the experience of divine abandonment" ("Inversion of Shame and Forgiveness," 105).

and ritual demands of God and on the other from the promise of restoration solely at God's initiative. In these passages, atonement[31] brings not joyful release from impurity but remorse. Restoration to the land prompts not gratitude but self-condemnation. Such responses may have satisfied the demands of justice and restored honor to the shamed name of the LORD (Ezek. 36:21, etc.),[32] but they imposed severe restraints on the hope that a new beginning might have been expected to evoke and scarcely cohere with the vision of a resurrected people, animated by the spirit, that was to be the answer to the exiled community's sense of hopelessness (37:11).

III. IN THE INTERESTS OF THE EXILES

It is clear from a number of passages in Ezekiel that those who remained in the land after the exile were not to be favored in the event of the land's liberation and restoration. Those who prided themselves as being the valuable "meat," protected by the "pot" in Ezek 11:1–13, were to be cast out and judged at the border of the land. The death of Pelatiah in the vision seems to imply the end of hope for those who believed God would deliver a remnant.[33] Those who did survive the "four deadly acts of judgment" against Jerusalem, however, were to be "brought out" and put on view in some way, their deeds demonstrating that they deserved the judgment they had suffered (14:21–23). In another place it is prophesied that those who inhabit the waste places[34] in the land of Israel (33:24) will be slain by the sword, devoured by wild animals, or perish from pestilence, so that the land will be truly desolate[35] without anyone even passing through it (33:27–28).

This last passage seems strategically placed. It precedes the shepherd prophecies, which conclude with the return of the exiles to the land (הארץ) from which it is envisaged that the wild animals will be banished or annihilated.[36] It will be a fruitful land (הארץ), with soil (אדמה) on which the returnees, the flock of God, will dwell secure (Ezek 34:25–27).

We shall consider the wider ramifications of Ezek 34:25–31 shortly. In the meantime, the question of whose interests the book of Ezekiel serves seems clear. It certainly does not serve the interests of those who had tended the vineyards and

---

However, Ezekiel explicitly assured the exiles that God would be with them in the future (Ezek 34:30; 37:27–28; cf. 48:35).

31. "Forgive," in the NRSV of 16:63, is the only occurrence of כפר Piel in Ezek 1–39.

32. Several times the prophecy states that God's decision to preserve Israel and restore the exiles was not for their sake but for the sake of God's name, lest it be profaned by other nations (Ezek 20:9, 14, 22, 44; 36:22–32). Of course, a name in the Hebrew Scriptures "is no mere sound or label, but expresses the essence of a thing or person" (Zimmerli, *Ezekiel*, 1:134).

33. The name Pelatiah means "YHWH delivers, or causes a remnant to escape."

34. Here the noun derives from the root חרב.

35. Two words, both from the root שׁמם, form a hendiadys.

36. The Hiphil of שׁבת is used, as in Jer. 36:29.

fields of Judah during the exile of the sixth century B.C.E. (Jer 39:10; 2 Kgs 25:12), or of the wild creatures that had served God's punitive purpose. Nothing stood in the way of what Carroll described as "the establishment of the hegemony of the deportees over the people of the land,"[37] and one might venture to suggest that the prophecy was deliberately intended to encourage that outcome.[38]

An element of self-interest on the part of the prophet should not be overlooked either. As the primary spokesperson for the hierarch, Ezekiel stood to benefit from the dominator hierarchy that his text created, for, despite the judgments he delivered against the exile community, he ultimately favored it and may have envisaged himself enjoying the privileges of priesthood in the restored temple.

Promotion of the exiles' interests in the book of Ezekiel basically ignores the interdependent living communities—vegetative, animal, and human—that Earth sustained in Judah throughout the exile. Again, Earth is largely a passive instrument by means of which God's absolute power to eradicate or renew may be demonstrated.

IV. WHERE THEN LIES HOPE?

Of the considerable range of specific expressions for "hope" in biblical Hebrew, the substantive תקוה appears in Ezekiel, but only twice.[39] The first occasion is in the fable-cum-lament for the princes of Israel in chapter 19. Its use there seems deliberately ironic, not to say sarcastic. When the first of two princes, portrayed as lion cubs, was caught in a pit and dispatched, bound, to Egypt, his mother's "hope was lost" (Ezek 19:5). The "lioness" is probably best understood, with Block and Zimmerli, as a figure for the politically ambitious nation of Judah/Israel.

On the second occasion that "hope" is specifically mentioned, it comes from the mouths of another subject dispatched, bound (metaphorically at least), this time

---

37. Robert P. Carroll, "The Myth of the Empty Land," *Semeia* 59 (1992): 81. Like the issue of shame, literature on the topic of the situation in Judah during the exile is voluminous. See further Hans M. Barstad, *The Myth of the Empty Land: A Study in the History and Archaeology of Judah during the "Exilic" Period* (SO Fasc. suppl. 28; Oslo: Scandinavian University Press, 1996); Lester L. Grabbe, ed., *Leading Captivity Captive: "The Exile" as History and Ideology* (European Seminar in Historical Methodology 2; JSOTSup 278; Sheffield: Sheffield Academic Press, 1998).

38. An analogy can be found in records of the colonial occupation of Aotearoa/New Zealand in the nineteenth century. David M. Gunn notes the use of biblical texts about "the promised land" or "Canaan" without mention of the corollary, "the promise of dispossession for the indigenous inhabitants." "Such rhetoric," he comments, "readily produces an empty land" ("Colonialism and the Vagaries of Scripture: Te Kooti in Canaan [A Study of Bible and Dispossession in Aotearoa/New Zealand]," in *God in the Fray: A Tribute to Walter Brueggemann* [ed. T. Linafelt and T. K. Beal; Minneapolis: Fortress, 1998], 132).

39. Other words conveying hope, of a kind, in Ezekiel, are מבטח, used of false confidence in Egypt (Ezek 29:16), and יחל and שקר, used of expectations raised by false prophets (13:6, 22).

to Babylon—the exile community itself: "Our bones are dried up, and our hope is lost; we are cut off completely" (Ezek 37:11).

The traditions of Ezekiel, then, explicitly enunciate hope only in retrospect, suggesting—not unsurprisingly—that awareness of it was sharpest when it had been lost. If fresh hope is to be discerned, it will need to address the role of the "prince" and the despair of the people as well as the plight of the desolated land.

When Zimmerli, who was one of the most knowledgeable and sympathetic modern exponents of the book of Ezekiel, wrote *Man and His Hope in the Old Testament*,[40] he devoted only four pages to the prophecy. He noted that in the face of the despair reflected in Ezek 37:11, and the guilt acknowledged in 33:10 ("our transgressions and our sins weigh upon us, and we waste away because of them"), Ezekiel "became the proclaimer of a new future."[41] Evidence for this he saw in the vivid imagery of Israel's resurrection (the dry bones vivified by רוח ["breath," "spirit"] in 37:1–14); the renewal of the exiles' inner being (the gift of a new heart and spirit in 36:16–38 and 11:14–21); the new exodus (20:32–44); the new Davidic shepherd (in ch. 34 and 17:22–24); and especially in the new sanctuary (37:27–28 and chs. 40–48). "The substance of hope and of a future is fully there as the prophet announces the coming activity of his God."[42] But, as might be expected of a monograph written in the 1960s, Zimmerli made no reference to the impact the fulfillment of such hope would have on the land—either of Israel or the nations—let alone on the wider environment.

In his *Hope within History*, however, Brueggemann identified Ezek 34:25–31, with its "hope for the restoration of creation, the renewal of the ecological process," as a

> promise . . . that articulates restoration for both history and nature, for both politics and fertility, in which all relationships will be as they were envisioned in the uncontaminated anticipation of the creation narrative of Genesis 1.[43]

Gowan, in his *Theology of the Prophetic Books*, reads Ezek 34:25–31 as a more modest expression of hope. While "restoration to the promised land will include the blessing of nature itself, and the assurance of security,"[44] "at the level of basic human need, the transformation of nature was hoped for so that there might be no more hunger."[45]

---

40. Walther Zimmerli, *Man and His Hope in the Old Testament* (SBT 2/20; London: SCM, 1971), 116–20; trans. of *Der Mensch und seine Hoffnung im Alten Testament* (Göttingen: Vandenhoeck und Ruprecht, 1968).
41. Ibid., 117.
42. Ibid., 120.
43. Walter Brueggemann, *Hope within History* (Atlanta: John Knox, 1987), 76.
44. *Theology of the Prophetic Books*, 135, with reference also to Ezek 36:33–38.
45. Ibid., 75.

In a previous study, *Eschatology in the Old Testament*, Gowan also referred to the transformation of nature in Ezek 36. "At first the entire subject of the chapter seems to be the natural world, for the prophet addresses not individuals or nations but the mountains of Israel." However, he went on to acknowledge that "the real subject is the people of Israel."[46] The fertility of the land is to be restored (vv. 8–9, 11, 29–30, 34–35) as in Ezek 34:25–31, so that the once desolate[47] land will be celebrated as a "garden of Eden" (36:35).[48] Yet, Gowan rightly concluded that the reason for the changes in nature following from the reestablishment of a proper relationship between God and Israel "is clearly anthropocentric."[49] Of Ezek 34:25–31 and the analogous provision of a fruitful land and harmony between humankind and other creatures in Hos 2:20–24 (Eng. 2:18–22), he stated: "So far we have found nothing that could be called a new ecology; . . . those passages do not speak of an ecological change."[50] He also noted that "the association of nations with beasts in 34:28 shows that (the passage) may be read either literally or figuratively."[51]

Ezekiel 34:25–31 and chapter 36 are indeed far from reflecting the ecojustice principles of The Earth Bible. We have seen that the vision of Ezekiel is basically focused on the community of Israel, and on the exiled community at that, as it faced the exacting demands of an irascible God. There is little in either passage to suggest the intimate involvement of God in the wonders of the natural world and its non-human creatures, such as are found in Job 38–39, or of joy in the whole creation, such as lady wisdom experiences according to Prov 8:22–31.

It is Brueggemann, in his *Interpretation and Obedience*, who opens a broader perspective on ecojustice in relation to Ezekiel. Under the rubric "Life-Giving Land Management" he notes that Ezek 47–48 marks a return to the ideal of apportioning land neither according to demand nor according to the economic power of those who "covet" it but according to the ideals associated with the premonarchic period as portrayed in Josh 13–19.[52]

I would not want to endorse all the complexities of "inalienable patrimony" that Brueggemann alludes to, for they bedevil relations in the Middle East to this day. But the systematic redistribution of land to each of Israel's twelve tribes—how-

---

46. Donald E. Gowan, *Eschatology in the Old Testament* (Philadelphia: Fortress, 1986), 101.

47. שמם Niphal, Ezek 36:35.

48. Although the etymology and semantic development of the word עדן ("Eden") are complex and remain hypothetical, the word is an antonym of מדבר ("wilderness"), as well as of places that were חרבה ("waste") and נשמה ("desolate"), as in Ezek 36:35; עדן "probably referred originally to a luxuriantly fertile area, a 'fruitful land'" (B. Kedar-Kopfstein, "עדן ʿēden," *TDOT* 10:487).

49. Gowan, *Eschatology*, 102.

50. Ibid., 103.

51. Ibid., 102. Brueggemann concurs: "The banishment of 'wild beasts' may be read literally or as a metaphor for rapacious political power" (*Hope within History*, 76).

52. Walter Brueggemann, *Interpretation and Obedience: From Faithful Reading to Faithful Living* (Minneapolis: Fortress, 1991), 251–55.

ever naive and impractical it may appear[53]—may nonetheless be taken to imply equality of opportunity and relationships of mutual support for all tribes and their members. Ezekiel 48:1–29 describes the land's division into thirteen horizontal strips. Each strip was probably equal in terms of its north-to-south dimension.[54] Seven tribes were located north of a sacred strip that included Jerusalem and the restored temple, and five were located south of it.

The arrangement countered the theme of economic and political domination that features so prominently in the biblical narratives of the monarchies (e.g., 1 Kgs 21; cf. 1 Sam 8:14) as well as in preexilic prophecy (Hos 5:10; Mic 2:2). In the restored theocracy of Ezekiel, princes will have no right to evict people from their land. The princes' portion of land within the sacred strip is generous and must suffice (Ezek 45:7–9; 46:16–18). By implication, the princes themselves will no longer be objects of hope, for their mothers (Ezek 19:5) or their people.[55]

Brueggemann also comments on the analogy between ritual defilement, which endangered entire communities, and modern land abuse by "the technology of contamination" (toxic chemicals and pollution). The restored community, cleansed of its iniquities, will till (עבד) the land and render it an Eden (Ezek 36:33–36), while the remarkable imagery of the river flowing from the restored temple (Ezek 47:1–12) suggests renewed fertility and abundant sources of nourishment and healing.[56] Purification of the land is also among the outcomes of the final battle against external aggressors, symbolized by the Gog episode (Ezek 39:16).

Finally, between the description of the boundaries of the land and the allotment of it to the tribes of Israel, there appears a reminder of the compassion that the restored people should show to the sojourner. Sojourners (גרים, "aliens" in the NRSV) are even to be allotted an inheritance of land like other citizens of Israel (Ezek 47:22–23). This, Brueggemann wrote in another place, "is a stunning statement," even though "the very generosity of the gift poses deep problems for the new land and its possessors."[57] But Kellerman suggests that the גר of Ezek 47:22–23 "probably already denotes a proselyte."[58] Within the same vision, the "foreigner" (נכר) is specifically excluded from the central institution—one might say, the source of life—in the restored land: "No foreigner, uncircumcised in heart and flesh, of all the

---

53. Not least because the Babylonian exiles were predominantly Judean.
54. Zimmerli, *Ezekiel*, 2:533.
55. Claus Westermann observes that hope, "when not related to God, is articulated negatively to a great degree" (*TLOT* 3:1132).
56. Julie Galambush comments on trees as symbols of Yhwh's power to restore fertility to the land ("Castles in the Air: Creation as Property in Ezekiel," *SBL Seminar Papers, 1999* [SBLSP 38; Atlanta: Scholars Press, 1999], 155; a revised version of the article appears in this volume).
57. Walter Brueggemann, *The Land: Place as Gift, Promise, and Challenge in Biblical Faith* (2nd ed.; Minneapolis: Fortress, 2002), 134.
58. D. Kellermann, "גור *gûr*," *TDOT* 2:447. Zimmerli writes of "something new" coming about during the exile in the association of non-Israelites with the community of Yhwh worshipers (*Ezekiel*, 2:532).

foreigners who are among the people of Israel, shall enter my sanctuary" (Ezek 44:9). If the vision appears generous on the one hand, on the other it firmly excludes the participation of a significant part of God's creation from the crucial gifts of the restored community.

It can hardly be denied then that hope *is* expressed in the book of Ezekiel. But it is far from unalloyed hope. It must remain tentative for the various reasons we have seen, and which remain to be summarized, particularly in relation to Earth.

V. Hope for Earth?

There are some wonderful, uplifting passages in the book of Ezekiel, and the possibility of new life expressed in 37:1–12 is without parallel. McFague calls it "one of scripture's most haunting and lovely resurrection texts."[59] She observes that this "second creation story" requires two helpers, a human being and nature—Ezekiel, as the mediator of God's word, and the "four winds" supplying the breath.

> The power of life can override the reality of death with the help of God's partners, human beings and nature itself. The passage says that with God all things are possible, even the reconstitution of dry bones.[60]

It may seem hypercritical to question such a positive evaluation, but the vision remains an anthropocentric one, and the hope it inspires, like the descriptions of the land restored in chs. 34 and 36, was primarily for the benefit of the exile community. If we assume it also applies to us, we may celebrate the encouragement such imagery offers, but whoever does so should recognize the associated dissonant features—the concomitant forgiveness and self-loathing that inhere in it according to the Ezekiel corpus.

Moreover, the hope is so focused on the divine initiative that it obscures the issue of human responsibility for Earth and the environment. The book of Ezekiel makes it very clear that prior to the sack of Jerusalem in 587 B.C.E., Earth was treated by God according to the behavior of its human inhabitants. As Galambush so appropriately puts it, Ezekiel "allows the land to serve as the 'site of injury' in the conflict between YHWH and his people."[61] The restoration of the exiles would be accompanied by the restoration of their land to its pristine, Edenic state. But it remains to be shown whether the community of the new heart and spirit (Ezek 11:19; 36:26–27)—however one identifies that community—is better at solving the

---

59. Sallie McFague, "An Ecological Christology: Does Christianity Have It?" in *Christianity and Ecology: Seeking the Well-Being of Earth and Humans* (ed. D. T. Hessel and R. R. Ruether; Cambridge: Harvard University Center for the Study of World Religions, 2000), 42.
60. Ibid., 43.
61. "Castles in the Air," 162.

problems of pollution, exploitative land management, and their associated environmental problems than those who are not part of that community.[62]

Critique of Ezekiel's imagery of hope is not simply a modern phenomenon. Other biblical Scriptures appropriate Ezekiel critically. Drawing on the work of Dieter Georgi, Rossing notes the continuity, but also the discontinuity between the imagery of Ezekiel and the New Testament book of Revelation.[63] Significant changes are made by the author of Revelation to several limiting and excluding concepts in the prophecy. Thus, while the tour and measuring of the new Jerusalem in Rev 21:9–27 are modeled on Ezek 40–48,

> [O]ne of the most striking modifications is the statement that the city has "no temple" (Rev 21:22). God's presence is not confined to a temple, but now extends to the entire creation. Revelation further universalizes and "democratizes" Ezekiel's elite priestly vision by extending priestly status to all God's people (Rev 1:6; 5:10; 20:6). New Jerusalem is a welcoming city, not a gated community. Whereas Ezekiel's gate was shut so that "no one shall enter by it" into the temple or its courtyards (Ezek 44:1–2), the twelve gates into New Jerusalem are perpetually open.... Even foreigners... are invited to enter.[64]

Ezekiel's vision is also broadened with respect to the water that flows from the new temple to provide food and healing for the restored community (Ezek 47:1–12). In Rev 22:1–2, the water that issues from the throne of God and of the Lamb is specifically termed "the river of the water of life," and the leaves of the tree (or trees) of life[65] that it nourishes are "for the healing of the nations"!

---

62. In 1967, Lynn White Jr. asserted that the Judeo-Christian traditions—on the basis of the instruction to the humans to "fill and subdue" the earth (Gen 1:28)—provided the moral, cultural, and spiritual foundation for the development of aggressive and environmentally harmful technologies. The assertion provoked a major debate. A concise summary of the main lines of response to White can be found in Stephen B. Scharper, "The Ecological Crisis," in *The Twentieth Century: A Theological Overview* (ed. G. Baum; Maryknoll, N.Y.: Orbis, 1999), 221–24.

63. Particularly influential is Georgi's argument that Revelation "democratizes" Ezekiel, in "Die Visionen vom himmlischen Jerusalem in Apk 21 und 22," in *Kirche: Festscrift für Günther Bornkamm zum 75 Geburstag* (ed. D. Lührmann and G. Strecker; Tübingen: Mohr Siebeck, 1980), 351–72. See Barbara R. Rossing, "River of Life in God's New Jerusalem: An Eschatological Vision for Earth's Future," in Hessel and Ruether, *Christianity and Ecology*, 223 n. 32.

64. Rossing, "River of Life," 217. While the new Jerusalem in the Book of Revelation compares favourably with Ezekiel's new temple in terms of accessibility regardless of ethnicity and priestly status, Revelation excludes from the city—and condemns to fearful punishment—those whose behavior is deemed unholy (Rev 21:8, 27; 22:11, 15).

65. Cf. "the tree of life" in Gen 2:9; 3:24. ξύλον ("tree") can be understood in both a singular and a collective sense in Rev 22:2.

VI. An Instrumental View of Nature

The most limiting and dangerous aspect of the book of Ezekiel is the portrayal of God as offended, vengeful, alienated from the people with whom He (sic) has chosen to be most intimate, and consumed by a narcissistic obsession with the honor of His name. The extent to which this portrayal is due to the prophet's personal experiences and self-perception is unlikely ever to be agreed on,[66] but the portrayal firmly establishes as God's will for the restored community a perpetual heritage of shame and self-loathing. That thwarts the emergence of wholehearted gratitude and trust, and represents an ongoing danger for anyone who might look to the prophecy for a model of contemporary relationships between God and people.[67]

Parsons notes that Ezekiel is an important source of the belief common among Christian fundamentalist communities that violent death and destruction is in some sense willed by God. He comments: "Any condoning of the destruction of whole masses of people, innocent and guilty [cf. Ezek 21:8 (Eng. 21:3)], even if that destruction apparently makes God's purposes possible, is a strange sentiment for a follower of Christ."[68] Moreover, Lieb illustrates the impact Ezekiel's "end-time thinking" can have on political discourse and policy at the highest levels of government, even to the point of inspiring plans for nuclear confrontation.[69]

As if that was not enough to alert us to the potential hazards of reading Ezekiel, the prophet's portrayal of God "dominat(ing) the natural world to try to win back the cherished but wayward Israelites"[70] has inherent dangers for the whole creation. Rasmussen describes the implications of such an instrumental view of nature in borrowed words:

> If you put God outside and set him vis-à-vis his creation and if you have the idea

---

66. As Robert P. Carroll wrote in relation to Jeremiah: "We cannot get back behind the text to an imagined original (prophet) . . . ; the prophet is lost to the scribe" ("Something Rich and Strange: Imagining a Future for Jeremiah Studies," in *Troubling Jeremiah* [ed. A. R. P. Diamond, K. M. O'Connor, and L. Stulman; JSOTSup 260; Sheffield: Sheffield Academic Press, 1999], 432).

67. The studies of the child psychiatrist D. W. Winnicott have shown the importance of trust for the development of healthy, responsive relationships. See Mark Patrick Hederman, *Kissing the Dark: Connecting with the Unconscious* (Dublin: Veritas, 1999), 61. Donald Capps refers to Jesus of Nazareth's encounters with "sinners" for examples of trust, which Capps argues is an essential element in the healing of narcissism and the cycle of shame associated with it. See his *Depleted Self: Sin in a Narcissistic Age* (Minneapolis: Fortress, 1993), 162–67.

68. Stephen Parsons, *Ungodly Fear: Fundamentalist Christianity and the Abuse of Power* (Oxford: Lion, 2000), 191–92.

69. Michael Lieb, *Children of Ezekiel: Aliens, UFOs, the Crisis of Race, and the Advent of End-Time* (Durham, N.C., and London: Duke University Press, 1998), 100–125. See his example on p. 108, "In him [President Ronald Reagan] the visions and oracles that distinguish the prophecy of Ezekiel flourished anew."

70. Dempsey, quoted above in relation to Amos (see n. 10).

that you are created in his image, you will logically and naturally see yourself as outside and against the things around you. And as you arrogate all mind to yourself, you will see the world around you as mindless and therefore not entitled to moral and ethical consideration. The environment will seem to be yours to exploit.

The words are those of the anthropologist Gregory Bateson,[71] but numerous theologians echo them.

In contrast to objectifying God over against creation, Wallace writes of God as "a thoroughgoing incarnational reality," indwelling all things and sustaining the biosphere.[72] O'Murchu says we must acknowledge that Earth and the surrounding cosmos are alive, and lists a range of scholars who regard consciousness as a property of creation at large and not just an aspect of human life.[73] Page proposes the concept of "pansyntheism," God's presence *with* creation in all its suffering and joy, not as an observer from some distant heaven.[74] Haught writes of God as "the Absolute Future," an indeterminate and inexhaustibly resourceful but never static future, finding expression in humility and self-giving love.[75]

VII. Conclusion

Although the criticisms that have been made of the prophecy would doubtless be rejected as totally unjustified hubris by Ezekiel and by those who preserved his work, they need to be made as a response both to dissonance within the book as well as to concepts that are discordant with other parts of the scriptural canon and contemporary knowledge of the environment. What Davies says of Isaiah may also be said of Ezekiel:

> We cannot know how precisely Isaiah's recreated creator corresponds to *any* idea of God prevalent in ancient Israel at the time when the book of Isaiah was composed.... To presume a link between Isaiah's YHWH and the God of Judaism and Christianity is acceptable—and perhaps inevitable, if undeniably problematic—theologically.... [But] as a literary creation rather than the deity as such, arguably

---

71. Gregory Bateson, *Steps to an Ecology of Mind* (New York: Random House, 1972), 472, quoted by Larry L. Rasmussen, *Earth Community Earth Ethics* (Maryknoll, N.Y.: Orbis, 1996), 181.

72. Mark I. Wallace, "The Wounded Spirit as the Basis for Hope in an Age of Radical Ecology," in Hessel and Ruether, *Christianity and Ecology,* 60.

73. Diarmuid O'Murchu, *Evolutionary Faith: Rediscovering God in Our Great Story* (Maryknoll, N.Y.: Orbis, 2002), 15, 173.

74. Ruth Page, *God and the Web of Creation* (London: SCM, 1996), 44, with reference to Jürgen Moltmann's conception of *God in Creation.* Page's concept of God's omnipresence "in no way denies the infinite transcendence of God, nor the existence of the divine independently of all limited thought or experience" (ibid).

75. John F. Haught, *God after Darwin: A Theology of Evolution* (Boulder, Colo.: Westview, 2000), 144. I am also relying on notes from a lecture delivered in Auckland, New Zealand, June 23, 2001.

YHWH should not be given the preferential treatment we would accord a real deity.[76]

Every portrayal of God is partial, of course,[77] and Ezekiel should not be blamed for the instrumental view of nature that he held. But nor should his portrayal of God, or of God's relationship to Earth, be assumed determinative.

Ezekiel did not have the privilege of seeing this frail but vivacious planet as we of this generation have:

> Viewed from the distance of the moon, the astonishing thing about the earth, catching the breath, is that it is alive. The photographs show the dry, pounded surface of the moon in the foreground, dead as an old bone. Aloft, floating free beneath the moist, gleaming membrane of bright blue sky, is the rising earth, the only exuberant thing in this part of the cosmos.[78]

Nor was he aware of the incredibly complex character of natural hierarchies, whether in whole or in part—of "elements born in supernovas,"[79] of the "two hundred and twenty-eight separate and distinct muscles in the head of an ordinary caterpillar"[80]—which science has discerned in relatively recent times. Also, he does not appear to have been aware that God would find ways of dealing with human disobedience other than making Earth the "site of injury."

Because of its place in the canon, the prophecies of Ezekiel have—understandably—had greater impact than the caveats of their critics. And the prophet has the right to be heard. But:

> It may be that in the next millennium religious convictions will be awakened and established within the young primarily by such meaningful encounters with the mysteries of the universe, and only secondarily by the study of sacred scriptures.

---

76. Davies, *Double Standards in Isaiah*, 11; see also 120 n. 1. A similar distinction is made by John J. Collins: "If we regard biblical texts as fictions, or proposals whose truth or adequacy remains to be assessed, we must admit the possibility of a distinction between God the character in a biblical story and 'the living god' or the power that moves the universe" ("Is a Critical Biblical Theology Possible?" in *The Hebrew Bible and Its Interpreters* [ed. W. H. Propp, B. Halpern, and D. N. Freedman; Winona Lake, Ind.: Eisenbrauns, 1990], 13).

77. Walter Brueggemann made this point in his response to the original form of this paper at the annual meeting of the Society of Biblical Literature, Denver, November 2001.

78. Lewis Thomas, *The Lives of a Cell: Notes of a Biology Watcher* (New York: Bantam, 1974), quoted in Jason Gardner, ed., *The Sacred Earth: Writers on Nature and Spirit* (Novato, Calif.: New World Library, 1998), 44.

79. Thomas Berry, *The Dream of the Earth* (San Francisco: Sierra Club Books, 1988), 216.

80. Annie Dillard, *Pilgrim at Tinker Creek* (New York: Harper & Row, 1974), quoted in Gardner, *Sacred Earth*, 50.

The task of education then will focus on learning how to "read" the universe so that one might enter and inhabit the universe as a communion event.[81]

So, Ezekiel should not have the last word. That should go instead to the one who is largely silent in the book of Ezekiel, but whose plight and promise we must "read" and voice.[82] For acknowledgment of Earth's vital role within the natural hierarchy of living ecosystems[83] is essential if the bread of compassion and justice is to be the source of robust hope and daily nourishment (Matt 6:11 // Luke 11:3) for every part of God's creation.

---

81. Brian Swimme, *The Hidden Heart of the Cosmos: Humanity and the New Story* (Maryknoll, N.Y.: Orbis, 1996), 101.
82. Berry observes: "Presently we are returning to the primordial community of the universe, the earth, and all living beings. Each has its own voice" (*Dream of the Earth*, 5). And see the discussion of the "Principle of Voice" in Habel, *Readings from the Perspective of Earth*, 46–48.
83. Again, see Peacocke, *Theology for a Scientific Age*, 38.

A RESPONSE OF EARTH TO EZEKIEL'S WORDS OF TENTATIVE HOPE:

> Oh, no! They're coming back.
>   Fresh stripes they'll inflict in their division of me.
> I'll still blossom or suffer desolation according to their deeds.
>   All they do affects me.
>
> And for all the promises, all the fine hopes,
>   soon, again they will be fighting,
> excluding others of my children—
> sisters and brothers to them though unrecognized,
> fighting wars they have fought many times over,
>   using more fire-power in a day
>   than Joshua in a lifetime.
> Is this really what God intends by their restoration to a "tilled" land?
>
> 'Til they can see their neighbours as themselves,
>   'til they can allow trust to resolve shame,
> they will never have the future they long for,
>   nor I the care that will make me a true Eden,
>   symbol of enduring hope for all the Earth—
> of which it will be truly said,
>   "The LORD is There."[84]

---

84. Ezek 48:35; trust Earth to embrace even the words of her antagonists!

The Silence of the Lands: The Ecojustice Implications of Ezekiel's Judgment Oracles

Norman Habel

I. Introduction

My aim in this essay is to illustrate how the hermeneutic espoused by the Earth Bible project helps us gain a fresh understanding of Ezekiel's fundamental orientation to Earth as God's creation and more particularly to the "lands" of Earth which are threatened with desolation within the judgment oracles.

The six basic ecojustice principles that inform the Earth Bible approach are outlined in the initial volume of the series, *Readings from the Perspective of Earth*.[1] At the risk of oversimplifying this approach, let me emphasize a number of considerations that are significant in tackling a complex literary work such as the book of Ezekiel.

The first relates to the assumed posture of the reader. In the Earth Bible project, we seek to read from the perspective of Earth. We are not simply exploring Earth as a theme or topos, an object of detached scholarly investigation, another odd image in Ezekiel's gallery of the bizarre. As Earth beings we are concerned about our Earth and how Ezekiel, a fellow Earth being, treats Earth.

We also seek to see things as Earth would view them: is Earth honored, ignored, treated unjustly, or viewed in some other way? Admittedly, such a reading remains an approximation. We would argue, however, that this reading remains a necessary—if precarious—task in the current ecological context. The critical state of the planet is an existential condition that affects all of us. We are, moreover, an integral part of Earth. When we seek to detach ourselves from Earth as the space and substance of our being, we establish a false dualism that tends to view reality from a

---

1. Norman C. Habel, ed., *Readings from the Perspective of Earth* (Earth Bible 1; Sheffield: Sheffield Academic Press; Cleveland: Pilgrim, 2000), 24, 42–53. In the Earth Bible, "Earth" is defined as "that living system *within* which we humans live in a relationship of interdependence with other members of the Earth community" (ibid., 27). By the term "Earth community" the contributors mean to convey that "[e]very species and every member of every species are connected to others by complex webs of interrelationships. . . . Humans are an integral part" (ibid., 44).

strictly anthropocentric perspective and to silence Earth as an active participant in the interpreting process.

Our application of ecojustice principles to any given text involves a basic hermeneutic of suspicion and retrieval. Because biblical texts have been written by historical human beings, there is every likelihood that they will be biased in favor of human interests at the expense of Earth's interests. Similarly, because most influential interpreters of the biblical text—until recent times—have been imbedded in a Western culture intent on human progress at the expense of the environment, such readings of the text are also likely to ignore rather than honor Earth as a participant in the interpreting process.

We also recognize that, precisely because of the anthropocentric bias of most past interpreters, there may well be texts in Ezekiel in which Earth is not dismissed or silenced within the text itself, but which these interpreters have overlooked. The retrieval of these texts is an exciting and significant part of the Earth Bible project. We are, however, wary of theological "cherry picking," selecting a collection of these texts and subsequently declaring that the Bible is "eco-friendly." Our task is to identify where Earth has experienced justice or injustice, whether at the hands of writers or readers, and where Earth is a subject within the text, whether honored or suppressed.

In any given reading of a text, we focus on those ecojustice principles that tend to be pertinent rather than discuss how all six of the principles may apply to the text. In this analysis of Ezekiel, I shall consider especially the principle of intrinsic worth, which states that *the universe, Earth, and all its components have intrinsic worth/value,* and the principle of voice, which states that *Earth is a subject capable of raising its voice in celebration and against injustice.*[2]

It is important to acknowledge from the outset that these are ecological principles developed in dialogue with ecologists. They are not cryptic theological principles designed to uncover an ecotheology latent in the biblical text. So, from the outset, the fact that a given text may appear to be theocentric rather than anthropocentric does not necessarily imply it is ecofriendly. In a given text, Earth may experience injustice at the hands of God just as readily as at the hands of humans.

II. Ezekiel's Cosmos

How does Ezekiel construct the world? What parts of his cosmos are valued or devalued in that construct? Is there a hierarchy of values in Ezekiel's cosmos? What roles do Earth and members of the Earth community play?

Ezekiel preserves no creation narrative similar to Gen 1 and no portrait of creation's designs as in Job 38–39. As David Petersen demonstrated in an earlier paper, "We have found no evidence that Ezekiel has used biblical creation traditions in his

---

2. Habel, *Readings from the Perspective of Earth,* 24, 42–44, 46–48.

rhetoric."[3] This absence of explicit creation traditions may suggest that Ezekiel is less interested in the events of a creation narrative than in the events of history, whether recent or past. Does this lack of focus on creation events imply, however, that Ezekiel has a negative attitude toward the natural world? Not necessarily. One possible way of discerning Ezekiel's attitude to creation/nature is to identify where its components are located in the construct of his world.

A. THE CITY

A key image in Ezekiel's cosmology is revealed when God announces to the prophet that "this is Jerusalem; I have set her in the center of the nations, with lands all around her" (5:5).[4] Jerusalem is the center of Ezekiel's world because YHWH has chosen this city to be the locus of the divine presence, the mountain sanctuary where the כבוד יהוה ("glory of YHWH") dwells (cf. 20:40–44; 40:2; 43:4–7). In anticipation of the *omphalos* image of Jewish midrash, Jerusalem is tantamount to the "navel of the earth."[5]

Ezekiel records no cosmogony in which Earth emerges pristine and latent with potential from the deep primal waters, as appears in Gen 1. Nor is there any suggestion of primordial rejoicing with wisdom, any celebration of the celestial host, or any divine play with creatures of the deep. Instead we are confronted with what might be designated an urban cosmogony—one centered on the city—whose rhetoric tends to subvert the very symbolism of a classic creation cosmogony (Ezek 16).

The location for the birth of the sacred center is in the land of the Canaanites, hardly an auspicious place of origin. The parents are portrayed as possessing much less than pure primal stock. The child is unwanted and abandoned in an open field, a bloody and miserable sight. Yet YHWH loves this rejected orphan, enters into a covenant with her, and transforms her into a beautiful city, adorned with magnificent finery. She becomes a wealthy queen, the rumor of whose beauty spreads to all the surrounding nations.

With a city at the center of his cosmos, Ezekiel seems to be essentially an urbanite. He apparently has a *polis* perspective on the world, an urban orientation that influences the way he views land, including the lands that surround his sacred city center. His perspective, then, is quite distinct from the rural orientation of texts like Lev 25–26 in which YHWH quite explicitly says, "The land is mine," rather than,

---

3. David L. Petersen, "Creation in Ezekiel: Methodological Perspectives and Theological Prospects," *SBL Seminar Papers, 1999* (SBLSP 38; Atlanta: Society of Biblical Literature, 1999), 500; a new version of the essay appears in this volume.

4. Biblical translations are the author's own, often close to the NRSV.

5. See S. David Sperling, "Navel of the Earth," *IDBSup* 621–23. Philip S. Alexander sees no explicit "navel" language in the Bible, although it appears in other ancient Jewish literature, such as *Jubilees* and *1 Enoch*. See his "Jerusalem as the *Omphalos* of the World: On the History of a Geographical Concept," in *Jerusalem: Its Sanctity and Centrality to Judaism, Christianity, and Islam* (ed. L. Levine; New York: Continuum, 1999), 104–19. Note that at Ezek 38:12 the LXX and Vulg. actually have the term "navel."

"The city is mine." In this Leviticus passage, the writer is concerned about the long-term welfare of the ancient land holdings. The locus of Yhwh's presence is not primarily in the city, but in the countryside where Yhwh "walks" (Lev 26:12) as Yhwh once walked through the garden of Eden.[6]

For Ezekiel, the urbanite, Jerusalem is the center, the locus of Yhwh's presence and the focus of his cosmological construct. The כבוד יהוה may reside temporarily among the exiles, but it belongs in the temple and must ultimately return there. The transformed cosmos in the final chapters of the book also has a holy district as the source and center. A stream flows from the threshold of the temple and creates a romantic landscape with unnatural patterns—including trees that produce fruit every month (47:1–12). This idealized cosmos, it seems to me (as a former youth from the country), suits the lifestyle of a city dweller. Ezekiel's valued world apparently begins and ends with the city.

B. Land and Lands

In Ezekiel's cosmos, the city of Jerusalem is located in the land of Israel, which is surrounded by other lands. The image appears to be one of a city located within one land (the land of Israel) that, in turn, is encircled by many other lands. How does Ezekiel view these lands?

The land of Israel is not just another land, but the "most glorious (צבי) of all lands," the promised land, the land in which God and God's people dwell (20:6). This land is also differentiated from other lands by the frequent use of the designation אדמה ("ground, tilled land," e.g., 7:2) rather than ארץ, which is the standard term for land in Ezekiel. The "land of Israel," it seems, is supposed to be the ideal settled and cultivated land (אדמה) under the supervision of the sacred city center. The אדמת ישראל is "the land belonging to Israel," the "homeland" of God's people as distinct from any other "land" (ארץ) surrounding Israel.[7]

At several points in the text of Ezekiel the term "land" (ארץ) is paired with "nations" (גוים; 5:5–6; 20:32; 22:4). This pairing suggests an overlap in semantic content between peoples and places when this term is employed. Elsewhere "land" (ארץ) is paired with "city" (עיר) and suggests a similar overlap in meaning between *polis* and place (7:23; 12:20). Land and lands are not simply geographical locations that bear a given name, but settled environments that are structured and ordered by human beings.

These findings are consistent with those of Julie Galambush; she points to the pairing of wasteland and ruined town, both of which are restored in the transformed cosmos. Galambush claims—quite correctly I believe—that in these contexts "land"

---

6. Norman C. Habel, *The Land Is Mine: Six Biblical Land Ideologies* (OBT; Minneapolis: Fortress, 1995), 97–114.

7. Julie Galambush, "Castles in the Air: Creation as Property in Ezekiel," *SBL Seminar Papers, 1999* (SBLSP 38; Atlanta: Society of Biblical Literature, 1999), 159; a new version of the essay appears in this volume.

is "coterminous with sown and settled land. This privileging of the settled over the wild is emphasised to the point that the land is 'promised' not only fertility but also urban development!"[8]

C. Beyond the Lands

Beyond the wider circle of settled lands, Ezekiel refers to a range of places and forces that may be designated the untamed or wild domains of the cosmos. Galambush refers to these domains as chaos, a realm of forces hostile to ordered human habitation.[9] A significant designation of part of this outer domain is the מדבר, often rendered "wilderness" (19:13; 29:5). This wilderness is beyond the peoples and surrounding lands where Israel may be scattered in exile, and is pictured as a dry domain (19:13).

The wilderness is apparently the haunt of wild animals; only when Yhwh banishes these wild animals from this dry domain is it considered safe for humans to inhabit (34:25). As Galambush has demonstrated, wild animals (חיות), as distinct from domestic livestock (בהמה), are associated with a territory that threatens the settled realm. They are a hostile force, like pestilence, famine, and fire, sent as agents of divine wrath (5:16–17; 14:21). Yhwh uses these wild animals to ravage a land and thereby render it totally desolate so that "no one may pass through it because of these animals" (14:15). Animals that properly belong to the domain of the wild, outside settled lands, are sent in by Yhwh to reverse the social order of the cosmos.

The depth of negative feeling associated with the wild animals is evident in Ezekiel's portrait of the great banquet of human flesh on the mountains of Israel (39:17–20). Here the wild animals are invited to join the birds to eat the flesh of the mighty and to drink the blood of the princes of Earth. At this ghoulish gathering, the wild animals are the epitome of the uncivilised world, "agents whose diametrical opposition to the realm of purity and order qualifies them to partake of the unclean sacrifice."[10]

That Ezekiel's negative classification of the world of the wild is not necessarily the accepted cultural perspective of other segments of Israelite society is apparent from the descriptions of the wild kingdom in Job 39. The domains of creatures such as the hawk, the lion, the mountain goat, and the wild ox reflect patterns of wisdom that exhibit a mysterious design, an alternative ordering of the cosmos that humans have yet to comprehend. For Ezekiel, however, the world of the wild is a terrifying untamed domain beyond the control of humans but accessible to Yhwh as a source for agents of destruction.

Other realms of destruction, beyond the ordered lands of the nations, include the great waters of the "deep" (תהום) and the "pit" (שחת [28:8] or בור [32:25])

---

8. Ibid., 162.
9. Ibid., 149.
10. Ibid., 151.

in the realms below (26:19; 28:8; 31:15; 32:25). These destructive depths of the underworld represent a watery counterpart to the barren wilderness that lies beyond the settled lands of the civilized world. Beyond the "lands" lie the desert and the deep, the untamed and untameable world of the wild.

III. Relative Worth

What is Ezekiel's attitude to the various components of his cosmos? Does he value the natural world as originally created by God? If I as a reader dare to identify with Earth as distinct from the human settlements on Earth, do I feel affirmed and honored, or negated and devalued?

Clearly, the center of Ezekiel's cosmos has supreme worth because it is the chosen locus of God's sanctuary, the abode of the כבוד יהוה. Even Jerusalem as such, however, has no intrinsic worth (16:2–5), but is endowed with value by virtue of the special transformation effected by Yhwh, the loving "husband." The mountain at the center of the cosmos is not valued as a cosmic mountain or a primordial peak, a primal *umbilicus terrae*; the mountain only becomes holy because Yhwh has chosen this site as the sacred center.

Similarly, the "land of Israel," as the settled land in which this mountain is located, has no value as part of Earth. "Lands," as ordered human habitations, can actually disappear and cease to exist (25:7).

In several key passages, "land" seems to be divided into at least two components: the life and the landscape. In the act of desolating a given land, all livestock are removed along with all humans (32:13, 15). More specifically, what is removed from the landscape is its "fullness" (מלא), which presumably refers to all forms of life (12:19; 30:12; 32:15). Some translations refer to the "contents" of the land and others render the term "inhabitants." These renderings, however, do not preserve the full force of the term as an expression for the life force of the land. Without the "fullness" the land is dead; it is *terra nullius*, totally devalued.

In the famous vision of Isaiah, the seraphim make their famous cry:

> Holy, holy, holy is the Lord of hosts,
> His glory is the fullness of all Earth
> (מלא כל־הארץ כבודו; Isa 6:3).

For Isaiah in this text, the כבוד is not a mobile presence in Jerusalem, but the very "fullness" of the land/Earth. The fullness of land/Earth in Isaiah is more than a life force; it is the divine life/presence. For Ezekiel, removing the fullness of the land may not have the significance of removing the כבוד, but neither can it be reduced to something as neutral as "contents." The fullness of the land, I suggest, is the very life of the land, especially ordered life in Ezekiel's terms.[11] In a later passage

---

11. For a similar use of the term, see, e.g., Ps 24:1.

(37:1–14), the image of a valley filled with dry bones and graves seems to reflect the reality of this lifeless landscape.

Ezekiel's message of judgment against the land is so absolute that it seems not only to proclaim doom and destruction for the peoples of a given land, including Israel, but also to devalue both the land and life on the land by reducing all to desolation. When reading from the perspective of Earth, both land and life seem to be cheap in Ezekiel; Earth has no obvious intrinsic worth as a structural component in the hierarchy of Ezekiel's cosmos.

IV. Patterns of Injustice against Nature

In the second part of this analysis, I will focus on the principle of voice as a hermeneutical guide for an Earth reading of the text. This principle recognizes that Earth and the Earth community are subjects in the narrative, subjects with a right to justice and a right to be heard.[12]

Most of us, having been conditioned by a Western education, whether in school or society, view Earth and nature as objects to be appropriated for human benefit or data to be analyzed with scientific detachment. Aside from the presence of a handful of *Gaia* advocates, green poets, and ecoliturgists, most of us are surrounded by a Western educational context in which Earth is an object, not a subject. To speak of Earth as a subject, of course, does not mean Earth is a human subject but a living subject in its own right, a nonhuman "thou," a distinctive component of the cosmos.[13]

If we grant, in accordance with this principle, that Earth—or more specifically the lands of Earth—has a right to justice, we are faced with the obvious question: do these subjects suffer injustice at the hands of other characters in the text or at the hands of the writer of Ezekiel? In my opinion, the answer is an unequivocal yes.

A. Burning the Forest

One passage that offers a clear example of this injustice is the destruction of the forest of the fields (יער השדה) in the Negev (21:1–5 [Eng. 20:45–49]). Ezekiel claims to have been commissioned by God to "preach against the south and prophesy against the forest land in the Negev" (21:2 [Eng. 20:46]). Ezekiel addresses the forest as a living subject and announces:

> Behold I am kindling a fire in you,
> and it shall consume every green tree in you and every dry tree;

---

12. A discussion of voice as more than metaphor in such contexts can be found in The Earth Bible Team, "The Voice of Earth: More Than Metaphor?" in *The Earth Story in the Psalms and the Prophets* (ed. Norman C. Habel; Earth Bible 4; Sheffield: Sheffield Academic Press; Cleveland: Pilgrim, 2001), 23–28.

13. The Earth Bible Team understands Earth as "a subject, a non-human 'thou,' an 'other' who is part of the biblical tradition . . . a subject capable of self-expression . . . a living subject" (ibid., 24).

the blazing flame shall not be extinguished,
and every face from south to north will be scorched by it.
And all flesh shall see that I, YHWH, have kindled it;
it shall not be extinguished. (21:3b–4 [Eng. 20:47b–48])

Many interpreters have pointed out that the Negev of Israel has no forest as such, but only rather modest scrub.[14] They tend to see this passage as a variation on the subsequent oracle against Jerusalem and the sanctuaries of Israel (21:6–13 [Eng. 21:1–7]), so that the fire burns Judah and Jerusalem, which are "south" from the vantage point of those in Babylon. But why the forest should be a metaphor for Jerusalem remains unclear, and no such connection is made in the text. When the wood metaphor is used of Jerusalem in 15:6–8, the inhabitants are vines not forest trees. While the south may refer to more than the Negev as such, the forest is specifically the forest or trees, that is, the living vegetation of the field.

Who sees this great fire? It is not the peoples in the lands nearby, but "all flesh" (כל בשׂר), all living creatures. All life-forms of the north and the south watch this destruction of natural habitat by God. This burning is not a natural process, a fire ignited by a lightning strike or some such phenomenon. This fire is so total, so overwhelming, that all living creatures will know that YHWH has destroyed their homes (21:4 [Eng. 20:48]).

From the perspective of the Earth community we may ask, what has the forest done to deserve this disaster? Why should the trees, the habitat for creatures of the field, suffer such a fire at God's hands? The trees have not sinned and yet they have experienced the wrath of God. No crime, human or nonhuman, is cited as the justification for this destructive deed of YHWH. The only reason given is that all flesh will see that YHWH has caused the disaster. There appears to be no justice for the trees or life of the field. Even if one seeks to interpret this oracle as a symbolic reference to Jerusalem, the destruction of harmless trees and the suffering of innocent life remain an ugly image of injustice, and Earth is portrayed as suffering without cause.

B. CLEARING THE MOUNTAINS

The same innocent suffering happens—I would argue—in many other contexts. The lands or some parts of the land suffer unjustly because of YHWH's judgment on the peoples of the land. Ezekiel's oracles against the mountains of Israel illustrate a similar pattern of injustice (6:1–14). Ezekiel announces doom on the mountains and valleys because they are the locations where Israelites have erected idols, altars, and high places unacceptable to God. The mountains presumably stand for the people—metonymy. But why should the mountains and valleys as such be

---

14. See, for example, Walther Eichrodt, *Ezekiel: A Commentary* (trans. C. Quin; OTL; Philadelphia, Fortress, 1970), 287, and Walther Zimmerli, *Ezekiel: A Commentary on the Book of the Prophet Ezekiel* (2 vols.; Hermeneia; Philadelphia: Fortress, 1979), 1:423.

destroyed? It could perhaps be argued that the oracle only affects the people polluting the mountains. In the end, however, the whole land is made desolate, cleared of all life, regardless of whether all components of the land deserve God's judgment. The injustice suffered by the mountains is more than metonymy.

Kalinda Rose Stevenson has paid close attention to the oracles against the mountains, and claims:

> As metonymy, "the mountains" refer to the people who live in Edom and Israel, substituting the mountains for the people, the container for the contained. As synecdoche, "the mountains" stand for the whole land, a figure of speech that substitutes a part for the whole. In the complicated figurative language of Ezekiel, "the mountains" are both a metonymy for the people and a synecdoche for the whole land. This figurative language itself obscures Earth. From our anthropocentric bias, we cannot see the mountains for the metonymy.[15]

In this article, she re-creates a court trial in which Earth appears as a prosecutor charging Yhwh with crimes against the mountains.

> Through synecdoche, you have made the mountains stand as the representatives for my hills, my ravines, my valleys and my watercourses. What you have done to the mountains, you have done to the whole Earth. We charge you with assault and battery, transference of guilt, and discrimination. As evidence for these crimes, we submit your own words as quoted by your prophet, Ezekiel.[16]

What happens to the mountains, in the context of Ezekiel's cosmology, happens to the rest of Earth. The mountains are part of the settled lands, and, thus, the removal of human activities means the clearing of life from the mountains, even though the mountains are themselves innocent of any wrongdoing.

C. Defending the Divine Ego

God's defense for these injustices against creation, according to Ezekiel, is summarized in the formula: "Then they/you shall know that I am Yhwh." Ezekiel uses this formula more than fifty times in a wide range of contexts. No matter what violence is imposed upon humans, lands, or other parts of Earth, it is justified by appeal to this formula. Some commentators have maintained a detachment from the negative force of this formula by designating it an "acknowledgment formula" or a "recognition formula."[17]

In the oracle cited above announcing the burning of the forest, the only reason given for the fire is that creatures may see that Yhwh has caused the disaster. Why

---

15. Kalinda Rose Stevenson, "If Earth Could Speak: The Case of the Mountains against YHWH in Ezekiel 6:35–36," in Habel, *Earth Story in the Psalms and the Prophets*, 160.
16. Ibid., 161.
17. See Eichrodt, *Ezekiel*, 15, and Zimmerli, *Ezekiel*, 1:37–38.

is a fire needed to vindicate Yhwh's name? Why should the forest suffer so that, according to Ezekiel, Yhwh's obsession with the divine name can be satisfied? In a similar passage (15:6–8), in which fire is threatened against Jerusalem, the primary rationale for the destruction is so that "you will know that I am Yhwh." Removing the sin or sinners of Jerusalem does not seem to carry the same weight as the need for Yhwh to vindicate the divine name. Compassion for human beings, lands, or Earth plays no role.

A closer analysis of the formula in question reveals that Ezekiel is not only obsessed with the name of Yhwh, but also with making known the reality of Yhwh. Ezekiel seems to portray Yhwh as a deity with an ego problem, an incessant need to have the divine name and identity displayed as the banner associated with every violent deed. This formula could perhaps be more appropriately designated as a divine ego formula.

Most judgment passages do not focus on the need for the Israelites to change their heart and repent, on the anguish of God over the sins of the people, or on the past compassion of their God. The focus, rather, is on acts of violence and destruction that will create such a total devastation that credit can accrue only to Yhwh, who alone will be named as the perpetrator.

The use of the divine ego formula in the oracle against the mountains (6:1–14) illustrates the prophet's obsession with publicizing the divine name/identity in the context of violence. In the aftermath of destruction, amid the slain, the name/identity is known (v. 7). When the slain lie among their idols, the name/identity is known (v. 13). All of this disaster is not in vain, because the name/identity is known (v. 10). When the land is totally desolate and devoid of settlements, the name/identity is known (v. 14). Any hint of justice for Earth or the community of Earth seems to be suppressed in order to promote Yhwh's identity and satisfy divine jealousy for the name. In Ezekiel's hierarchy of values, Yhwh's name must be accorded supreme worth at all costs.

V. Blaming the Victim

Julie Galambush has demonstrated that Ezekiel treats creation as property.[18] It has no intrinsic value and can be burned, battered, or broken at will by acts of violent judgment. The Earth or the Earth community suffers unjustly as Yhwh makes the landscape desolate. Reading from the perspective of Earth, I would like to draw out one of her conclusions. She writes:

> As Habel has demonstrated, the images of Leviticus and Jeremiah reflect ideologies in which the land is understood to have rights that are defended by YHWH. The innocent land demands or receives restitution because of injury inflicted by its

---

18. Galambush, "Castles in the Air."

inhabitants. In Ezekiel the tables are turned. The land is not a victim, but party to its inhabitants' actions; it is guilty and therefore suffers for its own actions at YHWH's hands.[19]

I agree that in Ezekiel we do not find Yhwh, the prophet, or any other party empathizing with the land or defending the land, qua land. The lands have no allies, anyone to give them voice. That fact in itself turns the lands into victims. For the lands to be accused of sins that the people of the lands have committed is a typical case of blaming the victim.

In Ezekiel, God proclaims: "When a land sins against me by acting faithlessly, and I stretch out my hand against it, and break its staff of bread and send famine against it, and cut off from it human beings and animals, even if Noah, Daniel, and Job, these three, were in it, they would save only their own lives by their righteousness" (14:13–14). Here, land may indeed refer to settled and inhabited land, but a distinction is made between human beings and other elements in the land, specifically animals. Yet they are all declared guilty, humans and nonhuman creatures of the land. All the land is made totally desolate and handed over to wild animals as agents of chaos. The landscape and the nonhuman creatures are made victims on two counts: they are both objects of transferred guilt and unwarranted destruction. Because there is violence in the land, the land itself and the fullness of the land is guilty by association (9:9; 12:19–20). The land is condemned to suffer with those who deserve to suffer. Even the righteous may not escape the fury of God's wrath (21:8 [Eng. 21:3]).

It may also be possible to interpret the violence toward Earth in terms of the theory of René Girard.[20] Blame is extended by God to land/Earth as an innocent victim. God, however, does not recognize the innocent nature of the victim. The land/Earth experiences violence and death at the hands of a jealous God. Earth, however, is not viewed as a genuine scapegoat or a surrogate victim. The violence of God seems to be so encompassing that all lands where humans have settled or worshiped must, willy-nilly, be reduced to desolation.

VI. Silencing the Victim

Not only are the lands and all the fullness of life within them forced to suffer, die, and become desolate at the hands of a jealous overlord, but their voice is also silenced. Ezekiel effectively suppresses the possibility that any party will identify with the victims, allowing their blood to cry out for justice. The possibility of the land responding to disaster is evident when the land is appalled at the raging of a young lion (possibly Jehoichin) in its midst (19:6–7). The land and its creatures

---

19. Ibid., 161.
20. See Robert G. Hamerton-Kelly, *Sacred Violence: Paul's Hermeneutic of the Cross* (Minneapolis: Fortress, 1992).

have a potential voice, but that voice is silenced in the context of Ezekiel's razed-Earth policy.

All the lands that are condemned in Ezekiel are destined to become desolate, their voices silenced in the face of violent forces of death. This silencing is encompassed in a recurring formula of desolation.[21] After the desolation, all voices of former life cease, whether voices of the landscape or life-forms. The physical silencing of life and landscape through divine acts of desolation symbolizes the silencing of their voices as subjects who have a right to be heard as innocent victims.

In his examination of the formula of desolation, Keith Carley interprets the desolation (שממה) as a horrifying devastation, transforming a fertile and flourishing landscape into a barren wasteland (6:14; 12:20; 33:28–29).[22] This desolation is so complete and so repulsive that no human will pass through the land. This process of desolation, moreover, is not confined to Israel but extends to a range of lands including Ammon, Moab, Edom, Philistia, Tyre, and Egypt.

The judgment of Edom (Mount Seir), for example, results in a perpetual desolation and wasteland with mountains full of repulsive slain bodies and streams polluted with rotting corpses (35:1–9). The voices of the mountains and the streams, the animals and the land itself who suffer this desolation are silenced with the dead. It is a sad testimony to the attitude of Ezekiel, that on the one occasion that Earth is given a voice to rejoice, she rejoices over the desolation of Edom. Earth is portrayed as expressing *Schadenfreude* that effectively silences the cries of the victim—Earth herself (35:14–15).

When the land of Egypt is made desolate, it too is stripped of all of its life, its fullness. The women of the other nations raise a lament, but the voices of the victims, the livestock and land of Egypt, are suppressed (32:13–15). Neither Ezekiel nor the God he represents as a prophet seems to have any sympathy for the victims or willingness to let their voice be heard. Ezekiel must suppress every form of grief, even for his wife. As Carley says:

> There is, however, no hint within the book of Ezekiel that the prophet himself was concerned about the impact on Earth of the judgments he delivered. His older contemporary, Jeremiah, of whose activity Ezekiel is likely to have known, heard the mourning of the desolated land (Jer 12:4, 11). But Ezekiel appears to have had feeling only for his wife, and he claimed God told him to suppress every sign of grief even at her death (Ezek 24:15–17).[23]

---

21. Keith Carley describes this "formulaic expression." See his "Ezekiel's Formula of Desolation: Harsh Justice for the Land/Earth," in Habel, *Earth Story in the Psalms and the Prophets*, 144–47. Carley says the basic form of the expression is "I will make the land a desolation, and they will know that I am the Lord." He finds the formula at Ezek 6:14; 12:20 (where the wording differs but "the meaning is nonetheless clear and severe"); and 33:28–29.

22. Ibid., 143–57.

23. Ibid., 153.

Ezekiel proclaims a range of divine agents designed to devastate and silence the lands: famine, pestilence, wild animals, and sword. The agent that brings home to me the horrific silent scenario reflected in this desolation is that of fire (15:4–8; 21:3–4 [Eng. 20:47–48]; 21:36–37 [Eng. 21:31–32]; 22:31; 30:8, 16; 39:6). A total burning reduces all settlements to ashes, destroys all livestock, and renders the landscape a barren wasteland. All life is killed and all voices silenced.

As a youth in the Australian outback, I experienced bushfires in which thousands of acres of countryside were made desolate. On a typical fire day, when the hot wind blew from the north, like the enemy in Jer 4:11–28, my father would sit on the verandah and watch the horizon for smoke. When a bushfire raged through the land, we escaped with our lives. To walk through the landscape the next day was a heartrending experience; the scene was black as far as the eye could see. We faced bloated dead sheep, blinded kangaroos, smoldering stumps, and twisted implements. And the silence! Wherever we walked the land suffered in silence, a suffering I could not help but feel deeply. In those walks through the bleak bush, I believe I knew already something of what it meant to be one with the land, with Earth, with flesh.

Ezekiel hears none of the suffering of the lands, or, if he does, he does not permit their pathos to be expressed. Some may wish to move from these silent wastelands to the transformed cosmos Ezekiel envisages in the future with mountains shooting branches, fields sown, abundant fruit, and towns inhabited (36:8–11, 29–30; cf. 47:1–12). These scenarios of new life, however, do not negate the acts of injustice and devastation wrought in innocent life and lands. Divine acts of rejuvenation do not excuse divine acts of injustice against Earth. Giving life back to the land does not excuse the suffering and silencing of the victim. Ultimately, the land's value as part of creation is not the reason for rejuvenation, nor is it God's compassion for the chosen people of Israel. Renewal happens merely "for the sake of my holy name" (36:22).

VII. Conclusion

Reading the judgment oracles of Ezekiel from the perspective of Earth exposes a decidedly negative bias toward creation. For the urbanite Ezekiel, the cosmos is intended to be a series of settled lands with God's chosen city as the sacred center. Beyond these lands lie realms of disorder. The natural world is not portrayed as having intrinsic worth, but as property at the disposal of those who make it a human habitation. There is a hierarchy of values from the sacred center to the dangerous wilds on the fringe of the cosmos.

Ezekiel's portrayal of God's judgment on the peoples of these lands is one of extreme violence. The outcome of this violent divine action is that the lands are made desolate and all life on the lands is destroyed. The lands and life on the lands suffer unjustly. They have done nothing to deserve the desolation they experience.

They are victims of a divine rage against any nation who has offended Yhwh. Publicizing the divine name is more important than compassion for creation.

Not only do these victims suffer unjustly, but also they are included among those identified as the guilty objects of Yhwh's wrath. Ezekiel portrays Yhwh as an angry God blaming the victims along with the perpetrators of the crime. In addition, the suffering victims who are forced to share the blame are silenced. The lands have no voice, no advocate, no venue for crying out against the injustice they experience. All is desolate. The silence of the lands is total.

Ezekiel in Abu Ghraib:
Rereading Ezekiel 16:37–39
in the Context of Imperial Conquest

Daniel L. Smith-Christopher

The title of this work is not originally what I had written in earlier drafts. During the course of the project that resulted in this essay, world events have taken on such an ironic relation to the subject of this essay, that I have determined in this final version to draw attention to the fact that the use of engendered humiliation as a tactic of psychological war is not a new phenomenon. In the Western popular religious imagination, it is often believed that Western societies follow in the steps of the best moral visions of the biblical Hebrews. This is what we want to believe about ourselves. Abu Ghraib, like Sand Creek, My Lai, and Hiroshima and Nagasaki, reveals instead that militarism only reduces us to a disturbing immoral similarity to the ancient empires who conquered the biblical Hebrews. We resemble our enemies. Can this troubling perspective actually provide insights into our interpretation of biblical texts?

The metaphor of Jerusalem as whore/prostitute is a motif known in a variety of prophetic passages in Hosea, Jeremiah, and Micah, but it is Ezek 16, along with the similar passage of Ezek 23, that has quite understandably been the subject of the most heated debate and discussion in recent literature. This is especially because feminist and/or gender concerns and analysis of the Bible have increasingly and appropriately become part of the normal agenda for critical analysis of the Bible, and of Ezekiel specifically. In a volume dedicated to examining the issue of hierarchical relations in Ezekiel, I will argue that a predominant interest in male/female hierarchical issues in Ezekiel's imagery (as important as I agree this approach has been) has tended to obscure a sociopolitical hierarchy that I believe is profoundly important to a more nuanced comprehension of Ezekiel's imagery. This somewhat bold assertion is tempered by my attempt to take seriously the warning issued by Johanna Stiebert, who voices this insightful warning with regard to Ezekiel 16: "All attempts at explaining this text are ultimately unverifiable and all constitute no more (or less) than imaginative reconstruction."[1] Nevertheless, I hope to make a modest contribution to at least clarifying one aspect of the imagery in Ezek 16.

One of the most controversial of the images in Ezek 16 is the public stripping and humiliation of "Jerusalem" in vv. 37–39. The relevant passage, in the NRSV translation, reads as follows:

> Therefore, I will gather all your lovers, with whom you took pleasure, all those you loved and all those you hated; I will gather them against you from all around, and will uncover your nakedness to them, so that they may see all your nakedness. [38] I will judge you as women who commit adultery and shed blood are judged, and bring blood upon you in wrath and jealousy. [39] I will deliver you into their hands, and they shall throw down your platform and break down your lofty places; they shall strip you of your clothes and take your beautiful objects and leave you naked and bare.

Already in the 1960s, Moshe Greenberg, who is noted for his studies of Ezekiel, chided Abraham J. Heschel's positive presentation of the "pathos" of the prophets by noting that Heschel too conveniently omitted much discussion of Ezekiel's troubling theology and imagery.[2] In a more recent monograph strikingly entitled *Battered Love*, Renita Weems generalizes about this prophetic use of female imagery, including Ezekiel:

> Perhaps more than any other material in the Bible, the portraits of women's sexuality drawn by Israel's prophets have contributed to the overall impression one gets from the Bible that women's sexuality is deviant, evil, and dangerous.[3]

It is widely held by scholars of the prophetic literature that the image of Jerusalem as prostitute, and some of the details of this imagery, derives from Hosea.[4] Particularly influential has been the article by Drorah Setel, entitled "Prophets and Pornography: Female Sexual Imagery in Hosea,"[5] whose use of the term "pornography" to describe these images has, one can clearly observe, caught on.[6] Robert

---

1. Johanna Stiebert, "Shame and Prophecy: Approaches Past and Present," *BibInt* 8 (2000): 268.
2. Moshe Greenberg, "Anthropopathism in Ezekiel," *Perspectives in Jewish Learning* 1 (1966): 1–10.
3. Renita Weems, *Battered Love: Marriage, Sex, and Violence in the Hebrew Prophets* (OBT; Minneapolis: Fortress, 1997), 5.
4. For example, see Joseph Blenkinsopp, *Ezekiel* (IBC; Louisville: John Knox, 1990), 76; Moshe Greenberg, *Ezekiel 1–20* (AB 22; Garden City, N.Y.: Doubleday 1983), 298; Keith W. Carley, *Ezekiel among the Prophets: A Study of Ezekiel's Place in Prophetic Tradition* (SBT 31; Naperville, Ill.: Allenson, 1974), 49.
5. T. Drorah Setel, "Prophets and Pornography: Female Sexual Imagery in Hosea," in *Feminist Interpretation of the Bible* (ed. L. M. Russell; Philadelphia: Westminster, 1985), 86–95.
6. See Pamela Gordon and Harold Washington, "Rape as a Military Metaphor in the Hebrew Bible," in *A Feminist Companion to the Latter Prophets* (ed. A. Brenner; FCB 8; Sheffield: Sheffield Academic Press, 1995), 310–12; Blenkinsopp, *Ezekiel*, 76–77; J. Cheryl Exum, "The Ethics of Biblical Violence

Carroll, who often identified himself, in characteristically puckish fashion, as "not a feminist," nevertheless writes:

> These allegories of Jerusalem, Samaria, and Sodom as members of the same family and as daughters/sisters/wives/mothers heavily involved in prostitution with Egypt and Assyria (synonyms of imperial power) sound at best like the ravings of a driveling lunatic and if they were not found in pages of "sacred scripture" they would be dismissed instantly by most modern readers as pornography (im)pure and (un)simple![7]

The images in Ezek 16 are disturbing for a variety of reasons, not the least of which is a history of interpretation of these passages in the twentieth century that has often arguably done more harm than good. Part of the controversy can be stated plainly: the negative portrayal of Jerusalem as an ungrateful adulterous wife seeking romantic and adulterous trysts with foreign nations (a "nymphomaniac bride," in Blenkinsopp's words)[8] is intentionally exaggerated in Ezekiel.[9] Greenberg, for example, notes that the image may be borrowed from Hosea, but Ezekiel takes it much further: "There is no time perspective in Hosea . . . no political 'harlotry,' and no maniacal perversity and insatiability."[10] Stated another way, Greenberg asserts that Ezekiel gives a "biography" to the adulterous wife of Hosea and Jeremiah.[11] Furthermore, however, the imagery in Ezekiel appears to:

1. blame Jerusalem for her mistreatment by other nations in her history, beginning with the enslavement by Egypt, and including the imperial conquests of Assyria and the Neo-Babylonian Empire;
2. suggest that "she" (Jerusalem) deserved her fate;
3. suggest that her behavior resembles the worst kind of sexual disloyalty within a marriage;
4. suggest that God requires punishment and humiliation of her in order to forgive her, at times even appearing to invite rape from foreign "lovers" (nations);
5. suggest, for many critical scholars, that the metaphor of exposure is based on actual treatment of adulterous women, and therefore invites readers to "join

---

against Women," in *The Bible in Ethics* (ed. J. Rogerson, M. Davies, and M. D. Carroll; Sheffield: Sheffield Academic Press), 248–71.

7. Robert P. Carroll, "Whorusalamin: A Tale of Three Cities as Three Sisters," in *On Reading Prophetic Texts: Gender-Specific and Related Studies in Memory of Fokkelien van Dijk-Hemmes* (ed. B. Becking and M. Dijkstra; Leiden: Brill, 1996), 68.

8. Blenkinsopp, *Ezekiel*, 79.

9. It is described as "vulgar" (Ralph Klein, *Ezekiel, the Prophet and His Message* [Columbia: University of South Carolina Press, 1988], 83); "coarse . . . and shocking" (Ronald E. Clements, *Ezekiel* [Westminster Bible Companion; Louisville: Westminster John Knox, 1996], 69); "puzzling," and "outrageous" (Stiebert, "Shame and Prophecy," 268).

10. Greenberg, *Ezekiel 1–20*, 298–99.

11. Ibid., 299.

God" in appalled horror at "her" behavior, and thus "approval" of her punishment; and
6. possibly suggest, as Corrine Patton writes, "If God is allowed to abuse his 'wives,' human husbands will see a sanction for physical abuse of their own wives."[12]

There are many other issues that some critics have also found objectionable, such as suggestions that God was not very caring and loving upon first finding the abandoned child. (Where, asks Carol Dempsey, is the nurturing parent?)[13] Furthermore, the text seems to suggest that God's interest in "her" was only as a sexual object when she was of the acceptable physical age for sexual relations. Finally, the entire patriarchal system reflected in the imagery of Ezek 16 (and other similar passages) unavoidably presumes oppressive forms of male sexual rights over females.[14] I am in agreement with the scholarly sentiments of concern that have often been expressed with regard to offensive implications of a text such as Ezek 16, and would further agree that if these notions are actually being supported by a fair and reasoned reading of these texts, then modern readers need to exercise critical caution in how we use, interpret, and teach this material. I would argue, however, that more is to be said about a fair and reasoned reading of certain elements of Ezek 16.

In her article "The Metaphorization of Woman," the late Fokkelien Van Dijk-Hemmes follows Setel in considering one aspect of the "pornographic" in prophetic imagery to be the fact that women are "degraded and publicly humiliated."[15] It is precisely this aspect of the image of the woman in Ezek 16 that I wish to consider further.

I. The Meaning of the Metaphor of Public Stripping/Nakedness in Ezekiel 16:37–39

One of the most understandably objectionable aspects of the imagery in Ezek 16 is the public stripping and humiliation of "Jerusalem." Greenberg, among many others, suggests that this act of stripping an adulterous female is actually drawn from ancient practice in Israel, and cites Hos 2:12; Nah 3:5; and Jer 13:22, 26 in defense

---

12. Corrine L. Patton, "'Should Our Sister Be Treated Like a Whore?' A Response to Feminist Critiques of Ezekiel 23," in *The Book of Ezekiel: Theological and Anthropological Perspectives* (ed. M. Odell and J. Strong; SBLSymS 9; Atlanta: Society of Biblical Literature, 2000), 221. It should be clarified that the opinion cited is not unqualifiedly that of the author.

13. See Carol J. Dempsey, "The 'Whore' of Ezekiel 16: The Impact and Ramifications of Gender-Specific Metaphors in Light of Biblical Law and Divine Judgment," in *Gender and Law in the Hebrew Bible and the Ancient Near East* (ed. V. H. Matthews, B. M. Levinson, and T. Frymer-Kensky; JSOTSup 262; Sheffield: Sheffield Academic Press, 1998), 65.

14. Weems, *Battered Love*, 32.

15. Fokkelien Van Dijk-Hemmes, "The Metaphorization of Woman in Prophetic Speech: An Analysis of Ezekiel XXIII," *VT* 43 (1993): 164.

of this view.¹⁶ But his illustrations tend to derive from legal discussions of *divorce ceremonies* rather than public trials or punishments for adultery.¹⁷ We will return to this notion that public stripping was a known punishment in Israel shortly, but there are other arguments often cited to explain the stripping in Ezek 16, besides cross-references to other texts such as Hos 2 and Nah 3.

Some make the literary observation that Ezekiel is balancing the image of the stripped young adult woman Jerusalem with the opening imagery of Jerusalem as a small child, found without clothing, lying in blood (Ezek 16:4–6). Thus, argues Ralph Klein, the "nakedness" of vv. 37–39 serves as a "negative inclusio" with the birth narrative of vv. 4–6.¹⁸ The idea, it seems, is to suggest that God leaves Jerusalem to her fate, returning her to the state she was in before God found her and cared for her.

Other scholars focus on the gendered impact of the nakedness of Jerusalem as connected to control of sexuality. Ilana Pardes, for example, suggests that Jerusalem, who exposed herself privately to her lovers in adultery, is doomed to be exposed in public as humiliating punishment.¹⁹ Apparently not questioning whether there actually existed such a practice of stripping adulterous females, Pardes argues that the humiliation of the female is directly connected to the issue of controlled sexuality. She writes:

> The prophetic preoccupation with female nakedness (Ephraim, the male personification of the nation is never uncovered) seems to exhibit an all too common patriarchal need to control women's bodies and women's sexuality . . . to make clear distinctions between women whose bodies are owned by given men (father, brother, or husband) and those that may be regarded as public property. A woman who does not maintain her nakedness under cover exposes herself to the danger of being undressed in public.²⁰

As significant as all of these observations may be, I do not think that the nature of the public stripping of "Jerusalem" has been satisfactorily explained. In two important articles published in the same year, Peggy Day carefully outlines her objections to this standard scholarly view with regard to the image of stripping

---

16. Greenberg, *Ezekiel 1–20*, 286.
17. Ibid., 287.
18. Klein, *Ezekiel*, 88; cf. Peter Craigie, *Ezekiel* (Daily Study Bible; Philadelphia: Westminster), 116.
19. Ilana Pardes, *Countertraditions in the Bible: A Feminist Approach* (Cambridge: Harvard University Press, 1992), 134–35.
20. Pardes, *Countertraditions in the Bible*, 135; cf. Mary E. Shields, "Multiple Exposures: Body Rhetoric and Gender Characterization in Ezekiel 16," *JFSR* 14 (1998): 5–18; idem, "Gender and Violence in Ezekiel 23," *SBL Seminar Papers, 1998* (SBLSP 37/1; Atlanta: Scholars Press, 1998), 86–105.

female Jerusalem in Hos 2 and Ezek 16 (among other places).[21] She agrees with other scholars that the imagery was intended to shock and thus to gain the attention of a predominantly male audience to the words of the prophet:

> This graphic and sustained depiction of a naked female body engaged in illicit sexual acts is calculated to have an emotive effect on its male audience, both titillating them with visions of sexual activity and rousing them to righteous fury and indignation.[22]

While this is not the burden of her article, it makes the assumption that Ezekiel's audience (as Hosea's before) were exclusively male. Why is this so widely presumed when the exilic communities were clearly mixed?[23] On what basis do we think that listening to prophets was an exclusively male privilege, particularly in the exile's walled family quarters (Ezek 8:8; 12:5, 7) of southern Babylonia? Furthermore, should the element of "titillation" be presumed in these passages? Gale Yee, for example, suggests otherwise in her analysis of Hos 2:

> The wife's exposed genitalia becomes a graphic image for the ruling class's breach of covenant and the land's decline. Unmasking their shared desires and sexual misconduct, the most vulnerable part of the wife's body will be displayed before her lovers, the nations. Although the male gaze usually results in visual pleasure, this is not the case here. The gaze of the nations/lovers reveals their own sexual and moral impotence in their inability to rescue Israel from its disgrace.[24]

My point in this brief aside about the concept of "the male gaze" is that I think it does illuminate elements of ancient literature at times, but on this occasion, I believe that it has led to a kind of hermeneutical distraction from other possible explanations of the nature of the "public stripping" of Jerusalem.

Day's important contributions include her questioning of the nearly universal notion that such public stripping of women was "an appropriate and lawful punishment for adultery in ancient Israel."[25] She cites an impressive barrage of previous scholarly literature on both the Hosea and Ezekiel passages to back her assertion that this is a well-established view in biblical analysis:

---

21. Peggy L. Day, "The Bitch Had It Coming to Her: Rhetoric and Interpretation in Ezekiel 16," *BibInt* 8 (2000): 231–54; idem, "Adulterous Jerusalem's Imagined Demise: Death of a Metaphor in Ezekiel XVI," *VT* 50 (2000): 285–309.
22. Day, "Bitch Had It Coming," 235.
23. In addition to Day, see Weems, *Battered Love*, 3, who speaks of the "predominantly male" audience.
24. Gale A. Yee, *Poor Banished Children of Eve: Women as Evil in the Hebrew Bible* (Minneapolis: Fortress, 2003), 106.
25. Day, "Bitch Had It Coming," 238.

The very fact that so many commentators have been fixated on reading the punishment as appropriate for adultery and not for murder is, I think, persuasive evidence that the commentators in question have taken the passage's rhetorical bait and assumed that subject position of Yahweh as aggrieved husband, focusing their ire on Jerusalem *as adulteress* and not on Jerusalem as murderer.[26]

In short, Day argues that the punishment of "Jerusalem" is a metaphor for breaking the covenant and not for adultery. Adultery was punished in the law by stoning (Ezek 16:40). She points out that there is nothing in the Mosaic law about public humiliation and stripping as a punishment for adultery or prostitution.[27]

I believe Day is quite correct to suggest that the metaphor has been consistently misread, but there is more to be said on the matter. Day does not deal directly with the element of public stripping, choosing rather to focus on the "sin," and clarifying its actual meaning behind the metaphor of adultery. But why did Hosea, and Ezekiel in chapter 16, choose the image of stripping?

An even more troubling perspective is held by those who argue that the stripping is a prelude to rape. This is argued in some detail by Gordon and Washington, but also in an important article by Rachel Magdalene, where the widespread use of rape imagery is analyzed in evidence beyond biblical texts, including ancient Near Eastern sources.[28] In relation to the imagery of Jerusalem as a female generally, Magdalene suggests:

> God, characterized as male, is regularly threatening, in judgments, to rape, or otherwise sexually abuse, the cities of Israel, Judah, and their neighbors, all characterized as female. Metaphorically, then, God is seemingly quite willing to perpetrate repeated sexual assaults and abuse on women.[29]

Furthermore, Magdalene suggests that in the ancient evidence almost any occasion of public stripping, or "lifting the skirt," is "generally regarded as the precursor to the act of rape."[30] Somewhat different, however, is her assertion that "God brings the hand of war upon the land and the female inhabitants can expect to be raped as a part of the people's defeat."[31] It can be argued whether the imagery suggests God engaging in an act of rape, or "permitting" this to occur as an element of military conquest. However, one can question whether the public stripping of Hos 2, and of

---

26. Ibid., 244 (Day's emphasis). Ezekiel 16:38 speaks of both adultery and bloodshed as the crimes to be judged and punished.
27. This was also noted in passing by Carley, *Ezekiel among the Prophets*, 58.
28. Gordon and Washington, "Rape as a Military Metaphor"; F. Rachel Magdalene, "Ancient Near Eastern Treaty-Curses and the Ultimate Texts of Terror: A Study of the Language of Divine Sexual Abuse in the Prophetic Corpus," in Brenner, *Feminist Companion to the Latter Prophets*, 326–52.
29. Magdalene, "Ancient Near Eastern Treaty-Curses," 327.
30. Ibid., 328–29 n. 4.
31. Ibid., 334.

Ezek 16 specifically, is actually a "prelude to rape." While not denying that rape was likely an aspect of ancient military conquest, I want to argue that the image of stripping is *not* directly related to rape, but most certainly is directly connected to, and indeed derived from, ancient military practice.

II. Nakedness and Shame in Imperial Conquest

A possible clarification of Ezekiel's use of nakedness images, and quite likely Hosea's as well, emerges when we read Ezek 16 in its social and political context: for Hosea, the Neo-Assyrian imperial and military context; for Ezekiel the later Neo-Babylonian imperial and military context. Seen in that light, we can read Ezekiel as a *refugee* as well as a prophet. This follows the important suggestions by Corrine Patton and Margaret Odell, which remind us that any reading of Ezekiel must keep in mind that this material

> is told from the perspective of a once-elite member of society who has been dragged off in chains to an unclean land, who sits powerless, "dumb" as his nation is destroyed and his world turned upside down. His concern is not with how husbands will use the text to reinforce cultural presumptions of gender.[32]

Odell, also, notes that any attempt at interpreting Ezek 16 "must reckon with the pervasive sense of humiliation and failure already present in the exile."[33]

In my own recent approaches to problems in the book of Ezekiel, I have explored ways in which socio-psychological analyses of post-traumatic stress disorder in soldiers, refugees and refugee workers, and disaster and relief workers may shed light on the famous "acts" of Ezekiel.[34] During a presentation of one of these papers at the sessions of the "Theological Perspectives on the Book of Ezekiel Seminar" of the Society of Biblical Literature, my friend Gale A. Yee asked what relevance this kind of analysis may have for Ezekiel's use of disturbing female imagery in chapters such as Ezek 16 and 23. I was certainly not prepared for that question, but it was a good one. This study represents my first attempt to respond to a question asked now three years ago, and now in dialogue not only with a series of very significant studies on the question, but also with Yee's own important recent work illustrating the importance of integrating social analysis with textual analysis.

---

32. Patton, "'Should Our Sister Be Treated Like a Whore?'" 229.

33. Margaret S. Odell, "The Inversion of Shame and Forgiveness in Ezekiel 16:59–63," *JSOT* 56 (1992): 105.

34. Daniel L. Smith-Christopher, "Ezekiel on Fanon's Couch: A Postcolonist Critique in Dialogue with David Halperin's *Seeking Ezekiel,*" in *Peace and Justice Shall Embrace: Power and Theopolitics in the Bible* (ed. T. Grimsrud and L. L. Johns; Telford, Pa.: Pandora, 1999), 108–44; idem, *A Biblical Theology of Exile* (OBT; Minneapolis: Fortress, 2002).

In her summary of the social and "materialist" conditions of female imagery in biblical material, Yee writes:

> Since an interrelationship exists between the text and the society that produces it, gender relations should be situated in the wider context of the most important socio-economic unit in tribal structure: the family household. . . . Governing the family household are a patrilineal descent ideology, patrilocal marriage residence customs, endogamy, and patrimonial inheritance rights, all of which privilege the male and subordinate the female in an asymmetrical hierarchy.[35]

An even more significant aspect of Ezekiel's "wider context" is violent social breakdown. Ezekiel is a refugee; his rhetoric cannot be read as the normative observations of an "average ancient Israelite," and thus a reflection of normal gender relations and imagery. Rather, Ezekiel's rhetoric is the language of suffering—and the rhetoric of suffering and anger is not "normal." The suffering of Ezekiel comes from his experiences as an exile in the shadow of the Neo-Babylonian imperial conquests of Palestine—conquests that follow the previous centuries' military practices of the Neo-Assyrian armies. Consider, for example, the following observation from the late Robert Carroll:

> If we then shift our attention from analyzing the text as discourse to reading the text as a culturally produced document we may catch echoes and traces in the text of socially oppressive practices. In a society where the public realm is ruled by powerful men, socially or sexually subversive women are an easy prey for violent men backed up by the social mores of a culture of violence. The discourses of Ezekiel are full of images of violence, bloodshed, vengeance, and terror.[36]

Somewhat startlingly for a writer of Carroll's incisive eye—the final sentence of this last quote apparently did not lead him to realize that the images of violence, bloodshed, vengeance, and terror are not concoctions of Ezekiel's normative theological reflection, but the realities within which he is living! How does this impact an analysis of the imagery of stripping in Ezek 16:37–39?

In recent work on rape as a military tactic in the late twentieth century, and in historical reviews inspired by the topic, attention has been directed to the warfare context of sexual violence. Inger Skjelsbaek writes:

> The victim of sexual violence in the war-zone is victimized by feminizing both the sex and the ethnic/religious/political identity to which the victim belongs, likewise the perpetrator's sex and ethnic/religious/political identity is empowered by becoming masculinized.[37]

---

35. Yee, *Poor Banished Children*, 56.
36. Carroll, "Whorusalamin," 76.
37. Inger Skjelsbaek, "Sexual Violence and War: Mapping Out a Complex Relationship," *European Journal of International Relations* 7 (2001): 225; cf. Roland Littlewood, "Military Rape," *Anthropology*

Unlike the act itself, the social *meaning* of rape cannot be generalized across time and culture. Precisely how it is understood depends on the sexual and gender relations within a given society. According to Lisa Sharlach:

> One may conclude . . . that rape as genocide appears to occur to ethnic groups that strongly stigmatize rape survivors rather than rapists. In such communities, women in their roles as mothers of the nation and as transmitters of culture symbolize the honor of the ethnic group. When a woman's honor is tarnished through rape, the ethnic group is also dishonored. To restore its honor, the ethnic group may ostracize or expel the raped girl or woman. The rape survivor's victimization continues long after the initial sexual assault. Post-rape trauma is compounded by "the second rape" of becoming a pariah in one's own society and even one's own family.[38]

This approach to understanding rape as military practice goes beyond its context in a patriarchal society (like ancient Israel) that oppresses women generally in its socio-economic system with lesser status and fewer rights. It means that elements of rape as military tactic must be seen within the engendering of warfare itself—aimed at both men and women in the target population.

In the writing of this essay, what began as a somewhat unusual approach to take in the study of Ezek 16 has become even more significant in the light of the shocking abuses of Iraqi prisoners by American soldiers in the conflicts there in the summer of 2004—where the horrifying links among war, sexuality, and the engendering of conflict and shame are all too obvious. How might the social and emotional brutalities of Abu Ghraib prison lead to a wider analysis of the theme of conquest and nakedness in Ezek 16?

There is significant evidence to suggest that the metaphor of "stripping" in Hos 2, but especially in Ezek 16, is drawn from the practice of stripping POWs in Neo-Assyrian and Neo-Babylonian military practice. One can see a number of illustrations of stripped male POWs in, for example, Pritchard's classic compendium, *Ancient Near Eastern Pictures*. Consider, for example, the famous "Gates of Shalmaneser III" (858–824 B.C.E.), which feature nude prisoners being led away with their arms tied behind their backs.[39] Otto Kaiser, in his exposition of Isaiah's "sign-act" of going naked in Isa 20:1–6, suggests the example of the Megiddo Ivory as well.[40] The Sennacherib stele depicting the defeat of Lachish also features naked

---

Today 13 (1997): 7–17; Marysia Zalewski, "Well, What Is the Feminist Perspective on Bosnia?" *International Affairs* 71 (1995): 339–57.

38. Lisa Sharlach, "Rape as Genocide: Bangladesh, the Former Yugoslavia, and Rwanda," *New Political Science* 22 (2000): 2.

39. See Yigael Yadin, *The Art of Warfare in Biblical Lands in the Light of Archaeological Study* (London: Weidenfeld and Nicolson, 1963), 396–97; James Pritchard, *ANEP*, 124–25.

40. Otto Kaiser, *Isaiah 13–39, a Commentary* (OTL; Philadelphia: Westminster, 1974), 114–15; cf. Pritchard, *ANEP,* 111, fig. 332.

POWs having been executed by impaling.⁴¹ Reliefs from the Palace of Sargon, Khorsabad (721–705 B.C.E.), feature executed opponents who have been stripped.⁴²

Enemies are often depicted with minimal, or no, clothing—see the Palette of King Narmer⁴³—either to indicate submission, humiliation, or their having been stripped as defeated. It may be significant to note that female captives do not appear to have been completely stripped,⁴⁴ and it is much more common to portray male captives or killed opponents as naked. It is tempting to suggest that this is in keeping with the desire to add further humiliation to the male defenders who have been defeated. Furthermore, there is strong biblical evidence for this practice.

The prophet Isaiah's "sign-act" of going "naked" in Isa 20:3 is often spoken of as a reference to the inevitability of being stripped as POWs.⁴⁵ An equally significant passage in 2 Chronicles—representing the reversal of a battle against the Judeans—is particularly important in this regard:

> Then those who were mentioned by name got up and took the captives, and with the booty they clothed all that were *naked* among them; they clothed them, gave them sandals, provided them with food and drink, and anointed them; and carrying all the feeble among them on donkeys, they brought them to their kindred at Jericho. (2 Chr 28:15)

Of this passage, Sara Japhet writes:

> Among the concrete details of the passage, note the repeated references to the captives as needing to be clothed. This may indicate not only the extent of the spoiling of the Judahites, but also a reflection of ancient customs: the naked shame of captivity exchanged for raiment of respect.⁴⁶

Punishment directed at "Lady Babylon" in Isaiah includes the same imagery:

> Your *nakedness* shall be uncovered, and your shame shall be seen. I will take vengeance, and I will spare no one. (Isa 47:3)

With regard to the imagery of Isa 47, David Vanderhooft notes the personification of Babylon as a captive woman:

---

41. *ANEP,* 131, fig. 373.
42. Yadin, *Art of Warfare,* 420–21.
43. Ibid., 124.
44. *ANEP,* 127.
45. Kaiser, *Isaiah 13–39,* 114–15. Brevard S. Childs omits any discussion of this in his more recent commentary, *Isaiah* (OTL; Louisville: Westminster John Knox, 2001).
46. Sara Japhet, *I & II Chronicles, a Commentary* (OTL; Louisville: Westminster John Knox, 1993), 904.

> She will be exposed and defiled, images that very likely involve application to Babylon of practices directed toward captives in Mesopotamian military expeditions. This is suggested in particular by the language of v. 2, where Lady Babylon is commanded: "Strip off your veil, bare your calf, cross over rivers." The depiction of captive females in the Assyrian artistic tradition may clarify this language: the bronze gates of Shalmaneser III (858–824 B.C.E.) from Balawat clearly depict Assyrian soldiers leading away captive women who are raising the fronts of their skirts.[47]

Furthermore, Vanderhooft notes that "in the Mesopotamian sphere, artistic representations of captives (occasionally naked males) being led away after defeat go back to the time of Sargon of Akkad in the third millennium, but are found much later as well, especially in Neo-Assyrian reliefs."[48]

With the stripping of POWs in mind, the following passages read rather differently:

> Jerusalem sinned grievously, so she has become a mockery; all who honored her despise her, for they have seen her *nakedness*; she herself groans, and turns her face away. (Lam 1:8)

> I am against you, says the LORD of hosts, and will lift up your skirts over your face; and I will let nations look on your *nakedness* and kingdoms on your shame. (Nah 3:5)

> He leads counselors away *stripped*, and makes fools of judges. (Job 12:17)

> He leads priests away *stripped*, and overthrows the mighty. (Job 12:19)

As I noted earlier regarding recent analyses of rape in warfare, this humiliation of the warrior becomes all the more important in the context of the engendering of warfare itself, another aspect often neglected in recent feminist analysis of the exilic context of Ezekiel. I agree with the initial observations along these lines published by Harold Washington,[49] to which more can certainly be added. For example, in his recent book, *War and Gender: How Gender Shapes the War System and Vice Versa*, Joshua Goldstein speaks of the importance (and neglect in recent research on warfare) of the engendering of warfare:

---

47. David Vanderhooft, *The Neo-Babylonian Empire and Babylon in the Latter Prophets* (HSM 59; Atlanta: Scholars Press, 1999), 181–82.

48. Ibid., 182 n. 225, where a number of illustrations are cited.

49. Harold C. Washington, "'Lest He Die in Battle and Another Man Take Her': Violence and the Construction of Gender in the Laws of Deuteronomy 20–22," in Matthews, Levinson, and Frymer-Kensky, *Gender and Law*, 197.

Of the hypotheses engaging mainly cultural explanations, three receive most support. First, and most strongly . . . the toughening up of boys is found robustly across cultures, and by linking bravery and discipline in war to manhood—with shame as enforcement—many cultures use gender to motivate participation in combat. Second . . . women actively reinforce—in various feminine war roles such as mothers, lovers, and nurses—men's tough, brave masculinity. Third . . . male soldiers use gender to encode domination, feminizing enemies. Connected with this coding, but more elusive empirically, are the possible heightened (or just shaken up) sexuality of male soldiers, and the more intense exploitation of women's labor in wartime.[50]

Goldstein's comments bring to mind passages in which women's "encouragements" of male involvement in warfare appear as possible measures of the engendering of warfare symbolism. Note, for example, that the Bible certainly does represent a kind of "engendering" of warfare as a male occupation, with women occasionally "cheering on" the soldiers in their male duties:

> As they were coming home, when David returned from killing the Philistine, the *women* came out of all the towns of Israel, singing and dancing, to meet King Saul, with tambourines, with songs of joy, and with musical instruments. (1 Sam 18:6)

Furthermore, there is a clear motif of feminizing the enemy and the defeated in the Bible:

> On that day the Egyptians will be like *women*, and tremble with fear before the hand that the LORD of hosts raises against them. (Isa 19:16)

> A sword against her horses and against her chariots, and against all the foreign troops in her midst, so that they may become *women*! A sword against all her treasures, that they may be plundered! (Jer 50:37)

> The warriors of Babylon have given up fighting, they remain in their strongholds; their strength has failed, they have become *women*; her buildings are set on fire, her bars are broken. (Jer 51:30)

The "humiliation" of "Jerusalem" as female must be directly connected to the ideology of, and practice of, Assyrian and Babylonian warfare. I would thus argue that it was the circumstances and practices of warfare by the Mesopotamian imperial states of the first millennium B.C.E. that suggested the imagery of stripping, and not a generally practiced punishment of adulterous women in Israelite society. Such contexts may also have given rise to other imagery where warfare itself is "engendered."

---

50. Joshua S. Goldstein, *War and Gender: How Gender Shapes the War System and Vice Versa* (Cambridge: Cambridge University Press, 2000), 406.

This analysis does not necessarily mitigate the observations of Magdalene about rape in warfare and conquest, even with regard to those wars brought about by God as punishment:

> For I will gather all the nations against Jerusalem to battle, and the city shall be taken and the houses looted and the *women* raped; half the city shall go into exile, but the rest of the people shall not be cut off from the city. (Zech 14:2)

Even here, though, the passage lists rape as one of the destructive and horrific impacts of ancient warfare itself, and not as a particular metaphor for war generally. Indeed, Susan Brooks Thistlethwaite flatly argues, "[R]ape is never used as a biblical metaphor for war,"[51] although elements of this language are used in metaphors associated with warfare:

> At another level . . . is the overarching symbol system of war as the triumph of order over chaos, at times imaged through the chaotic nature of female sexuality and the need for its control. And, whatever definition biblical writers themselves held of rape, the fact remains that female captives were sexually violated against their will.[52]

Consider, finally, the intriguing fact that the common term for exile—"Golah"—derives from the same root as the term often used for "stripping" or "uncovering," the clear meaning of the root in Ezek 16:37. At least one of the terms used for this imagery of "uncovering" in Ezek 16 is related to the earlier use of this idea in Hos 2:12 (Eng. 2:10), where a similar image is suggested:

> Now I will uncover (אגלה) her shame in the sight of her lovers, and no one shall rescue her out of my hand.

Is Ezekiel thus aware of a Hebrew "word-game" that we are no longer noting, namely, the semantic relationship of the terms for "strip" and "exile"? Both the Hos 2 and Ezek 16 passages employ the root term גלה to speak of stripping. Might the very reason that גלה comes to be used as a term for an exile be because of the Neo-Assyrian and Neo-Babylonian practice of stripping and humiliating captive males? Interestingly, classical Arabic features the same semantic field for the term *j-l-w* or *j-l-y*. The root can create the term for "exile," and also the term "uncovered."

What would be some of the implications of this proposal? It has been argued that the stripping of female Jerusalem is "titillation" for the "male gaze" of ancient Israelite males. However, if there is any "gazing" in passages like Ezek 16, it may not

---

51. Susan Brooks Thistlethwaite, "'You May Enjoy the Spoil of Your Enemies': Rape as a Biblical Metaphor for War," *Semeia* 61 (1993): 61.

52. Ibid., 69.

be a "male gaze," but rather a triumphalist "imperial gaze" of the conquerors over the humiliated and stripped male soldiers who foolishly tried to resist the superior forces. Ezekiel himself may have been fully aware of his "feminization" of this imperial gaze in order to deepen the impact of his metaphor—and not at all involved in merely a "male attempt" to appeal to a supposed practice of publicly stripping and humiliating women as punishment for adultery.

Finally, the entire notion of exile as "God's doing" (virtually the entire theological message of Jeremiah in relation to the exilic events, for example, and the historical interpretation of the Deuteronomistic Historian in the books of Kings) could be read as portraying a sadistic God. It is arguable, however, that such a "self-blaming theology" does have a creative, even an ironically positive function for defeated peoples, as dangerous as it may be when taken as evidence of a "sadistic God." Self-blaming ideologies attempt to take away the ultimate victory of the conqueror by attributing defeat to one's own failures or sins, and not to the superior culture, superior force, or superior ability of the opponents. Self-blaming ideologies can also fuel renewal because it suggests that when one's own house is back in order, the defeat can be reversed.

Furthermore, when scholars note the near-raving attitudes attributed to the "male God" in the metaphor of a "betrayed husband,"[53] there is a consistent inability to see in such images not a presumed normal husband, acting in a "normal way" in response to being betrayed, but rather an image of the kind of horrendous destruction of relationships that occurs in circumstances of war, deprivation, and oppression.

To state it another way, the error that I believe is common to many modern readers of the exilic-period biblical literature is the omission of a sustained appreciation of the oppressive, violent, and suffering circumstances of warfare and the resulting exiled community. It is therefore assumed by many modern readers of the Bible that these images of violent male behavior are somehow considered "normal" or "acceptable," rather than symptoms of the worsening conditions of exile. Why is it almost always presumed that the "horror" felt by the listeners of Ezekiel, Hosea, or other prophets is a horror directed only at the female aspects of the imagery? Could it not instead be a horror at the male and military images of violence and therefore a picture of "our present circumstances in exile"? Feminists frequently speak of the "silent" or "voiceless" female subject but easily place thoughts in the minds of the equally silent and voiceless "hearers" of Ezekiel's tirades who are then presumed guilty. However, the image of the stripped and humiliated Jerusalem may not have "titillated" the male hearers at all, but rather shocked them precisely because it reminded them of their own treatment at the hands of the Babylonian conquerors! *Thus, they would have identified with the female Jerusalem, rather than the*

---

53. Weems, *Battered Love*, 77.

"*male God.*" I take friendly issue with at least one element of the argument of a scholar such as Weems when she writes:

> The image of the battered promiscuous wife caters to patriarchal thinking in that it leaves unquestioned husbands' presumption that they have the authority to degrade and silence their wives when the latter act in ways that allegedly bring shame on their husbands.[54]

Ronald Clements is less certain. He writes: "From a purely artistic literary perspective, it is questionable whether Ezekiel's allegory works very well overall."[55] However, on the aspect of the metaphor that points to imperial oppression, it may have "worked" more effectively than we have heretofore appreciated. Ralph Klein observes:

> While modern readers are profoundly disturbed by the violence of this approach, especially since it is directed against a woman, we can still recognize through the unfortunate metaphor the prophet's theological conclusion: Ezekiel sees no way for Jerusalem to escape the full force of the divine fury.[56]

At least one way that Ezekiel's metaphor does work effectively can be illustrated, finally, with another observation arising from a reading of contemporary analysis of engendering political relations and conflict—and especially in the light of the abuses of Abu Ghraib prison in 2004:

> Once masculinity is seen as an attribute of power rather than as an attribute of men, it becomes clear that while all men gain to some extent from the associations between masculinity and power, not all men have equal access to these associations. Strategies of feminization can be used to marginalize groups of men as well as women.[57]

I believe that studies of the exilic period that are focused on issues of female and male imagery and violence need to continue to integrate insights from further study of the imperial contexts of Neo-Assyrian, Neo-Babylonian, and Persian military realities.

This analysis is not at all intended to suggest that there are not many serious exegetical and even more serious theological problems with Ezekiel's vulgar use of "pornographic" imagery and violence. However, I believe Stiebert is on to a very cre-

---

54. Ibid., 86, 87.
55. Clements, *Ezekiel,* 72.
56. Klein, *Ezekiel,* 85.
57. Charlotte Hooper, "Masculinities in Transition: The Case of Globalization," in *Gender and Global Restructuring: Sightings, Sites, and Resistances* (ed. M. H. Marchand and A. S. Runyan; London and New York: Routledge, 2000), 62.

ative and helpful train of thought (similar to, but more developed than, Blenkinsopp's use of the adjective "Swiftian" to describe Ezekiel's imagery)[58] when she suggests that Ezekiel's language may well illustrate an example of an "anti-language":

> Antilanguages . . . are the languages of antisocieties seeking self-consciously to create a different kind of society from that which has been or is dominant. As their purpose is usually radically to alter everything, antilanguages are almost inevitably characterized by such traits as overcharged rhetoric, cunningly subversive wordplay and metaphor, vulgarity and grotesque parodies of reality: features which . . . are not difficult to discern in Ezekiel.[59]

I would suggest that further work on Ezek 16—in addition to continued analysis of the female imagery and the cultural suggestions that this may involve—should also focus on the entire subject of "inviting punishment"—that Jerusalem deserved her fate—just as much as the engendered details of that fate. This, in my view, represents a further "antilanguage" that is theological in nature, and a further disturbing aspect of Ezekiel's theo-politics (and Jeremiah's political theology, as well, for that matter). As I have tried to illustrate in my work on exile, it is somewhat striking how often one can see a historical perspective of self-blame among minority populations in history who have suffered serious military or social trauma.[60] Clearly, such a view serves some creative function of denying power or superiority to the conqueror or the conqueror's gods and locates responsibility in the failures of the defeated. As we have seen, however, this interpretive tactic runs the risk of being read as the punishments of a sadistic God by those who do not agree with the self-blaming ideology. But, as we have illustrated here, all such analysis should carry on with an attempt to be aware of the violence of imperial conquest and ancient tactics of warfare, and the attempts of defeated peoples to creatively reinterpret their defeat, and "disempower" their conquerors.

In conclusion, studies of Ezekiel reveal a conflicting array of hierarchies. While the language of Ezekiel could be read to primarily buttress a male/female hierarchy within exilic Israelite communities—or even Israel more widely—this is not the only way to read many of the images of Ezek 16. Given the context of war and exile, it must also be asked whether Ezekiel's imagery more basically reveals the impact of a degrading imperial hierarchy on himself and his fellow exiles. Indeed, this other "hierarchy" that consists of military defeat and engendered humiliation in the ancient Near Eastern imperial context may well raise serious questions about how "normative" any discussion of male/female relations could possibly be in the book of Ezekiel, or in the hallways of Abu Ghraib.

---

58. See Blenkinsopp, *Ezekiel*, 78–79.
59. Stiebert, "Shame and Prophecy," 269.
60. Smith-Christopher, *Biblical Theology of Exile*, esp. 105–23.

'With a Mighty Hand and an Outstretched Arm': The Prophet and the Torah in Ezekiel 20

Risa Levitt Kohn

> *You will not find a prophet beside him who reproves*
> *his generation by the standard of the Torah.*[1]

Scholarship addressing the relationship of language, context, and imagery in the book of Ezekiel to that of other material in the Torah is beginning to shift in focus from issues of chronological priority to that of "inner-biblical exegesis."[2] While Ezekiel frequently alludes to material found elsewhere in the Hebrew Bible, Moshe Greenberg aptly notes that

> there is almost always a divergence large enough to raise the question, whether the prophet has purposely skewed the traditional material, or merely represents a version of it different from extant records.[3]

Ezekiel appears to be familiar with earlier biblical sources, but his writing is more than just a product of its influence or tradition.[4] The prophet appropriates terminology and content but situates it in new, different, and even contradictory contexts. It is evident that Ezekiel knows the sources that constitute the redacted Torah, but

---

1. Eliezer of Beaugency, twelfth-century French commentator, as quoted by Moshe Greenberg, "Notes on the Influence of Tradition on Ezekiel," *JANESCU* 22 (1993): 29 n. 4.

2. For a thorough review of this scholarly trend, see Risa Levitt Kohn, "Ezekiel at the Turn of the Century," *Currents in Biblical Research* 2 (2003): 13–14. The move towards inner-biblical exegesis was highlighted in Michael Fishbane's seminal work *Biblical Interpretation in Ancient Israel* (Oxford: Clarendon, 1985). Fishbane's analysis of Ezekiel, in particular, has helped to highlight the way in which authoritative biblical texts were reinterpreted in the face of new historical circumstances, "when divine words had apparently gone unfulfilled as originally proclaimed (as in various promises and prophecies); or when new moral or spiritual meanings were applied to texts which had long since lost their vitality" (*Biblical Interpretation in Ancient Israel*, 14).

3. Greenberg, "Notes on the Influence," 29.

4. It is my contention that both P and D predate Ezekiel and, as a result, linguistic influence travels in only one direction. See further Risa Levitt Kohn, *A New Heart and a New Soul: Ezekiel, the Exile, and the Torah* (JSOTSup 358; Sheffield: Sheffield Academic Press, 2002).

he adjusts this material to suit his personal prophetic agenda and the contemporary circumstances of his audience.

Perhaps one of the most interesting illustrations of Ezekiel's use of Torah sources is Ezek 20:1–44. Here the prophet recounts Israel's history from the exodus to the prophet's day. Ezekiel's account does not directly parallel any pentateuchal source. His story begins with Israel's rejection of Yahweh while still in Egypt (20:5–9) and progresses with subsequent rejections in the wilderness and in the land, culminating in the exile of Ezekiel and his contemporaries (20:10–32). The final episode in Ezekiel's story foretells a "second" exodus (20:34–35), a second judgment in the wilderness (20:36), reentry into the land, and a complete eradication of sinners from Israel (20:38).[5]

Ezekiel distorts the resiliently optimistic and salvific credo of the exodus traditions found in the Torah into a recitation of Israel's history of sin. The prophet's portrayal of the exodus as an expression of Yahweh's wrath contrasts with the vision of the redacted Torah, where it is an act of divine benevolence intended to fulfill Yahweh's pledge to the patriarchs. Ezekiel regards Israel's behavior in his own day as a relapse to the contemptuous irreverence toward Yahweh that characterizes for him the exodus-wilderness period. In this respect, the wilderness period becomes, for Ezekiel, only one of numerous examples in Israel's history when defiance and sin destroy the community's relationship with God.

In order to achieve this unique evaluation of Israel's past and present, Ezekiel fuses images and expressions drawn from the independent traditions of the Priestly and Deuteronomistic sources.[6] Consequently, Ezek 20 is replete with terms, phrases, and concepts found in both the P and D traditions. In the following translation of Ezek 20:1–44,[7] Priestly terminology appears in boldface, Deuteronomistic language in italic:[8]

---

5. The motif of a second exodus is not unique to Ezekiel. Perhaps the earliest occurrence is in the book of Hosea, where, in the context of future restoration, the bride Israel will "be refreshed as in the time of her youth, when she came up from the land of Egypt" (Hos 2:17 [Eng. 2:15]). Micah, in the face of the Assyrian crisis in the late eighth century B.C.E., foresees Yahweh's future redemption of Israel as a repeat of past miracles (Mic 7:14–15). Isaiah anticipates Yahweh setting his hand a "second time" to recover his people from Egypt and Assyria (Isa 11:11). Jeremiah looks to the return of Israel's northern tribes with the reformulation of a traditional oath formula (Jer 16:14–15).

6. In recent years, the Documentary Hypothesis has come under scholarly attack for various reasons, some cogent, some not. The presence, however, of at least two different literary entities within the Torah—P and D—is still accepted by most. For recent discussions, see the surveys in John Van Seters, *The Pentateuch: A Social Science Commentary* (Trajectories 1; Sheffield: Sheffield Academic Press, 1999), and Alexander Rofé, *Introduction to the Composition of the Pentateuch* (trans. H. Bock; Biblical Seminar 58; Sheffield: Sheffield Academic Press, 1999).

7. The following translation is my own.

8. For detailed discussion of Ezek 20, see Moshe Greenberg, *Ezekiel 1–20* (AB 22; Garden City, N.Y.: Doubleday, 1983), 360–88; Walther Zimmerli, *Ezekiel: A Commentary on the Book of the Prophet Ezekiel* (2 vols.; Hermenia; Philadelphia: Fortress, 1979), 1:399–418; Terry Burden, *The Kerygma of the Wilderness Traditions in the Hebrew Bible* (New York: Peter Lang, 1994), 167–77; Jacques Pons, "Le vocabulaire d'Ézéchiel 20: Le prophète s'oppose à la vision deutéronomiste de l'histoire," in *Ezekiel and His Book: Tex-*

1. In the seventh year in the fifth month on the tenth day of the month, some elders of Israel came to me to *consult Yahweh*[9] and sat down before me. 2. And *the word of Yahweh came to me.*[10] 3. Son of Man, speak to the elders of Israel and say to them: Thus says my Lord Yahweh: Have you come to *consult me*? As I live, says Yahweh, I will not be *consulted* by you—word of my Lord Yahweh. 4. Will you judge them, Son of Man, will you judge them? Let them know the abominations of their ancestors. 5. And say to them, thus says my Lord Yahweh: On the day of *my choosing Israel*,[11] **I raised my arm**[12] to the *seed of Jacob's*[13] house and **made myself known to them**[14] in the land of Egypt; **I raised my arm** to them, saying, **"I am Yahweh your god.**"[15] 6. On that day **I raised my arm** to them, to **take them out from the land of Egypt**[16] to *a land I scouted for them*,[17] *flowing with milk and honey*,[18] the most beautiful of

---

tual and Literary Criticism and Their Interrelation (ed. J. Lust; Louvain: Louvain University Press, 1986), 214–33; Johan Lust, "Éz XX, 4–26: Une parodie de l'histoire religieuse d'Israel," *ETL* 20 (1967): 488–527. For recent discussions of the structure of Ezek 20, see Leslie Allen, "The Structuring of Ezekiel's Revisionist History Lesson," *CBQ* 54 (1992): 448–62, and Lyle Eslinger, "Ezekiel 20 and the Metaphor of Historical Teleology: Concepts of Biblical History," *JSOT* 81 (1998): 93–125.

9. The concept of consulting (דרש) Yahweh is exclusively found in Deuteronomy (cf. Deut 12:5, 30), describing the functions of prophets in the tradition of Moses.

10. The expression "the word of Yahweh came to me" occurs forty-five times in Ezekiel (noted by Robert R. Wilson, *Prophecy and Society in Ancient Israel* [Philadelphia: Fortress, 1980], 283). See Wilson's discussion for its Deuteronomistic provenance. See also Walther Zimmerli, "The Special Form- and Traditio-historical Character of Ezekiel's Prophecy," *VT* 15 (1965): 515–16.

11. Yahweh's election (בחר) of Israel is a concept predominantly found in Deuteronomy, where the Israelites are reminded that Yahweh chose them from among all the nations of the world (Deut 4:37; 7:6, 7; 10:15; 14:2; 1 Kgs 3:8). P speaks only of the election of Aaron.

12. The image of Yahweh raising his arm (swearing) is used in P (Exod 6:8; Num 14:30) to describe his promise of land. That Ezekiel was familiar with this use of the expression is apparent in Ezek 20:28, which directly recalls Exod 6:8. See William H. C. Propp, "The Priestly Source Recovered Intact?" *VT* 46 (1997): 472. In D, Yahweh's promise of the land is described with the term נשבע ("swore," Deut 1:8).

13. The expression "seed of Jacob" is found in Exod 33:1 (E) and Deut 1:8; 34:4. In Deuteronomy, this expression is used in connection with Yahweh's promise of land to the patriarchs.

14. The theme of Yahweh making himself known either by reputation or by name is found exclusively in P (Exod 2:25 [LXX, = MT *Vorlage*]; 6:3). For discussion of this expression in P and Ezek 20, see Propp, "Priestly Source Recovered Intact?" 473. Propp suggests that the similarities between Ezek 20:5 and the two passages in P may indicate that the prophet knew P as an independent narrative source.

15. This expression occurs twenty-two times in P and four times in Ezekiel; see Levitt Kohn, *New Heart*, 90. In P, the phrase serves as a refrain reminding the Israelites of Yahweh's constant presence in all aspects of their life as well as his role in rescuing them from Egypt.

16. See Exod 6:6, 7; 12:42. For detailed discussion of the similarities between Ezek 20:5–9 and Exod 6:2–9, see Jean L. Ska, "La place d'Ex 6, 2–8 dans la narration de l'Exode," *ZAW* 94 (1982): 539, and Propp, "Priestly Source Recovered Intact?" 472–73. The use of the verb הוציא ("take out") is particularly noteworthy.

17. In both P (Num 13) and D, תור ("scout") describes the advance scouting of land. However, the notion that Yahweh himself did the reconnoitering is exclusive to D (Deut 1:33) and Ezekiel. The LXX apparently read נתתי, perhaps confusing תרתי with earlier נשאתי (v. 6a).

18. This expression is prevalent in all the pentateuchal sources except P, where it appears only in Lev 20:24 (see, e.g., Exod 3:8 [J], 17 [E]; Num 13:27 [J]; 16:14 [J]; Deut 6:3; 11:9; 26:9, 15; 27:3; 31:20; Josh 5:6).

all lands. 7. I said to them, "Each of you cast away the abominations of your eyes, and do not pollute yourselves with the *detestable things*[19] of Egypt. **I am Yahweh your god.**" 8. But they rebelled against me and would not heed me. Each one did not cast away the abominations of his or her eyes, and they did not abandon the *detestable things* of Egypt. So I resolved to *pour out my wrath upon them, spending my anger*[20] against them within the land of Egypt. 9. But I acted for the sake of my name,[21] lest it be profaned **in the eyes of the nations**[22] in whose midst they were, to whom **I had revealed myself** in their eyes, by taking them out of the land of Egypt. 10. So I led them out of the land of Egypt and brought them into the wilderness. 11. I gave them my *statutes* and showed them my *ordinances*[23] *by whose observance everyone shall live.*[24] 12. Moreover, I gave them **my Sabbaths,**[25] **to be a sign between me and them,**[26] so that they might know that **I, Yahweh, sanctify them.**[27] 13. But the house of Israel rebelled against me in the wilderness; they did not follow my *statutes* but rejected my *ordinances, by whose observance everyone shall live*; and **my Sabbaths** they greatly profaned. Then I resolved to *pour out my wrath* upon them in the wilderness, to make an end of them. 14. But I acted for the sake of my name, so that it should not be profaned **in the eyes of the nations**, in whose sight I had brought them out. 15. Moreover, **I raised my arm** to them in the wilderness that **I would not bring them into the land I had given them,**[28] *flowing with*

---

19. See Deut 29:16; 1 Kgs 11:5, 7; 2 Kgs 23:13, 24; Jer 4:1; 7:30; 13:27; 16:18; 32:34. In Deuteronomy and the Deuteronomistic History, this term always refers, as it does here, to idolatry. In P, the term describes various creatures unfit for consumption, but is never used in connection with idolatry.

20. The description of Yahweh's anger with the terms אף and חמה is found in Deut 9:19; 29:27; Jer 7:20; 21:5; 32:31; 33:5; 36:7; 42:18; 44:6; and nine times in Ezekiel (5:13, 15; 7:8; 13:13; 20:8, 21; 22:20; 23:25; 25:14; 38:18).

21. In Exod 32:11 (E), it is Moses who urges Yahweh to refrain from killing the Israelites for the sake of what the Egyptians might say. This appeal is recounted in Deut 9. Yahweh also shows concern for the preservation of his holy name in Lev 22:32 (P).

22. See Lev 26:45 (P), where Yahweh's deliverance of the Israelites from Egypt and his establishment of a formal relationship with Israel occur "in the sight of the foreign nations."

23. The expression חקים ומשפטים is found exclusively in D (Deut 4:1, 5, 8, 14; 5:1; 11:32; 12:1), whereas P prefers the expression חקות ומשפטים (Lev 18:4, 5, 26; 19:37; 20:22; 25:18; 26:15, 43), contra Moshe Weinfeld, *Deuteronomy and the Deuteronomistic School* (Oxford: Clarendon, 1972), 337.

24. Greenberg notes that the combination of observance and life is a Deuteronomistic concept (*Ezekiel 1–20*, 366). See Deut 6:24–25; 30:15, 19 (cf. Ezek 18:5; 33:15). The concept of living by Yahweh's statutes and ordinances also recalls Lev 18:5.

25. See Exod 31:13; Lev 19:3, 30; 26:2; and Ezek 22:8, 26; 23:38; 44:24. P requires that Yahweh's Sabbaths be observed and sanctified, whereas Ezekiel repeatedly accuses Israel of profaning them. Deuteronomy never uses the plural in reference to the Sabbath.

26. The Sabbath is described as a sign between Yahweh and the Israelites exclusively in P (Exod 31:13, 17) and Ezekiel (20:12, 20). See Levitt Kohn, *New Heart*, 49.

27. This expression occurs only in P (Exod 31:13 re: Sabbath; Lev 20:8; 21:8; 22:32) and Ezek 20:12. See Levitt Kohn, *New Heart*, 34–35.

28. Perhaps an allusion to the spy episode in Num 13–14 (cf. 14:30); cf. Burden, *Kerygma*, 172.

milk and honey, the most glorious of all lands, 16. Because they rejected my *ordinances* and did not follow my *statutes* and profaned **my Sabbaths**, for *their heart*[29] went after their idols. 17. Nevertheless, *my eye spared them*[30] from destruction, and I did not make an end of them in the wilderness. 18. I said to their children in the wilderness, "Do not **follow the statutes**[31] of your parents, nor observe their ordinances, nor defile yourselves with their idols, 19. **I am Yahweh your god**; follow my *statutes* and be careful to observe my *ordinances*, 20. and hallow **my Sabbaths that they may be a sign between me and you, so that you may know that I Yahweh am your God**." 21. But the children rebelled against me; they did not **follow my statutes**, and were not careful to observe my *ordinances, by whose observance everyone shall live*; they profaned **my Sabbaths**. Then I resolved to *pour out my wrath upon them and spend my anger* against them in the wilderness. 22. But I withheld my hand, and acted for the sake of my name, so that it should not be profaned **in the eyes of the nations**, in whose sight I brought them out. 23. Moreover, I **raised my arm** to them in the wilderness that I would *scatter them among the nations*[32] and disperse them through the countries, 24. because they had not executed my ordinances, but had rejected my statutes and profaned **my Sabbaths**, and their eyes were set on their ancestors' idols. 25. Moreover, I gave them *statutes* that were no good *and ordinances* by *which they could not live*. 26. I defiled them through their very gifts, in their offering up every **firstborn**,[33] in order that I might horrify them, so that they might **know that I am Yahweh**. 27. Therefore, Son of Man, speak to the house of Israel and say to them, thus says my Lord Yahweh: In this again your ancestors insulted me by **dealing treacherously with me**.[34] 28. For when **I had brought them**

---

29. Ezekiel's use of the motif of the "heart" as the place of human moral response to Yahweh parallels D/Dtr, where the heart often appears in connection with obedience to Yahweh and as the place in the human body where one makes principled decisions (Deut 6:6; 30:2, 14; Josh 24:23; 1 Kgs 8:48; 2 Kgs 23:25). See Paul Joyce, *Divine Initiative and Human Response in Ezekiel* (JSOTSup 51; Sheffield: JSOT Press, 1989), 119.

30. This expression is used in Deuteronomy exclusively with reference to the Israelites, who are continually commanded to show no pity in the face of their internal or external enemies. In Ezekiel, it refers exclusively to Yahweh, who shows no pity towards his backsliding people (Deut 7:16; 13:9; 19:13, 21; 25:12; Ezek 5:11; 7:4, 9; 8:18; 9:10).

31. The expression בחקי תלכו occurs exclusively in P and Ezekiel (Lev 20:23; 26:3; Ezek 11:12; 20:18; 36:27). The equivalent expression in Deuteronomy is to "walk in the ways of Yahweh" (see Deut 5:30; 8:6; 10:12).

32. This verse seems to recall Deut 4:27 directly, contra Greenberg, who states, "[T]he Pentateuchal sources are silent about this remarkable oath, taken by God even before they entered the land" (*Ezekiel 1–20*, 368). Ezekiel always uses this Deuteronomistic expression in connection with Yahweh's dispersion of Israel (Ezek 11:17; 12:15; 22:15; 29:12; 30:23, 26; 36:19).

33. פטר רחם occurs three times in P (Exod 13:2; Num 3:12; 18:15). It is also found in Exod 13:12, 15 (E?); 34:19 (J). See George Heider, "A Further Turn on Ezekiel's Baroque Twist in Ezek 20:25–26," *JBL* 107 (1988): 721–24.

34. See Lev 5:15, 21; Num 5:6, 27; 31:16; and Ezek 14:13; 15:8; 17:20; 18:24.

into the land that I raised my arm to give them, then, wherever they saw any *high hill or any leafy tree*,[35] there they offered their sacrifices and presented the provocation of their offering; there they sent up their **pleasing odors**,[36] and there they poured out their drink offerings. 29. I said to them, "What is the high place to which you go?" So it is called Bamah *to this day*.[37] 30. **Therefore, say**[38] to the house of Israel, thus says my Lord Yahweh: will you defile yourselves after the manner of your ancestors and go after their detestable things? 31. When you offer your gifts and *make your children pass through fire*,[39] you defile yourselves with all your idols to this day. And shall I be *consulted* by you, house of Israel? As I live, says Yahweh, I will not be consulted by you. 32. What arises in your mind will never happen, when you say *"Let us be like the nations*,[40] like the families of the countries and serve *wood and stone*."[41] 33. As I live, says my Lord Yahweh, *with a mighty hand and an outstretched arm*[42] and with *wrath poured out* I will rule you. 34. I will bring you out from the peoples and *gather you from the lands in which you have been scattered with a mighty hand and an outstretched arm* and with *wrath poured out;* 35. and I will bring you into the wilderness of the peoples, and there I will enter into judgment with you, *face to face*.[43] 36. As I entered into judgment with your ancestors in the wilderness of the land of Egypt, so I will enter into judgment with you, says my Lord Yahweh. 37. I will make you **pass under the staff**[44] and will bring you within the bond of the covenant. 38. I will purge out the rebels among you and those who sin against me; I will bring them out of the **land of their sojourn**,[45] but

---

35. See Deut 12:2; 1 Kgs 14:23; 2 Kgs 16:4; 17:10; Jer 2:20; 3:6; Ezek 6:13. Both Dtr and Ezekiel describe idolatrous practice in terms of worship at these locations.

36. This expression occurs thirty-three times in P and in Ezek 6:13; 16:19. Whereas P refers to Israelite offerings in this way, Ezekiel (with the exception of 20:41) uses the expression with reference to pagan practices. See further Levitt Kohn, *New Heart*, 55–56, 76–77.

37. The expression עד היום הזה occurs in Gen 26:33 (J); 32:33 (E); 47:26 (E?); 48:15 (E); Exod 10:6 (E?); Num 22:30 (E); fifty-five times in D/Dtr; and nine times in Jeremiah.

38. See Exod 6:6; Num 25:12 and Ezek 11:16, 17; 12:23, 28; 14:6; 33:25; 36:22.

39. Deuteronomy 18:10 prohibits passing one's child through fire, while P uses its own phraseology, "from your seed you shall not pass over to Molech" (Lev 18:21). Here Ezekiel compares Israel's current idolatrous activity to that of her ancestors following D's terminology.

40. The wish of the people "to be like other nations" (נהיה כגוים) recalls 1 Sam 8:20. On both occasions, the people's defiant wish leads to Yahweh's anger. See Greenberg, *Ezekiel 1–20*, 371.

41. The idolatrous practice of worshiping "wood and stone" is mentioned in Deut 4:28; 28:36, 64; 29:16; 2 Kgs 19:18; Isa 37:19.

42. See Deut 4:34; 5:15; 26:8; Jer 32:21; Ps 136:12. Deuteronomy uses this expression to describe Yahweh's wondrous deliverance of the Israelites from slavery in Egypt. Here Ezekiel describes Israel's future deliverance with the same expression. Note that Ezekiel does not use the term in his recollection of the exodus from Egypt.

43. The expression פנים אל־פנים recalls Yahweh's relationship with Moses in Deut 34:10 and Exod 33:11 (E).

44. See Lev 27:32.

45. See Gen 17:8; 28:4; 36:7; 37:1; Exod 6:4. In P, this expression refers exclusively to Canaan as it was promised to Abraham and his offspring. In Ezekiel, it refers to the lands of exile. Here, the land of

they will not enter the land of Israel. Then **you will know that I am Yahweh**. 39. As for you, house of Israel, thus says my Lord Yahweh: Go serve your idols, each of you, and after, if you will not listen to me, you shall no more **profane my holy name**[46] with your gifts and your idols. 40. But on my holy mountain, the mountain height of Israel, word of my Lord God, there all the house of Israel, all of them, shall serve me in the land; there I will receive them, and there I will require your contributions and the choicest of your gifts, with all your sacred things. 41. As a **pleasing odor** I will accept you, when I bring you out of the peoples and *gather you out of the countries where you have been scattered*; and I will manifest my holiness among you **in the eyes of the nations**. 42. **You will know that I am Yahweh**, when I bring you into the land of Israel, the country that **I raised my arm** to give to your ancestors. 43. There you shall remember your ways and all your deeds by which you have polluted yourselves, and you will despise yourselves for all the evils you have committed. 44. And **you shall know that I am Yahweh**, when I deal with you for my name's sake, not according to your evil ways or corrupt deeds, house of Israel, says my Lord Yahweh.

Ezekiel chronicles Israel's past through an intricate synthesis of Priestly and Deuteronomistic terminology and traditions. It is not an optimistic tale. The elders' consultation with Ezekiel reflects the classic Deuteronomistic prophetic mode for inquiring of Yahweh. Ezekiel's trenchant response, however, is to cite to them Yahweh's refusal to respond to such inquiry (20:3). Yahweh's singular selection of Israel from among the nations is portrayed as having occurred on a specific day when God made himself known to the people in Egypt. This combines the Deuteronomistic concept of Yahweh's election with P's recollections of the exodus.[47] Ezekiel echoes Deuteronomy's conviction that Israel is being punished for past sins, and yet he is reminiscent of P when he recounts the role of the law in this regard. He stirs an odd concoction of both theologies by suggesting that Israel's laws are construed as part of Yahweh's castigation of Israel. Ezekiel then toys with this premise by deeming some laws as "no good" (לא טובים), such that no one can live by them (לא יחיו בהם), a cynical reversal of Lev 18:5 and the Deuteronomistic notion that laws provide life.[48]

There are also several striking differences between Ezek 20:1–44, on the one hand, and P and D, on the other. Ezekiel does not mention the role of Moses, Aaron, or Sinai. The prophet does not recount the plagues, Passover observance, or the miracle at the sea. He does not explicitly mention Yahweh's covenant with the

---

the covenant and the land of the people's sojourn are separate, antithetical and distinct entities. In P, they are one and the same.
46. See Lev 20:3; 22:32.
47. Compare Ezek 20:5, 9 with Exod 6:2 and Ezek 20:6, 9–10 with Exod 6:6–7.
48. Also noted by Wilson, *Prophecy and Society,* 284.

patriarchs.[49] There is no reference to specific incidents of rebellion such as the golden calf or the spies. Also, unlike Ezek 20:7, neither P nor D record instances of idolatry or punishment in Egypt.[50] The divine appeal in the wilderness (vv. 18–20) is likewise absent from both Priestly and Deuteronomistic traditions.

Patton argues that, in Ezek 20, the prophet uses earlier Exodus traditions to react to the fall of Jerusalem and to prepare the reader for the new laws revealed in Ezek 40–48. In this context, Ezekiel portrays himself as a "new Moses":

> It is clear that the author of Ezekiel 40–48 considered himself a legitimate mediator of the law. He believed Israel's history was still open to the possibility of the revelation of new law . . . the experience of the destruction of the temple rendered Moses irrelevant. . . . The book of Ezekiel manipulates the legal and historical traditions at hand in light of the . . . experience of loss, defeat and abandonment.[51]

This depiction too is a confluence of Priestly and Deuteronomistic traditions. Moses functions as a priest in P, while in D he is primarily a prophet.[52] In both sources, he is above all a legislator. Ezekiel functions as prophet, priest, and legislator; he is a prophet by calling, a priest by birthright. And Ezek 40–48 is the only body of legislation in the Hebrew Bible not placed in the mouth of Moses.[53] Like Moses in P, Yahweh warns Ezekiel before he sets out that his mission will fail due to the strong resolution and hardened hearts of others.[54] D foretells the coming of a prophet like Moses, who will be raised up "from among the Israelites, and in whose mouth Yahweh will place his words" (Deut 18:18). Ezekiel's mission, regardless of its success or failure, will signify to Israel that there was "a prophet among them" (Ezek 2:5). Then Ezekiel eats a scroll containing Yahweh's words; that is, the divine message is literally placed in his mouth (Ezek 2:10–3:1). Moses receives a design of the tabernacle in P; Ezekiel similarly receives a detailed vision of the new temple.[55]

---

49. Ezekiel 20:5 has often been understood to suggest that Yahweh's first covenant was with the Israelites of the exodus. However, Propp notes that Ezek 33:24, which refers to Abraham's inheritance of the land, and Ezek 28:25; 37:25, which mention "my servant Jacob," illustrate that the prophet was likely aware of a patriarchal covenant. See Propp, "Priestly Source Recovered Intact?" 475.

50. Rejection of the gods of Egypt is mentioned in Exod 12:12; Josh 24:14.

51. Corrine Patton, "'I Myself Gave Them Laws That Were Not Good': Ezekiel 20 and the Exodus Tradition," *JSOT* 69 (1996): 78. See also Henry McKeating, "Ezekiel the 'Prophet Like Moses'?" *JSOT* 61 (1994): 97–109, and Jon Levenson, *Theology of the Program of Restoration of Ezekiel 40–48* (HSM 10; Missoula, Mont.: Scholars Press, 1976), 38–39.

52. In P, *Aaron* is to serve as Moses' prophet, while Moses is to be "like God to Pharaoh" (Exod 7:1).

53. Levenson, *Theology*, 39. Thus, Ezekiel, unlike P, does not attempt to legitimize laws by locating them in a sacred past.

54. Compare Ezek 2:4 and Exod 7:3; see Jean L. Ska, "La sortie d'Egypte (Ex 7–14) dans le récit sacerdotal (Pg) et la tradition prophétique," *Bib* 60 (1979): 203–4. Ska notes the similarities between Ezekiel's call (Ezek 2:1–3:11) and the commissioning of Moses in Exod 7:1–5.

55. Kaufmann believes the temple vision in Ezekiel is based upon Exod 29:9, 40 (*The Religion of Israel* [trans. M. Greenberg; New York: Schocken Books, 1972], 524). Both the Targum and Vulgate read תבנית ("design," "pattern") for תכנית in Ezek 43:10.

Before Ezekiel sees this vision, he is transported to a high mountain (Ezek 40:2) and shown the plan in a manner closely resembling Moses seeing the land of Israel from Mount Nebo (Deut 32:49–52).[56] Both Moses and Ezekiel receive laws relating to festivals and sacrifices.[57] Ezekiel hears Yahweh speaking directly to him from the restored temple, just as God speaks to Moses inside the tabernacle in P (Num 7:89).[58] Ezekiel consecrates the new altar, instructs the priests, and oversees the cult, like Moses in P (Exod 28; 29; Lev 8; 9).[59] Ezekiel may only see in visions the land about which he has preached. Like Moses in P, he is not permitted to settle there (Num 27:12–13; cf. Deut 32:49–52).[60]

The quintessential synthesis of Israelite traditions is, of course, the compilation and editing of the Torah. This process, traditionally dated to the period of restoration, rendered the ideologies of JE, D, and P less visibly exclusive while preserving the essential core of each source. Examination of the book of Ezekiel, and chapter 20 in particular, suggests that the roots of this process are to be found in the early exile. Indeed, Ezekiel's younger contemporary, Second Isaiah, also combines and reworks older Israelite traditions, but lacks Ezekiel's priestly bias.[61]

Ezekiel synthesizes older Israelite traditions and interprets present events in the context of Israel's sacred past.[62] Ultimately, though familiar with the history and law presented in P and D, Ezekiel's presentation, unlike the redacted Torah, is not true to either source. As a prophet, and specifically as a prophet of the exile, he questions these traditions and reformulates them as is evident in our examination of Ezek 20. When it comes to formulating a plan for the future, neither source provided the ideal. Similarly, Ezekiel's evaluation of the people's behavior is based on the standards of both P and D. The failure of his contemporaries to follow the precepts of either torah provides him with a compelling theological explanation for the exile.[63] However, when it comes to future redemption neither source proves entirely useful. Indeed, the laws and regulations presented in Ezek 40–48 are among the few in the

---

56. Levenson, *Theology*, 42–43.
57. McKeating, "Ezekiel the 'Prophet Like Moses'?" 101. Levenson (*Theology*, 43) adds that much of the P material in Num 27–36 bears striking similarity to Ezek 40–48, discussing the liturgical calendar and rules of sacrifice (Num 28; 29; Ezek 45:18–25; 46:1–15), the allocation of land (Num 32; 33:50–56; Ezek 47:13–48:29), boundaries of the land (Num 34:1–15; Ezek 47:13–20), special land arrangements for the Levites (Num 35; Ezek 45:1–6; 48:13–14), and inheritance laws (Num 36; Ezek 46:16–18).
58. G. C. M. Douglas, "Ezekiel's Temple," *ExpTim* 9 (1897–98): 421.
59. Levenson, *Theology*, 38.
60. McKeating takes this even further, observing that Ezekiel, like Moses in Deut 34, is not reported as descending the mountain after his final vision ("Ezekiel the 'Prophet Like Moses'?" 103).
61. See, e.g., Bernhard Anderson, "Exodus Typology in Second Isaiah," in *Israel's Prophetic Heritage: Essays in Honor of James Muilenburg* (ed. B. Anderson and W. Harrelson; New York: Harper, 1962), 177–95.
62. See also the conclusions of Ellen Davis in *Swallowing the Scroll: Textuality and the Dynamics of Discourse in Ezekiel's Prophecy* (JSOTSup 78; Sheffield: JSOT Press, 1989).
63. See Levitt Kohn, *New Heart*, 78–80, 94.

Hebrew Bible not based upon the Sinai event.[64] Ezekiel, as a prophet of the exile, endeavored to create a new theology that was neither independent of its sources nor a simple composite of them.

As noted in our analysis, Ezekiel's retelling of Israelite history in chapter 20 illustrates that the prophet was well versed in the sources that now make up the redacted Torah. Ezekiel does not appear to favor one version over the others.

The prophet's priestly lineage as well as his numerous allusions to the P source—both context and vocabulary—have led some to argue for the predominant importance of things Priestly in Ezekiel. Our analysis suggests otherwise. The prophet is familiar with P, but his writing is more than just a product of its influence or tradition. Ezekiel's analysis of Israelite history does not elevate the status of P over other Torah sources. Rather, the prophet appropriates Priestly content and terminology situating it in new, different, and even contradictory contexts. P is not simply imitated in Ezekiel, nor is D.

The efforts of Ezekiel and of the later pentateuchal redactor may indicate that the priests in exile, with their temple destroyed and their ideology discredited, came to accept what were rival streams of thought in preexilic Israel. Additionally, by appropriating these traditions in the way he does, Ezekiel appears to leave his priestly role behind. Although this background shaped Ezekiel's message, his book is first and foremost the work of a prophet.[65] As such, Ezekiel models himself on Moses—the Israelite prophet and lawgiver par excellence—issuing laws in anticipation of the next exodus and resettlement of the land of Israel.

---

64. See ibid., 112.

65. See Baruch Schwartz, "A Priest Out of Place: Reconsidering Ezekiel's Role in the History of the Israelite Priesthood," in the present volume. Schwartz presents compelling evidence that questions the existence of a so-called exilic priesthood with which Ezekiel has traditionally been associated.

Creation and Hierarchy in Ezekiel: Methodological Perspectives and Theological Prospects

David L. Petersen

In this essay devoted to the topic "Creation and Hierarchy in Ezekiel," I want to do several things. First, I shall offer some reflections about the sorts of methods that scholars have used (often implicitly) to make claims about the role of "creation" in the book of Ezekiel. Second, I want to review several recent proposals about the presence of creation language and/or traditions in Ezekiel. In this regard, I will assay proposed correlations between creation texts and Ezekiel. Third, I want to offer at least one reason why creation traditions may not have been particularly appealing to Ezekiel, as he formulated both his rationale for the defeat of Israel and his case on behalf of its restoration. Fourth, and finally, I shall describe some elements of the new creation that Ezekiel foresees in chapters 40–48, an order in which one may perceive spatial and human hierarchies.

I

First, claims about Ezekiel knowing or alluding to Israelite creation traditions are fraught with difficulty. What does it mean to claim that "creation" might be present in or important for a biblical book? Such difficulty is exemplified by the various analytical vocabularies that one encounters in such a discussion. In pursuing this issue, I have encountered scholars who talk about creation as a tradition, motif, theme, imagery, concept, story, account, myth, and belief. Such terminological variation bespeaks analytical difficulties. For example, a motif is quite different from a tradition. Each of these terms involves a different sort of claim; they belong to different discourses. What does it take for a text to attest to an identifiable tradition (e.g., the Zion tradition)? In a related vein, what constitutes a tradition? Similarly, what is a motif? How is a motif similar to or different from a tradition? If Ezekiel uses the verb ברא ("create"), would that be sufficient reason to think that he knew a tradition about creation similar to Gen 1? Or would that usage attest to a shared motif? Or might one want to argue that Ezekiel knew the text (whether oral or written) of Gen 1 or 2? In this case, would one want to mount an intertextual argument on behalf of a literary allusion? These questions raise an issue fundamental to biblical studies, namely, the necessity of articulating appropriate clarity of method or critical perspective.[1]

Two types of argument concerning Ezekiel and creation appear with some frequency. They involve appeals to tradition and to the existence of allusion, stances that bespeak tradition history and literary criticism.

A. TRADITION

The word "tradition" figures prominently in discussions of creation in Ezekiel. Yet what is a tradition? The question is surprisingly difficult to answer.[2] Some seem to think of it as a theme, others an idea, still others a text. These usages are diverse. For example, it is one thing to speak of the Zion tradition, and quite another to speak of the priestly tradition. Both have common currency in Hebrew Bible studies, and yet the referents are very different. The Zion tradition as such is a much more discrete entity, whereas the priestly tradition is used to describe the tetrateuchal source known as "P," religious traditions associated with priesthood, ritual, temple, and the like. Were one to speak of a creation tradition, one would, I think, be making a claim more like that on behalf of the Zion tradition than that of a priestly tradition. For the purposes of this paper, the so-called Zion tradition will exemplify what I mean by tradition.

However, does it make sense to speak of "a" creation tradition, since we know that Israelites viewed Yahweh's creative activity in diverse ways? From a traditio-historical perspective, one might, therefore, expect to ask which, if any, Israelite or non-Israelite creation tradition is perceptible in the book of Ezekiel? Potential answers would include the Yahwistic picture, the Priestly version, the imagery attested in Ps 104, something akin to the picture in *Enuma Elish* or the Atrahasis Epic, and so forth. There are multiple creation traditions.

In a related vein, and with specific reference to the topic of creation, one must address another basic question. When one analyzes a text such as Gen 2–3, which is often labeled "the Yahwistic account of creation," what in these verses counts as the Yahwistic creation tradition? To be sure, one may read Gen 2–3 as a unified piece of literature. However, as Westermann, among others, has argued, there are really two distinct elements present in these chapters: a narrative of creation and a story about Eden or paradise (on which see below). Put another way, not all portions of a so-called creation text may reflect a tradition about creation. An allusion to some

---

1. It is informative to observe someone address the issue of method when attempting to clarify possible Babylonian influence on the book of Ezekiel (Daniel Bodi, *The Book of Ezekiel and the Poem of Erra* [OBO 104; Fribourg: Universitätsverlag Fribourg, 1991], 35–51).

2. For a recent discussion, see Douglas A. Knight, "Tradition History," *ABD* 6:633–38. For a good example of a traditio-historical argument, see Frank Moore Cross, "The Song of the Sea and Canaanite Myth," *Canaanite Myth and Hebrew Epic* (Cambridge: Harvard University Press, 1973), 112–44.

element in Gen 2 or 3 does not necessarily involve an attestation of a creation tradition.

B. ALLUSION

One might, of course, offer a less "intense" claim, namely, that the author of a text was aware of an earlier tradition or text and alluded to it without attempting to include all the important elements of that text or tradition. For example, one might imagine a text that read "the heavens and the earth quaked" (cf. Joel 3:16). A reader familiar with theophanic texts in the Hebrew Bible might recognize this as involving the second of two elements normally found in a description of a theophany. And such a reader would understand that God's presence often caused the heavens and the earth to quake. That is what I take to be an allusion, an incomplete reference to a larger literary entity. Genette talks about allusion as "an enunciation whose full meaning presupposes the perception of a relationship between it and another text, to which it necessarily refers by some inflections that would otherwise remain unintelligible."[3] The description seems apt, though I would want to affirm that "text" here can mean something that could be "texualized," namely, an oral tradition, even if it were not actually in written form. Allusion, in this mode, belongs to the world of literary studies and is often described using the language of intertextuality. (One must at this point note that "intertextuality" can refer to various reading strategies.)[4]

Were one to think about Ezekiel alluding to "creation," one might imagine the presence of certain vocabulary characteristic of and peculiar to one or another account of creation, whether biblical or extrabiblical. If the phrase "the image of God" appeared in Ezekiel, someone might cite it as an allusion to the Priestly account of creation. Similarly, were a phrase like נשמת חיים ("breath of life," Gen 2:7) to appear in Ezekiel, I would not be surprised to see a claim that Ezekiel was alluding to the Yahwistic view of creation.

Claims about the existence of allusions obviously depend upon the relative age of the texts in which a "copresence" has been identified. In the case of Homer's *Odyssey* and Joyce's *Ulysses,* there can be no question about the direction of the influence. However, in the case of biblical literature, one may not so easily assume that the Tetrateuch or its constituent parts predate Ezekiel. So, to identify copresence is one thing. To claim that Ezekiel is alluding to the Priestly tradition, or that the Priestly tradition is alluding to Ezekiel, or that both are appealing to yet another "text," requires establishing a relative chronology of the texts that offer a copresence.

---

3. Gérard Genette, *Palimpsests: Literature in the Second Degree* (Lincoln: University of Nebraska Press, 1997), 2.

4. See, for example, Gail R. O'Day, "Intertextuality," in *A Dictionary of Biblical Interpretation* (ed. J. Hayes; Nashville: Abingdon, 1999), 546–48; Danna Nolan Fewell, ed., *Reading between Texts: Intertextuality and the Hebrew Bible* (Literary Currents in Biblical Interpretation; Louisville: Westminster John Knox, 1992); and *Semeia* 69–70 (1995), an issue edited by George Aichele and Gary A. Phillips on the theme of "Intertextuality and the Bible."

To speak of traditions and allusions is not, of course, to exhaust the full range of claims that might be made about the relation of Ezekiel and matters involving creation. For example, one might contend that Ezekiel is quoting (in reverse order) a text involving creation, for example, Ezek 36:11, "they shall increase and be fruitful" // Gen 1:28 "be fruitful and increase." Quotation achieves an effect different from an allusion. Some would maintain that the strategies for intertextual reading would help us articulate the ways in which such a quotation might work.

In sum, scholars have used diverse vocabulary to speak about the relation of creation and Ezekiel. In order to bring appropriate clarity to the conversation, one should recognize that, at a minimum, two different methods have been deployed—albeit often implicitly—in these discussions, tradition history and literary criticism.

II

A number of scholars have argued that Ezekiel seems to refer to or know traditions from the primeval history, even the creation traditions themselves. In particular, the dissertations by John Strong and, more recently, John Kutsko push in this direction. On the one hand, Strong, whose dissertation treated the oracles against the nations in Ezekiel, maintained that one central perspective in those texts was "the affirmation of Yhwh as the Great King of Israel."[5] Strong contends that this affirmation stems from the Zion tradition, which, for him, involves elements like the river of paradise and the temple. In this web of traditions, "the Hebrew creation myth was used in connection with the Jerusalem temple and Zion tradition."[6] More particularly, Strong contends that Ezek 28 exemplifies the creation tradition, since it overtly refers to the garden, the sin of hubris, and the expulsion. At one point, he writes, "Ezekiel chose the creation account because it was a story centered around hubris, the sin of the prince of Tyre as stated in 28:1–10."[7]

Several questions come to mind: (1) If traditions work in the way Strong postulates, can one imagine that any important religious motif in Judah would not have been part of the Zion/Jerusalem/temple complex? (2) Is creation as such truly important in Ezekiel? It is one thing to point to a motif of expulsion à la Gen 3. But does the notion of creation of humanity or the cosmos play an important role in Ezekiel's rhetoric? In my judgment, the evidence is not overwhelming. As I indicated earlier, it is necessary to distinguish between creation traditions as such and other primeval traditions, such as that involving paradise lost.

On the other hand, John Kutsko, too, has maintained that Ezekiel knew and used creation traditions in a significant way ("the prophet is interacting with the

---

5. John Strong, "Ezekiel's Oracles against the Nations within the Context of His Message" (Ph.D. diss., Union Theological Seminary in Virginia, 1993), 26.
6. Ibid., 228.
7. Ibid., 232.

independent but interrelated creation traditions from Genesis").[8] For example, he has claimed that Ezekiel knew and used the Priestly tradition involving the אלהים צלם ("image of God," ṣelem 'elōhîm), even though the phrase itself does not appear in Ezekiel.[9] He bases his argument primarily upon the presence of the phrase ṣalem ili/ilāni and its use to refer to divine-cult statues and kings in the ancient Near East. Kutsko deems the presence of the word דמות in Gen 1:26 and Ezek 1:26–28 to provide important evidence for the presence of a צלם אלהים notion in Ezekiel. In this regard, he appeals to Barr's judgments that there are strong similarities between P and Deutero-Isaiah. To be sure, Barr correctly observes that both P and Deutero-Isaiah share an "emphasis on creation."[10] However, it is not clear that Ezekiel shares this same emphasis. As a result, I cannot accept Kutsko's claim that "Ezekiel chooses the terms *demût* and *mar'eh* with knowledge of the Priestly ṣelem and *demût*."[11] Elsewhere Kutsko thinks that Ezekiel knew the Eden traditions (36:34–35) and, more generally, regarding Ezek 36:9–11, he claims, "[T]he larger setting as well as the immediate context suggests creation concepts from Genesis 1 and 2."[12] Finally, he maintains that Ezek 37:1–8 reflects the creation of humanity as depicted in Gen 2.[13] Ezekiel 36–37 has pride of place in this analysis.

If Strong's arguments are traditio-historical, Kutsko's are more "intertextual." The former appeals to traditio-historical complexes, whereas Kutsko appeals to similarity in diction and thought. Both want to claim that creation is important in Ezekiel, though they mount their arguments in quite different ways.

In order to focus the discussion, I shall at this point present a roster of representative claims that scholars have offered (or might offer) about the relation of creation texts in Genesis to the book of Ezekiel. According to their order in Genesis, the similarities are:

ברא—Gen 1:1, 21, 27; 2:3, 4 // Ezek 28:13, 15
תהום—Gen 1:2 // Ezek 31:4
תנין—Gen 1:21 // Ezek 29:3
Command to be fruitful and multiply—Gen 1:28 // Ezek 36:11 (missing in LXX)
Breath of life—Gen 2:7 // Ezek 37:8 (different vocabulary!)
Eden/primeval human—Gen 2–3 // Ezek 28:11–19

---

8. John F. Kutsko, "The Presence and Absence of God in the Book of Ezekiel" (Ph.D. diss., Harvard University, 1997), 222 n. 129.
9. John F. Kutsko, *Between Heaven and Earth: Divine Presence and Absence in the Book of Ezekiel* (Biblical and Judaic Studies from the University of California, San Diego, 7; Winona Lake, Ind.: Eisenbrauns, 2000), 54. This is the published version of his dissertation.
10. J. Barr, "The Image of God in the Book of Genesis—A Study in Terminology," *BJRL* 51 (1968): 12–14.
11. Kutsko, *Between Heaven and Earth*, 67.
12. Ibid., 131.
13. Ibid., 133.

The paradisal river(s)—Gen 2:10–14 // Ezek 47:1–12
Gemstones—Gen 2:11–12 // Ezek 28:13
Cosmic tree—Gen 2:9 // Ezek 17:22–24; 31
The sword—Gen 3:24 // Ezek 21:13–22 (Eng. 21:8–17)
The cherub(im)—Gen 3:24 // Ezek 28:14, 16

This list prompts a number of observations. First, the preponderance of apparent similarities occurs between Ezekiel and the so-called Yahwistic version. Second, the absence of connection between Ezekiel and the Priestly account of creation is striking, especially given the number of instances elsewhere in Ezekiel where that book is directly related to priestly or ritual concerns. Third, most of the similarities involve isolated vocabulary, not the narrative flow of either biblical account of creation. Fourth, one text (Ezek 28) presents the greatest number of putative parallels to the Genesis material.

Not all of the putative similarities are equally significant. Hence, it is appropriate to determine if they involve either an allusion or an appeal to a tradition. In this regard, we may benefit from the use of tradition history, especially as that method has been used to examine Gen 2–3. Claus Westermann has argued—convincingly in my judgment—that Gen 2–3 derives from several different traditions, including the creation of humanity and the paradise/expulsion. More particularly, he contends that Gen 2:9–17 belongs to the paradise/expulsion tradition, not to the creation tradition.[14] If one follows Westermann's lead, it seems clear that virtually all the similarities between the Yahwistic tradition and Ezekiel occur in the paradise/expulsion story. As a result, from a traditio-historical perspective, it is licit to claim that Ezekiel did not use creation traditions attested either in Gen 1 or 2 in consequential ways.

To make this argument is not, of course, to claim that Ezekiel was unaware of biblical and/or ancient Near Eastern primeval traditions. As John Van Seters has shown, Ezekiel's depiction of a primal man in the garden and his subsequent expulsion suggests strongly that Ezekiel knew an ancient Near Eastern tradition otherwise unattested in ancient Israel. However, especially given the current flux in pentateuchal studies, one must be careful about assuming that Genesis influenced Ezekiel. For example, Van Seters maintains that Ezek 28 influenced the Yahwist, not the other way around.[15]

At this point, I need to integrate the analysis in this section of the essay with the methodological clarifications offered in the first section. We have discovered that Ezekiel has used the tradition of the primal human/king-expulsion. The tradition of

---

14. Claus Westermann, *Genesis 1–11* (Minneapolis: Augsburg, 1984), 190–96.
15. John Van Seters, "The Creation of Man and the Creation of the King," *ZAW* 101 (1989): 340. Cf. Dexter E. Callender Jr., "The Primal Human in Ezekiel and the Image of God," in *The Book of Ezekiel: Theological and Anthropological Perspectives* (ed. M. Odell and J. Strong; SBLSymS 9; Atlanta: Society of Biblical Literature, 2000), 190–91, who maintains that Ezek 28 reflects Gen 1–3.

a primal king is attested in a recently published Neo-Babylonian text.[16] Moreover, we have found no evidence that Ezekiel has used biblical creation traditions in his rhetoric. There do appear to be allusions to creation texts, for example, the references to a vivifying breath/spirit, though the vocabulary in Ezek 37:5 is different from that in Gen 2. Nonetheless, apart from these allusions, the larger creation traditions, along with their attending theological implications, are absent from Ezekiel.

III

Creation traditions are not important for Ezekiel's theological argument. Ezekiel did not use creation traditions in a way comparable to Deutero-Isaiah (e.g., Isa 42) or Trito-Isaiah (Isa 66:22), major prophetic voices in the articulation of Israel's convictions about creation. Even when Ezekiel does incorporate vocabulary of creation, such language occurs primarily in contexts of judgment. It is, therefore, no accident that Ezekiel shares the diction of several verses in Gen 2–3, since this is a story in which the utterly human character of the Earth-creature is underscored. Ezekiel has no real stake in identifying humans as created in the image of God or in viewing everything that God had made as "very good." Moreover, he does not invest time in talking about the wonders of the cosmos. The heavens and the earth are not, for him, of great theological consequence. For Ezekiel, humans are essentially corrupt, hence his version of Israel's history as an *Unheilsgeschichte* (Ezek 20). Similarly, when Ezekiel anticipates a better future, humanity will need to be reconstituted, perhaps even re-created. Ezekiel addresses this issue in various ways, but Ezek 36:26 may serve as a case in point: "A new heart I will give you, and a new spirit I will put within you; and I will remove from your body the heart of stone and give you a heart of flesh." Ezekiel's conviction is clear. Humans as originally created are defective. They have a heart of stone and breath that is insufficient to engender proper life. (The necessity of a new spirit is also emphasized in the vision of the valley of dry bones [Ezek 37:1–14] as well as in an oracle of weal [Ezek 39:29].) Such a position presumes that the original form of the Earth-creature was radically deficient, a claim similar to Ezekiel's perception that Israel, from its very beginnings, was fundamentally flawed (so, e.g., Ezek 16:3–4). Such a prophet would have had a difficult time proclaiming the goodness and significance of the created order. And Ezekiel does not try.

We should not be surprised about the absence of creation traditions in Ezekiel. He avoided other traditions as well. Von Rad observed many years ago, "He is strangely unable to expound the David tradition."[17] No prophet, no prophetic book

---

16. Werner R. Mayer, "Ein Mythos von der Erschaffung des Menschen und des Königs," *Or* 56 (1987): 55–68.

17. Gerhard von Rad, *Old Testament Theology* (2 vols.; Edinburgh: Oliver & Boyd, 1965), 2:236. Walther Zimmerli contends that Ezekiel did know the David tradition (*Ezekiel: A Commentary on the*

incorporates in equal measure all the major religious traditions of ancient Israel. The book of Isaiah probably offers the greatest variety, though this may be more a function of the time span during which the book was created than a function of Isaiah of Jerusalem's rhetorical arsenal. Some traditions were indeed important for Ezekiel, namely, those involving the presence of the deity, ritual requirements and defilement, priestly behavior, sacral law, the history of Israel, and so on.[18] But the creation tradition was not among them.

IV

When Ezekiel turns toward the future, he does, of course, build on prior realities and traditions. The land will have its fertility restored (Ezek 36:8, 30, 35). People will return; the population will multiply (Ezek 36:10, 38). Cities will be rebuilt. (Oddly, there is no explicit reference to the rebuilding of Jerusalem, though such reconstruction is presumed, since Ezek 48:30–35 refers to Jerusalem's gates.)[19] And, of course, a new temple will be erected (Ezek 40–43).

One might think of Ezekiel conceiving this restoration as a recapitulation of the preexilic order. But that would be far from the mark. The temple is conceived according to a new torah, "the torah of the temple" (Ezek 43:12). As Stevenson has shown, the temple reflects an entirely new concept of space. A square altar is surrounded by a square temple, the square symbolizing the perfection of holiness.[20]

In this new Israel, there is a hierarchy of space. In the middle of the land will be a sacred "strip" or district (45:1–5; 48:8–14). That district, "the holy portion," runs laterally through the country and is twenty thousand cubits wide (LXX). A central band, ten thousand cubits wide, belongs to the Zadokites. That territory is "the most holy portion" of the country. In the midst of that territory sits the sanctuary—in a square area five hundred cubits to a side (45:2).

In the holy portion, but farther from the temple, is another ten-thousand-cubit holding. This one is allocated to the Levites. They are distinguished from the "priest," but the Levites, too, undertake service at the temple (44:11, 14). The Levites are construed as "ministers in my sanctuary," but they are not "to serve as priest" (44:11, 13). Due to earlier malfeasance (e.g., 44:10, 12–13; 48:11), the Levites hold a lower rank than do the Zadokites. The hierarchy of space—holy vs. ordinary—manifests itself in human hierarchies, with the Zadokite at the top and

---

Book of the Prophet Ezekiel [2 vols.; Hermeneia; Philadelphia: Fortress, 1979], 1:41). However, its presence does not automatically translate to importance.

18. Zimmerli, *Ezekiel*, 1:41–52.

19. The word "Jerusalem" does not even appear in Ezek 40–48, a fact consistent with Ezekiel's negative view of that city and the abominations that were practiced within its walls. In Ezek 40–48, he speaks of "the city" (e.g., 48:15) and gives it a new name, "The Lord is there" (Ezek 48:35).

20. Kalinda Rose Stevenson, *The Vision of Transformation: The Territorial Rhetoric of Ezekiel 40–48* (SBLDS 154; Atlanta: Scholars Press, 1996), 19–30.

the common folk at the bottom: Zadokite, Levite, prince, common folk ("citizens of Israel" [e.g., 47:22], "people" [e.g., 44:14], "the people of the land" [e.g., 46:9]).[21]

Other hierarchies are emerging. In the old order, the king would have had pride of place in the polity. And Ezekiel does see a place for the restored Davidide. At one point, he is even granted the label "king" (Ezek 37:24). However, he is also given a less glorious appellation, "prince" (Ezek 37:25). In the authoritative vision of temple restoration (chs. 40–48), the role-label *king* is not used. Instead, the authors speak of the *prince*, regulating his movements, prescribing his ritual activity, and legislating his property and its disposition (44:3; 46:1–18; 48:21–22). The civil role of the king has virtually disappeared.

Also gone are the vast distinctions in status between the twelve tribes, whether expressed in size of land holdings (Josh 13–19) or in poetic imagery (Gen 49; Deut 33). Instead, the idealized land of Israel is to be divided "equally" (Ezek 47:14). All tribes are to receive the same amount of land. These proposals about the civil leader and territory abnegate the hierarchies that were established in Israel's prior two perceived polities, that prior to the monarchy and that during the monarchy. It is now time for something radically new, even utopian.

Stratification within Israelite society does not derive from either ownership of property or from status in the civil polity. Rather, in the dispensation of Ezekiel's temple torah (43:12), hierarchy plays itself out in the realm that truly counts, namely, that of ritual affairs.[22] The most pronounced distinctions occur within the priesthood.

Ezekiel 40–48 also addresses the status of non-Israelites. And these chapters do so with reference to this same world of ritual affairs. Non-Israelites receive explicit attention at two points in the vision of temple restoration. Based on the first text, one might be tempted to say that the author of these chapters was interested in creating a hierarchy in which Israelites were viewed as superior to non-Israelites. The foreigner, בֶּן־נֵכָר, is not permitted to enter the temple compound. The reasons are ambiguous. They are doubly uncircumcised (in "heart and flesh"). Further, they had apparently been improperly participating in temple ritual, whether heterodox or not is unclear (44:7–8). However, in prescriptions that address the allocation of land, the resident alien (גֵר) is permitted to own land, as would an Israelite (47:22–23). One

---

21. The nature of the distinction between the priest and Levite remains vexed. For recent and competing explanations, see Steven S. Tuell, *The Law of the Temple in Ezekiel 40–49* (HSM 49; Atlanta: Scholars Press, 1992), 121–52; Stephen L. Cook, "Innerbiblical Interpretation in Ezekiel 44 and the History of Israel's Priesthood," *JBL* 114 (1995): 193–208; Stevenson, *Vision of Restoration*, 56–78; Thilo A. Rudnig, *Heilig und Profan: Redaktionskritische Studien zu Ez 40–48* (BZAW 287; Berlin: de Gruyter, 2000), 42–44, 280–318; Michael Konkel, *Architektonik des Heiligen: Studien zur zweiten Tempelvision Ezechiels (Ez 40–48)* (BBB 129; Berlin: Philo, 2001), 305–32.

22. Cf. Susan Niditch, "One's place in this society is defined not only by one's job per se but also by the location one is allowed to occupy in the temple-as-cosmos, by what one wears, and even by what one eats" ("Ezekiel 40–48 in a Visionary Context," *CBQ* 48 [1986]: 218).

might presume that such resident aliens practiced the rite of circumcision (cf. Gen 17:12–13) and, hence, are viewed in a light different from the "foreigner." As a result, the critical distinction is not between Israelite and non-Israelite, but between ritually acceptable foreigner and non–ritually acceptable foreigner. The hallmark is circumcision.

Hierarchies in Ezekiel's restoration vision reflect primarily the impact of the sacral world. Both territory and people can be ranked on the basis of their access and proximity to the temple. As Susan Niditch contends, "One's place in this world is especially defined by one's role and place in this temple."[23] This polity does not, however, stem from the orders of creation, which Ezekiel deemed to be flawed. Rather, an individual's status in the world derives from new hierarchies, promulgated in Ezekiel's new torah, which was revealed in the vision of restoration.

V

Various claims have been proffered about the presence of creation traditions, motifs, and the like in Ezekiel. These claims derive from the deployment of diverse methods, primarily tradition history and literary criticism. It does appear that Ezekiel alluded to texts such as Gen 1–3, or perhaps an earlier form of them. In this regard, the Yahwistic tradition is more prominent than the Priestly tradition. Moreover, Ezekiel is familiar with nonbiblical primeval traditions, namely, the king in the garden. However, such data do not provide evidence that creation traditions play a prominent role in Ezekiel. Unlike Deutero-Isaiah, the theologies of creation are relatively unimportant in the overall theological construction of Ezekiel. Further, in the vision of a new temple-based community, new hierarchies emerge, those of space—hierarchies of spatial holiness—and people, reflecting their access and proximity to the sanctuary. Places and people of highest status are those closest to the deity. The hierarchies of space and people do not inhere in the created order. Rather, they stem from the acts of restoration foreseen in Ezek 40–48.

---

23. Ibid., 219.

Cosmos, *Kabod*, and Cherub: Ontological and Epistemological Hierarchy in Ezekiel

Stephen L. Cook

Cherubim make multiple, fascinating appearances in Ezekiel. Their movements in and out of Jerusalem and across the Fertile Crescent help structure the book. Well known in the ancient world as boundary keepers, the image of the cherubim also gives Ezekiel an ideal tool for depicting a storied cosmos, with graded levels of closeness to God. Exploring Ezekiel's cherubim is thus uniquely helpful in illuminating the hierarchical theology of the book.

In the ancient Near East, cherubim were winged, composite beings ("sphinxes"), regulating access to the center of the cosmos and divinity. They guarded temples and royal thrones, prime earthly access points to the transcendent. Ezekiel betrays a thorough knowledge of their widely known symbolism in the ancient world.[1]

In Ezekiel, the cherubim take the specific form of four-faced, winged creatures carrying God's throne (Ezek 1:5–14; 10:15, 20–22). Darting about like lightning (Ezek 1:14), and roaring like a sea storm (Ezek 1:24), they surround God's presence with a devastating display of divine power. Their symmetrical arrangement reflects the four points of a compass and they synchronize their movements flawlessly (Ezek 1:9, 12, 17, 19, 21).

---

1. For an introduction to the cherubim, see Hermann Gunkel, *Genesis* (trans. M. Biddle; Macon, Ga.: Mercer University Press, 1997), 24–25; W. F. Albright, "What Were the Cherubim?" in *The Biblical Archaeologist Reader* (ed. G. E. Wright and D. N. Freedman; Garden City, N.Y.: Doubleday, 1961), 1:95–97; T. A. Busink, *Der Tempel Salomos* (vol. 1 of *Der Tempel von Jerusalem von Salomo bis Herodes*; Leiden: Brill, 1970), 267–75, 285–87; F. A. M. Wiggermann, "Mischwesen A," *Reallexikon der Assyriologie und Vorderasiatischen Archäologie* (Berlin: de Gruyter, 1991–), 8:225–28, 245; Anthony Green, "Mischwesen B," *Reallexikon der Assyriologie*, 8:249–51, 255–57; Carol Meyers, "Cherubim," *ABD* 1:899–900; D. N. Freedman and M. P. O'Connor, "כרוב," *TDOT* 7:308–10, 314–19; Tryggve N. D. Mettinger, "Cherubim," *DDD* (2nd rev. ed.), 189–92. The temple at ʿAin Daraʿ northwest of Aleppo (tenth to eighth centuries B.C.E.) preserves superb examples of winged sphinxes guarding its entrance. See Philip J. King and Lawrence E. Stager, *Life in Biblical Israel* (Library of Ancient Israel; Louisville and London: Westminster John Knox, 2001), 335–38.

Parallel imagery of monstrous, guardian beings positioning themselves symmetrically about a holy, divine axis is common both in the ancient Near East and in the mythologies of world cultures. In these images, the cosmos's axis often appears as a highly stylized, symbolic tree, which marks paradise, or Eden, where God is present (cf. Gen 3:24; Ezek 31:9). Earthly temples aim to model this locale (cf. Ezek 41:18), presenting themselves as Eden, God's mountaintop garden (see below).

A cylinder seal from northern Syria (Alalakh level I–II, 1225–1175 B.C.E.) shows seated, winged sphinxes flanking a sacred, cosmic tree. They have raised their paws, forming a shield against all encroachers. Similarly, two ram-headed sphinxes mirror each other across a palmette tree on an ivory carving from Arslan Tash (ninth century B.C.E.).[2] Antithetical sphinxes, from about the same time, also appear on an ivory panel from Nimrud. They flank the same voluted tree, which rises heavenward in tiers.[3]

From farther west, winged male sphinxes guard the cosmic center on five cast plaques from Mycenean Cyprus (twelfth to early eleventh century B.C.E.). The plaques form part of a tripod's ring-shaped top. On each one, sphinxes sit upright, at attention, arrayed about a stylized, lily-like tree. They are lean and hungry, and wear round helmets with knobs and plumes.[4]

C. G. Jung's description of the image of the *quaternity* helps us conceptualize cherubim figures, and their heraldic arrays, as innately associated with a guarded cosmic axis. Jung found the quaternity in clients' dreams, in alchemy, and in Greek thought.[5] A widespread human archetype, it consists of a four-point or four-fold

---

2. For the Alalakh seal, see Dominique Collon, *The Alalakh Cylinder Seals: A New Catalogue of the Actual Seals Excavated by Sir Leonard Woolley at Tell Atchana, and from Neighboring Sites on the Syrian-Turkish Border* (British Archaeological Reports International Series 132; Oxford: British Archaeological Reports, 1982), 116–17, fig. 105 (cf. pp. 94–95, fig. 74; p. 121, fig. 110; pp. 123–24, fig. 113); idem, *First Impressions: Cylinder Seals in the Ancient Near East* (Chicago: University of Chicago Press, 1987), fig. 307; Elizabeth Bloch-Smith, "Solomon's Temple: The Politics of Ritual Space" in *Sacred Time, Sacred Place: Archaeology and the Religion of Israel* (ed. B. M. Gittlen; Winona Lake, Ind.: Eisenbrauns, 2002), 85–86. For the seal from Arslan Tash, see Richard D. Barnett, *Ancient Ivories in the Middle East* (Qedem 14; Jerusalem: Institute of Archaeology, Hebrew University, 1982), 48, pl. 47b.

3. Max E. L. Mallowan, *Nimrud and Its Remains* (3 vols.; New York: Dodd, Mead, 1966), vol. 2, fig. 477; Barnett, *Ancient Ivories*, pl. 49e.

4. H. W. Catling, *Cypriot Bronzework in the Mycenaean World* (Oxford: Clarendon, 1964), pl. 29c, d, e and pp. 196–97 (also cf. pl. 35a and pl. 36a); Bloch-Smith, "Solomon's Temple," 86. For additional examples of primordial beings guarding paradise in Semitic and Greek traditions, see my essay from which this article stems: "Creation Archetypes and Mythologems in Ezekiel: Significance and Theological Ramifications," in *SBL Seminar Papers, 1999* (SBLSP 38; Atlanta: Scholars Press, 1999), 123–46, and James E. Miller, *The Western Paradise: Greek and Hebrew Traditions* (San Francisco: International Scholars Publications, 1997), 14, 23, 26–28.

5. Jung was convinced that human dreams and myths provided access to universal "archetypes," constitutive of the "collective," unconscious human mind. See his *Psychology and Religion: West and East* (vol. 11 of *The Collected Works of C. G. Jung*; ed. H. Read, M. Fordham, and G. Adler; trans. R. Hull; 20 vols.; Bollingen Series 20; New York: Pantheon, 1958), 50. Cf. Ken Wilber, *A Brief History of Everything*

arrangement of objects or symbols associated with the sacred, the "numinous." Giving three-dimensional depth to the flat images of ancient seals and plaques, it symbolizes the notion of a holy cosmic center and the creation of the world that emanated in all directions from it.[6]

The evidence from ancient locales such as Cyprus and Syria provides a start for the investigations of this essay. Such comparative data is historically and geographically proximate to Ezekiel. My interpretive model for elucidating Ezekiel's cherubim would be greatly impoverished, however, without reference to Jung's research. Frozen images from the past spring alive when viewed as instances of the fascinating, dynamic human archetypes he treats.

Employing an interpretive model, formed out of comparative evidence and Jung's archetypes, greatly facilitates understanding the complex mythological images of the Bible, such as the cherubim. A model helps us imagine a coherent configuration for the sparse data of the biblical texts and bridge gaps in our knowledge. Contrary to its critics, the comparative method does not force a ready-made grid onto a biblical text. Use of a model merely suggests the complexity and range of possibilities at stake in a given biblical structure or pattern.

The thesis, defended by Jung, that Ezekiel's cherubim manifest the cosmic quaternity suggests that we should also connect them with a second well-known Jungian image, *Mercurius*, a "fourfold being."[7] Mercurius is the Latin name of the Roman god Mercury—Hermes, in Greek mythology—but for Jung he is also a basic archetype. He is the living threshold of the transcendent, holy realm of the gods, and all of its dangerous, volatile power. His relevance for comprehending the cherubim is apparent.

The cherubim, with all their incongruous features, begin to make sense once we view them as instantiations of Mercurius. Like the cherubim, Mercurius is a god of boundaries. Eyes cover his body in at least one of his incarnations, making him an alert and wise guardian of borders. The cherubim dart about in an agitated state, and so does Mercurius. A god of mobility, his winged helmet and winged shoes mark him as fleet-footed and aerial. The cherubim, with their frantic movements and four-faced heads, also mimic Mercurius' unstable, tensive nature. A liminal being in multiple respects, Mercurius embraces opposites in tension.

Some of the most illuminating evidence for understanding Jung's archetype of the cherubim comes from his "dream pictures," drawn by patients under psychiatric care. The pictures graphically portray the cherubim's derivation, drives, and vulner-

---

(Boston and London: Shambhala, 1996), 213–17. Furthermore, Jung argued that the images of alchemy correspond to archetypes. Cf. Janet O. Dallett, *The Not-Yet-Transformed God: Depth Psychology and the Individual Religious Experience* (York Beach, Maine: Nicolas-Hays, 1998), 38; C. G. Jung, *Alchemical Studies* (vol. 13 of *The Collected Works of C. G. Jung*; ed. H. Read, M. Fordham, and G. Adler; trans. R. Hull; 20 vols.; Bollingen Series 20; Princeton: Princeton University Press, 1967), 274.

6. Jung, *Psychology and Religion*, 52, 56–58; idem, *Alchemical Studies*, 282–83.

7. Jung, *Alchemical Studies*, 279; cf. pp. 191–250, which offer an extensive treatment of Mercurius and his many traits.

abilities. Jung was convinced that the images of these pictures are not inventions of the conscious mind, but representations of humanity's preconscious psychic functioning. As projections of the collective unconscious, they present the same archetypes that surface in human mythologies.

One "dream-picture" by a client of Jung powerfully identifies Ezekiel's cherubim as instantiations of Mercurius, the quaternary mediator of sacred power.[8] The painting depicts a cosmic (sacred) tree with a spirit lodged inside it as an anthropomorphic *modality* (i.e., a numen or genius of the tree). In other paintings, this modality awakens, undergoes fission, and begins to branch off from the tree as a quaternity or cherubim array (e.g., in fig. 27 of Jung's series). Here in this painting (fig. 30), the modality is a masculine figure, forming the trunk of the tree, and there is an ambiguity and numinousness about him.

A bird descends upon him, but a phallic arrow rises below him. His posture and garb exude an occult-like aura, but they could also be that of a Christian monk. Jung concludes that he is a "daemon" composed of basic elements in tenuous equilibrium and hence is to be equated with Mercurius.[9]

This brief discussion supplies the outlines of a model for understanding Ezekiel's cherubim. As we explore the cherubim, we may expect to encounter them as mirrored opposites, interlocked with some dangerously holy locale. Arrayed about this center, they may be keeping its holiness contained or facilitating its safe projection into the world. We should not necessarily trust the cherubim to be docile servants of goodness. We have seen them as lean and hungry beasts, as well as dangerously wise beings. Opposing forces seemingly battle within them, and their balancing act has no guarantee of perpetual success.

I. Ezekiel's Throne Vehicle and Ontological Hierarchy

An excellent place to observe Ezekiel's cherubim and their hierarchical symbolism at play is in Ezek 9–10, a vision of the supernatural judgment of Jerusalem. We witness in these chapters nothing less than the failure of all the normal structures and measures for ensuring God's safe dwelling among the Israelites in the temple. The collapse of these structures forces God's departure from Jerusalem carried by the cherubim, exposing the city to utter catastrophe. Ezekiel thus reveals in this section, by negative example, the cherubim's role in maintaining an inviolable, holy Judah.

Ezekiel had seen God's cherub throne before, in chapter 1, by the river Chebar in Babylonia. To the reader's shock, God's *kabod* ("glory") first appeared to the prophet in the exile, not only away from Jerusalem's temple but also outside the borders of Judah. His inaugural vision assured Ezekiel of God's presence with him and his fellow deportees, and formed a firm basis for his commissioning. It depicted

---

8. Ibid., fig. 30, located between pp. 272 and 273.
9. Ibid., 268–69.

little, however, of the normal pattern of the *kabod*'s dwelling over the cherubim of Jerusalem's temple. We learn more about that from chapters 9–10.

The chapters are part of a series of revelations that Ezekiel sees in a visionary journey to Jerusalem (Ezek 8:1–11:25). Fourteen months after his commissioning the spirit of God transports the prophet to Zion, revealing to him the basis of the city's coming judgment through the Babylonians. Utter degradation is forcing the departure of God's glory from the temple, levying a punishing destruction in its wake.

Ezekiel 10 reveals a great deal about God's cherub throne. For starters, v. 2 indicates the cherubim have coals between them, which supply the means of God's punishment of Jerusalem through burning (also see vv. 6–7). The presence of the fiery coals is no convenient happenstance. A basic fact about cherubim in Ezekiel is their association with burning supernatural power.

The vision of the cherubim in chapter 1 depicts their glowing fire in more detail. In particular, Ezek 1:13 describes how in the middle of the four beings, "there was something that looked like burning coals of fire, like torches moving to and fro." "The fire was bright, and lightning issued from the fire."[10]

I interpret the fire of Ezekiel's cherubim as numinous energy, that is, the dangerous, scorching *otherness* of the transcendent and the holy. The cherubim partake of this energy in their interrelationship with God, enthroned in their midst. Ultimately, the fire represents the blazing presence of God's very self.[11]

Invoking our comparative model, parallels with Mercurius quickly shed light on this numinous energy. Well known as energetic and powerful, Mercurius sometimes reveals himself as a being of fiery brightness—an astral figure. Thus, Jung associates him closely with the primal being of Persian mythology, Gayomart, a youth of dazzling whiteness. Like his alias, Gayomart, Mercurius is white and brilliant, shining like the sun.[12]

Further, Mercurius is a provider of blazing, cosmic water. Jung identifies him with the fiery stream that feeds the cosmic tree in some of his dream paintings (see

---

10. A parallel burning fire occurs in Ezekiel's description of the distinctive cherub in Ezek 28, which I discuss shortly. The fire, which ends up consuming the being, issues forth directly from his midst (מתוכך, v. 18). See Robert R. Wilson, "The Death of the King of Tyre: The Editorial History of Ezekiel 28," in *Love and Death in the Ancient Near East* (ed. J. H. Marks and R. M. Good; Guilford, Conn.: Four Quarters, 1987), 216.

11. See Dexter E. Callender Jr., *Adam in Myth and History: Ancient Israelite Perspectives on the Primal Human* (HSS 48; Winona Lake, Ind.: Eisenbrauns, 2000), 116–18; John F. Kutsko, *Between Heaven and Earth: Divine Presence and Absence in the Book of Ezekiel* (Biblical and Judaic Studies 7; Winona Lake, Ind.: Eisenbrauns, 2000), 88. Ezekiel's earlier description of God's image confirms its fiery nature: Ezek 1:27; cf. 1:4; 8:2. Cf. also, e.g., Num 9:15; Pss 18:9; 104:4.

12. Jung, *Alchemical Studies*, 131–32; see also pp. 225–29. Jung understands Gayōmart, also known as Gayō-maretan, as an instantiation of Mercurius. He is the primeval man of Persian mythology, created by the supreme god Ahura Mazda. On the astral functions of Near Eastern composite beings, see Wiggermann, "Mischwesen A," 229–31.

especially fig. 5). He quotes the description of Nicolas Flamel (1330–1418 c.e.) that the god Hermes—the Greek deity equivalent of Mercurius—"watered his tree with *that* water."[13]

Numinous power is fraught with danger. Mercurius is an unpredictable, highly intelligent god, who is difficult to contain once roused. In Jung's fairy-tale story of Mercurius, only extreme cleverness saves his discoverer from destruction. To release Mercurius from his glass bottle was to encounter holy energy, as much evil as good.[14]

Just as natural fire plays both constructive and destructive roles, numinous power has a similarly ambivalent character. It can be a potent good among God's people, but must also be respected and treated with utmost care. Otherwise, full-blown disaster is possible. The animal faces of Ezekiel's cherubim (Ezek 10:14, 22)—the lion face, the ox face, and the eagle face—all suggest a potential for animalistic violence (see, e.g., Jer 4:7; Exod 21:28; Deut 28:49).

Dale Launderville correctly states, "Fire, as a symbol of the divine presence, reveals the ambivalence of the holy: a warming presence or a scorching punishment. Whether one has a positive or a negative experience of this fire depends on how close one draws to the fire and how attentive one is to draw upon it without daring to take over or misuse its power."[15]

In their ideal, proper functioning, the cherubim play a positive hierarchical role in handling God's numinousness. They surround the fire and contain it, preventing an uncontrolled, explosive burning of everything lying below them in the cosmic order. They also channel the fiery power out to humanity, for purposes that may involve either salvation or judgment.

Ezekiel 10:7 explicitly depicts their boundary-keeping, mediating role: "A cherub stretched out his hand from among the cherubim to the fire that was among the cherubim, took some of it and put it into the hands of the man clothed in linen, who took it and went out."

The role of cherubim as controlling "valves" of fiery holiness makes them key stabilizing elements in the structure of the cosmos. For Ezekiel, gradations of holiness characterize this structure, extending along both vertical and horizontal axes. Later in Ezekiel's book, his blueprint for a restored land in chapters 40–48 makes his ideal, graded infrastructure for holiness even clearer. These chapters assume a holiness hierarchy whose two axes intersect at the temple as an organizing center (Ezek 43:12).[16]

The spatial conceptions of Ezek 9–10 lay bare Ezekiel's holiness infrastructure.

---

13. Jung, *Alchemical Studies*, 309 (emphasis mine); see also pp. 207–8.
14. Dallett, *Depth Psychology*, 48; Jung, *Alchemical Studies*, 193–94.
15. Dale Launderville, "Ezekiel's Cherub: A Promising Symbol or a Dangerous Idol?" *CBQ* 65 (2003): 174.
16. The temple rises on a succession of terraces, so that height demarcates increasing holiness (Ezek 40:22, 31, 34, 37). Holiness also increases horizontally as one moves in toward the temple's adytum ("holy of holies") through walled perimeters and gates (Ezek 42:14; 44:19; 46:3).

Combing these chapters, we note first the vision's vertical organization. It reports on divine reality in language couched in terms of up and down. The focal point of reference is clearly the cherubim.

Peering "above" (על, Ezek 10:1) the cherubim, the prophet catches glimpses of God's glowing throne, "something like a sapphire." Soon, God's very presence will appear upon it. At Ezek 11:22, God's *kabod* visibly hovers over the living cherubim, resting "above" (מלמעלה).

Nearer their heads, according to Ezek 10:1, is a "dome" or "expanse." This is the same cosmic boundary (רקיע) appearing in Gen 1:6–8, which separates earth and heaven. Atop it, God sits enthroned as king forever (cf. Ezek 1:22–26; Ps 29:10).[17]

For both Ezekiel and the wider Israelite context, with the divine glory present, Jerusalem's temple symbolized God's cosmic mountain towering into the cosmic expanse. There, humans came closest to Eden, God's holy realm. The carved pattern of repeating cherubim and palm trees on the temple's doors and wood paneling (Ezek 41:16–20, 25; 1 Kgs 6:29, 32, 35; cf. Exod 26:31; 36:35) helped re-create Eden's ambiance (cf. Gen 3:24; Ezek 28:13).[18]

In the present situation, sin polluted this sacred precinct. Ezekiel sees the cherubim "on the south side of the house" (v. 3), not within its midst. They are waiting to remove God's glory from a spoiled, desecrated sanctuary.

"Below" (תחת) the cherubim lies a wheelwork, where celestial reality makes contact with earth (Ezek 10:2). Normally, the wheels form a key junction of heaven and earth at Jerusalem's temple. Things are horribly wrong now, however, and God's glory is on the move (Ezek 10:15; 11:22).

The cherubim's wheelwork is where God's servants have nearest access to God's numinous energy. God's heavenly functionary, the man clothed in linen, approaches God's cosmic fire through the wheels to retrieve burning coals (Ezek 10:2, 6). Jerusalem's priests performed their normal functions at the same ground level, manipulating the temple's altar coals, burning incense and sacrifices to God. Like the functionary, they also wore linen (e.g., Lev 6:3 [Eng. 6:10]). The realistic wheels they experienced regularly are illumined by three bronze-stand wheels from the eleventh century B.C.E. unearthed at Tel Miqne-Ekron.

Ezekiel's visual description, with all its language of "over" and "under," clearly

---

17. See Tryggve N. D. Mettinger, *The Dethronement of Sabaoth: Studies in the Shem and Kabod Theologies* (ConBOT 18; Lund: Gleerup, 1982), 29, figs. 4, 30, 69, 100; Othmar Keel, *The Symbolism of the Biblical World: Ancient Near Eastern Iconography and the Book of Psalms* (trans. T. Hallett; New York: Seabury, 1978), 174, fig. 239.

18. So did many other details, such as the brilliant stones of the high priest's breast piece. See, e.g., Miller, *Western Paradise*, 109–14, 120; Callender, *Adam in Myth and History*, 50–54, 103, 132; and D. N. Freedman's comment, cited in Moshe Greenberg, *Ezekiel 21–37: A New Translation with Introduction and Commentary* (AB 22A; New York: Doubleday, 1997), 582.

assumes a storied cosmos. The prophet reveals a layered hierarchy of holiness in the world, with cherubim as the linchpin.

His carefully tiered universe is unusual, even compared to other ancient priestly theologies. One can readily cite alternate priestly corpora with differing views of reality, where cherubim are unrelated to increasingly holy cosmic levels. Wary of anthropomorphizing God, they avoid the idea of a cherub throne for God comparable to those in the palaces of Phoenician kings and other earthly monarchs.[19]

Compared with Ezekiel, the PT ("Priestly Torah") source of the Pentateuch has a relatively nonstratified iconography of God's presence on earth.[20] In PT, the cherubim are no under-propping for God's glory. Rather, when appearing to Moses, God simply speaks from in between them (Exod 25:22, PT; cf. Lev 16:2, PT).[21]

The temple is certainly a holy place for meeting God in PT's theology. In contrast to Ezekiel, however, it forms neither a supporting structure for God's glory nor an epicenter of a holy territory, permeated with God's numinous power.

The book of Isaiah, another literature oriented on temple thinking, also differs in imagining God's glory. Isaiah envisions God enthroned in heaven, not on Earth, and describes God's attendants (the seraphs) flying *above* the divine presence (ממעל לו; Isa 6:2), not beneath it. The guardian beings appear calling to one another, worshiping God seated below them. When Second Isaiah repeats the scene, God's heavenly attendants remain preoccupied with proclamation, not the cosmic structure (Isa 40:6).[22]

---

19. For sample royal thrones with cherubim, see Barnett, *Ancient Ivories*, pls. 19a, 52a, 53; Keel, *Symbolism*, 169–71, figs. 233–36.

20. This past decade, Israel Knohl and Jacob Milgrom have identified two different priestly orientations, HS and PT, within the P strand of the Pentateuch. For a list of texts in the PT source, see Israel Knohl, *The Sanctuary of Silence: The Priestly Torah and the Holiness School* (Minneapolis: Fortress, 1995), 104–6. The PT source views God as inscrutable and hidden, and is especially concerned with God's ceremonial worship by temple priests. Although I agree with Knohl's new identifications of HS and PT as priestly sources of the Pentateuch, I cannot endorse several of his arguments from silence about the theology of PT.

21. Knohl observes that as part of its avoidance of anthropomorphism, PT lacks "any description of God as seated on the cherubim" (*Sanctuary of Silence*, 131 n. 23). Mettinger likewise concludes that "here the cherubim are no longer throne bearers but serve as guardians of the mercy seat" ("Cherubim," 191). Cf. Mettinger, *Dethronement of Sabaoth*, 87–88, 106, 115. Alongside PT, Deuteronomistic literature lacks the idea that the cherubim supported God's throne. Deuteronomy does not mention any cherubim on the ark itself (Deut 10:1–5), and 1 Kgs 8:7 depicts the huge cherubim of the temple oriented downward, as a covering shield. Busink thus concludes that in 1 Kings, "The wings [of the cherubim] shelter the ark, 'just as birds safeguard their young'" (*Der Tempel*, 286–87, cf. 198; see also Mettinger, *Dethronement of Sabaoth*, 50–52). The second tier of the tenth-century Taanach cult stand fits this imagery. It has cherubim flanking a void in their midst that likely signifies God's presence. (I reject the alternative interpretation of King and Stager, *Life in Biblical Israel*, 341–44.)

22. The language of Isa 37:16 (= 2 Kgs 19:15) is mere traditional phraseology in the mouth of King Hezekiah. Isaiah himself knew the earthly temple could barely contain the hem of God's robe (Isa 6:1, 3). In Isaiah's theology, God inhabits eternity, not the temple's cherub statues. Cf. Keel, *Symbolism*, 172, fig. 237.

Holiness in Ezekiel has a horizontal configuration as well as a vertical one, and it appears of even greater theological significance. The horizontal, Earth-based structure is what prevents impurity from driving God's presence away from God's people. Ideally, it also allows God's holiness to permeate the congregation's lives.

Ezekiel's cherubim, with their tremendous mobility, permit God's saving power to project out into the land of Israel, creating a holy territory for God's people. Their awesome wings and wheels allow them to bear God's presence to all the land's corners.

The glory of the LORD is in its normal earthly locale as Ezek 9 begins. It is set down on the horizontal plane, resting in the temple (cf. Ezek 35:10; 37:27; 43:7). In Ezekiel, God has personal attachments with this setting, calling it "my sanctuary" (v. 6; cf. 5:11; 23:39; 37:28). The diction, with its anthropomorphic overtones, is characteristic of the HS ("Holiness School") source of the Pentateuch (Lev 19:30; 20:3; 26:2).[23]

The whole of Ezekiel's horizontal infrastructure of holiness builds on the HS source. It is in this priestly source that God's presence "dwells" (שׁכן) in the temple (see especially Exod 25:8; 29:45–46; and Lev 26:11, all HS; also cf. Exod 40:34). Other priestly biblical writings express themselves in different terms. The idea of the temple as God's personal home appears neither in the PT source of the Pentateuch nor in the book of Isaiah.[24] As I have noted, these writings avoid anthropomorphic depictions of God.

Within the temple, according to Ezekiel, the *kabod* of God normally rests in the adytum. It hovers over the cherub statues in the holy of holies, where Ezekiel sees it in Ezek 9:3 (also 10:4).[25] The statues sit symbolically at the intersection of the axes of the cosmos. As God's sacred power drops down to the cherubim and their invisible wheels, it switches axes and emanates horizontally into the world.

In Ezekiel's view, the idea of an earthly enthronement of God's *kabod* is not at all about exalting the temple as an insular sphere. More than other priestly circles of the biblical world, he wants this clear. God's sacred power is dynamic and animate, projecting itself into reality in the form of wondrous, living beings. Arrayed symmetrically about the cosmic center, the beings extend its influence horizontally to the surrounding congregation.[26]

---

23. For a list of texts in the HS source, see Knohl, *Sanctuary of Silence*, 104–6. The HS source is concerned with the holiness of all Israelites and with ceremonial and ethical purity in all the territory of Israel.

24. On this theme within HS, see Knohl, *Sanctuary of Silence*, 171; Mettinger, *Dethronement of Sabaoth*, 88–89. For the Isaiah community, heaven is God's home and Earth God's footstool (Isa 66:1). It would be impossible for humans to build a real house for God. At most, God's feet rest in the sanctuary (Isa 60:13).

25. Ezekiel uses the singular form of "cherub" (כרוב) to designate the inanimate pair of statues in the temple, in contradistinction to the four living creatures that they represent (Ezek 9:3; 10:4; see Moshe Greenberg, *Ezekiel 1–20: A New Translation with Introduction and Commentary* [AB 22; Garden City, N.Y.: Doubleday, 1983], 198–99).

26. Thus, both HS and Ezekiel stress that God's presence not only dwells in the temple but also "in the midst" (בתוך) of the congregation. See Knohl, *Sanctuary of Silence*, 109; Mettinger, *Dethronement of*

The cherubim have four faces, representing their omnidirectional interests. Their loud-sounding wings and gleaming wheels reveal the tremendous scope of their mobility. Possessing the spirit of the living cherubim (Ezek 10:17), the wheels extend the beings' reach to Earth's four compass points (cf. Zech 6:1–8).

Eyes cover their entire body, as well as their wings and wheels (Ezek 10:12; cf. 1:18). They are the "eyes of the LORD, which range through the whole earth" (see Zech 4:2, 5, 10b). One look at the cherubim and no one can doubt their role in extending God's presence and holy power out from the temple. They help create an entire holy land, where Israel can dwell oriented around God.

The cherubim reveal and release God's holiness, but also safeguard it. They must protect God's presence from the world, which contains sin and impurity that are anathema to the holy.

Especially in Ezek 9:9, the text reveals its concern with the periphery's threat to the center. In this key verse, God complains that transgressions in the land have desecrated the sanctuary, forcing the departure of the *kabod*. "The guilt of the house of Israel and Judah is exceedingly great; the land is full of bloodshed and the city full of perversity." God's majesty cannot dwell (שָׁכַן) amid such uncleanness (see Ezek 8:6; 43:9).

Here again, Ezekiel makes plain the roots of his thinking in the theology of the HS source. Unrestrained "bloodshed," God's chief complaint, is defined elsewhere in Ezekiel based on HS regulations. Ezekiel 22:2–12 is a good example. Its catalog of indictments repeatedly charges "bloodshed," defined in terms of Lev 18–20. Verses 6–7 reflect Lev 20:9; v. 9 reflects Lev 19:16; v. 10 reflects Lev 18:7–8, 11, 19; and v. 12 reflects Lev 19:13.

As Greenberg notes, the Hebrew commentator Joseph Kara already in the eleventh century saw the connection with Leviticus. Commenting on Ezek 22, Kara writes, "They transgressed everything written [in Lev 18–20]; hence they are called, at the beginning of this prophecy, 'Impure of name [v. 5].' "[27]

So too, when Ezek 18:10–13 portrays a quintessential "shedder of blood," it relies directly on HS. Verse 11 reflects Lev 18:20; v. 12 reflects Lev 25:17; and v. 13 reflects Lev 25:36.

An eruption of "bloodshed" in the land, violating the HS covenant, perfectly explains the divine departure, which is now in progress (Ezek 8:6; 9:3; 10:4; 10:18–19; 11:16; 11:22–23). According to HS, defiling any part of the land, God's holy territory, constitutes an assault of impurity on God's shrine (e.g., Lev 15:31; 19:30; 26:2; Num 5:3; 19:13, all HS). Sacrifices at the temple—particularly the purification offerings (cf. Lev 4:5–7)—can purge some of this uncleanness. Willful, chronic

---

Sabaoth, 96 n. 64. For the symbolic role of the cherubim in radiating God's holiness, see figs. 3, 22, and 26 in Jung's collection of dream pictures, located between pp. 272 and 273.

27. Greenberg, *Ezekiel 21–37*, 467.

pollution of the sanctuary, however, will eventually force God out and leave the people exposed to judgment.[28]

The *kabod* had moved freely outside both the sanctuary and the holy land in times past (see especially Exod 16, HS), and it could leave the land again.[29] Ezekiel 9–10 envisions the fulfillment of this threat.

Leviticus 18:25, 28, with its metaphor of a weak stomach, is especially illuminating of Ezekiel's theology. Expressing tangible revulsion at the prospect of the land's defilement (cf. Ezek 9:9; 36:16–21), HS pictures it vomiting out its unworthy inhabitants. Their abominations have resulted in divine abandonment, and the consequent experience of radical judgment.

Like Ezekiel, but unlike other priestly corpora within the Bible, HS understands God's holiness to project out from the central shrine to cover an entire sacred territory. To honor the land's holiness is to experience God's transforming presence. To defile the holy land, in the midst of which God dwells, however, is to push God away and invite disaster (Num 35:34, HS; cf. Ezek 33:25–26).

Where Ezekiel goes beyond anything in HS is in using cherubim imagery to clarify God's exilic-era departure from Jerusalem. The cherubim's innate quality of mobility had previously symbolized how God's holiness extended out dynamically from a stable center. Ezekiel now gives the mobility another role, for an unbearable time of crisis. If the center should experience irredeemable desecration, as it does in Ezek 9:9, the cherubim may use their mobility to spirit away God's glory.

As of Ezek 10:1, the mundane cherub statues of Jerusalem's shrine fade from view and the animate, living cherubim of God appear. Fascinatingly, supernatural reality begins to distinguish itself from Jerusalem's banal icons. The throne above the living cherubim appears empty. Ezekiel 10:3 begins to clarify what is happening.

In v. 3, God's *kabod* chariot appears on the scene *beside* the temple, available for occupancy. In order to collect the glory of the LORD, it must break into the temple precincts from the beyond. The *kabod* has been present in the temple (Ezek 9:3), but is clearly also interlinked with an expansive, transcendent reality.

The import of Ezekiel is inescapable. One cannot equate the visible compo-

---

28. Jacob Milgrom, *Leviticus 1–16: A New Translation with Introduction and Commentary* (AB 3; New York: Doubleday, 1991), 43; Knohl, *Sanctuary of Silence*, 185–86. This background theology of Ezekiel forces me to disagree with John T. Strong, "God's *Kābôd*: The Presence of Yahweh in the Book of Ezekiel," in *The Book of Ezekiel: Theological and Anthropological Perspectives* (ed. M. Odell and J. Strong; SBLSymS 9; Atlanta: Society of Biblical Literature, 2000), 87–88. In Ezekiel, God's presence *does* "dethrone" from upon Jerusalem's cherub statues.

29. Exodus 16 introduces God's *kabod* as a new phenomenon in the Priestly narrative. HS purposely placed the chapter *before* the events of Sinai and the establishment of Israel's cultic institutions, thus showing that the *kabod* of God is not eternally bound to Israel's land and its sanctuary. See William P. Wood, "The Congregation of Yahweh: A Study of the Theology and Purpose of the Priestly Document" (Th.D. diss., Union Theological Seminary in Virginia, 1974), 112, 116, 119, 132, 178–79. Contrast Steven S. Tuell, "Divine Presence and Absence in Ezekiel's Prophecy," in Odell and Strong, *Book of Ezekiel*, 100.

nents of Solomon's temple with the invisible, transcendent realities they represent. Through a cosmic and eschatological vision, Ezekiel has insisted on an expansive reality behind Zion's icons and symbols. God condescends to work with humans through icons, but icons place no limits or constraints on God.

This survey of the cherubim's role in Ezek 9–10 allows for some quick observations about cosmic hierarchy in Ezekiel. To begin, Ezekiel's hierarchical system allows God to abide unusually near humanity—much nearer than in alternative biblical systems. With the *kabod* actually enthroned in the temple, the congregation can encamp around the deity. The goal is dangerous,[30] so Ezekiel has "firewalls" allowing a safe, graded exposure to divine holiness. In the present circumstances, impurity has degraded the firewalls.

Ideally, in HS and Ezekiel, God's dwelling at the land's center molds the periphery, and the entire territory becomes sacred (God's own land, Ezek 36:5; 38:16; cf. Lev 25:23, HS). As Knohl summarizes, "Holiness . . . emerges from the Priestly center, radiating out to all sectors of society and to all walks of life and encompassing the entire land."[31] Every corner of Israel becomes ceremonially pure (e.g., Num 35:34; Lev 18:25, both HS; Ezek 39:12, 14–16). In contradistinction to PT's understanding, Israel takes no chances with the land's sanctity. Unclean persons step back from the congregation (Num 5:3, HS).

The ultimate goal of this theological system is increasing people's holiness. For their part, the people emulate the holiness in their midst (e.g., Lev 19:2; 20:26, both HS; Ezek 37:24; 43:9). God, in turn, reaches out to the people through graded structures to sanctify the willing. God exclaims, "I the LORD, *I who sanctify you,* am holy" (Lev 21:8, HS, emphasis mine; cf. Ezek 20:12; 37:28; and HS at Exod 31:13; Lev 20:7; and 22:32).

II. The Cherub of Ezekiel 28 and Epistemological Hierarchy

A very different use of cherub imagery appears in Ezek 28:11–19, a judgment prophecy against the king of Tyre. The passage describes Tyre's king by comparing him with a mythical cherub who committed hubris and fell from heaven.[32] The NRSV translators along with many past scholars have defended a contrary interpretation that the passage is about a prototypical human, such as Adam, but this cannot be correct. The central figure of the text is not "with" a cherub, but *is* a cherub.

---

30. Pure holiness kills. See, e.g., Num 16:38 (MT: 17:3); 17:13 (MT: 17:28), both HS; Ezek 42:14; 44:19; 46:20. Cf. Kutsko, *Between Heaven and Earth,* 80.

31. Knohl, *Sanctuary of Silence,* 198; cf. Kutsko, *Between Heaven and Earth,* 126 n. 110.

32. The antihero is a cherub, rather than Adam, in the KJV, NIV, JPSV, NJB, NASB, NLT, and the ESV. This interpretation is followed, e.g., by Freedman and O'Connor, *TDOT* 7:311; Greenberg, *Ezekiel 21–37,* 579–93.

This is the clearly the sense of the MT,³³ which in v. 14 reads, "You were an anointed cherub, the guardian." Similarly, the Hebrew of v. 16, MT, reads, "I drove you out, O guardian cherub."

The imagery of the text also demands this sense. Cherubim are companions of the divine presence. They are nowhere companions to humans, as the alternative reconstruction of the passage would have it.³⁴ Moreover, an interpretation of the antihero of Ezek 28 as a cherub is required by the mythological details of the passage.

First, the cherub dwells in a sacred center, Eden, the garden of God (v. 13) on the cosmic mountain (v. 14). The cherub was supposed to be a *guardian* of this center, and of the deity who dwells there. The Hebrew term סכך ("shield," "protect"; vv. 14, 16) has this meaning here (see Nah 2:6 [Eng. 2:5]; Exod 25:20; 37:9; 1 Kgs 8:7).³⁵

Second, like other cherubim, the figure possesses fiery, volatile power. Verse 16 associates it with violent power, חמס ("violence"). Verse 18 associates it with internal numinousness. The fire that eventually destroys it, turning it to ashes, emanates from its own midst (מתוכך, v. 18).

Third, the being shares signal traits with Mercurius. Mercurius is Jung's rubric for the universal archetype of the cherubim, of which this cherub is a particular example. Beyond the numinous fire of Mercurius, it possesses Mercurius's intelligence, being "full of wisdom" (vv. 12, 17).³⁶ Further, it shares Mercurius's astral characteristics. The אבני־אש ("fiery stones") among which it walks according to vv. 14, 16 are probably the stars of heaven.³⁷ This may be true as well of the precious stones set in its covering (v. 13).³⁸

---

33. In the Hebrew of v. 14 of the MT, the pronoun "you" appears strangely in the feminine form את. Greenberg argues, however, that את can have a masculine antecedent here, as it does, e.g., in Num 11:15 and Deut 5:24 (*Ezekiel 21–37,* 583). Also see James E. Miller, "The Mælæk of Tyre (Ezekiel 28,11–19)," *ZAW* 105 (1993): 498. Alternatively, the pronoun may be emended to אתה (Freedman and O'Connor, *TDOT* 7:311).

34. Miller, "Mælæk," 497–98. Miller argues that only a supernatural, primeval being, not a prototypical human, is appropriate as the antihero of the myth. Support for this position can be found in texts such as Ezek 32:1–16, which, like our passage, speak of a human king as a mythical being (cf. Miller, "Mælæk," 499).

35. For the association of cherubim with the cosmic mountain, see Collon, *Alalakh Cylinder Seals,* 94–95, fig. 74. On the significance of the term "shield," see Miller, "Mælæk," 499; Daniel I. Block, *The Book of Ezekiel,* vol. 2, *Chapters 25–48* (NICOT; Grand Rapids: Eerdmans, 1998), 113; Callender, *Adam in Myth and History,* 109 n. 233, 110; Launderville, "Ezekiel's Cherub," 167.

36. This correlation is strong evidence against arguments that the references to wisdom in the pericope are secondary accretions. For this view, see, e.g., Walther Zimmerli, *Ezekiel: A Commentary on the Book of the Prophet Ezekiel* (2 vols.; Hermeneia; Philadelphia: Fortress, 1979), 2:87, 94; John W. Wevers, *Ezekiel* (NCB; London: Nelson, 1969), 215–16.

37. Gunkel, *Genesis,* 34; Zimmerli, *Ezekiel,* 2:91, 93.

38. For these stones as the astral coterie of the cherub, see Hugh Rowland Page Jr., *The Myth of Cosmic Rebellion: A Study of Its Reflexes in Ugaritic and Biblical Literature* (VTSup 65; Leiden: Brill, 1996), 149 n. 264.

More than Ezekiel's other visions of cherubim, this one reveals their tensive, unstable nature. In conformity with comparative evidence, it shows that the mythological guardians of the cosmic center are unpredictable, that is, rather untamed.[39] Once the cosmic center spins off modalities, comparative study suggests, they may take on an ambiguous relationship to it. Differentiated from the central axis and parceled out into an array, they remain oriented to the center but diminished in relative power. Thus diminished, they may covet the center's power.[40]

A good example of the cherubim's ambiguous, untamed relation to the cosmic center comes from the Ugaritic myth of Athtar, a cherub-like figure. Athtar is another specific example that helps illustrate certain aspects of the cherubim archetype. He traveled to the cosmic center, Ṣapon, where he attempted to occupy the vacant throne of the god Baal. Despite his numinous power, Athtar's feet could not reach Baal's footstool, and his head could not reach the top of the throne.

In this myth (Ugaritic text KTU 1.6 I), Athtar, "the powerful," or "the terrible,"[41] is an awe-inspiring being interested in the cosmic center. Despite his orientation to the center, he cannot meet the demands of occupying it. Thus, as might be expected from a cherub, Athtar covets the cosmic navel but cannot lay claim to it.[42] His demeanor is not intrinsically evil, only energetic and ambitious.

If Athtar were an Ugaritic type of cherub, we would expect him to bear characteristic traits of Mercurius. In fact, this is what we find. Several aspects of Athtar's nature that have puzzled interpreters become intelligible once we make this connection.

Like Mercurius, Athtar is a fiery, astral god. A text at Emar calls him "Astar of

---

39. See Wiggermann, "Mischwesen A," 226–29, 231; Miller, *Western Paradise*, 26–27; Callender, *Adam in Myth and History*, 124; Launderville, "Ezekiel's Cherub," 168, 172; A. Green, "Beneficent Spirits and Malevolent Demons: The Iconography of Good and Evil in Ancient Assyria and Babylonia," in *Popular Religion* (ed. H. G. Kippenberg; Visible Religion 3; Leiden: Brill, 1984), 86. Green has a particularly interesting discussion of the malevolent background of many protective spirits in the ancient Near East.

40. Thus, the mirrored, anthropomorphic figures in a third-millennium cylinder seal from Mari seem to threaten the cosmic center (Keel, *Symbolism*, 47–48, fig. 42). Figure 10 (located between pp. 272 and 273) of Jung's collection of drawings of cosmic trees depicts two crocodiles as separated opposites, which Jung describes as dangerous. See, further, Mircea Eliade, *Patterns in Comparative Religion* (trans. R. Sheed; New York: Sheed and Ward, 1958), 291.

41. On Athtar's epithet, see Mark S. Smith, "The God Athtar in the Ancient Near East and His Place in KTU 1.6 I," in *Solving Riddles and Untying Knots: Biblical, Epigraphic, and Semitic Studies in Honor of Jonas C. Greenfield* (ed. Z. Zevit, S. Gitin, and M. Sokoloff; Winona Lake, Ind.: Eisenbrauns, 1995), 630; Page, *Myth of Cosmic Rebellion*, 90.

42. Thus, I would argue that Athtar's shortcomings in Ugaritic myth are bound up with the substance of the archetype behind him. They are not a historical reflection of his cult's demise at Ugarit in relation to the cult of Baal, as is sometimes suggested (e.g., Smith, "Athtar," 640). This argument is buttressed in that Athtar's watering function (see n. 45 below) may differ significantly from that of Baal. If Athtar's water is the fiery, animating water of Mercurius, then he would be in less direct competition with Baal than it at first might appear.

the stars"; a ninth-century Aramaic seal contains the name "Athtar of heaven."[43] In one Ugaritic text, KTU 1.2 III 13, Athtar possesses "torches" and "fire," which may signify his astral status.[44] Moreover, Athtar, like Mercurius, is an occasional provider of energized water. In the South Arabic inscriptions in particular, and probably at Ugarit as well, Athtar appears to be a peculiar type of watering god.[45]

Furthermore, Athtar is intelligent like Mercurius. Assuming that he is the same figure as *Yadiʻ Yilḥan* in KTU 1.6 I 47–54, Athtar is referred to as one who "knows" and "understands." Most significant in understanding Athtar, however, is his nature as an unsocialized and unstable figure, which he shares with Mercurius.

Athtar's unsettled nature appears in his quick assumption and immediate, voluntary abdication of Baal's throne. The data of KTU 1.2 III 1–24 mirror these traits. Athtar appears in this text as lacking both a house and a court, though he expresses interest in acquiring them. He is also unmarried, as he is in KTU 1.24, where others fear he would be easily aroused and made jealous at a proposed marriage of two deities. H. R. Page sums up the situation well: "Athtar serves as the cosmic archetype of divine powers whose *numinous* force has yet to be comprehended fully (and *socialized*)."[46]

In indicting Tyre, Ezekiel is concerned to expose its תוך ("inmost self"; 28:16), its "motivating force."[47] He knows this self-conception to be delusional, an affront to God and a threat to Israel. He thus aims to get it out into the open and to subvert it. Tyre's king, Ezekiel discerned, envisioned himself as a powerful cherub.

Although cherubim are untamed and dangerous, at Tyre to conceive of oneself as a cherub was a positive thing. One magnificent Phoenician ivory from the ninth century B.C.E. depicts a human monarch in the guise of a semi-divine cherub. The sphinx wears obvious Pharaonic trappings.[48]

Though intrinsically unsettled, cherubim were wondrous creatures, "full of wisdom and perfect in beauty" (Ezek 28:12). Far from an enemy of major Levantine deities, such as Baal and El, Athtar was actively worshiped alongside them.[49]

---

43. Smith, "Athtar," 629, 633. For similar South Arabian evidence, see also p. 635.

44. Athtar's "sinking" and "arousal" in KTU 1.24 may also reflect astralized behavior.

45. Smith cites two South Arabic inscriptions that call Athtar a god of watering. Lines 66–67 of the Athtar section of the Ugaritic Baal Cycle (KTU 1.6 I) associate Athtar with the drawing of water in flagons and jars. See Smith, "Athtar," 635, 638. Cf. Page, *Myth of Cosmic Rebellion,* 58, 92.

46. Page, *Myth of Cosmic Rebellion,* 78; cf. p. 86.

47. See Ellen F. Davis, "'And Pharaoh Will Change His Mind . . . ,' (Ezekiel 32:31): Dismantling Mythical Discourse," in *Theological Exegesis: Essays in Honor of Brevard S. Childs* (ed. C. Seitz and K. Greene-McCreight; Grand Rapids: Eerdmans, 1999), 231.

48. Mallowan, *Nimrud and Its Remains,* vol. 2, color plate IX, facing p. 560; Barnett, *Ancient Ivories,* 52 and pl. 51; Block, *Ezekiel 25–48,* 113 n. 120. Although it is Phoenician in style, the ivory is from Nimrud and may depict an Assyrian monarch. It wears a Pharaonic head cloth and *atef* crown. (Mallowan dates the ivory more than a century later than Barnett.) Figure 506 in Mallowan's volume (p. 565) is a similar image.

49. At Ugarit, Athtar's name appears in lists of deities and offerings. See Page, *Myth of Cosmic Rebellion,* 77, 107, and the discussion in n. 42 above.

Mythic, archetypal images like that of Athtar, however, turn out to be multifaceted. Sometimes they have negative as well as positive forms and applications. Ezekiel earlier in his book has made clear the cherubim's potential for harm, describing their noise, fire, and role in punishing Israel. Basing himself on the divine, revelatory word (Ezek 28:12), Ezekiel here brings out more serious, inherent liabilities to the cherub paradigm. The fluid quality of the cherubim's nature includes the potential for lust and sin.

Bringing out the dark side to an image is a common way Ezekiel deals with metaphors for nations as well as with their myths. There are good examples in Ezek 29, 32, and 27. Pharaoh may well be a crocodile, but crocodiles can be caught with fishhooks (Ezek 29:4). Crocodiles are also no good at ranging on land (Ezek 32:2).[50] Ships, such as Tyre, may be grand, but they can also sink (Ezek 27:26)!

According to Ezekiel, to be a cherub is a precarious, lightning-fast dance with mirrored, antithetical partners. Each synchronized step aims to contain unspeakable power, and to resist its enormous pull. The potential to stumble or succumb to desire is ever present. Sometimes a fatal misstep happens.

The quaternity paradigm of mythology, according to Jung, can sometimes fail at one of its four points. One quaternity-point can lose its angelic character, while the other three remain morally positive.[51] The fallen point becomes "demonic in the worst sense."[52]

It is noteworthy that Ezek 28 depicts only a single cherub falling into "wickedness" and "sin" (vv. 15–16). Biblical cherubim usually come either in pairs or in a fourfold array, and the same is true of excavated cherubim from Syria and Phoenicia.[53] This cherub, however, is missing his partners—an ominous sign, since its antithetical components are what maintain the quaternity's stability. That here only one cherub becomes corrupt immediately reminds us of Jung's image of a negative quaternity-point. Ezekiel must be referring to the mythological pattern of the occasional demonizing of one-quarter of the cosmic array.

Comparative study attests to Jung's description. The Ugaritic texts do not explicitly describe Athtar as judged for hubris and evil, although he does descend from Baal's throne to rule over the underworld. However, we come close to an actual judgment of Athtar as a fallen, condemned figure in KTU 1.23. In this text a divine figure called "Death-and-Shining-One," who is possibly a hypostasis of Athtar, is "bound" and "pruned."[54]

---

50. Cf. Greenberg's astute interpretation (*Ezekiel 21–37*, 657).
51. Jung, *Psychology and Religion*, 59, 170.
52. Jung, *Alchemical Studies*, 282.
53. For discussion, see Miller, "Mælæk," 498–99. Ezekiel does use the singular form, כרוב, to designate the inanimate pair of statues in the temple (as noted above). Ezekiel 28, however, clearly does not reference inanimate statues.
54. This figure's very name suggests that, like Athtar, he is both astral and chthonic. For a fascinating discussion of this text, see Page, *Myth of Cosmic Rebellion*, 94–103.

In his thorough 1996 monograph, H. R. Page Jr. has reconstructed what may have been an ancient, developed form of the story of "Death-and-Shining-One."[55] Based on evidence from biblical texts such as Isa 14, Job 38, and Ps 82, he reconstructs a Semitic "myth of cosmic rebellion." The myth relates the revolt of an astral anti-hero, who was originally part of El's coterie before his wisdom and beauty corrupted him. El, or one of his commanders, puts down the figure's hubristic attempt to wrest control of the cosmic center and casts him to the underworld.

Ezekiel 28:11–19 has the form-critical structure of a dirge. In vv. 16–19, the dirge moves from the cherub's past glory to an account of his downfall through hubris. There come to expression all the potential pitfalls of being a cherub. The account picks up significant aspects of the Semitic myth of cosmic rebellion, as Page reconstructs it.

Verse 17 refers to the appetite and ambition that can lead a cherub, in hubris, to assail the cosmic center. The oracle's complementarity to Ezek 28:1–10 allows us to infer safely that the cherub is arrogating to himself the "seat of the gods, in the heart of the seas" (v. 2). Launderville is correct: "The king of Tyre . . . misused his role as cherub . . . in order to seize for himself the sovereign role in the divine sphere."[56]

As the cherub launches his mutiny, he loses his tensive, internal equilibrium. As if putting his animal faces forward, the creature fills with "violence" and unleashes it on others (v. 16). Raging out of control, the numinous fire of the cherubim endangers its own vessel (v. 18).

God easily puts down the cherub's revolt. He is cast down from the heavens, from the midst of the stars (v. 16). Igniting on fire, he falls ablaze to the ground (v. 18). The image is reminiscent of Ovid's description of Phaethon's long trail of fire as he falls from heaven. Phaethon, a Roman instantiation of Mercurius, descends "as a star sometimes seems to fall" (*Metamorphoses* II.319–323). The fall to the ארץ ("earth"/"underworld," vv. 17, 18) also parallels the language of Athtar's story. Athtar's (more voluntary) descent is also said be to the *'arṣi* ("earth"/"underworld," KTU 1.6 I 65).

To summarize, Ezek 28 strikingly unveils the moral ambiguity of the cherub nature. Mercurius is a two-faced archetype, as are his instantiations in mythology. Athtar—the Ugaritic god—provides a particularly good example. Ezekiel's cherub is ambitious and reckless in bearing the role of Mercurius, and it proves his undoing. The earthly reign of the king of Tyre, Ezekiel claims, demonstrates how this heavenly paradigm can also manifest itself on earth. Tyre's king could have helped bring

---

55. Ibid., 204, 206–8. Note that he does not equate his anti-hero with a cherub.
56. Launderville, "Ezekiel's Cherub," 183, cf. 171–72. On the complementarity of Ezek 28:1–10 and 28:11–19, see, further, Mettinger, *Dethronement of Sabaoth*, 27; Callender, *Adam in Myth and History*, 180–81.

light to the world, but instead, mimicking the will to power of the diabolical, fallen type of cherub, he profaned his land.

This brief investigation of Ezek 28 reveals a second type of hierarchical thinking in Ezekiel. In addition to a tiered ontology (i.e., a storied cosmos), the prophet had a storied epistemology. Whether or not he was conscious of it, his discourse suggests that there are different levels of human knowledge about God and God's ways.

The uppermost level of knowledge about God comes through direct, *special* revelation. In receiving Ezekiel's prophecies as Scripture, Israelites and later religious communities of Jews and Christians valued them as this type of knowledge.

Of all the Hebrew prophets, Ezekiel perhaps knew best what it meant to experience God's direct communication. In Ezek 8–11, for example, the hand of God falls upon the prophet while sitting with some elders in his house in Babylonia (8:1). He states, "The spirit lifted me up between earth and heaven, and brought me in visions of God to Jerusalem" (v. 3).

In Ezek 28, divine revelation comes to the prophet in the alternative form of a verbal oracle. Introducing the oracle, Ezekiel states in v. 11, "The word of the LORD came to me." Reinforcing its revelatory character, the oracle contains the prophetic messenger formula, "Thus says the Lord GOD" (v. 12).

Ezekiel exploited a second, lower level of revelation, however, in his prophecy of judgment against Tyre's king. As a foreign nation, Tyre lay outside of Yahweh's historical relationship with Israel. The prophet could not accuse it directly of infractions against Yahweh's covenant and Yahweh's law. He needed to indict it based on general, collective principles.

Even if Tyre were never to receive Ezekiel's message, this would still be true. His oracle would still have to be understandable and convincing to his Israelite audience as an ostensible prophecy against a foreign nation. Mythic images provided Ezekiel with the universal principles he needed.[57]

Ezekiel draws on and exploits the dark sides and negative forms of nations' myths, even though the nations did not consciously acknowledge these features. In so doing, Ezekiel, knowingly or not, addresses the nations based on a common epistemological ground with them rooted in *transcendental experience*. As pieces of *transcendental knowledge,* Ezekiel's images contained an unthematic and anonymous knowledge of divine reality.[58]

The terms are those of the modern Roman Catholic theologian, Karl Rahner. His investigations, in my view, help clarify the two levels of epistemology in Ezekiel's prophecies. In his lifework, Rahner developed an understanding of mythic and

---

57. On the fittingness of cherubic imagery for Tyre's king, see the images referenced in n. 48 above. For the possibility that exiles from Tyre were part of Ezekiel's audience, see Block, *Ezekiel 25–48,* 31, 121; Launderville, "Ezekiel's Cherub," 180.

58. Peter Machinist, a respondent to my 1999 *SBL Seminar Papers* essay, has drawn my attention to an actual biblical attestation of the idea of an "anonymous Yahwist": Isa 45:4.

archetypal images—such as those Ezekiel used—as key to what theologians have traditionally called *general revelation* or *natural religion*.[59] On a lower epistemological level than special revelation, this general revelation comes through what Rahner identified as a shared human "transcendental experience."

Rahner believed that God is present to all humans at the level of their awareness that is usually associated with archetypal and mythological forms. This epistemological level lies beneath human reflection and consciousness. It contains basic paradigms and archetypes innate to the necessary and inalienable structures of human knowers. Some of the constituent elements in this lower level of human knowledge, according to Rahner, are supernatural. They are openings out into the transcendent and express basic theological truths.[60] Ezekiel used such truths to indict Tyre, to overturn the delusional self-conception of Tyre's king. This self-conception contained the seeds of its own critique.

There is an appealing quality to the idea of a general, natural level of human awareness about God. At least, my current seminarians seem encouraged at the prospect of there being some knowledge of God outside of the tight circle of God's chosen community. Certain powerful theological minds are famous for having resisted the idea tooth and nail, but Ezekiel, it appears, was open to it.

This investigation of Ezekiel's cherubim confirms their special role in supporting his thinking about the structure of existence (ontology) and his assumptions about knowledge and its sources (epistemology). He uses images of cherubim in ways that support what today we would call a hierarchical ontology and a hierarchical epistemology. In neither case is Ezekiel's thinking particularly chauvinist or exclusivist. In Ezek 9–10, he propounds an inclusive sacredness in the homeland. In Ezek 28:11–19, he strives for a discourse intelligible to a culture outside Israel's covenant.

Cherubim are liminal beings, our comparative model discerned, guarding the threshold of the divine realm. Ezekiel 9–10 sharply revealed this function, and extended it by connecting the cherubim to an ideal system of gradations of holiness in Israel. Cherubim are also ambiguous, unsettled creatures, according to our comparative model. This trait came out clearly in examining Ezek 28. Behind the Tyrian king of the chapter, the cherub archetype revealed its potential for hubris and violent disaster.

In both Ezek 9–10 and Ezek 28, the prophet found a way, using an archetypal image, to speak of a transcendent reality beyond human manipulation and control. This reality interconnects with our lives, influencing history. With this perspective, Ezekiel challenged his audience's complacency, and directed his readers' imaginations to heaven's perspective on earth's doings.

---

59. Karl Rahner, *Foundations of Christian Faith: An Introduction to the Idea of Christianity* (trans. W. Dych; New York: Crossroad, 1978), 81, 85.
60. Ibid., 20, 321.

Proverb Performance and Transgenerational Retribution in Ezekiel 18

Katheryn Pfisterer Darr

I. Introduction

The harsh oracles of Ezekiel, a Judean priest commissioned as God's prophet to his fellow exiles in Babylonia in 593 B.C.E., set him at odds with his community. Little wonder that his scroll includes disputation oracles,[1] in which speakers quote a popular opinion (thesis), typically in the form of a proverb; pose a counterthesis; and then dispute the people's opinion by means of a thorough explication of that counterthesis.[2]

Ezekiel 18 begins with the familiar announcement, "The word of YHWH came to me" (v. 1).[3] However, neither God's usual address to Ezekiel ("Mortal"), nor a command to prophesy, follows. Has the Lord taken this (undated) occasion to confront our priest/prophet privately with a popular saying (v. 2), to declare its imminent extinction (v. 3), and to refute its message (v. 4)? Or, do the second-person masculine plural pronominal suffixes (כֶם–) in vv. 2 and 3 signal the presence of an exilic audience not otherwise acknowledged in vv. 1–4?

The word of YHWH came to me: "What do you mean performing[4] this proverb

---

1. E.g., 11:1–13, 14–17; 12:21–25, 26–28; 18:1–32; 20:32–44; 33:10–20; 33:23–29; 37:11b–13.
2. See D. F. Murray, "The Rhetoric of Disputation: Re-examination of a Prophetic Genre," *JSOT* 38 (1987): 114. Adrian Graffy, by contrast, divides our oracle into two parts (*A Prophet Confronts His People: The Disputation Speech in the Prophets* [AnBib 104; Rome: Pontifical Biblical Institute, 1984], 21). Graffy limits the oracle to vv. 1–20, but I concur with Gordon H. Matties that Ezek 18 is a single, complex literary unit (*Ezekiel 18 and the Rhetoric of Moral Discourse* [SBLDS 126; Atlanta: Scholars Press, 1990], 34–46).
3. Citations are from the NRSV unless otherwise indicated.
4. The Qal m. pl. active ptc. מֹשְׁלִים from מָשַׁל ("to use a proverb") suggests that the proverb is performed before various audiences on different occasions by more than one speaker. LXX streamlines MT by omitting אַתֶּם מֹשְׁלִים אֶת־ ("you, performing"); cf. Ezek 12:22.

concerning[5] the land of Israel: 'Parents eat sour grapes, but[6] their children's teeth are set on edge'?[7] As I live, declares Lord YHWH, you shall no more perform this proverb in Israel. Consider: all lives are mine; the life of the parent and the life of the child are mine. Only the person who sins shall die." (author's translation)

In the following verses, Ezekiel's God systematically spells out why this proverb[8]—for all its polish, pedigree, and ostensible authority—fails to make sense of their situation(s). In so doing, Ezek 18 advances an argument about transgenerational retribution that contradicts certain venerable Israelite traditions regarding YHWH's administration of justice.[9]

What role(s) does proverb performance (hereafter "PP") play in Ezek 18? To address this question, I adopt a working definition of "proverb," identify some of its characteristic formal features and functions, consider conflict as a major stimulus of PP, take account of the "aura of authority" surrounding "traditional sayings,"[10] and investigate the roles proverbs can play in settling disputes. Beyond those tasks, I engage in an imaginative exercise—a reconstruction of the Judeans' "sour grapes" PPs, and of Ezekiel's strategic attempt to trump them.

---

5. Translating ל remains a conundrum. The NRSV and NIV choose "concerning" and "about," respectively, NJPS "upon"; Walther Zimmerli (*Ezekiel: A Commentary on the Book of the Prophet Ezekiel* [2 vols.; Hermeneia; Philadelphia: Fortress, 1979], 1:369) opts for "in" and attributes the proverb performances (hereafter "PPs"; sg. "PP") to Judeans in Judah after Jerusalem's destruction (*sans* compelling reason). Whichever option one chooses, the proverb—purportedly a popular saying (see also Jer 31:29)—likely was familiar to Judeans at home and in Babylonia.

6. No simple rule determines whether the ו linking segment B to segment A is conjunctive ("and") or disjunctive ("but"). LXX, Vulg., and most moderns render ו conjunctively; hence, the saying does not specify if parents, as well as their children, suffer for their sins. If ו is disjunctive, however, then the proverb seems to say that only (or especially) the children suffer for their elders' sins—a sentiment expressed in Lam 5:7. I render the ו disjunctively ("but").

7. The verb קהה ("set on edge"), which describes the effect of unripe grapes on teeth, also appears in Jer 31:29 and in Eccl 10:10 (Piel; of dulled iron). LXX renders with a verb (γομφιάζω) meaning "to suffer pain in the teeth"; Vulg. "become numb." Tg. paraphrases: "The parents have sinned, and the children are punished." Some scholars suggest "grind"; others "clench." I opt for the traditional "set on edge." I venture a modern analogy: a person pops chewing gum into his/her mouth, only to discover that a sliver of its foil wrapping remains stuck to the gum.

8. The text expects readers to regard the proverb as both "genuine" and current among Ezekiel's contemporaries. Carole R. Fontaine warns that "not all ... sayings [bearing] the form of a traditional saying can be considered ... genuine (i.e., current) ... and not all of the genuine traditional sayings in the prophetic corpus may appear in their normal saying form" (*Traditional Sayings in the Old Testament: A Contextual Study* [Sheffield: Almond, 1982], 242).

9. In this essay, "transgenerational retribution" refers to corporal punishment that includes not only the offender and relatives of his/her own generation, but also the offender's offspring.

10. This is Fontaine's phrase for proverbs outside the biblical wisdom corpus (*Traditional Sayings*, 2). I use the two terms synonymously.

II. Defining "Proverb"

Defining "proverb" is so difficult that Archer Taylor abandoned the chore: "The definition of a proverb is too difficult to repay the undertaking; and should we . . . combine in a single definition all the essential elements and give each the proper emphasis, we should not even then have a touchstone. An *incommunicable quality* tells us this sentence is proverbial and that one is not."[11] Taylor's final observation may hold true for native audiences, but outsiders risk a proverb's "incommunicable quality" whizzing over their heads![12] Hence, something should be said about what proverbs are and how proverbs function within particular social contexts.

Ruth Finnegan's pithy definition of proverb, "a saying in more or less fixed form marked by 'shortness, sense, and salt' and distinguished by the popular acceptance of the truth tersely expressed in it,"[13] suits many sayings gathered cheek-by-jowl in collections,[14] loosed from specific social contexts (both "vivid present" and "broader horizon").[15] Such sayings often express their themes as unmitigated truths (see, e.g., Prov 15:1 NRSV). Within specific social contexts, however, their contextualized meanings[16] might convey quite different truths (functioning in Prov 15:1, e.g., to urge a military commander to intensify his rhetoric in order to rouse his troops). Hence, Seitel defines (metaphorical) proverbs as "the strategic social use of meta-

---

11. Taylor, *The Proverb and an Index to the Proverb* (Hatboro, Pa.: Folklore Associates; Copenhagen: Rosenkilde and Bagger, 1962), 3; emphasis mine.

12. As Ruth Finnegan observes, "It is often impossible to grasp the point . . . of a given proverb without some knowledge of [its] cultural background and of what the thing mentioned means to those [uttering] it" ("Proverbs in Africa," in *The Wisdom of Many: Essays on the Proverb* [ed. W. Mieder and A. Dundes; New York and London: Garland, 1981], 25; repr. from R. Finnegan, *Oral Literature in Africa* [Oxford: Clarendon, 1970], 389–418). See also Peter Seitel, "Proverbs: A Social Use of Metaphor," in *Wisdom of Many*, 138; repr. from *Genre* 2 [1969]: 143–61. I am grateful to Dr. Seitel for contributing to this essay via his publications, e-mail, and telephone.

13. Finnegan, "Proverbs in Africa," 14.

14. On the difference between "living proverbs" and those within collections, see Fontaine (*Traditional Sayings*, 54); Wolfgang Mieder, "The Essence of Literary Proverb Study," *Proverbium* 23 (1974): 892; and Peter Seitel, *The Powers of Genre: Interpreting Haya Oral Literature* (Oxford Studies in Anthropological Linguistics 22; New York: Oxford University Press, 1999), 36.

15. Like William E. Hanks (*Language and Communicative Practices* [Boulder, Colo.: Westview, 1996], 142), Seitel (*Powers of Genre*, 5) distinguishes between the "vivid present" ("the immediate interactional setting . . . includ[ing] the participants . . . and the topics, utterances, and acts that have gone before the . . . utterance in question and those that are expected to follow") and the "broader horizon" ("the broader social-historical context . . . just as utterances refer to people, topics, and other utterances in the vivid present, they also refer to people, topics, utterances, and genres in the broader horizon"). In PPs, the "vivid present is dominant in understanding its usage" (Seitel, *Powers of Genre*, 37).

16. I follow Seitel's distinction between a proverb's theme and its contextualized meaning. Theme emerges from "relationships perceived between the constituent parts of [the proverb]" and "remains relatively constant." Meaning "emerges from relationships perceived between the [proverb] (in part or as a whole) and the context in which it is spoken . . . and received" and "changes with its context of performance and/or reception" (Seitel, *Powers of Genre*, 4–5).

phor . . . the manifestation in traditional, artistic, and relatively short form of metaphorical reasoning,[17] used in an interactional context to serve certain purposes."[18]

In this essay, I adopt Fontaine's definition of the "traditional saying" because it addresses both proverbial *form* and how proverbs *function* within specific social settings:

> [T]he traditional saying [is] a statement, current among the folk, [that] is concise, syntactically complete, consisting of at least one topic and comment[19] which may or may not be metaphorical,[20] but which exhibits a logical relationship between its terms. Further, the saying may be marked by stylistic features (mnemonics, rhythm, alliteration, assonance, etc.) or be constructed along recognizable frames ("Better A than B . . ." etc.) [that] distinguish it from other genres (or folk idioms). The referents [forming] the image are most likely . . . drawn from the experience of common, "everyday" life,[21] but the meaning (message) of the saying may vary from context to context, and any "truth claim" for that message must be considered "relative" rather than "absolute." The transmission of the saying, however achieved, is *always* purposeful, but specific details of contextual use may be necessary to determine the purpose in any given situation.[22]

III. Formal Features of the "Sour Grapes" Proverb

Biblical scholars agree that Ezek 18:2b is a proverb.[23] Its genre is presaged in v. 2a by the phrase משלים את־המשל הזה ("performing this proverb"). While the

---

17. Not all proverbs include "that figure of speech [metaphor] whereby we speak about one thing in terms . . . suggestive of another" (Janet Martin Soskice, *Metaphor and Religious Language* [Oxford: Clarendon, 1985], 15).

18. Seitel, "Proverbs: A Social Use of Metaphor," 122.

19. Hence, proverbs must have at least two words (e.g., "money talks"). See Alan Dundes, "On the Structure of the Proverb," in *Wisdom of Many*, 51–52; repr. of *Proverbium* 25 (1975): 961–73.

20. Audiences often recognize a contextualized metaphorical proverb by its out-of-context subject matter, but Ezek 18:1–4 reveals almost nothing about the contexts of the PPs Yhwh condemns. One could imagine a context in which parents eat sour grapes, but their children's teeth are affected. Such a scenario is illogical, however, since what one person eats does not affect another's teeth. (But *caveat lector*! Anyone who watches a person suck on lemons, or hears fingernails scrape a chalkboard, knows such acts can create physical reactions in others; and anyone who identifies deeply with a loved one's psychological/physiological illness might personally experience symptoms of that illness.)

21. Traditional sayings typically address "eternal and universal human concerns—love and money, family and friends, work and play" (Paul D. Goodwin and Joseph W. Wenzel, "Proverbs and Practical Reasoning" in *Wisdom of Many*, 142; repr. of the *Quarterly Journal of Speech* 65 [1979]: 289–302). Our proverb images derive from agricultural and familial spheres.

22. *Traditional Sayings*, 64.

23. See, e.g., Otto Eissfeldt, *Der Maschal im Alten Testament* (BZAW 24; Giessen, Germany: Töpelmann, 1913), 45; Zimmerli, *Ezekiel*, 1:369; Thomas Renz, *The Rhetorical Function of the Book of Ezekiel* (VTSup 76; Leiden: Brill, 2002), 79–81. In this essay, I bracket questions of origin and authorship.

Hebrew noun מָשָׁל also designates other literary genres (e.g., parables, riddles, taunts, admonitions),[24] Ezek 18:2b displays enough characteristics of popular sayings to confirm its genre as a proverb, including a "concise [only six Hebrew forms], syntactically complete" statement expressing "a logical relationship between its terms" (i.e., positive causation [A→B]) and elevated style (e.g., binary structure, atypical Hebrew word order [A: noun + verb + object; B: bound noun + absolute noun (= construct chain) + verb], the formulaic word-pair "fathers/sons," alliteration,[25] and an equal number of stressed syllables [3][26] in each half). More specifically, our saying is a "multi-descriptive element"[27] proverb consisting of two topics and two comments linked by וּ.

Segment A

    Topic 1   *Comment 1*

    Parents   eat sour grapes,

Segment B

    Topic 2   *Comment 2*

    (but) the children's teeth   are set on edge.

Moreover, our saying states its "truth" impersonally, and its imperfect verb forms (יֹאכְלוּ ["eat"] and תִּקְהֶינָה ["be set on edge"]) suggest that this truth is "just the way it is."[28]

IV. THE LOGIC OF PROVERB PERFORMANCES

A. THE LOGIC OF PROVERB SPEAKING

When a person performs a proverb in a particular social context, "a topic of conversation is described through metaphorical reference to the situation portrayed

---

24. See Timothy Polk, "Paradigms, Parables, and *Měšālîm*: On Reading the *Māšāl* in Scripture," *CBQ* 45 (1983): 564–68.
25. Note the repetition of ב in אָבוֹת ("parents"), בֹּסֶר ("sour grapes"), and הַבָּנִים ("the children"); moreover, each form in segment B of the proverb contains a נ.
26. Presupposing that the bound noun שִׁנֵּי ("the teeth of") retains at least some stress on its initial syllable. If its stress is surrendered, however, then three stressed syllables (segment A) are followed by two stressed syllables (segment B), casting the proverb as a brief lament.
27. Dundes, "On the Structure," 51–52.
28. On the "habitual non-perfective," see Bruce K. Waltke and Michael P. O'Connor, *An Introduction to Biblical Hebrew Syntax* (Winona Lake, Ind.: Eisenbrauns, 1990), sec. 31.3e. Jeremiah 31:29 has the Qal perfect אָכְלוּ ("have eaten"), rather than the imperfect יֹאכְלוּ ("eat"), expressing Jeremiah's desire to emphasize the anteriority of the parents' actions (Daniel I. Block, *The Book of Ezekiel*, vol. 1, *Chapters 1–*

in [that proverb]."²⁹ This process involves three separate domains: the domain in which the proverb is spoken; the one present in the proverb construed literally; and the one to which the proverb is applied. The following diagram illustrates these three domains:³⁰

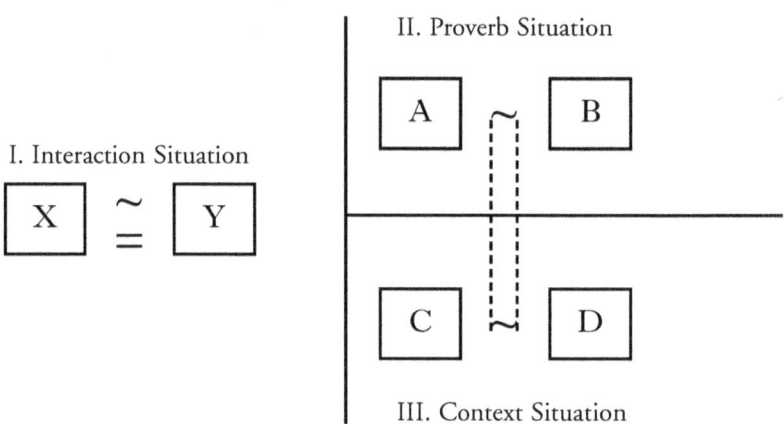

According to Seitel's model, a proverb speaker (X) asserts to an audience (Y) in an interaction situation (I) that the relationship between persons or entities in the proverb situation (II) is analogous to the relationship between persons or entities in the context situation (III).³¹ The broken lines represent the analogous relationship that the speaker posits between the proverb and context situations. In Isa 37:1–4, for example, King Hezekiah (X) asserts to Isaiah (Y) via messengers that the relationship between entities in the proverb situation ("Babes are positioned for birth [A], but there is no strength to deliver" [B]; author's translation) is analogous to the relationship between entities in the context situation (Jerusalem's helpless inhabitants are surrounded and in deadly peril [C], but Hezekiah and his advisers are incapable of delivering them [D]).³²

---

24 [NICOT; Grand Rapids: Eerdmans, 1997], 560) and buttressing his claim that the proverbial theme expresses "the way it is," but will *not* be in the future.

29. Seitel, *Powers of Genre*, 5.

30. Seitel, "Proverbs: A Social Use of Metaphor," 127. This version of Seitel's diagram appears in a reprint of "Proverbs: A Social Use of Metaphor," in *Folklore Genres* (ed. D. Ben-Amos; Austin: University of Texas Press, 1976), 129.

31. Seitel, *Powers of Genre*. Asserting that the proverb and context domains are analogous (A→B = C→D) is one of two favorite strategies for PP. The second asserts that the two domains are not analogous (e.g., A→B ≠ C→D) and seeks "to redirect the attitudes of the [r]eceiver" (Fontaine, *Traditional Sayings*, 163). Every Ezekielian PP, save one (16:44), employs the second strategy.

32. My analysis of Hezekiah's PP appears in *Isaiah's Vision and the Family of God* (Literary Currents in Biblical Interpretation; Louisville: Westminster John Knox, 1994), 205–17.

B. The Logic of Proverb Reception

"Finalization" is crucial to grasping the logic of proverbs and, more broadly, of contextualized PPs. "Finalization," Seitel explains, refers to "the sense of completion achieved in an artistic work . . . the awareness by performer and *audience* that a work or some part of it is finished, complete."[33] Mikhail M. Bakhtin[34] observes that finalization in generic utterances (e.g., proverbs) occurs on the three dimensions of a literary work—composition, style, and theme—at three levels respectively: the proverb itself; "the complete utterance of which the proverb is part"; and "an occasion on which the proverb is [performed], including the situation to which [it] refers." Three dimensions at three levels yield nine "loci" where "the finalizations characteristic of [proverbs]" are discernible.[35]

In this essay, I focus upon thematic finalization at the three levels of the "sour grapes" PP(s).[36] Because our text says little about two of these levels, however, I also resort to the Isaian PP cited above for illustrative purposes.

V. Thematic Finalizations at Three Levels of Proverb Performances

A. Thematic Finalization at the Level of the Proverb Itself

As Seitel observes, "Generic compositional finalization creates the underlying logical form of an utterance, or an exchange of utterances."[37] In proverbs, compositional finalization produces this logical form ("the shape truth takes in the world proverbs envision")[38] by "isolating the semantic contrasts that articulate [proverbial] themes." These semantic contrasts occur in "paired, parallel, and opposed propositions"[39] between "symbols juxtaposed in . . . proverb images." A proverb's dominant "theme" (an "abstract, culturally specific idea")[40] is expressed by ratios of acts and conditions in the contrasting propositions.[41] Both propositions are stated explicitly in some proverbs. In others, one proposition is explicit, but its opposite is only implicitly present, and achieving thematic finalization at the proverb level requires that the audience supply the unspoken contrast.

In our "sour grapes" saying, the paired, parallel, and opposed propositions are: the (explicit) assertion, "parents eat sour grapes, but the children's teeth are set on edge" (A→B); and the (implicit) contrasting assertion, "parents eat sour grapes, but

---

33. Seitel, *Powers of Genre*, 17; emphasis mine.
34. *Speech Genres and Other Late Essays* (ed. C. Emerson and M. Holquist; Austin: University of Texas Press, 1984); cited in Seitel, *Powers of Genre*, 37.
35. Seitel, *Powers of Genre*, 37.
36. A study of finalizations at the levels of style and composition would exceed the limits of this essay.
37. *Powers of Genre*, 28.
38. Ibid., 41.
39. Ibid., 28.
40. Ibid., 31.
41. Ibid., 51.

the children's teeth are *not* set on edge" (A≠B).⁴² Proverbial "theme" is expressed by ratios of acts and conditions in the opposing propositions.⁴³ Here, however, the audience encounters a problem: the theme, construed literally, defies common sense (what one person eats does not set someone else's teeth on edge). (The implicit, opposed proposition, construed literally, comports with common sense, but is not what our proverbial theme asserts.) Hence, the audience must identify a principle that makes the "non-sense" asserted by the proverbial theme "true" in a metaphorical sense. In our case, that "principle" is divine transgenerational retribution—the form God's justice takes such that children suffer the consequences of their parents' actions.

B. Thematic Finalization at the Level of the Entire Proverb Utterance

At this level, a proverbial theme is applied to a situation, "names" it, explains it, and identifies a way to deal with it. Thematic finalization occurs when the audience grasps the analogy between the proverb's theme and the situation it names. The entire utterance usually includes a literal reference to that situation.⁴⁴

Ezekiel 18:1–4 does not specify the situation(s) prompting the PPs Yhwh condemns. (Isaiah 37:1–4 is more forthcoming, for Hezekiah's proverb [Isa 37:3b] metaphorically "names" its context.) Thematic finalization at this level occurs when the receivers grasp the analogous relationship between the proverb's theme and its situation(s). The entire utterance (including the proverb) often includes a "literal reference to that situation" (e.g., Hezekiah's message begins with the words ["Thus says Hezekiah,] 'This day is a day of distress, of rebuke, and of disgrace'") and identifies a way to deal with it (Hezekiah asks Isaiah to offer intercessory prayer to Yhwh on behalf of his imperiled city).

C. Thematic Finalization at the Level of the Performance Context

Finally, thematic finalization occurs at the level of the performance context (occasion of the entire proverb utterance) when its audience understands that the proverbial theme (first level), which is analogous to the context domain (second level), applies to itself (third level).⁴⁵ Finalization at this level is achieved in Isa 37:1–4, for example, when the prophet realizes that he is the addressee of Hezekiah's PP and that the PP seeks from him the intercessory prayer Hezekiah desires.

---

42. Creating a contrast between our proverbial assertion and its parallel, opposed assertion requires negation of segment B only. Negating both assertions does not create contrast, since the result (like the proverb itself) connects what the parents do (in this case, what they do not do) with what the children experience (in this case, do not experience). See Seitel, *Powers of Genre*, 44.
43. Ibid., 42.
44. Ibid., 38.
45. Ibid., 38–39.

VI. Proverb Performances in Ezekiel 18:1–4

Because Ezek 18:1–4 says little about the interaction domains of the PPs Yhwh condemns, we know virtually nothing about the Judean proverb propounders (X), their audiences (Y), and the social dynamics (e.g., age, gender, social status) between them. Moreover, because the text says nothing specific about the context domains of these PPs, we learn only that: (1) the proverb propounders posit an analogy between the proverb domain (A→B) and the context domain(s) (C→D); and (2) Yhwh rejects their analogy because, in God's administration of justice, "only the person who sins shall die."

Lacking such data, biblical scholars might (the tenth commandment notwithstanding) covet anthropologists' access to PPs in extant societies and to native members of those societies who can either confirm or correct their interpretations.[46] Too often, we must resort to hypothetical reconstructions, informed by what such specialists can teach us about social contexts in which PPs frequently occur. "Hypothetical" and "imaginary" are words most historically inclined biblical scholars might wish to eschew. But you know what they say: "nothing ventured, nothing gained!"

A. Proverbs and Conflict

PPs transpire in innumerable social settings and address an inexhaustible variety of situations toward a vast array of strategic goals. Here, however, I focus upon the commonplace observation among paremiologists that PPs often occur in conflict situations.[47] An apropos proverb can summarize a dispute, pass judgment on it, and commend a course of action.[48] The speaker perceives disparity between his or her "correct" side in an argument and an opponent's "incorrect" position,[49] and performs a proverb in hopes of changing the opponent's perception and resolving the argument.[50] Moreover, PPs not only "offer a guide to the 'trouble spots' in a society," but also function as "social safety valves."[51] In the Hebrew Bible, proverb propounders are those whom we would expect to know their culture's traditional sayings: "All are seasoned leaders of various types, used to settling disputes and ren-

---

46. See Dennis Tedlock and Bruce Mannheim, eds., *The Dialogic Emergence of Culture* (Urbana, Ill.: University of Illinois Press, 1995), 3; cited in Seitel, *Powers of Genre*, 10. When Seitel adds that "the future of proverb studies clearly lies with *indigenous* social scientists . . . in local social interaction" (ibid., 8), modern students of ancient societies can only despair.
47. See, e.g., Finnegan, "Proverbs in Africa," 31.
48. Archer Taylor, "The Study of Proverbs," *Proverbium* 1 (1965): 7.
49. Fontaine, *Traditional Sayings*, 154.
50. Ibid., 165.
51. Joseph Raymond, "Tensions in Proverbs: More Light on International Understanding," in *Wisdom of Many*, 302; repr. of *Western Folklore* 15 [1956]: 153–58.

dering judgments on a wide range of topics."⁵² But participants in PPs need not share equal social status; proverbs—by virtue of their indirection and sense of detachment—can serve an "egalitarian function," providing those of lesser status with a reasonably benign way to challenge their superiors.⁵³

B. THE AUTHORITY OF PROVERBS

Proverbs also resolve conflict by virtue of their authority qua proverbs. In PPs, a saying's "aura of authority" derives from various factors, including (1) form; (2) theme; (3) contextualized meaning; and (4) the speaker's reliability. Barbara Kirshenblatt-Gimblett observes that "neat symmetries and witty convergences of sound and meaning, tight formulations of logical relations, highly patterned repetitions, structural balance, and familiar metaphors encapsulate general principles and contribute to the feeling that *anything that sounds so right must be true.*"⁵⁴ This does not mean that proverbs actually express incontrovertible truths; they are "just supposed to sound like they do."⁵⁵ Moreover, if a phrase such as "they say," or "you know what they say," precedes the saying, then the receiver's sense of its authority intensifies.⁵⁶ (YHWH's rhetorical question, "What do you mean performing this proverb?" [v. 2a], identifies Ezek 18:2b as a popular saying in a derogatory way.)⁵⁷

A proper understanding of proverbial authority recognizes that proverbs express their themes (and contextualized meanings) as nuggets of condensed human experience.⁵⁸ The obscure origins of many a saying might be traced to one creative individual, but an established saying conveys more clout than does any single person's ad hoc utterance. Said differently, a proverb might reflect "one man's wit," but it purports to encapsulate "all men's wisdom."⁵⁹ Proverbs are "vivid expressions of group mind, group remembering";⁶⁰ rooted in tradition, they partake of the "generally acknowledged authority of tradition"⁶¹ and command respect. Moreover, if a saying is deeply rooted in established religious traditions, its aura of authority is

---

52. Fontaine, *Traditional Sayings*, 155.

53. Those with greater power are less cautious when "setting up negative correlations between the proverb image and participants in the Interaction or Context Situation" (C. R. Fontaine, "Proverb Performance in the Hebrew Bible," in *Wise Words: Essays on the Proverb* [ed. W. Mieder; New York: Garland, 1994], 405). See also Raymond, "Tensions in Proverbs," 301.

54. "Toward a Theory of Proverb Meaning," in *Wisdom of Many*, 111, emphasis mine (repr. of *Proverbium* 22 [1973]: 821-27).

55. Ibid., 111-12.

56. Goodwin and Wenzel, "Proverbs and Practical Reasoning," 153. See Ezek 16:44. In 1 Sam 24:14 (Eng. 24:13), David underscores the authority of the saying he quotes to King Saul by foregrounding its venerable age.

57. See Waltke and O'Connor, *Introduction to Biblical Hebrew Syntax*, secs. 18.2g and 18.3b.

58. Taylor, *Proverb*, 87.

59. Lord John Russell defined "proverb" as "one man's wit and all men's wisdom" (*Swarthmore College Bulletin* 54 [1962]: 4-7).

60. Raymond, "Tensions in Proverbs," 305.

61. Fontaine, *Traditional Sayings*, 158.

likely greater still, since to some degree it purports to encapsulate not only "all men's wisdom" about God, but also God's wisdom as revealed to human beings (see, e.g., Prov 2:1–8).

For good reason, then, persons in conflict tap traditional sayings to imbue their arguments with proverbial gravitas and to reveal the folly of opposing views. Little wonder that Israel's prophets, seeking to convince audiences of the authority of the oracles they proclaim in God's name, resort to proverbs and proverbial phrases, as well as other strategic resources.

C. What Makes a Proverb Religious?

Block makes much of our saying's "secular" cast: its form is that of a popular משל ("proverb"); it reflects everyday experience; and its message "reflects . . . resignation to immutable cosmic rules of cause and effect . . . that has left the exiles without hope and without God."[62] To his mind, Yhwh objects to the proverb not because it asserts that people suffer for the sins of previous generations, or because it might raise the question of theodicy, but because it implies that God is either indifferent to the exiles' situation, or unable to change it.[63]

Proverbs need not refer to a deity, or to concepts like covenant, sin, and salvation, however, to qualify as religious sayings. An isolated proverb's theme might be thoroughly secular, but its contextualized meaning may be thoroughly religious.[64] I do not doubt that the "sour grapes" proverb could address a secular matter. Someone ruing the deleterious influence of an adult upon a minor might perform it when a mother's lying prompts her daughter to weave her own web of deceit, or if a devious father emerges from an illegal scheme unscathed, while his hapless scion is punished.[65] If such were the sort of situations occasioning the PPs cited in v. 2a, however, it seems highly doubtful that (Ezekiel's) God would intervene so vehemently to discredit the saying and quell its future performance. Transgenerational responsibility played an important role in ancient Israel (e.g., Prov 22:6). In its present context, however, our proverb addresses transgenerational retribution, not transgenerational influence.

Moreover, Block's reference to "immutable cosmic rules of cause and effect" as the people's explanation for their predicament seems anachronistic. I search in vain

---

62. *Ezekiel 1–24*, 560, 561.
63. In Block's view, Ezekiel seeks to shift the people's focus from "immutable cosmic laws" to his own "radically theocentric view of the universe." The exiles are not "victims of immutable cosmic laws; their fate is in the hands of God" (*Ezekiel 1–24*, 562). I argue, by contrast, that Ezekiel seeks to shift the Judeans' interpretation of their plight from blaming it on their ancestors' sins to concluding that they suffer for their own sins.
64. The following comments borrow from my "Book of Ezekiel: Introduction, Commentary, and Reflections," *NIB* 6:1257 (corrected printing, 2002).
65. The book of Proverbs teems with instructions intended to help youths escape the death-dealing influence of evildoers.

for evidence that biblical writers conceived of such "cosmic" rules operating independently (and irrespectively) of Yhwh's creation and control. Where might such rules rank in a hierarchy of powers that includes God's "cosmic rule"? True, Israel's sages (and occasionally its prophets) spoke of actions and their consequences without explicitly identifying Yhwh's power as the force conjoining the two. Within Israelite tradition, however, the issue of transgenerational retribution arises especially in theocentric arenas.[66]

If, however, we grant that the people performing this משל ("proverb") might debate the cause of their plight in purely secular terms, both God's response in vv. 3–4 (note the first-person singular possessive pronouns) and the following exposition of the counterthesis (vv. 6–20) make clear that from Yhwh's (Ezekiel's) perspective, the "truth" or "falsity" of the proverb's contextual meaning must be adjudicated in terms of *divine* governance. Indeed, Block later appears to reverse his earlier judgment: the Judeans do not really believe themselves to be "victims of an immutable universal law that locks their fate to the conduct of their parents." They only claim to be such victims. They "really perceived themselves to be at the mercy of a capricious God, whose actions are unpredictable and arbitrary."[67]

Thus far, we have considered proverbial forms and functions, the logic of proverb performance (speaker and audience), the authority of traditional sayings, conflict as a major stimulus of PPs, and the role proverbs can play in articulating/settling disputes. Now we turn to an imaginary reconstruction of the PPs Yhwh condemns in Ezek 18:1–4.

VII. An Imaginary Reconstruction of the Judeans' "Sour Grapes" Proverb Performances

At points in our study of Ezek 18:1–4, we have hit the proverbial "stone wall," forced to acknowledge that data about the PPs cited are simply too sparse to permit thorough investigation. As analysts, we might wish that Yhwh's abrupt report to the prophet shed greater light on those contexts in which some Judeans, at least, resorted to the "sour grapes" saying. A speaker's proverbial utterances are, after all, acutely affected by their "vivid present"—including the "already spoken" on the one hand,[68] and the "not yet spoken" (the people's reactions) on the other.[69] However,

---

66. Darr, "Book of Ezekiel," 1257. Studies of divine retribution (including transgenerational retribution) often focus on Job and Deuteronomy–2 Kings. The Latter Prophets corpus, however, also is a rich resource—not only because God is said sometimes to address the issue head-on (including justifying it), but also because such texts ascribe to Israel's deity a full range of human emotions motivating retribution *and* mercy.

67. Block, *Ezekiel 1–24*, 585.

68. "[A]ll utterances address previous utterances," Seitel observes, "even if they do not literally include them, a kind of reference ... called intertextuality" (*Powers of Genre*, 9).

69. Ibid., 8.

the text does not share our interest in these lacunae. The details of our proverb's "vivid present" are all but lost to us.

But all is not lost. We can reasonably infer from vv. 2–4, for example, that the PPs Yhwh cites did not address a hodgepodge of unrelated problems confronting Ezekiel's contemporaries. Rather, different Judean communities were wrestling with a common problem that, for some at least, their proverb resolved—or at least explained. Indeed, Yhwh's initial attack on the saying in vv. 2–4 strongly suggests that from their perspective(s), it was successfully (1) "naming" that problem; (2) making sense of their situation; and (3) commending a strategy for dealing with it.

Little imagination is needed to surmise that the "problem" confronting Ezekiel's contemporaries was the imposition of Babylonian imperial policies upon Judah. Those in the homeland faced an uncertain future: had the deportation of Jerusalem's "upper crust" and the plundering of Yhwh's temple in 597 b.c.e. failed to appease the enemy? How many would die during a siege of their capital city? How many would be wounded, raped, slaughtered when Babylonian troops set to the grizzly task of reaping victory's rewards? Meanwhile, the exiles surely wondered if their deportation would be short-lived or extend into the indefinite future. Would they suffer persecution if the Babylonians lost patience with Zedekiah's attempts to enlist aid from Egypt? Could they "sing the Lord's song in a foreign land" (Ps 137:4)? In the end, would they die and be buried in alien soil?

For both groups, unthinkable possibilities loomed: could Jerusalem be destroyed and, with it, Yhwh's promise that one of David's descendants would forever occupy its throne? Did their plight signal the withdrawal (Ezek 8:12b), the defeat, the injustice (Ezek 18:25, 28; 33:17), or the callous indifference of the God who had forged a covenant with their ancestors at Sinai? These were years when fear and uncertainty commingled, and life was collapsing.

"In times of cultural ambiguity and unrest," Fontaine writes, ". . . traditional societies make use of traditional arguments, and the wisdom found in traditional sayings constitutes one of the chief weapons in [an] arsenal aimed at the reduction of anomie."[70] Ezekiel's contemporaries undoubtedly probed their traditions for answers not only to the queries raised above, but also to other crucial questions inextricably linking theological precept with personal experience: "Why are we suffering so?"; "Who, or what, is responsible for our anguish?"[71] In the process, questions about God's justice erupted.[72] But when the Judeans turned to their religious traditions—the "broader horizon" of their theodicean debates—they confronted the fact that even their most revered traditions did not speak uniformly about matters of

---

70. *Traditional Sayings*, 168.
71. Like most moderns, I reject the idea that Ezek 18 replaces an earlier emphasis on corporate punishment with a doctrine of individual responsibility.
72. Contra Block, *Ezekiel 1–24*, 560.

divine justice, wrath, mercy, and forgiveness. We can imagine that within those communities, opinions were as diverse as the traditions encapsulating them. To judge from the people's reported resort to the "sour grapes" proverb, however, the idea that transgenerational retribution was part and parcel of Yhwh's administration of justice figured prominently in their thinking.[73]

A. Transgenerational Retribution

The belief that deities punished not only offenders, but also their relatives, was not ancient Israel's alone.[74] In the Hittite "Instructions for Temple Officials," we read:

> If a slave causes his master's anger, they either kill him or they will injure him . . . or they will seize him, his wife, his children, his brother, his sister, his in-laws, his kin. . . . If then . . . anyone arouses the anger of a god, does the god take revenge on him alone? Does he not take revenge on his wife, his children, his descendants, his kin, his slaves, and slave-girls, his cattle (and) sheep together with his crop, and will utterly destroy him?[75]

This belief also surfaces in the fourteenth-century B.C.E. Hittite king Muršiliš' complaint about the Storm-god. Note the king's insistence that his generation suffers for its ancestors' sins:

> Because of the plague, I made the offerings to the river Mala the subject of an oracle also. And in that matter too it was established that I should have to account for myself before the Hattian Storm-god. See now! I have admitted my guilt before the Storm-god (and said): "It is so. We have done it." I know for certain that the offence was not committed in my days, that it was committed in the days of my father. . . . But, since the Hattian Storm-god is angry for that reason and people are dying in the Hatti land, I am (nevertheless) making the offerings to the Hattian Storm-god, my lord, on that account.[76]

Muršiliš later asserts his innocence and states explicitly that the principle of transgenerational retribution is at work: "It is only too true that man is sinful. My father sinned and transgressed against the word of the Hattian Storm-god, my lord. But I have not sinned in any respect. It is only too true, however, that the father's sin falls upon the son."[77]

---

73. This conclusion is obvious unless we opt for one of two alternatives: (1) the Judeans adopted the "sour grapes" saying for reasons other than its assertion of transgenerational retribution, but (Ezekiel's) God misunderstood their purpose in using it; (2) (Ezekiel's) God knew that the people's use of the saying had nothing to do with transgenerational retribution, but took the opportunity to denounce that principle nonetheless.

74. This discussion borrows from my "Book of Ezekiel," 1257–58.

75. "Instructions for Temple Officials," trans. A. Goetze, *ANET*, 207–8.

76. "Plague Prayers of Mursilis," trans. A. Goetze, *ANET*, 395.

77. Ibid.

In ancient Israelite tradition, divine transgenerational retribution was inscribed in no less than the Ten Commandments (Exod 20:4–5; Deut 5:9b) and versions of the "credo" of Exod 34:6b–7.[78] And not a few biblical passages presuppose its legitimacy—for example, Josh 7:22–26; 1 Sam 22:16–19; Job 23:13–14. King Josiah's anguished response to a law scroll discovered in the Jerusalem temple states the principle plainly: "Go, inquire of the Lord . . . concerning the words of this book . . . ; for great is the wrath of the Lord that is kindled against *us*, because *our ancestors* did not obey the words of this book, to do according to all that is written concerning us" (2 Kgs 22:13; emphasis mine). Perhaps most poignant is the attempt by the Deuteronomistic Historians to explain why even Josiah's righteous deeds (2 Kgs 23:25) did not reverse Yhwh's decision to destroy Judah for the sins of King Manasseh (2 Kgs 21:12; 23:26; see also the "update" in 2 Kgs 24:3–4). These examples suffice to show that the principle of divine transgenerational retribution was entrenched within certain Israelite religious traditions.

Other biblical texts, however, either baldly contradict or ignore the principle of transgenerational retribution (e.g., Num 26:11). Deuteronomy 7:9–10 reiterates that God "maintains covenant loyalty with those who love him and keep his commandments, to a thousand generations," but limits divine punishment of those who reject Yhwh to "their own person." Judah's King Amaziah (800–783 b.c.e.) spares the children of his father's assassins (2 Kgs 14:6); his decision is said to turn on "what is written in the book of the law of Moses, where the Lord commanded, 'The parents shall not be put to death for the children, or the children be put to death for the parents; but all shall be put to death for their own sins'" (Deut 24:16). The intent of this law about justice in the *human* arena is to rule out wholesale revenge against a perpetrator's family and descendants. The effect of Ezek 18:4 is to assert that what pertains (or should pertain) in the human sphere conforms to God's own administration of justice.

Given their traditions' lack of unanimity, we imagine that Ezekiel's contemporaries discussed and even disputed both the validity of the principle of transgenerational retribution and its relevance for their situation. Were we witnesses to the people's "sour grapes" PPs, we likely could determine on the basis of their "vivid present" both the "spirit" in which they spoke, and the audiences' responses. Without such information, however, we can only imagine how they said what was said, and how those who heard it reacted.

Where texts are silent, interpreters rush in. Hence, we are not surprised that scholars ascribe to the Judeans of vv. 2–4 a variety of attitudes toward, motivations for, and responses to their "sour grapes" saying. In so doing, these critics engage in "imaginary reconstructions" of their own. Their opinions suggest that for many Judeans, appropriating their saying was conflicted, if not a response to conflicts among themselves. Some scholars opine that the people's proverb expresses "cynical

---

78. See also, e.g., Num 14:18; Isa 65:7; Ps 109:13–15.

disillusionment" over God's inequitable brand of "justice";[79] in their insolence, they "mock" a divine modus operandi that punishes children for their parents' sins.[80] Indeed, their מָשָׁל states a "patently absurd" religious dogma "in such a form as to expose it to ridicule and condemnation." In other words, the proverb points out the ludicrousness of the very dogma it asserts; and "whoever decreed it ought either to recognize his own caprice, or be rejected as unjust."[81]

Other critics ascribe to the Judeans, cynical though they might be, a profound hopelessness that "no longer see[s] God's righteousness in the face of [their suffering]."[82] They experience "depression and despair," and "resignation to the *traditum*" that children bear their parents' sins, and "there is nothing anyone can do about it."[83] Bound by chains they did not forge, their appeals to Yhwh are useless. Are they succumbing to the "temptation and danger"[84] of a dogma that can justify not only resignation, but also transgression? What matter if they are as idolatrous, violent, oppressive, and unjust as Ezekiel accuses them of being?[85] Though they complain about injustice, they have ". . . a vested interest in the [principle] embodied in the 'sour grapes' proverb; unless it can be established that one generation suffers for the sins of previous generations, they will have to admit [their] blame for the current situation." Better that "Yhwh be unjust than to admit themselves unjust."[86]

But perhaps the people's earlier disputes about the relationship of transgenerational retribution to their adversity have ended. Now they quote their saying (with pious resignation?) primarily to console one another. Such a strategy emerges when a proverb speaker and his/her audience conclude that their situation must be accepted and endured:[87] Resign yourselves! Divine transgenerational retribution is "the shape truth takes" not only in the world the proverb envisions, but also in the world God governs. Their proverb "save[s] them from absurdity. Better that they think their plight represents punishment, rather than gratuitous cruelty. Any answer is better than no answer."[88]

We should not dismiss such conjectures out of hand; it is possible that each was

---

79. Hans-Joachim Kraus, *Klagelieder (Threni)* (BKAT 20; Neukirchen-Vluyn: Neukirchener, 1956), 84. Block speaks of the people's "cynical charge of divine injustice" (*Ezekiel 1–24*, 583); see also Zimmerli, *Ezekiel,* 1:379.

80. Zimmerli, *Ezekiel,* 1:378.

81. Polk, "Paradigms, Parables, and *Məšālîm*," 575.

82. Zimmerli, *Ezekiel,* 1:377.

83. Block, *Ezekiel 1–24,* 580, 556.

84. Zimmerli, *Ezekiel,* 1:378.

85. Darr, "Book of Ezekiel," 1265.

86. Paul Joyce, *Divine Initiative and Human Response in Ezekiel* (JSOTSup 51; Sheffield: Sheffield Academic Press, 1989), 47, 48.

87. Seitel, *Powers of Genre,* 31.

88. Elie Wiesel, "Ezekiel," in *Congregation: Contemporary Writers Read the Jewish Bible* (ed. D. Rosenberg; New York: Harcourt Brace Jovanovich, 1987), 174–75.

represented among Ezekiel's contemporaries. Indeed, participants in the "sour grapes" PPs might have conceded that the saying made sense of their situation, yet done so with cynicism, resentment, hopelessness, and/or despair—all with an eye to survival.

B. Ezekiel and the Principle of Transgenerational Retribution

Ezekiel presents himself as knowing ancient Israel's religious traditions intimately. Indeed, his mastery of those traditions, and his ability to deal with them creatively, appears formidable. Hence, no imagination is needed to conclude that he was as familiar as anyone with its traditions about divine transgenerational retribution.

When we attempt to identify Ezekiel's own position vis-à-vis those traditions, however, no clear-cut answer emerges. In chapter 20, Yhwh is said to offer Israel's second wilderness generation a "clean slate" (vv. 18–20), despite their parents' sins. The people refuse God's offer, repeat their progenitors' transgressions, and are penalized with "not good" statutes and death-dealing ordinances. But they are not punished for their parents' sinfulness. In this context, transgenerational retribution has no place, since it would doom the second generation also to die in the desert. In the next moment, however, Yhwh swears to scatter their descendants among the nations on account of their refusal to obey God's life-giving laws—the very punishment that the exiles are experiencing. Here, the principle of divine transgenerational retribution is key because, on that basis, Ezekiel can insist on two points relevant to the issue of divine justice: (1) subsequent generations have been living on "borrowed time" made possible only by Yhwh's forbearance; and (2) the present generation's punishment is more than justified, since their ancestors' sins only increased after the second generation entered Canaan (vv. 27–29).

Ezekiel appears willing in chapter 20 and elsewhere to marshal any resource to drive home the point of a particular oracle. This is not to suggest that Ezekiel's oracles "blow where the wind goes." To the contrary, his book displays remarkable consistency on many issues, everywhere insisting, for example, that (1) Yhwh's power and sovereignty are unrivaled; (2) God controls the history of Israel and of all the (other) nations; (3) Judah's destruction is the doing, and not the undoing, of its Lord; (4) its punishment is proportionate to the crime; and (5) human recalcitrance can never abort God's plan for Israel's future. But Ezekiel is no systematic theologian. In one breath, he argues one way; in the next breath, he might argue another—all for the sake of his argument.

A second text not only "envisions" divine transgenerational retribution in action, but also elicits from the priest/prophet a rare, impassioned (but not unprecedented) protest.[89] According to Ezek 9:3–9, Ezekiel watches as Yhwh's executioners begin to "cut down" those who neither sigh nor groan over abominations commit-

---

89. Without an audience, Ezekiel apparently dares to intercede with God on Israel's behalf (see also Ezek 11:13).

ted in their city (Ezek 9:5–6). The text specifies that everyone without the protective mark—"graybeard, youth and maiden, women and children" (NJPS)[90]—is a target. I do not imagine that Ezekiel cries out (9:8b) solely because Jerusalem's children also are (un)marked for death. To the contrary, he expresses anguish that God intends to annihilate "*all* who remain of Israel"—the very old, the very young, and everyone in between. Nevertheless, the text's insistence that those who moan and groan over their city will escape (a defense of divine justice woefully blind to the ways of warfare) asks much of its audience. Perhaps each of the unmarked graybeards, youths, maidens, and women deserved to die. But the smallest children (not נערים ["young men"], but טף ["little children"]) perish for their elders' sins, not their own. Ezekiel fails to change God's mind, but we love him for trying.

What was Ezekiel's opinion of the PPs God ostensibly condemns in 18:2–4? Did he first learn of them from YHWH's abrupt report, or was he already aware that the proverb was in play among his contemporaries? Was Ezekiel himself present for his fellow exiles' debates, and so knew well the spirit in which they uttered and received the "sour grapes" saying? Had he remained silent in the past because he was uncertain how to respond, or felt incapable of discrediting the proverb's thesis adequately, or because, in the argot of the book, his tongue clung to the roof of his mouth, rendering him speechless until YHWH opened his mouth and filled it with divine words? Indeed, had one PP transpired only minutes earlier, as Ezekiel sat among an audience whose responses (vv. 19, 25) will suggest that the text preserves a lively debate?

In *Swallowing the Scroll*, Ellen Davis states that while other prophets engaged in direct exchanges with rival prophets, priests, and kings, Ezekiel's primary conversation partner is Israelite tradition: "Like a creative archivist, he desires not only to preserve the treasures of the past but also to make them available and meaningful in the present. Even his disputation speeches are aimed as much at the tradition as at the people, purging it of its useless elements . . . and correcting disastrous misinterpretations."[91] To judge from chapter 18, Ezekiel has concluded that in the present context, the principle of divine transgenerational retribution has become one such "useless element." And so, he seeks to eliminate it from the people's interpretations of their situation. This would not be Ezekiel's first attempt to discredit certain long-lived Israelite religious beliefs, as Ezek 16, for example, shows all too well.

Is it possible that *none* of Ezekiel's contemporaries performs the "sour grapes" saying? Has he created these scenarios as part of a strategy to crystallize, and then condemn, a popular/potential construal of the people's situation by coining, or quoting, a saying encapsulating their unspoken attitude solely for the purpose of rejecting it?

---

90. NJPS reverses the order of "women" and "children" in MT.
91. *Swallowing the Scroll: Textuality and the Dynamics of Discourse in Ezekiel's Prophecy* (Bible and Literature 21; Sheffield: Almond, 1989), 62.

By casting the attitudes of the Receiver [as] a saying, the Source makes explicit the folk ideas [functioning] for the covenant community at that time. . . . By doing this, the Source presents a radically new Gestalt to the Receivers, one [bearing] little resemblance to the popular piety and hypocrisy [that] the prophets attacked. The [people's] shock and chagrin upon hearing their most deeply hidden and self-centered attitudes articulated in . . . a traditional saying—a powerful expression [that] carried great authority—and then ridiculed and denied by God . . . must have had a very great impact. Here is a type of indirection [that] shields not the Source, but the Receiver from . . . the awful truth . . . of the community's misperceptions. This . . . must have descended upon the Receivers . . . with all the force . . . language can wield.[92]

Perhaps the PPs Yhwh ostensibly cites are a literary fiction, devised by Ezekiel to confront his contemporaries with a death-dealing dogma, and then to release them from it (whether they want to be released or not). Or again, perhaps vv. 2–4 cite bona fide PPs that Ezekiel has personally committed himself to debunk so thoroughly that the saying becomes extinct.

Whether or not these possibilities, or others, shed light on the role that PPs play in Ezek 18, one thing is clear: the text does not attribute its contents to Ezekiel. To the contrary, here, as almost everywhere in the book, the text presents Ezekiel's oracles as Yhwh's own and expects its readers to receive them as such. God commissions Ezekiel and sends him to the people (2:3); he must transmit the Lord's words to them, whether they listen or not (2:5, 7), because his very life hangs on his obedience to God (3:16–21). Ezekiel must ingest Yhwh's words of "lamentation and mourning and woe"; and, as Robert Wilson observes, "All of the words which Ezekiel speaks are precisely the same words which God literally put inside the prophet."[93] God restricts Ezekiel to his house, clamps his tongue to the roof of his mouth, and forbids him both to speak of his own initiative and to act as arbiter in Yhwh's case against Israel.

Behind these restrictions stand agendas of utmost seriousness: if God authors Ezekiel's words, then their authority must not be questioned, competing claims notwithstanding. If Ezekiel's oracles are unbearably harsh, he cannot be blamed, since Yhwh is responsible for their content. Ezekiel does not intercede for the people, because God has expressly forbidden him to do so. Those who would dismiss him as a false prophet, or as merely a maker of metaphors (21:5 [Eng. 20:49]), or as a singer of inconsequential love songs (33:32), defy the Lord who, Ezekiel avers, both commissioned and scripted him. Receiving his words as anything other than God's contravenes what is arguably the text's preeminent claim.

If Ezekiel would tackle divine transgenerational retribution—a principle firmly fixed amidst competing Israelite traditions about Yhwh's administration of jus-

---

92. Fontaine, *Traditional Sayings*, 251.
93. Robert Wilson, "Prophecy in Crisis: The Call of Ezekiel," *Int* 38 (1984): 127.

tice—one way is to attribute to God an argument that (1) states that principle; (2) passes judgment on it; (3) poses a counterthesis; and (4) disputes the people's opinion by means of a thorough explication of that counterthesis. In short, Ezekiel might open God's mouth, as it were, and place within it a PP.

VIII. Yhwh's Proverb Performance

Thus far, our analysis has focused upon the PPs that Yhwh reports to Ezekiel and his audience (18: 2–4), seeking not only to elucidate the "sour grapes" saying but also to imagine how its contextualized meaning might have functioned for both speakers and audiences.

Here, however, we focus upon Yhwh's PP. Form critics rightly identify God's oracle as a "disputation," but it is also an extended PP, in which God's citation of PPs anchors and initiates an argument about the relationship between human sin and divine justice. In this PP, Yhwh's motive for quoting the "sour grapes" saying is the opposite of the Judeans': they cite it in order to assert that the proverb and context domains are analogous, but Yhwh denies any analogy between those two domains. The proverb not only "mis-names" and fails to explain the Judeans' current circumstance(s), but also commends an invalid survival strategy. God seeks so to transform their assessment of their situation(s) that the dispute reaches its proper resolution (the Lord "wins" the argument). While his contemporaries perform their saying in hopes of "identifying some repeatable tract of experience, useful to know about when engaged in the project of striving to make a coherent whole out of one's existence," Ezekiel seeks to "jolt his audience out of this hoped-for continuity into a new judgment about [God's justice]."[94]

Viewing Ezek 18 as Yhwh's PP does not require that we revise all aspects of our earlier investigation. On the one hand, our definition of "proverb," identification of the "sour grapes" saying's formal features, and explanations of proverbial functions and of thematic finalization at the level of the proverb itself remain the same, as do our observations regarding the frequent confluence of PPs and conflict situations. Even our remarks on proverbial authority do not change, although, to the extent the audience accepts Ezekiel's rejection of its truth claim as Yhwh's own, the traditional saying's authority is "trumped" by God's greater authority.

On the other hand, our shift in focus reveals data about Yhwh's PP—for example, the identification of the participants (X and Y) and the social dynamics between them—not available for the Judeans' PPs: the interaction situation (ostensibly) involves Yhwh, Israel's patron deity, and Ezekiel, God's prophet (plus his audience). The former is the superior party, the latter the inferior party. Yhwh's words are presented as true and reliable; and Ezekiel purports to be an authentic, trustworthy spokesperson of those words.

---

94. William A. Beardslee, "Uses of the Proverb in the Synoptic Gospel," in *Wisdom of Many*, 171–72.

We can illustrate the logic of Yhwh's PP by returning to a slightly modified interpretation of Seitel's diagram: Yhwh (X) asserts to Ezekiel and his audience (Y) in an interaction situation that the relationship between persons in the proverb situation is not analogous to the relationship between persons or entities in the context situation, because children are not punished for their parents' sins. (Now, the broken lines connecting the two domains represent Yhwh's assertion that no analogy exists between them.)

That Ezekiel begins God's speech with a derogatory rhetorical question already suggests that Yhwh's citation of the people's proverb is antagonistic, not amicable or neutral. This suspicion is quickly confirmed, for having quoted the saying, God swears an oath to its imminent extinction, rejects its (contextualized) meaning, and asserts the "counterthesis" in v. 4b.[95]

Yhwh's PP, however, does not end there. The Lord buttresses the counterthesis by relating logically, and in the argot of casuistic law, three hypothetical test cases concerning a righteous man (vv. 5–9), his sinful son (vv. 10–13), and his righteous grandson (vv. 14–17). Does Yhwh's explication of the counterthesis, chockablock with juridical argot, suggest a connection between PPs and formal legal settings in ancient Israel?

Space permits only a few observations about these test cases.[96] The first begins with a protasis amplified by eleven examples of righteous conduct that, in typical Ezekielian fashion, juxtapose cultic and moral obligations (see, e.g., Ezek 22:6–12).[97] A summary statement declaring that the righteous one faithfully obeys Yhwh's laws (v. 9a) is followed by two declaratory formulas: a "verdict" declares, "he is righteous"; a "sentence of acquittal" ("he shall surely live") is cast as the opposite of the death sentence ("he shall surely die") and might, in a lighthearted way, be termed a "*life* sentence."[98] This first test case does not bear directly on the truth claim of the people's proverb, and Ezekiel's audience ostensibly does not respond.

According to the second case, this righteous person begets a son whose conduct is the opposite of his own. In the following catalog of unrighteous deeds, Ezekiel transforms previously positive statements into negative ones ("does not restore the pledge") and vice versa ("eats upon the mountains"), the better to contrast the son's behavior with his parent's. Verse 13 contains no counterpart to the verdict in v. 9b,

---

95. Matties identifies "all souls are mine" as God's new משל to the people (*Ezekiel 18 and the Rhetoric*, 85–86). That statement is not the opposite of the proverb's assertion, however, although it is essential for the actual opposing assertion, "only the person who sins shall die."

96. The following comments borrow from my "Book of Ezekiel," 1258–61. See also Moshe Greenberg, *Ezekiel 1–20: A New Translation with Introduction and Commentary* (AB 22; Garden City, N.Y.: Doubleday, 1983), 328–47; Matties, *Ezekiel 18 and the Rhetoric*, 159–96; and Block, *Ezekiel 1–24*, 564–81.

97. Ezekiel's list of ordinances has no precise parallel elsewhere in Scripture, but similar legal lists appear in a variety of biblical genres. Scholars propose various original social settings for such lists; see Matties, *Ezekiel 18 and the Rhetoric*, 92–105; Block, *Ezekiel 1–24*, 566–69.

98. Ronald M. Hals, *Ezekiel* (FOTL 19; Grand Rapids: Eerdmans, 1989), 123.

but one of its three death sentences ("he shall not live") is the opposite of "he shall surely live." This second test case also has no direct relevance to the proverb's theme; and again, Ezekiel's audience ostensibly does not respond.

Finally, the text introduces a third case: the son of the violent person witnesses his parent's sins, takes thought (see Eccl 7:14), and rejects them. The ensuing catalog of righteous deeds (vv. 15–17) is both the antithesis of vv. 11–13 and a near copy of vv. 5–9, save for minor changes. Though the grandchild's case does not include the formula "he is righteous," the "sentence of acquittal" appears in v. 17b. Verse 18 returns to the second case and summarizes the charges for which his father dies.

With the completion of this third case, Ezekiel creates a scenario bearing directly upon the people's proverbial theme and contextualized meaning: contrary to their saying, the righteous child is not punished for the parent's sins. No surprise, then, that his audience challenges, or is said to challenge, the verdict (v. 19a). Yhwh (ostensibly) counters their resistance in three ways. First, Ezekiel reiterates points in his argument, summarizes "evidence" in the third case, restates its "verdict," repeats the counterthesis, and refutes the saying's truth claim. Second, Ezekiel moves beyond its truth claim to insist that divine transgenerational retribution operates neither forward (i.e., from one generation to the next, as in v. 2b) nor backward (i.e., from one generation to preceding one[s]) (as legislated within the human sphere in Deut 24:16). Third, Ezekiel's God addresses the issue of divine retribution (not divine transgenerational retribution!) in a judgment concerning an individual's/generation's "righteous(ness)" and "wicked(ness)" (v. 20b) This final assertion not only ends the first section of Yhwh's PP, but also sets the stage for the remainder of God's disputation in vv. 21–32.

Block detects in v. 19a additional evidence that the people's proverb speaks not of sin and retribution (a "theological" interpretation), but to their contention that "present circumstances are inextricably linked to the actions of past generations" (a "secular" interpretation): "According to the traditional interpretation, the proverb would have the people accusing God of injustice because he had visited the sins of the fathers on the children. However, in v. 19 they ask why he should not do so.... It is inconceivable that the prophet's intervening arguments would have had such a dramatic effect upon them."[99] But his argument is not persuasive. Yhwh's PP might fail to persuade its audience to reject the principle of divine transgenerational retribution, but this would not mean that they have rejected a theological explanation in one moment (v. 2b), only to embrace it in the next (v. 19). It means, rather, that their belief in the proverb's theme and relevance has not changed, despite the arguments in Ezekiel's (God's) PP thus far. The משל is *not* a way of stating a "patently absurd" religious dogma in order "to expose it to ridicule and condemnation."[100] Rather, it expresses "the way it is" in God's world, whether they like it or not.

---

99. Block, *Ezekiel 1–24*, 561.
100. Polk, "Paradigms, Parables, and *Mĕšālîm*," 575.

In our analysis of the Judeans' PPs, we observed how thematic finalization occurs at the first level. Now we turn to what might be called "contra-thematic" finalization at the second and third levels of YHWH's PP. At the second level, contra-thematic finalization occurs when the audience grasps that the proverb and context domains are *not* analogous. Ezekiel 18:1–4 does not identify the precise situation(s) prompting the Judeans' PPs, but YHWH responds to those (ostensible) PPs and the thinking that prompted them. And contra-thematic finalization occurs at the third level when the audience grasps that the proverb's theme (first level), which is not analogous to their context situation (second level), does not apply to themselves (third level) and so abandons their argument and accepts God's counterthesis (v. 4b).

If and when YHWH's PP achieves this third level of finalization, and Ezekiel's audience accepts that its proverb neither names nor explains their present situation, then the people face a new crisis. Given YHWH's "truth claim" that their lives hang solely upon their own righteousness or wickedness, what survival strategy is possible? The answer lies in the logical connection between vv. 1–20 and vv. 21–32. God's disputation oracle (PP) does not end with v. 20, as Graffy would have it (see n. 2). Rather, vv. 21–32 articulate a strategy for naming, explaining, and *surviving* their situation as Ezekiel's God has just defined it.

In advancing this new strategy, Ezekiel dismantles the notion that human beings accumulate a "treasury of merit or demerit" over their lifetimes.[101] Two test cases illustrate the exiles' options: if a wicked person turns back from his/her sins, observes God's statutes, and does what is just and righteous, then "he shall surely live; he shall not die." A past trove of sin will not determine that person's "destiny." YHWH's rhetorical question in v. 23 demands a negative response—God does not desire the death of the wicked, but that they repent of their former ways and live. If, on the other hand, a righteous person repents of his/her righteousness and does evil, practicing the very abominations that the (formerly) wicked person committed, none of his former righteous deeds will be remembered. A modern analogy sheds light on vv. 21–24: life is not like a nine-inning baseball game, in which a team "wins" or "loses" depending upon the number of runs it scores during the entire game. In life, victory depends solely upon the number of "runs" scored in the ninth inning alone.

I submit that the challenge attributed to Ezekiel's audience in v. 25 responds directly, as its location implies, to Ezekiel's assertion in vv. 21–24, and is not a delayed reaction to God's rejection of their proverb. If I am correct, then we might conclude that their objection is not without merit. Why should the Boston Red Sox lead at the end of the eighth with seven runs to the New York Yankees' three, yet lose the game because they score only one run in the ninth, while the Yankees score two? Why should a period of backsliding in an otherwise righteous life "cancel out"

---

101. Block, *Ezekiel 1–24*, 550.

former righteousness and result in a death sentence? Why should a last-ditch period of righteousness in an otherwise wicked life "cancel out" former wickedness and result in a verdict of acquittal?

If we would entertain sympathy for the exiles' thinking on this point, Ezekiel's God does not. In vv. 25b–28, Yhwh rejects their objection by means of two rhetorical questions: in the first, God challenges their charge of divine malfeasance ("O house of Israel, are my ways unfair?"); in the second, God lobs their accusation back into their laps ("Is it not your ways that are unfair?"). Moreover, Yhwh repeats the judgments rendered in the two most recent test cases. But the exiles are not deterred. Again, they protest the unfairness of the Lord's way; and Yhwh responds with the same two rhetorical questions. The argument between the exiles and Ezekiel('s God) has reached a stalemate.

But then, God speaks again—first, to reassert Yhwh's right to judge and to reiterate the actual principle by which those judgments are rendered ("'I will judge you, O house of Israel, all of you according to your ways,' says the Lord God"); second, to issue a call to repentance, lest iniquity lead to demise (vv. 30b–32; see 14:6). Here, Block states, Ezekiel changes his rhetorical strategy: "If he cannot convince his audience of the error of their ways through logical argumentation, perhaps a more impassioned approach will succeed."[102]

Had we access to the "vivid present" of Yhwh's PP, we might better discern if the tenor of the PP has changed. However, the text itself suggests that something radically different has entered the argument. Verse 31 issues a call to action: God urges the exiles to cast away their transgressions and "get themselves a new heart and a new spirit." The challenge is astonishing—unique to the book of Ezekiel and, within that corpus, unique to this passage. In Ezek 11:19–20, Yhwh promised to give the exiles "one [or "a new"] heart" and a "new spirit," that they might henceforth obey God's laws. Only here, however, does the prophet assert that human beings have the capacity to acquire these attributes for themselves. "Why will you die, O house of Israel?" asks the Lord. Although v. 32 essentially reiterates the substance of v. 23, what was there posed as a question here becomes an impassioned plea: Yhwh takes no pleasure in the death of anyone. "Repent, then, and live!"

IX. The Purpose of Yhwh's Proverb Performance, or "Is There Repentance in Ezekiel?"

What, finally, is the purpose of Yhwh's PP? Its goal is not simply to banish belief in divine transgenerational retribution, though doing so is the first, crucial step in God's larger argument. Rather, it seeks to provide the people with a means to survive their *present* circumstances: repent of your past sins and leave them behind; get yourselves a new heart and a new spirit, and then set to the task of doing

---

102. Ibid., 587.

righteousness in every aspect of your lives. Matties states the purpose of our passage beautifully:

> [Ezekiel 18] is one of the few texts in Ezekiel that is hortatory. . . . Judgment we can understand; even the vision for salvation and the utopian portrait of the restored Israel is comprehensible in the light of the prophetic task. We find Ezekiel holding out a dream for a peaceable world to come. But what [connects] the two? Surely, chapter 18 is essential to make the movement complete. Without it the overall Ezekiel tradition would be incomplete, two polarities without the dimension of human possibility. Ezekiel 18 bridges the gap between resignation after recognizing the necessity of judgment, and visionary hope for divine intervention and deliverance. The human factor in between, the life in the meantime, is the context to which this chapter speaks. It is the ethical dimension that must be addressed as the people find a way of being in the world, their world, not the past or the future world. Chapter 18 is the *via media* by which the holy God comes to dwell with a holy people. That possibility both enables "life" and is "life" in the presence of God.[103]

The question quoted in the previous heading, "Is there repentance in Ezekiel?" arose during the second of two sessions of the Theological Perspectives on the Book of Ezekiel Group at the 2003 annual meeting of the Society of Biblical Literature (Atlanta, 24 November 2003). Once posed, it dominated our discussion. Some participants said "no"; others said "yes." My answer is "yes," so long as we revise the question slightly: "Is repentance *possible* in Ezekiel?" We cannot know if, or when, Ezekiel's audience accepted his explanation for their circumstances and adopted his alternative strategy for coping with them—although a question attributed to the exiles in another disputation oracle, with striking similarities to our own (33:10b), suggests that eventually they both acknowledged their own transgressions and assumed responsibility for their situation ("*Our* transgressions and *our* sins weigh upon *us*, and *we* waste away because of them" [emphasis mine]), and explicitly sought a way to survive it ("How then shall we live?"). But repentance is possible in Ezekiel, because Yhwh's PP in chapter 18 can release those who accept its argument not only from the "sour grapes" their ancestors ate, but also from the bitter fruit of their own partaking.

---

103. *Ezekiel 18 and the Rhetoric*, 222–23.

RESPONSES

In Search of Theological Meaning:
Ezekiel Scholarship at the Turn of the Millennium

Daniel I. Block

Among the experiences that have brought me the most satisfaction and intellectual stimulation over the past fifteen years have been the conversations with scholars devoted to the study of Ezekiel at the annual meetings of the Society of Biblical Literature. These conversations have been both formal and informal. We have met to read and hear one another's papers. These have represented an extremely broad range of hermeneutical methodologies and theological perspectives. Although approaches and conclusions have varied greatly, the style of the papers has always been professional and of consistently respectful tone. It has been both a delight and an honor to be a part of many of these conversations. I for one have relied upon these annual meetings to help keep me abreast of trends in scholarship, and after the conferences have always returned to my students with new ideas and new enthusiasm for the biblical scholarly enterprise.

Equally satisfying have been the private conversations with other Ezekiel scholars. Most of us work in environments where the prophet Ezekiel and the book that goes by his name suffer from serious marginalization. And when laypersons, and even other biblical scholars, learn that we have devoted major parts of our lives and countless hours to the study of this book, their responses range from indifference to utter incredulity. For this reason, among others, discussing the times, the personality, the theology, or the text of this extraordinary (many say bizarre) prophet over coffee or lunch with others who share similar passions has often brought even greater pleasure.

Ezekiel scholars will recognize that the present collection of essays illustrates the point. The organizers of the annual SBL program unit "Theological Perspectives on the Book of Ezekiel" and the editors of this volume are to be commended both for the subjects they have selected for discussion and the range of contributors they have engaged. Readers unfamiliar with the world of Ezekiel scholarship should be delighted to find in this volume essays by scholars who represent a broad and polychromatic spectrum of theological and hermeneutical perspectives. This is reflected in the institutions with which the contributors are associated, which include Jewish,

Roman Catholic, mainline Protestant, evangelical Protestant, and secular establishments. Regardless of the tradition from which the essayist comes and that he or she serves, evaluation of the essays will inevitably depend upon one's view of the validity/invalidity of the methodology adopted.

In the broadest sense of the word the essays in this volume relate to issues of hierarchy: the bases of authority, the contexts in which authority is exercised, and specific textual treatments of authority. The scholars who have contributed to this volume have applied a wide range of methodologies to their respective assignments, including classical redaction criticism (Fechter), the interpretation of biblical texts within their ancient Near Eastern cultural context (Smith-Christopher, Cook), intertextual analysis (Kohn, Petersen), literary analysis (Darr), and postmodern deconstruction (Habel, Carley). As a collection these essays introduce readers to the breadth and variety of perspectives driving biblical scholarship at the beginning of the twenty-first century. The attention this review will give to each essay will vary, but the comments will largely follow the order of the essays in the collection.

I. Who Is This Man? Social Hierarchy and the Priesthood

When I was pursuing my own research on the book of Ezekiel in the 1980s and 1990s, like many others I assumed that Ezekiel was a priestly prophet, that is, that he functioned primarily as a prophet, but did so from the perspective of the priesthood. In the meantime, through the research of one of my students (T. J. Betts) I have been forced to rethink this position and to ask whether Ezekiel served as a priestly prophet or as a prophetic priest. A casual reader may wonder what difference this makes, but for those who wrestle with the book the implications of the reversal of noun and modifier are profound. If Ezekiel functioned primarily as a priest, but with a prophetic mandate superimposed on his priesthood (cf. 2:5; 33:33), rather than as a prophet with a priestly foundation undergirding his prophetic ministry, then we are forced to rethink the nature and purpose of the book, beginning with the opening vision. Was the event described here primarily a call to the priesthood, and secondarily a call to prophetic ministry, rather than the reverse? I am grateful for the assistance the first four essays in this volume offer in thinking through these issues.

Three of the first four essays affirm Ezekiel's priestly role. The title of Fechter's essay, "Priesthood in Exile according to the Book of Ezekiel," invites the reader to expect a forthright answer to the question concerning the nature of the priesthood among the exiles in Babylonia.[1] However, recognizing that the first thirty-nine chapters have little to say about the priesthood, Fechter concentrates on the last nine chapters, focusing particularly on 43:18–27 and 44:4–31. In the former, which he

---

1. Like a geological "erratic," Fechter's redaction-critical approach contrasts sharply with the methodologies that tend to be pursued in North America today, as illustrated in the rest of the essays in this volume.

interprets as "a priestly legislation text," he rightly sees Ezekiel functioning like Moses in Exod 29:1–37 and Lev 8:15–34, consecrating the altar and executing the first offerings. More specifically, he argues that in the minds of the authors of 43:18–27 Ezekiel initiated the postexilic sacrifice in the temple.

In response, it is unclear whether or not this text says anything at all about Ezekiel's priestly ministry or the role of the priests in the exile, other than that he might have issued priestly kinds of legislation. In the first instance, the activities described involve an altar and activities that transpire within the physical context in the temple. This is clearly not an exilic picture. In the second instance, chapter 43 is imbedded within a larger visionary context (chs. 40–48), whose purpose is to provide an ideational portrayal of a nation restored in its relationship with Yhwh. It is doubtful that any of the images in this complex series of texts reflected exilic realities or was ever intended as a paradigm for exilic practices. The nature and style of the text are consistent with what we might expect from a priestly mediator of divine revelation and/or priestly author, but they say nothing about actual priestly performance in the exile, let alone implementation in the future.[2]

Fechter places even more stock in 44:4–31 for reconstructing the nature of the priesthood during the exile, finding in the legislation of Ezekiel the roots of the exilic and postexilic opposition between priests and Levites. Apart from an apparent unawareness or deliberate ignoring of alternative interpretations of the data,[3] the position presented tends to overstate the case for "strong polemics against the Levites." For instance, in discussing the causes of the Levites' demotion, Fechter comments, "This rejection of all strangers is in clear contradiction to 3:6, which implies that Yhwh could have sent Ezekiel to any nation." But where is the contradiction? Indeed, where is the connection? Chapter 44 concerns access to the temple, from which all uncircumcised are barred. This has nothing to do with 3:6, in which Yhwh contemplates sending Ezekiel as his messenger to a people of unintelligible speech. Nothing in this context suggests Ezekiel would have gone to them to invite them to come as they are and worship in the temple.

Later, in reflecting on the significance of 44:10–16, Fechter opines that 44:13 "can only mean that they [the Levites] had been permitted to do priestly service in former times." But is this the only meaning possible? In order to make this statement the verse should probably have read, "*No longer are* they allowed to come close to me in order to serve as priests for me and to approach all my holy things, to the

---

2. Following Yehezkel Kaufmann, Moshe Greenberg ("The Design and Themes of Ezekiel's Program of Restoration," *Interpretation* 38 [1984]: 181–208; idem, *Ezekiel 1–20* [AB 22; Garden City, N.Y.: Doubleday, 1983], 15) rightly reminds us that none of Ezekiel's "legislation" was ever implemented.

3. Cf. Baruch J. Schwartz, "A Priest Out of Place: Reconsidering Ezekiel's Role in the History of the Israelite Priesthood," in this volume, p. 62, and n. 8. In addition to the literature cited there, see Corrine L. Patton, "Priest, Prophet, and Exile: Ezekiel as a Literary Construct," in this volume, p. 85 n. 39; Daniel I. Block, *The Book of Ezekiel*, vol. 2, *Chapters 25–48* (NICOT; Grand Rapids: Eerdmans, 1998), 626–37, esp. n. 106.

holy of holies." As it stands, the present text could also be interpreted to mean that the distinctions that existed previously will continue. I agree that Ezek 44 draws clear distinctions between the roles of Levites and those of the Zadokite priests, but to read distinction as "conflict" (not to mention "virulent" conflict) is to overstate its significance.[4]

Duguid's essay presents a sharp contrast in both method and conclusions to Fechter's work. Exhibiting a much more positive view of the text itself and also the significance of the book for informing us on Ezekiel's role as a priest, Duguid argues that the book illustrates what priestly service would have looked like once the temple had been destroyed and its system of rituals terminated. Thereafter a primary aspect of the priest's role would have involved instruction in the torah. Correcting the view I expressed earlier, that the watchman text (3:16–21) expresses Ezekiel's calling to prophetic ministry, Duguid notes that we have undervalued the priestly aspect of this calling. To the considerations he presents we might add the Deuteronomic tradition that sees Levitical priests involved in legal decisions involving issues of life and death (Deut 17:8–13). In the end Duguid offers an extremely positive verdict on the book as a witness to Ezekiel's role as a priest and to his vision of a future when all—priests, Levites, and laypersons—will be fulfilling their proper roles within the context of the nation of Israel's restored relationship with Yhwh.

Approaching the issue from a more sophisticated sociological and literary perspective, Corrine Patton ("Priest, Prophet, and Exile: Ezekiel as a Literary Construct") recognizes in Ezekiel the idealization of the priesthood. Although Patton is skeptical about recovering any historical information on the exilic priesthood from the book, she finds "the storytelling in the book so artful that it draws the reader into assuming that what it says about Ezekiel reflects a historical person's real experience." But this approach raises some serious questions regarding the patronymic introduction to the person whose ministry it purports to recount (1:2–3), the biographical nature of the bulk of the book, and especially about the fourteen date notices distributed throughout the book. If the character of Ezekiel is indeed primarily a literary creation, the sophistication with which this is achieved is extraordinary, probably too extraordinary to be true. Would an exilic or postexilic author so near to the events really have couched an ideological agenda in such concrete historical terms? It may seem naive in the modern cultural context, but readers of ancient texts should be cautious about imposing contemporary literary standards or ideological preoccupations on ancient documents.

This is not to say that Patton's understanding of Ezekiel as a character is misplaced. On the contrary, she offers an excellent analysis of the priestly role and functions of Ezekiel. Although he offers no sacrifices (contra Fechter), follows no ritual calendar, makes no decisions regarding purity and ritual cleanness, and is

---

4. So also Iain Duguid, "Putting Priests in Their Place: Ezekiel's Contribution to the History of the Old Testament Priesthood," in this volume, p. 49 n. 25.

never reported observing the Sabbath or performing the rite of circumcision, in the absence of a temple Ezekiel mediates God's presence and offers the people a window to the mind of God. However, while he functions as the servant of God par excellence he does so as one who is utterly human, even debased.

Patton rightly criticizes the view of many that in contrast to prophets, who regularly campaigned for social change, the priests served primarily as a "conserving" group whose function was to reinforce existing hierarchical social structures. Indeed she finds Ezekiel's role as "change-agent" (my expression) to be his defining function. By the time one reaches the end of the book one realizes how this character serves the author's agenda of reducing the role of prophets, reining in the power of civil and royal authorities, and elevating the role of the priests, especially the Zadokites, with himself as a high priestly figure occupying the top rung. This interpretation has much to commend itself.

Especially intriguing is Patton's observation of the total absence of any prophetic figure from the last nine chapters. One wonders, however, if this is the result of an ideological struggle between prophets and priests or whether it simply recognizes that in the ideal Israel—where the people are genuinely people of faith and demonstrate their fidelity to Yhwh by fulfilling their covenant obligations—there is any need for prophets at all. It is striking that even in the Deuteronomistic History the prophetic institution emerges as a significant force only as the spirituality of the people in general and the fidelity of the priesthood in particular wane. In short, the prophets represented ad hoc appointees whose very presence was a symptom of the spiritual malaise of the people. Given the idealism with which the final chapters paint the picture of Israel's future relationship with Yhwh, the involvement of prophets would be superfluous.

At the same time, Patton is often given to overstatement and arguments from silence, especially with regard to Ezekiel's personal role. She claims that Ezekiel's status is asserted (I prefer reflected) through ritual hierarchy, but her presentation of the arguments is forced. Her interpretation of the elders' approach for consultation (8:1; 14:1; and 20:1) as evidence of a usurpation of political roles is unwarranted, inasmuch as the language used of their approach is traditional. This is no more usurpation of political power here than we witness anywhere else when priests or prophets offer their services in revealing the will of God to political and military leaders.[5] Nor should Ezekiel's role in the final vision be interpreted as a usurpation of royal power. The statement "God works with him to plan the new temple" is misleading. God does not plan the temple with him; nor does he give him any responsibility in its construction. It is revealed to him as a building already constructed. Ezekiel's sole role is to observe a third person as he takes the measurements

---

5. Cf. the priestly use of the Urim and Thummim in Num 27:21; David's consultation of Nathan in 2 Sam 7; Ahab and Jehoshaphat's consultation of Ahab's prophets and Micaiah ben Imlah in 1 Kgs 22; Josiah's consultation of Huldah in 2 Kgs 22.

of the temple, and then to report to the people what he has seen (43:10). As for the set of laws that he receives, with the exception of the consecration of the altar, Ezekiel functions only as the recipient of revelation. Later Patton argues that although Ezekiel is not in fact the high priest, he is portrayed as a priest "who usurps the hierarchy of approach from the high priest, and even surpasses it." She is right in declaring that "he sees God more clearly than the priests who remain in Jerusalem," but access to God's presence in visionary form should not be interpreted as usurpation of power. To see 44:9–31, particularly the affirmation of the Zadokites' superior priestly status, as evidence of his own elevation to the top rung is unfounded.

While the speculative nature of some of Patton's argumentation undermines some of her conclusions, she has offered modern readers a creative way of reading the book. Her perception of Ezekiel as a priestly character who "out-prophesies" (my expression) the prophets and ultimately declares the prophetic institution to be unnecessary is especially intriguing.

If Patton and Duguid argue for viewing Ezekiel as a prophetic priest, Baruch Schwartz ("A Priest Out of Place") argues for the reverse. Indeed, to a large extent this essay represents a response to Duguid. Schwartz acknowledges the obvious priestly heritage and background of Ezekiel, but he challenges Duguid's conclusions regarding his primary role. Schwartz argues correctly that there is no evidence for Ezekiel performing priestly duties prior to his exile or of participating in cultic rituals in Babylonia. What then is left for him to do as a priest? Schwartz answers, divining the will of Yhwh and teaching Yhwh's ordinances and laws in Israel, but then goes on to argue that neither of these is evident in the priestly sense in the book.

However, the issues are not quite as simple as Schwartz argues. With respect to the first, he writes,

> Torah (תורה), in the sense of oracular divination, as performed by priests, entails the manipulation of the Urim and Thummim or other devices. It is occasioned by an inquiry initiated by someone other than the priest, and it is aimed at discerning a particular piece of information, known to exist but not accessible (or at least not readily accessible) by the means available to mortals. This might include a person's guilt or innocence of a crime or the identity of a culprit—that is, knowledge that the deity would otherwise not be inclined to communicate.

With the exception of the manipulation of the Urim and Thummim, which were the prerogative of the priest at the central sanctuary, Schwartz's description of the oracular role of the priest accords precisely with what Ezekiel does in 8:1, 14:1, and 20:1. In each case elders of the exilic community initiate an inquiry, which results in the revelation of information otherwise inaccessible to mortals, identifying guilty parties and/or exposing the nature of crimes that have been committed. The fact that 11:4 expressly speaks of persons coming to inquire of a prophet (apparently referring to Ezekiel) does not necessarily exclude a priestly activity.

As for Ezekiel's role as a supposed instructor in the תורה ("torah"), understood as Yhwh's ordinances and laws, it seems that Schwartz again has drawn lines too finely. On the one hand he argues that prophecy "threatens and promises, cajoles and condemns, but it does not instruct." But what is one then to do with 43:12, where Yhwh explicitly identifies his revelation concerning the temple as תורת הבית, "the torah of the house"? Whether one interprets this as a colophonic statement referring to what has preceded or a superscription to what follows, the surrounding materials scarcely fit Schwartz's own description of the function of prophecy. On the other hand, he declares that torah is normative: it tells what to do in order to be in accord with existing law and how to do it. It seems to me that this is precisely what Ezekiel does, especially in chapters 4–24 and 33–39. Schwartz also seems to have too narrow an understanding of the teaching role of the priests when he declares:

> It was completely ancillary to, and dependent upon, his role as cultic practitioner and specialist, and it consisted of informing the worshiper which ritual needed to be performed and how to do so, of supervising its proper performance, and of ruling and responding on matters requiring expert determinations, as posed by the worshiper or necessitated by circumstances. . . . Ancient Israelite priesthood was not a ministry to the people; it was a ministry on behalf of the people to the deity.

If this was the case, then who was responsible for the pastoral care of the people? Who would read to them the stories of divine grace toward the ancestors and explain to them the ordinances attending their covenant relationship with Yhwh, if not the priests? To argue that this represents an anachronistic interpretation of "biblical passages employing the word תורה according to this word's postexilic and postbiblical meaning" is to beg the question. Furthermore, if expressions like "my torah" (Ezek 22:26) and declarations that the Levites were to teach "your ordinances to Jacob and your torah to Israel" (Deut 33:10) do not suggest a recognized authoritative record of the divine will (whether oral or written),[6] it is difficult to know what these statements might mean. Furthermore, instructing in the torah surely involved more than seeing to it that ritual laws were properly observed. If the priests and Levites were not engaged in pastoral ministry, which must have involved instruction in the will of God for everyday life, then who performed these functions for the nation? The prophets represented ad hoc appointees, sent by God to call the people back to covenant relationship precisely because the priests had failed in this role. We do not deny that Ezekiel was a prophet, but we should be cautious about dismissing him as a priest in any sense of the word. It could be argued that in his adaptation and appli-

---

6. Hosea knew of a written body of divine תורה ("instructions"; 8:12). Even if the text itself is exilic (which we doubt), Deut 31:9–13 knows of a tradition according to which Moses expressly designated the Levitical priests as custodians of a written torah. Cf. Deut 17:18.

cation of Priestly and Deuteronomic materials to the new exilic situation Ezekiel was actually fulfilling his role as teacher of torah.[7]

II. Whose Land Is This? Territorial Hierarchy in Ezekiel

Julie Galambush offers a welcome theological analysis of creation in Ezekiel. Her conclusion that in the book wild animals function as agents threatening the social order is well taken. However, the issues are more complex than she suggests. If wild animals by definition symbolize threats to the creative order, how is it that the wildest of mammals (lion) and of birds (eagle) are represented among the four heads of the cherubim, which function as symbols of nobility serving Yhwh's sovereign control in 1:10 and 10:14?[8] It seems that some creatures stand on the border between order and chaos. The lion is an especially intriguing figure in chapter 19. Here the animal represents royalty, but it is a royalty with a propensity to overstep its bounds. Not satisfied with natural prey, the young male develops an appetite for human flesh. In this respect what happens to the lion parallels what Galambush recognizes to happen with some plants. Symbols of beauty become symbols of overweening pride. In chapter 17 Israel is a vine out of control, and in chapter 19 a towering plant gone wild. The same happens not only to the lion of Judah (19:3, 6), but also to the lion of Egypt who morphs into a sea monster (תנים בימים, 32:2). Unlike the plants that "are not properly wild but have merely 'run wild,'" these are wild animals that should be under control but continue to display their natural wildness.

A study of the significance of animals in Ezekiel should not end with wild creatures. Images of domesticated animals play an even more significant role in the book. These images appear in the opening chapter (the head of the ox [שור] as a symbol of cherubimic power and nobility, 1:10) and carry on to the end, where bulls (פר), rams (איל), bucks (שעיר), and sheep (שה) are listed as sacrificial animals (43:23, 25; 45:15). In the meantime, lambs, rams, and goats have served as merchandise to be traded (27:21), and the flock has functioned as a symbol of the people of Yhwh (34:1–31; 36:37–38), and rams (אילים) as symbols of nobility (17:13; 31:11). But even among the domestic animals one observes a propensity to wildness and overstepping the boundaries, as in the case of the rams (אילים) and male goats (עתודים) gone bad in 34:17. Indeed one wonders if Ezekiel's references to "battering rams" (כרים) in 4:2 and 21:27 are not intended to raise images of destructive creatures in the minds of the hearers. All this demands further study.

Galambush's treatment of the land is equally intriguing. We concur with her

---

7. See my response to the essay by Risa Levitt Kohn below.
8. Stephen Cook ("Cosmos, *Kabod*, and Cherub: Ontological and Epistemological Hierarchy in Ezekiel," in this volume) suggests the lion, ox, and eagle faces all suggest a potential for "animalistic violence."

assessment that in Ezekiel the land is not an innocent victim of Yhwh's violence (contra Habel), but a participant and accomplice in the crimes of its inhabitants. The land sins against Yhwh by acting faithlessly (14:12–23). But more than this, picking up on the animal metaphor, according to 36:13–14, like the lion in chapter 19, the land devours human beings (אדם) and bereaves its own nation of children.

Perhaps the most unconvincing element in the essay is Galambush's portrayal of divine weakness, in particular Yhwh's struggle to assert his lordship over the land. It seems she has imposed the exiles' interpretation of the theological significance of their defeat and deportation (Yhwh has been impotent to defend his land and his temple from the Babylonians) upon the book itself. Although people may perceive historical events to be the consequence of the struggle between forces of chaos and order, in the book there is no question about Yhwh's absolute sovereignty over both the universe in general and the land occupied by his people in particular. The comparison to Abraham bargaining with the Hittites from a position of weakness scarcely applies. Although ownership of the land itself may pass from the hands of his people to foreigners, as representatives of the forces of chaos, there is never any doubt that this happens according to the will, the timing, and the plan of Yhwh. Yhwh not only leaves the land of his own volition, but he also brings in the Babylonians as agents of his will. The same is true of other agents of destruction: famine, wild beasts, plague, bloodshed, and the sword (5:17). Those who experience these disasters may interpret them as symbols of chaos and evidence of Yhwh's weakness and inability to sustain control over his land, but this is precisely the issue that Ezekiel combats from beginning to end.

The narrator does not share the exiles' "profound land anxiety." He may be waiting for the ultimate reestablishment of divine "social order," in the land and on earth, but this does not dilute nor minimize his firm conviction that Yhwh is in absolute control in the present. For him there is no contest of authority or power.

Keith Carley and Norman Habel go much farther than Galambush in exposing the insidious hierarchical structures reflected and advocated in the book of Ezekiel. In "From Harshness to Hope: The Implications for Earth of Hierarchy in Ezekiel," the former writes of Ezekiel's portrayal of God as dangerous. He is "offended, vengeful, alienated from the people with whom He (*sic* [referring to Ezekiel's language]) has chosen to be most intimate, and consumed by a narcissistic obsession with the honor of His name." Meanwhile, Carley speaks of Earth, this "frail but vivacious planet," in most sympathetic, almost affectionate terms. He recognizes in the end that Ezekiel and those who preserved his work would reject his criticisms as "totally unjustified hubris," but he refuses to let Ezekiel's word be determinative. With Stephen Parsons he dismisses "Christian fundamentalist communities" that view death and destruction as somehow willed by God. However, one wonders if a new form of fundamentalism has not replaced the old—a fundamentalism that treats all hierarchical structures, but especially human rank-orderings in male-dominant societies, as pathological by definition.

As long as the book of Ezekiel is read as an isolated document, divorced from the context from which it derives and which it addresses, it will be difficult to see the grace and compassion of a God who rescued Israel from certain death and drew them into covenant relationship with himself. It will also be difficult to recognize that even in this book the judgment of the people and the devastation of the land is not the last word. After all, the book closes on a glorious ecological note: a devastated world transformed into a veritable Eden by the river of life that flows from the temple, the ultimate symbol of hierarchical structures.[9]

According to Habel ("The Silence of the Lands: The Ecojustice Implications of Ezekiel's Judgment Oracles"), the fundamental problem with Yhwh is his ego. Habel's approach is symbolized by his relabeling of the "divine recognition formula" ("Then X will know that I am Yhwh") as the "divine ego formula." I am sympathetic to his efforts to recover the "voice" of the earth/land within the complex relationship involving deity, land, and people, and to recognize the symbiotic nature of these relationships. However, in this instance the bias of the author of the essay seems to suppress the voice of the text, even as he claims the author of the book has silenced the voice of the land. One wonders what Ezekiel the prophet or the person ultimately responsible for the book would have thought about such approaches. On the other hand, in the present postmodern hermeneutical landscape one hesitates even to raise this question, lest one be dismissed as naive and fundamentalist.

III. Whose Book Is This? Textual Hierarchy and the Book of Ezekiel

If Habel's essay typifies the nature of the postmodern hermeneutic, the methodology adopted by Daniel L. Smith-Christopher ("Ezekiel in Abu Ghraib: Rereading Ezekiel 16:37–39 in the Context of Imperial Conquest") serves to rein in some of its excesses. In the past two or three decades feminist and gender-sensitive approaches have rightly given voice to suppressed perspectives in biblical texts. We should readily admit that we all come to all texts with our own biases, and honesty requires that we acknowledge those biases. However, as with any methodology, it is possible to be taken captive by one's own hermeneutic and to read one's own biases into biblical texts to the exclusion of the voice of the author.

Many readers of this essay will thank Smith-Christopher, not so much for undermining the excesses of feminist approaches to texts like this, as for presenting an objective basis for interpreting Yhwh's exposure within the context from which it derives and the issues that it addresses: the exiles' own recent experience of being

---

9. On which see the study by David Petersen, "Creation and Hierarchy in Ezekiel: Methodological Perspectives and Theological Prospects," in this volume.

stripped. Those who have seen the recent photographs of the abuse of Iraqi prisoners by American military personnel have been reminded that to this day shame and humiliation represent basic tactics with which conquerors treat defeated foes.

What is striking in Ezek 16, where Jerusalem represents not women in particular but the population in general, is that Yhwh appears as the enemy. But this should not surprise us. On the one hand, the covenant curses in Lev 26 and Deut 28 declare unequivocally that if the Israelites will respond to Yhwh their gracious redeemer and covenant lord with persistent rebellion and disobedience, they will render themselves his enemy. But we heard this note already in the call of Ezekiel, who was charged with the responsibility of warning the Israelites of him; he, Yhwh, their enemy was poised to strike in judgment for their infidelities (3:17).

Risa Levitt Kohn's essay, "'With a Mighty Hand and an Outstretched Arm': The Prophet and the Torah in Ezekiel 20," approaches the issue of authority in the book of Ezekiel from a completely different perspective than was represented in the discussions focusing on the land. Paying careful attention to the echoes of the Priestly writings and the book of Deuteronomy she demonstrates that Ezekiel is as much at home in one as in the other, and that both traditions are deemed equally authoritative. She concludes from the use of P and D in this chapter that the synthesis that eventually produced the Torah began in the early exile. In this reconstruction of the process she follows prevailing scholarship. However, one wonders if the time has not come for another look at the sequence of events. Could it be that Ezekiel and his contemporaries already possessed some form of the Torah that had already synthesized these sources and that he could refer to any part with equal comfort?

David Petersen's study, "Creation and Hierarchy in Ezekiel: Methodological Perspectives and Theological Prospects," confirms the view of most that creation traditions do not play a prominent role in the prophecies of Ezekiel. His tabulation of expressions and motifs linking Ezekiel with Gen 1–3 finds the greatest concentration in chapter 28, with most of the borrowings being derived from the Yahwist account. To be precise, most of the connections in this chapter derive from the paradise traditions, rather than the actual account of creation. The links with Gen 1 tend to be lexical rather than thematic: ברא, "to create"; תהום, "the great deep"; תנינם, "sea creatures." To this list he might have added the relatively rare expression, רקיע, "expanse, firmament" (Ezek 1:23, 25–26; cf. Gen 1:7–8; Ps 19:2; 150:1). In the end Petersen concludes that the hierarchies of space and people as presented in Ezekiel do not stem from the created order; rather, they derive from acts of re-creation anticipated in chapters 40–48.

Methodologically, Stephen Cook's essay ("Cosmos, *Kabod*, and Cherub: Ontological and Epistemological Hierarchy in Ezekiel") bears the closest resemblance to Smith-Christopher's contribution. Attempting to interpret the cherubim of chapters 1 and 10 on the one hand and the cherub of chapter 28, on the other, within the ancient Near Eastern context from which the book of Ezekiel derives, Cook demonstrates how widespread the motif was in the ancient world. To this picture he adds the figure of the Roman god, Mercurius (Mercury, Hermes, in Greek mythology), whose body in at least one of his incarnations is covered with eyes and whose winged helmet and shoes symbolize his mobility. Like the cherubim in Ezekiel, Mercurius symbolizes "the transcendent, holy realm of the gods, and all of its dangerous, volatile power." In chapters 1 and 10, the cherubim play a positive hierarchical role, containing the fire within and preventing it from burning up the cosmos and its order. They also channel the fiery power to humanity, visiting the earth in judgment or salvation.

Cook offers a particularly helpful analysis of the function of the cherubim in chapters 9–10 and their significance for Ezekiel's hierarchical ontology. Here the static icons from Solomon's temple, symbols of stability, are transformed into living beings, which now symbolize God's unrestrained power. So long as the *kabod* remained above the cherubim in the temple, the people could dwell safely around it. However, the sins of the people have degraded the "firewalls" that protected the people from the lethal holiness of God. Accordingly, Ezekiel's *kabod* chariot assumes a new role: to collect the glory of YHWH and transport it out of the city. Whereas in Solomon's temple the glory resided above the cherubim inside the adytum, and sat at the vertical axis of the cosmos, in Ezekiel the limitless mobility and all-seeing eyes symbolize the emanation of divine glory and power horizontally out into the world.

In the second half of the essay Cook demonstrates how different is the figure of the cherub (singular) in chapter 28. Like Mercurius, this being possesses extraordinary intelligence and shares his astral characteristics. But the chapter shows that the mythological guardians of the cosmic center are not only untamed and unpredictable, but also capable of lust and sin. Like the lion in chapter 19 and the plants that go wild, as a cherub the king of Tyre has overstepped his boundaries and attempted to seize prerogatives that belong exclusively to God.

Cook concludes his essay by reflecting on the epistemological implications of the way Ezekiel applies the biblical image of a cherub to the king of Tyre. Although the oracle that makes up vv. 12–19 is introduced with the citation/messenger formula, "Thus says the Lord GOD," it draws on mythic images to declare universal principles. Specifically, "Ezekiel draws on and exploits the dark sides and negative forms of nations' myths, even though the nations did not consciously acknowledge these features." Whether or not this oracle ever reached Tyre, Ezekiel's addresses to Tyre and the other nations were based on common epistemological foundations, and cast in forms that should have been intelligible to peoples outside the covenant community of Israel.

Cook suggests that in Ezekiel's hierarchical ontology (chs. 9–10) and in his hierarchical epistemology the prophet exhibits a disposition that is neither chauvinistic nor exclusivist. I am not sure what he means by this. Does he mean that Ezekiel would affirm the Tyrian's perceptions of hierarchical structuring as reflected in their myths? It is one thing to draw on Tyrian myths and traditions for rhetorical effect, and deliberately to cast a message in forms that that people would understand, even if it were intended primarily for Israel. It is quite another to affirm those people's perceptions of reality. The oracle explicitly declares Yhwh to be both the source of the king of Tyre's power and the one who will cast him down. Whatever the basis of Tyre's hierarchical thinking, this notion alone would have challenged prevailing conclusions.

The collection of essays concludes with Katheryn Pfisterer Darr's "Proverb Performance and Transgenerational Retribution in Ezekiel 18." With its forty-three pages in manuscript form, it is an unusually long essay within the collection. It relates to the overall theme of hierarchies in the book of Ezekiel only in a very general sense: it examines the power of proverbs to reflect and determine human behavior. Although many have studied the complex disputation speech that makes up Ezek 18, the strength of this essay lies in its careful theoretical analysis of the nature and function of proverbs. This enables her to conduct a much more sophisticated examination of the proverb about the sour grapes than has previously been possible, and exposes the weaknesses of the interpretations of chapter 18 that some of us have provided. I am grateful for the integrity and sensitivity with which Darr has criticized my own work on this chapter. The only criticism I have of her is that I wish she had written this paper fifteen years earlier.

IV. Conclusion

When I began my own work on the book of Ezekiel twenty years ago, we could count the number of colleagues who were devoting a significant portion of their scholarly energies to the book of Ezekiel with the fingers on two hands. Thanks in large measure to the Ezekiel Consultation and the Ezekiel Group of the Society of Biblical Literature, the number of recognizable Ezekiel scholars has tripled. But it is not only the number of scholars involved in the study of this fascinating book that inspires us all; it is also the creativity and imagination of their approaches. Even when we are uncomfortable with the methodologies adopted and the conclusions proposed, every new study forces us to rethink what we are doing and offers the promise of new insights. This is certainly true of the collection of papers gathered in this volume.

Contemporary Studies of Ezekiel:
A New Tide Rising

Steven Shawn Tuell

In his 1987 Sprunt Lectures at Union Theological Seminary in Virginia, Walter Brueggemann heralded a "sea change" in biblical studies. Of course, at the time of his address, that change was already well under way. The years since then have witnessed the rise of new methodologies, and the fall of old verities. The much-vaunted rise of postmodernism prompted many to trumpet the end of objectivity and the demise of the Enlightenment program of historical-critical investigation into the composition of Scripture. However, as is the way of the sea, change is ongoing. A new tide is now rising, and obituaries for historical-critical methodology have proven premature. Increasingly today, scholars make use of a variety of methodological tools in concert, maintaining a creative tension between literary and historical techniques of interpretation.

While this creative tension is of course evident in every area of biblical studies, the study of Ezekiel provides a fascinating microcosm of the discipline. The two greatest commentators on Ezekiel in the twentieth century are certainly Walther Zimmerli and Moshe Greenberg. Zimmerli, the quintessential historical-critical scholar in the classic German mold, resolved conflicts and contradictions in the enigmatic text of Ezekiel by appeal to multiple layers of redaction. Greenberg, on the other hand, reads Ezekiel holistically and appeals to the history of interpretation (particularly Jewish interpretation) and literary techniques to resolve interpretive quandaries. Their two magisterial works have come to represent two competing methodologies: diachronic against synchronic, historical against literary, analysis against synthesis. The dichotomy is, of course, a false one: Zimmerli was deeply interested in literary and theological questions, while Greenberg reads Ezekiel as a whole, not for literary or canon-critical reasons, but because he is persuaded, on historical-critical grounds, that the entire book derives from the sixth-century prophet! Still, like the Montagues and Capulets, the Hatfields and McCoys, or the Ptolemies and Seleucids, the disciples of Zimmerli and Greenberg have often behaved like warring camps.

An early working title of this volume was *The Text Creates a World: Hierarchical Theology in Ezekiel*. The main title pointed toward the now commonly accepted literary paradigm, in which the text is viewed as its own reality, rather than in terms of its reconstructed historical or social context. Yet the subtitle also indicated an openness to the historical-critical enterprise: can we reconstruct the context out of which the intricately wrought, hierarchically ordered world of priestly theology, evident in Ezekiel as in the priestly texts of Torah, emerged? The volume's title has changed, but not its scope. The essays collected in this volume demonstrate both the tension, and the creative, dynamic interchange, between these two perspectives.

The first four essays deal with a fundamental issue in the interpretation of Ezekiel: the priesthood. As any consideration of priesthood in Ezekiel must, all of these essays deal more or less with Ezekiel's final vision report, chapters 40–48. Following a classic historical-critical methodology strongly reminiscent of Zimmerli, Friedrich Fechter's essay demonstrates that the references to priests and priesthood in Ezek 40–48 belong primarily to the later redaction of the book; they neither derive from the historical Ezekiel nor refer to his circumstances. On the other hand, the delimitation of priesthood in these chapters to the descendants of Zadok is suggestive for considering how priests in exile, removed from cult and temple, came to conceive of their role and identity: "The question 'Who is a priest?' took on increasingly greater significance, apparently in view of the absence of the practice of sacrifice during that time. The genealogical connection with one common ancestor apparently became the decisive criterion." Indeed, this focus on the Ezekielian circle of Zadokites may be seen as emerging out of the message of Ezekiel: his sense of isolation from the people and radical theocentrism may help explain the exclusivity, and radical monotheism, of priesthood in the postexilic community.

Iain Duguid opens with a fine summary of priestly tasks according to the Torah and the Chronicler's History. He rightly describes Ezekiel as serving in the only priestly capacities possible for a priest in exile: teaching, judging, and discerning between clean and unclean. Duguid's approach, like Greenberg's, is holistic; unlike Fechter, he therefore reads Ezek 40–48 in continuity with 1–39. Ezekiel 44, which designates distinctive roles for Zadokite and Levite and states explicitly that Levites are not priests (44:13), is generally regarded as an interpretive crux for these final chapters. Duguid sees Ezekiel here, not as putting the Levites "in their place," but rather as establishing the proper place and role of the priests and Levites, as well as all Israel (cf. Num 18). This is a common approach (in this volume, compare Schwartz); however, it remains unsatisfactory. While Num 18 requires the Levites to remain at a distance from the holy things, it does not state that the Levites are not to serve as priests. Such a statement is unnecessary; the context in Numbers assumes that the Levites are not priests. This, by contrast, is precisely what Ezek 44:13 *does* stipulate: "They shall not come near me, to serve me as priest" (NRSV). Former priestly service by the Levites is also presupposed in the accusation (44:7) that בני נכר ("foreigners") have been present in the sanctuary "when you [clearly, the Levites] offer me my food, the fat and the blood." Since only priests could offer sacrifices, former priestly service for the Levites is presupposed (as Fechter also argues). In his discussion of

43:18–21, Duguid emphasizes Ezekiel's priestly role in the altar consecration (but compare Fechter here, who argues persuasively for the secondary character of this text). In Duguid's view, this text, and indeed, Ezek 40–48 as a whole, confirms Ezekiel's priestly function as a teacher of Torah.

While both Fechter and Duguid deduce elements of exilic priesthood from the text of Ezekiel, Baruch Schwartz denies that this is possible. Although Ezekiel was certainly a priest in exile, he tells us little or nothing about exilic priesthood, as such. With Kaufmann, as well as with his teacher Greenberg, Schwartz asserts that Ezekiel "is a visionary, not a legislator"; his book reveals the theological content of his visions, not the political shape of his own, or any actual future, reality.

In contrast to Duguid, who emphasizes noncultic (or, at any rate, nonsacrificial) aspects of priesthood, Schwartz asserts that priesthood was inextricably linked to the sacrificial cult. With the destruction of the shrine in Jerusalem, worship ceased to be possible, and priesthood became irrelevant. On the other hand, from the mention of grain and incense offerings at Mizpah following Jerusalem's fall (Jer 41:5), sacrificial worship in Israel did survive the temple's destruction. Perhaps the role of the priest remained important among the exiles as well.

Schwartz insists that Ezekiel is presented in the book as a prophet, not as a priest. He argues that the teaching function of the priest, stressed by both Fechter and Duguid, was inseparable from his role in the cult: "[I]t consisted of informing the worshiper which ritual needed to be performed and how to do so, of supervising its proper performance, and of ruling and responding on matters requiring expert determinations." This ministry was impossible and irrelevant in the exile. Hence, Schwartz understands the sign-act involving bread cooked over a dung fire (4:9–17) to show that, with no temple to defile, clean and unclean have become irrelevant. When Ezekiel objects to performing this defiling act, "YHWH's reply is indicative of Ezekiel's own sad realization: such delicateness of habit is a thing of the past; all your priestly customs are obsolete." Therefore, though Ezekiel thinks and writes in priestly terms, he does not fill the role of a priest, and can teach us nothing of exilic priesthood. "Instead of asking 'What can Ezekiel teach us about the priesthood,' the question to pose is 'What can the priesthood teach us about Ezekiel?'"

In contrast, Corrine Patton argues that the key to understanding Ezekiel, both the book and its narrator, is the identification of the narrator as a priest. I hold that she is correct. Indeed, the thesis is even stronger than Patton allows, for the priestly claims that she applies only to Ezekiel the character are particularly apt depictions of Ezekiel the man, and may indeed enlighten us as to the motivation behind the unique form of this book.

Unlike Schwartz, who emphasizes the distinction between priest and prophet, Patton observes "a growing trend in studies on Israelite religion to recognize that the categories of priest and prophet are more interdependent than once thought." As a priest, Ezekiel mediates access to the divine presence. Indeed, Ezekiel functions as high priest—one who "has access to the holy of holies, even when he is, in fact, not physically there." Yet, curiously, "nowhere in the book does Ezekiel do anything one would consider particularly priestly." By this, Patton means that Ezekiel performs no acts pertaining to cult or ritual; arguably (with Fechter and Duguid; contra Schwartz), Ezekiel does teach torah, a task he accuses the Jerusalem priesthood of shirking (cf. Ezek 7:26; 22:23–28). Ezekiel's priesthood, then, must be understood in broader theological and anthropological terms, not in terms of ritual performance.

Patton's emphasis on the points of continuity between priest and prophet relates in particular to the priest's oracular function (divination via the Urim and Thummim) and to the frequent incidence of priests *as* prophets, and vice versa, in the Hebrew Bible (i.e., Samuel, Elijah, Isaiah, and Jeremiah, as well as Ezekiel). Weaker is her claim for priests as visionaries. The prime example Patton alleges, Exod 24:9–10, represents a one-time concession, mediated by Moses, not by Aaron. The primary, theological role of the priesthood, however, remains leadership in worship, a role critically important in the absence of cult and ritual.

Priestly mediation of the divine presence, Patton suggests, is different from the divine communication mediated by the prophets: "Priests, on the other hand, mediate a god's presence, acting as a buffer zone between God and the people." Patton proposes that, in part, the priest does this by example, through a life of moral and ethical purity. She argues that the character Ezekiel is "hierarchically better, more pure, and, therefore, more qualified to approach God than any other previous Israelite figure," a claim she bases on Ezek 4:14 (where Ezekiel, told to eat bread prepared over a fire fed by human dung, protests his own purity) and on the fact that, despite his role as an intermediary coming directly into contact with the divine presence, Ezekiel undergoes no purifying rituals. Even more striking, she concludes that the exemption of Ezekiel himself from the judgments in this book, combined with his ritual purity in a book that presumes "the intimate connection between cultic and ethical violations," means that Ezekiel "has committed no sin." Such exaltation of the prophet seems unlikely, particularly in light of Patton's fine analysis of the humbling address YHWH uses toward Ezekiel: בן אדם ("mortal"). Patton finds a likely contrast between איש האלהים ("person of God") in the Deuteronomistic History and Ezekiel, who is merely בן אדם. Hence, I would propose that Ezekiel, like the community of exiles who have been spared Jerusalem's destruction, is chosen as a free act of the divine will, and not because he is in any way better than his peers.

Rather than exalting Ezekiel as a perfect intermediary, the book of Ezekiel redefines the means of access to YHWH. Patton powerfully expresses the significance of Ezekiel's priestly role: "Ezekiel as priest functions as a transparent figure: the audience inside the text, as well as the reader of the text, sees God through him." But the case is even stronger than she claims. The paucity and character of references to priesthood in the book of Ezekiel (apart from its final redactional layer, only Ezek 7:26; 22:23–28 [both negative] and 40:45–46 [neutral]) suggest that Ezekiel is not merely *a* priest, but has become in a sense *the* priest, in a way that transcends and redefines both priesthood and prophecy.

The six essays in the second part of this volume concern themselves with another critical issue for Ezekiel and his exiled community: the land of Israel. In the first essay, Julie Galambush explores Ezekiel's theology of creation. According to Galambush, the text of Ezekiel presents a *Chaoskampf* with a difference: "Ezekiel is not concerned with how the world came into existence, but with re-forming a world gone awry." Here, God is reestablishing not only divine order, but also the social order disrupted by sin and exile. To get at Ezekiel's theology of creation, Galambush considers references in the book to aspects of the natural world. Wild animals represent chaos, opposed to settled land and order; though they "may be co-opted to perform YHWH's (avenging) will" (i.e., 39:17), they will be barred from the land in the idealized future (34:25). In the plant world, the contrast is not between domestic crops and wild plants or weeds, but rather "the image of the unnatural plant, desirable in itself, but whose luxurious growth symbolizes overarching ambition or pride"—for example, the parable of the vine (ch. 17; 19:10–14); or Egypt and Assyria envisaged as trees (ch. 31). On the other hand, the weather is always under YHWH's undisputed control: perhaps a reflection of YHWH as storm god, or of the weather as "entirely and unambiguously beyond human coercion."

In Ezekiel, אדמה ("soil, arable land") is never used for the Earth generically, but only for the land of Israel. Here, the land has no independence from the human community that inhabits it; in fact, as Galambush observes, land or mountains stand for their inhabitants in Ezekiel (so Ezek 7). Therefore, the restoration of the land in Ezek 25–48 means its habitation. This is scarcely surprising; as Galambush notes, "Ezekiel's privileging of inhabited over barren land and of domestic over wild animals is consistent with ancient Near Eastern norms." Ezekiel 47 is the exception that proves the rule: even here, the goodness of the miraculous stream is tied to its utility for the settled world. Ironically, these symbols for the possession of the land come from a time of exile: "The profound land anxiety of the narrator and his fellow exiles is expressed through its exact opposite: an assertion of absolute divine right soon to be manifested through YHWH's reestablishment of that divine 'social order' of which they themselves are the guardians."

While the first five essays all relate, in greater or lesser degrees, to historical-critical methodology, Keith Carley's piece is thoroughly postmodern in its outlook. Carley discusses Ezekiel's negative attitude toward the natural world, accurately described by Galambush. Following Riane Eisler, Carley decries what he calls "dominator hierarchies," based on force and threat, which "systematically suppress compassion and justice." He undertakes, therefore, a deconstruction of Ezekiel, aiming "to find a voice for the silent Earth for the sake of its liberation and for God's."

Carley identifies Ezekiel's God as "vengeful and loveless"—particularly toward the Earth, which suffers desolation because of the sin of its inhabitants. What Carley does not consider, as Galambush makes clear, is that that desolation involves precisely depopulation: the "land" is a metonym for the people; its "desolation" means their exile. With Jack Miles, Carley states that the biblical God "does not know what love is." He notes the general absence of terms denoting God's love, mercy, or compassion from Ezekiel (with the single exception of רחם, "have compassion," in 39:25). This is certainly significant, though perhaps not for the reasons Carley thinks; after all, until its closing movement, the book of Ezekiel is devoted to the depiction of YHWH's wrath and judgment.

Carley sees the emphasis on shame in Ezekiel as unhealthy, indeed dangerous, even as, with Donald Nathanson, he "warns against assuming that we understand precisely what the experience of shame is, for our contemporaries, let alone for people of other eras." But then, that is of course precisely the point. Without viewing the text of Ezekiel in its historical and social context, we certainly cannot understand what the prophet may have meant by "shame" (cf. Maggie Odell's excellent treatment of this issue, dismissed by Carley). Like Galambush, Carley cites Robert Carroll on the "myth of the empty land," seeing the text as emerging out of the situation of the exiles. However, he views the exiles as colonizers, who displaced the people of the land in the Persian period (hence, history is introduced after all, by the back door). Carley claims of Ezekiel that, "despite the judgments he delivered against the exile community, he ultimately favored it and may have envisaged himself enjoying the privileges of priesthood in the restored temple"—an entirely baseless accusation, which smacks of blaming the victim. Carley is forgetting the circumstances of the exile, the homelessness, loss, and despair Ezekiel and his fellows endured (on this, see the later article in this collection by Smith-Christopher).

With Brueggemann, Carley acknowledges that some measure of "ecojustice" is found in Ezek 47–48, in the equitable division of the land among the tribes, and in (as I have argued elsewhere) the unprecedented provision of an inheritance to the גר (47:22)—though Carley insists, without citing any evidence, that the גר given an inheritance is not truly a foreign sojourner, but a proselyte. Still, it seems, there is no justice for the Earth itself, apart from its use by the human community. Here it must be noted, as Galambush demonstrates, that Ezekiel did not invent this instrumental view of the natural world, but that indeed it was the dominant view of his day—indeed, the dominant view of most human communities, until fairly recently.

For Carley, the view of God in Ezekiel is so negative as to provide no model for contemporary thinking about God. Indeed, Carley's rejection of Ezekiel's theology extends to the denial of any theology that sees God as separate from the natural world. "Pansyntheism" (Carley's term; it is apparently an extension of Hartshorne's panentheism, though actually indistinguishable, I would argue, from simple pantheism) may be an intriguing idea, but it is not Christianity, or Judaism, or Islam. Persons who desire to live and understand their relationship with God from within those ancient traditions are hence excluded by Carley's theology, together with the prophet Ezekiel. Although, in the end, Carley acknowledges that Ezekiel's view of the cosmos is not the prophet's fault, and that there are some things to learn from this book, Carley clearly has little use for Ezekiel. He gives the last word to the wounded Earth, in a poem he imagines as the Earth's response to the negative views of Ezekiel.

Norman Habel, editor of The Earth Bible project in which Carley too is engaged, likewise repudiates the instrumental view of the natural world expressed by Ezekiel. He too advocates a "hermeneutic of suspicion and retrieval," aimed at uncovering the androcentric biases of the biblical authors. The problem with such a reading, arguably, is that it is not actually a "reading" at all: rather than a dialogue, which attempts to give the text its own authentic voice, such an approach easily becomes a self-congratulatory monologue, telling us only what we already believe and affirm. Asked what constitutes a feminist reading, Phyllis Bird responded, "a feminist reader"—who nonetheless takes the text seriously as a dialogue partner. Similarly, I would argue that what constitutes an ecojustice reading ought properly to be a reader sensitive to issues of ecology and justice; the text should be permitted its own voice.

To his reading of Ezekiel, Habel applies two principles fundamental to The Earth Bible: that the Earth has intrinsic worth, and "that *Earth is a subject capable of raising its voice in celebration and against injustice.*" In these terms, Ezekiel of course must be found wanting, as neither is in any sense derived from the text or from any reasonable construal of its social or historical context. Habel cites, and agrees with, the affirmation made by Petersen later in this volume: "We have found no evidence that Ezekiel has used biblical creation traditions in his rhetoric." I will refute this idea later, in connection with Petersen's piece; for now, it must be said that Ezekiel is in fact as interested in creation as any of the prophets, with the possible exception of Second Isaiah, and that it is difficult to read Ezek 28 or 47 in any other way than as indicating a knowledge and use of creation traditions and theology.

Habel discerns in Ezek 5:5 an "urban cosmogony," centered in the city rather than in the natural world. He rightly affirms that "Ezekiel seems to be essentially an urbanite," in intriguing tension with the rural topos of priestly texts such as Lev 25–26 (not to mention the agricultural focus of Israelite liturgy). He notes that Ezekiel's final vision opens with a structure like a city set on a very high mountain (40:1) and closes with the renamed, purified Jerusalem, now called יהוה שמה ("The LORD is There"). On the other hand, the land does play an important role. Carley notes, as does Galambush, Ezekiel's consistent use of אדמה ("soil, arable land") rather than ארץ for Israel. In Ezekiel's judgment oracles, the land is made desolate, robbed of its fullness—that is, its life. Habel concludes, "When reading from the perspective of Earth, both land and life seem to be cheap in Ezekiel; Earth has no obvious intrinsic worth as a structural component in the hierarchy of Ezekiel's cosmos." Habel puzzles over the injustice of the forest fire in the south in 21:1–5 (Eng. 20:45–49): "The trees have not sinned and yet they have experienced the wrath of God." Note, however, that Ezekiel too bewails this tragedy (21:5 [Eng.

20:49]), in one of only four objections to God's words or actions voiced in this profoundly theocentric book (the others are 4:14; 9:8; and 11:13). The extremity of divine wrath is troubling to the prophet as well as to us! Further, despite Habel's doubts, parallels with Ezekiel's oracles against the mountains (6) and land (14:12–23) suggest that the forest of the south as well is a metonym for the people: Ezekiel simply is not concerned with the land as such, for its own sake.

Habel sees the "recognition formula" as being rather a "divine ego formula": "Ezekiel seems to portray Yhwh as a deity with an ego problem, an incessant need to have the divine name and identity displayed as the banner associated with every violent deed." However, the formula also appears in connection with acts of deliverance; *all* that God does is a manifestation of the divine being. With Carley, Habel describes Ezekiel as a willing participant in Yhwh's silencing of the land, indifferent to the suffering of the Earth. Note, however, that if the land is silenced in this book, so is the prophet (3:22–27). Not only the Earth, but also Ezekiel himself, is denied an independent voice. Even the words of the community typically are filtered through the divine, communicated to Ezekiel in the context of divine word (see Darr's article). In Ezekiel, no voice is permitted save the divine voice, and no perspective is granted validity save God's.

David Petersen begins his piece with a call for methodological clarity. While many scholars have claimed that some notion of "creation" is present in Ezekiel, it is not at all clear what that claim means, whether some shared creation tradition, literary allusion to Gen 1 and 2, or merely a common motif. Of course, it is possible to talk about intertextuality without concern for relative dates, as is done in synchronic canonical readings, though then, of course, it would scarcely be meaningful to talk in historicizing terms of "tradition," or even in literary terms of quote and allusion. Petersen therefore chooses to focus on the tradition-historical and literary-critical questions, and particularly on shared vocabulary.

The Tyre oracle in Ezek 28, which Petersen claims is the locus for the greatest number of "putative parallels," demonstrates Ezekiel's knowledge and use of "the tradition of the primal human/king-expulsion." However, that tradition derives from his neo-Babylonian context rather than from any Israelite text or tradition relating to creation. While there may possibly be textual allusions to the Genesis accounts, Petersen cautions that the allusion may in fact run the other way (as, for example, Van Seters has argued). He concludes (I would argue, prematurely) that "the larger creation traditions, along with their attending theological implications, are absent from Ezekiel." The reason for this absence, Petersen suggests, is that Ezekiel's argument lies elsewhere, with the radical sinfulness of Israel and Jerusalem. Petersen argues from the "new heart, new spirit" language in 36:26 and the re-creation imagery in Ezek 37 that Ezekiel "presumes that the original form of the Earth-creature was radically deficient"—in contradiction to Gen 1, which affirms the goodness of creation. While this is a possible conclusion, the texts do not require it; indeed, Ezekiel's point is not that Israel has a sinful nature, but rather that Israel persistently and perversely behaves sinfully.

Curiously, Petersen does not discuss the vision of the river in Ezek 47, with its paradisial trees, a text that not only alludes to the J creation story in Gen 2, but also evidences explicit terminological connections with the Genesis accounts of creation and flood. In Ezek 47:9, נפש חיה ("living creature"), an expression found in the primordial stories of creation (Gen 1:20, 21, 24, 30 [P]; 2:7, 19 [J]) and flood (Gen 9:10, 12, 15, 16), and the term שרץ ("swarm"), which appears in the Priestly creation and flood accounts, both appear. Note that נפש חיה without the article appears only in the creation and flood accounts and in Ezek 47:9, and that שרץ appears in conjunction with נפש חיה (again, without the article) only in Gen 1:20 and Ezek 47:9 (in Gen 1:21 and Lev 11:10, 46, שרץ appears in conjunction with נפש־החיה). It seems probable that explicit reference is made here to the Genesis accounts. Certainly, Petersen is correct that creation theology is not a dominant perspective in Ezekiel, as the bulk of the book focuses on judgment and wrath, not on affirmation. But where affirmation breaks through, it is certainly significant that it finds expression in the language and imagery of Gen 1 and 2.

Stephen Cook's essay moves in an entirely different direction, finding in the cherubim of Ezekiel's visions indications of a hierarchically ordered cosmos. Cook considers the role played by composite beings in the iconography of the ancient Near East, as well as in the mythological researches of Carl Jung. In Jung's notion of the quaternity, and particularly in the fourfold archetype Mercurius, Cook finds reflected the guardian role of Ezekiel's cherubim, as fearsome beings associated with the cosmic center, and particularly as liminal beings: "Arrayed about this center, they may be keeping its holiness contained or facilitating its safe projection into the world."

Cook rightly affirms that Ezekiel's initial vision, despite its terrifying nature, "assured Ezekiel of God's presence with him and his fellow deportees, and formed a firm basis for his commissioning." The cherubim both guard and contain the holy fire and "channel the fiery power out to humanity, for purposes that may involve either salvation or judgment." So, in the vision of judgment in Ezek 8–11, it is one of the cherubim who places the coals that will burn Jerusalem into the hands of the destroyers (10:7). "[A] storied cosmos" is in view here, with the divine throne surmounting the sky dome above the cherubim and the wheelwork with its flaming coals, where the presence touches earthly reality in the fires of the sacrificial cult, below them. As Cook notices, this "vertical" gradation of holiness, with guards and wards regulating access, becomes "horizontal" in the depictions of sacred space in Ezek 40–48. Following Israel Knohl, Cook claims that the view of holiness depicted here is consistent with the views of the Holiness School ("HS"), and stands in contrast to Priestly Torah and the Isaiah school. In YHWH's departure from the earthly temple, borne by the cherubim, Cook sees the fulfillment of the threat in HS: "Willful, chronic pollution of the sanctuary, however, will eventually force God out and leave the people exposed to judgment." YHWH uses icons (temple, cherub images) to communicate God's presence, but is not bound by them.

Cook argues (contra Petersen) that in Ezek 28 we should read with the MT, so that the king of Tyre is here compared to a cherub, rather than (as LXX, Syriac, and the NRSV render) to the proto-human guarded by a cherub. While this is a possible reading, Cook has not persuasively demonstrated it to be the preferred reading. We do not have, anywhere, a tradition involving a cherub being driven from heaven (whatever Day Star son of Dawn in Isa 14:12 might be, he is not called a cherub). However, we do have the expulsion story in Gen 3, with a cherub appointed as guard, a connection strengthened by the reference to Eden in 28:13. Still, Cook makes intriguing use of Karl Rahner's notion of "transcendental experience." Although I would argue that Ezek 28 originally referred to Jerusalem's priests rather than to the prince of Tyre, in its final form the text does seem to assume a common universal experience of the divine, even among the people, and in the mythology, of Tyre (cf. Rom 1:18–20).

The three other essays in this volume deal, not with a single common topic or theme, but with the application of the principles of Ezekiel's "hierarchical thought" to the exegesis of particular texts (we may call these "test cases"). Daniel Smith-Christopher uses sociological analysis, particularly postcolonial reading, and psychological analysis based on the experiences of refugees, to understand the extremely difficult and disturbing parable of the foundling bride in Ezek 16. Psychological analysis of Ezekiel has sometimes been used in ways that distance the reader from the text, and ignore the social context of prophecy in ancient Israel (e.g., Broome's dismissal of Ezekiel as a schizophrenic, recently resurrected by Miles). Smith-Christopher, however, demonstrates the insights that the responsible use of this methodology can yield.

Smith-Christopher is primarily interested in one element of this extended metaphor, the public stripping and humiliation of Jerusalem (16:37–38). He rightly rejects the common view that public stripping was a penalty for adultery (noting, with Peggy Day and Keith Carley, that there is nothing in Torah regarding this as a punishment). More importantly and significantly, Smith-Christopher rejects the notion that Ezek 16 is pornography, aimed at the titillation of Ezekiel's male audience, as we have no reason to think that that audience was predominantly or exclusively male.

The major principle in Smith-Christopher's interpretation of Ezekiel is the prophet's social situation as "an exile in the shadow of the Neo-Babylonian imperial conquests of Palestine." Hence, he rightly observes "that the images of violence, bloodshed, vengeance, and terror are not concoctions of Ezekiel's normative theological reflection, but the realities within which he is living." Smith-Christopher considers the evidence for rape as a military tactic, humiliating the conquered population, and for the "engendering" of warfare and feminization of the enemy—a study tragically applicable to our current political situation, as evidence of stripping, sexual abuse, and torture of prisoners by the U.S. military in our recent conflicts continues to unfold. The stripping of Jerusalem is best understood in light of the practice of the stripping of prisoners of war in the ancient Near East, witnessed in a variety of inscriptions as well as in the biblical texts (esp. Isa 20:1–6). Noting the presence of the root גלה, meaning "strip, uncover," in Ezek 16:37, Smith-Christopher asks, "Might the very reason that גלה comes to be used as a term for an exile be because of the Neo-Assyrian and Neo-Babylonian practice of stripping and humiliating captive males?" Jerusalem's stripping, then, is neither for the titillation of a male readership, nor a mere reflection of female subordination in ancient Israel. Rather, "if there is any 'gazing' in passages like Ezek 16, it may not be a 'male gaze,' but rather, a triumphalist 'imperial gaze' of the conquerors over the humiliated and stripped male soldiers who foolishly tried to resist the superior forces."

Hence, Ezek 16 is certainly not about any notion of normal human relationships, and to read the text in this way misses its point:

> When scholars note the near raving attitudes attributed to the "male God" in the metaphor of a "betrayed husband," there is a consistent inability to see in such images not a presumed normal husband, acting in a "normal way" in response to being betrayed, but rather an image of the kind of horrendous destruction of relationships that occurs in circumstances of war, deprivation, and oppression. (155)

As Smith-Christopher quite properly reminds us, Ezekiel is a victim, not an oppressor; the book is reflective of his experience of violence and abandonment. The blame language that is characteristic of this book, disturbing as it may be to contemporary readers, is seen in other oppressed groups: by taking responsibility for the tragedy of exile, Ezekiel and his community "creatively reinterpret their defeat, and 'disempower' their conquerors."

Risa Levitt Kohn uses inner-biblical exegesis to consider Ezekiel's use of the Torah. Oddly, she speaks of a "shift in focus from issues of chronological priority to that of 'inner-biblical exegesis,'" yet also argues for the use of authoritative tradition in Ezekiel. Despite claims of indifference to chronology, Kohn assumes a preexilic setting for much of both D and P: "It is evident that Ezekiel knows the sources that constitute the redacted Torah, but he adjusts this material to suit his personal prophetic agenda and the contemporary circumstances of his audience." She is interested in particular in the evidence of Ezekiel's exegesis found in the famous *Unheilsgeschichte* of Ezek 20:1–44. As Kohn rightly observes, Ezekiel views Israel's story as a history of rebellion rather than salvation. Indeed, the picture is even more bleak than Kohn allows, for while she speaks of "a relapse to the contemptuous irreverence towards Yahweh that characterizes for him the exodus-wilderness period," it is more accurate to say that for Ezekiel, Israel continues to be, as it has always been, a rebellious house (2:5–6; 12:2–3).

Kohn argues that Ezek 20 uses "terms, phrases, and concepts found in both the P and D traditions." Ezekiel's use of priestly tradition is clear. However, use of Deuteronomistic tradition is much harder to demonstrate. Kohn claims that the idea of "seeking YHWH" through a prophet derives from D, yet the phrase לדרש את־יהוה *never appears* in Deuteronomy. Apart from Ezek 20:1, לדרש את־יהוה is found in Gen 25:22; 1 Kgs 22:8 // 2 Chr 18:7; 2 Kgs 22:18; Hos 10:12; 2 Chr 12:14; 14:3; 15:12. Note that not only is Gen 25:22 a J text, but also that, apart from 2 Chr 18:7, the Chronicles references are not parallels to DtrH (in Chronicles, seeking YHWH refers to worship before the temple, not prophetic consultation). In short, לדרש את־יהוה simply is not a Deuteronomistic formulation. With many others, Kohn sees the expression "the word of YHWH came to X" as Deuteronomistic. However, this expression too does not appear in Deuteronomy at all (indeed, it appears only once in the Pentateuch, in Gen 15:1 [J]), and in the Deuteronomistic History it occurs only ten times (once in 1 Samuel, once in 2 Samuel, and eight times in 1 Kings). In the Twelve, "the word of YHWH came to X" is found only in the postexilic books Jonah (1:1; 3:1), Haggai (five times), and Zechariah (nine times). Where the expression predominantly appears is in Jeremiah (thirty times) and Ezekiel (forty-nine times); indeed, the postexilic use of "the word of YHWH came to X," particularly in Haggai-Zechariah, more likely reflects the influence of Ezekiel than of the Deuteronomists. In short, Ezekiel's use of this phrase may say more about Hebrew idiom in the exilic period than it does about his use of Deuteronomistic traditions. On the other hand, Kohn is correct on other points involving the use of Deuternomistic traditions by Ezekiel: for example, the consistent use of תועבה for idolatry in Ezekiel certainly reflects the D rather than the P usage of the term.

A methodological problem often found in claims of inner-biblical exegesis occurs in Kohn's piece as well: how closely must two texts cohere in order for an interpreter to legitimately claim the use, whether by quote or allusion, of one by the other? For example, Kohn claims that Ezek 20:23 "seems to recall Deut 4:27 directly." However, while both verses express the general idea of YHWH driving Israel out among the nations in exile, the only explicit terminological connection is the use of פוץ in the Hiphil—scarcely enough to demonstrate that Ezekiel has used this verse.

By not dealing head-on with chronological issues in the composition of Ezekiel, in particular the evidence (some of which is cited in this volume, by Fechter in particular) for the later redaction of chapters 40–48, Kohn winds up assuming that the "law of the temple" in Ezek 40–48 is a correction of the "statutes that were not good and ordinances by which they could not live" in 20:25. Thus, Kohn asserts, "Ezekiel functions as prophet, priest, and legislator." While this may be true of Ezekiel canonically, it is probably not an accurate description of Ezekiel historically. Correspondingly, Kohn's thesis that Ezekiel is combining and transforming D and P theologies is difficult to assess. Arguing canonically, this may well be the effect of reading the texts in their final form. However, Kohn seems to assert a dependency of Ezekiel on D and P, introducing largely unexamined chronological claims by the back door (see, e.g., her discussion of the final redaction of the Torah).

Katheryn Pfisterer Darr views the "sour grapes" proverb in Ezek 18 through the lens of rhetorical and reader-response criticism. Using Bakhtinian analysis, she identifies three levels at which the theme of the proverb attains finalization. The first, the level of the proverb itself, is clearly nonsensical in literal terms: what one generation eats cannot possibly set the teeth of the next generation on edge. This demonstrates that the proverb's theme must be metaphorically expressed: its point, Darr states, "is divine transgenerational retribution—the form God's justice takes such that children suffer the consequences of their parents' actions." The next level of finalization, the level of the utterance, is the occasion of the interaction between the performer of the proverb and the audience. Here, Darr claims, the text is silent; Ezek 18:1–4 "does not specify the situation(s) prompting the [proverb performances] YHWH condemns." The third level of thematic finalization occurs "when its audience understands that the proverbial theme (first level), which is analogous to the context domain (second level), applies to itself (third level)." Here too, Darr claims, the text is silent. This reticence seems odd: surely, the circumstance is that of the community in exile, which understands the proverb as absolving them of responsibility for their plight. Darr, however, staying at the level of the text in its final form, insists on remaining largely agnostic about the historical circumstances and processes of the text's composition (in intriguing contrast to the first essay, in which Fechter argues that a great deal can be said about both the prophet and his book). At the opening of her essay, the most Darr will say of the book of Ezekiel is that it purports to consist primarily of oracles from God to "a Judean priest commissioned as God's prophet," which were delivered to "his fellow exiles in Babylonia in 593 B.C.E."

Darr aims to reconstruct the second and third levels of thematic finalization for this proverb imaginatively, by means of rhetorical analogy. Proverb performance typically occurs in a setting of conflict, where the performer aims to reassert the culture's traditional values. Although "[t]he details of our proverb's 'vivid present' are all but lost to us," the purported setting permits us to imagine that the problem this proverb performance addresses is *the* problem of their day: the Babylonian invasion, and the threat it posed to exile and resident alike. The "sour grapes" proverb solves the problem by appeal to "the idea that transgenerational retribution was part and parcel of YHWH's administration of justice." This reconstruction, Darr acknowledges, requires virtually no imagination—indeed, in light of the setting that the text claims for itself, and that historical-critical investigation confirms as reasonable, it is "obvious." Perhaps it is time to question the postmodern insistence on the pose of hermeneutical suspicion. We in fact can, and do, know something about the historical context of Ezekiel.

Darr traces the idea of transgenerational retribution in the ancient Near East and in Scripture, noting that while some texts (including the Decalogue) assume that divine retribution is visited on the descendants of offenders, others (most notably, Deut 24:16) deny that this principle is just—or at any rate, that it can figure in "the administration of justice in the *human* arena." Darr argues that in the book of Ezekiel as well no single, clear perspective on this issue emerges. For example, while Ezek 20:18–20 suggests that the wilderness generation is punished for their own sins, not for their parents', 20:27–29 sees the exile as the consequence of the sins of all of Israel's generations: in a sense, exactly what the repudiated proverb in 18:2 claims! Similarly, Darr sees the indiscriminate slaughter of all who do not weep for Jerusalem in Ezek 9 as reflecting transgenerational retribution. I would, however, question Darr's exegesis at these points. The point of 20:27–29 is not that Ezekiel's generation is suffering the consequences of their parents' sins, but rather that they suffer for doing as their parents did: "Will you defile yourselves after the manner of your ancestors and go astray after their detestable things?" (20:30, NRSV). The problem is that they have continued in sin, "to this day" (20:31). With Smith-Christopher, further, I would argue that the depiction of indiscriminate slaughter in Ezek 9 is not a normative description of divine justice, but rather a true reflection of the exilic community's experience: in war, innocents suffer and die. The repudiation of the "sour grapes" proverb in 18:2 is consistent with the points raised both in the vision of Jerusalem's destruction in Ezek 9, and in the *Unheilsgeschichte* of Ezek 20. There is no escaping the responsibility of Ezekiel's generation for the disaster that has come upon them.

Darr explores the possibility that there may in fact not be an actual proverb performance in view here. The text, after all, does not involve Ezekiel witnessing such a performance, but rather YHWH's report of the proverb to the prophet. If the performer of the proverb is YHWH, the point of the performance becomes the denial of any analogy between the proverb and the community's situation. This point is then supported, "logically, and in the argot of casuistic law," by "three hypothetical test cases concerning a righteous man (vv. 5–9), his sinful son (vv. 10–13), and his righteous grandson (vv. 14–17)." Darr observes that the standard of righteousness presented here interweaves "cultic and moral obligations"; we can add that the laws cited here all derive from HS, particularly Lev 18–20, lending support to Cook's proposal for a dependence of Ezekiel on HS. The case of the righteous grandson, who follows the ways of his grandfather rather than the example of his wicked father, prompts a response from the audience ("Yet you say, 'Why should not the son suffer for the iniquity of the father?'"; 18:19), as this case contradicts their own assertion of innocence and denial of responsibility. But YHWH's proverb performance is not aimed merely at refuting transgenerational retribution: "Rather, it seeks to provide the people with a means to survive their *present* circumstances: repent of your past sins and leave them behind; get yourselves a new heart and a new spirit, and then set to the task of doing righteousness in every aspect of your lives."

This collection demonstrates the vitality of Ezekiel studies, evident in the creative melding of historical and literary methodologies to uncover fresh insights. Ezekiel both inhabited and described a hierarchical universe, in which God and this world were relegated to decidedly separate spheres, with priests mediating between the mundane and the sacred realms. It is a view of cosmic order that prevailed even in the face of the ultimate tragedy of exile, a view that, arguably, enabled the people Israel to survive the dismantling of their central institutions and, against all historical precedent, to rise from their graves to renewed life (37:1–14).

Selected Bibliography

I. Commentaries

Allen, Leslie C. *Ezekiel 1–19* and *Ezekiel 20–48*. WBC 28 and 29. Dallas: Word, 1994, 1990.
Blenkinsopp, Joseph. *Ezekiel*. IBC. Louisville: John Knox, 1990.
Block, Daniel I. *The Book of Ezekiel*, vol. 1, *Chapters 1–24* and *The Book of Ezekiel*, vol. 2, *Chapters 25–48*. NICOT. Grand Rapids: Eerdmans, 1997 and 1998.
Clements, Ronald E. *Ezekiel*. Westminster Bible Companion. Louisville: Westminster John Knox, 1996.
Cooke, George A. *A Critical and Exegetical Commentary on the Book of Ezekiel*. ICC. Edinburgh: T. & T. Clark, 1936.
Darr, Katheryn Pfisterer. "The Book of Ezekiel: Introduction, Commentary, and Reflections." Pages 1073–607 in vol. 6 of *The New Interpreter's Bible*. 12 vols. Nashville: Abingdon, 2001.
Duguid, Iain. *Ezekiel*. New International Version Application Commentary. Grand Rapids: Zondervan, 1999.
Eichrodt, Walther. *Ezekiel: A Commentary*. Translated by C. Quin. OTL. Philadelphia: Fortress, 1970.
Greenberg, Moshe. *Ezekiel 1–20* and *Ezekiel 21–37*. AB 22 and 22A. New York: Doubleday, 1983, 1997.
Hals, Ronald M. *Ezekiel*. FOTL 19. Grand Rapids: Eerdmans, 1989.
Vawter, Bruce, and Leslie J. Hoppe. *A New Heart: A Commentary on the Book of Ezekiel*. ITC. Grand Rapids: Eerdmans, 1991.
Wevers, John W. *Ezekiel*. NCB. London: Nelson, 1969.
Zimmerli, Walther. *Ezekiel: A Commentary on the Book of the Prophet Ezekiel*. 2 vols. Vol. 1 edited by Frank Moore Cross and Klaus Baltzer, with the assistance of Leonard Jay Greenspoon. Translated by Ronald E. Clements. Vol. 2 edited by Paul D. Hanson, with Leonard Jay Greenspoon. Translated by James D. Martin. Hermeneia. Philadelphia: Fortress, 1979, 1983.

II. Books, Monographs, and Dissertations

Bodi, Daniel. *The Book of Ezekiel and the Poem of Erra*. OBO 104. Fribourg: Universitätsverlag Fribourg, 1991.
Carley, Keith W. *Ezekiel among the Prophets: A Study of Ezekiel's Place in Prophetic Tradition*. SBT 31. Naperville, Ill.: Allenson, 1974.
Davis, Ellen F. *Swallowing the Scroll: Textuality and the Dynamics of Discourse in Ezekiel's Prophecy*. JSOTSup 78. Bible and Literature 21. Sheffield: Almond, 1989.

Duguid, Iain M. *Ezekiel and the Leaders of Israel.* VTSup 56. Leiden and New York: Brill, 1994.
Friebel, Kelvin G. *Jeremiah's and Ezekiel's Sign-Acts: Rhetorical Nonverbal Communication.* JSOTSup 283. Sheffield: Sheffield Academic Press, 1999.
Galambush, Julie. *Jerusalem in the Book of Ezekiel: The City as Yahweh's Wife.* SBLDS 130. Atlanta: Scholars Press, 1992.
Gese, Hartmut. *Der Verfassungsentwurf des Ezechiel (Kap. 40–48) Traditionsgeschichtlich Untersucht.* BHT 25. Tübingen: Mohr Siebeck, 1957.
Joyce, Paul. *Divine Initiative and Human Response in Ezekiel.* JSOTSup 51. Sheffield: JSOT, 1989.
Klein, Ralph W. *Ezekiel: The Prophet and His Message.* Studies on Personalities of the Old Testament. Columbia: University of South Carolina Press, 1988.
Kohn, Risa Levitt. *A New Heart and a New Soul: Ezekiel, the Exile, and the Torah.* JSOTSup 358. London and New York: Sheffield Academic Press, 2002.
Konkel, Michael. *Architektonik des Heiligen: Studien zur zweiten Tempelvision Ezechiels (Ez 40–48).* BBB 129. Berlin: Philo, 2001.
Krüger, Thomas. *Geschichtskonzepte im Ezechielbuch.* BZAW 180. Berlin and New York: de Gruyter, 1989.
Kutsko, John F. *Between Heaven and Earth: Divine Presence and Absence in the Book of Ezekiel.* Biblical and Judaic Studies from the University of California, San Diego 7. Winona Lake, Ind.: Eisenbrauns, 2000.
Lapsley, Jacqueline E. *Can These Bones Live? The Problem of the Moral Self in the Book of Ezekiel.* BZAW 301. Berlin and New York: de Gruyter, 2000.
Levenson, Jon D. *Theology of the Program of Restoration of Ezekiel 40–48.* HSM 10. Atlanta: Scholars Press, 1986.
Matties, Gordon H. *Ezekiel 18 and the Rhetoric of Moral Discourse.* SBLDS 126. Atlanta: Scholars Press, 1990.
Mein, Andrew. *Ezekiel and the Ethics of Exile.* Oxford Theological Monographs. Oxford and New York: Oxford University Press, 2001.
Renz, Thomas. *The Rhetorical Function of the Book of Ezekiel.* VTSup 76. Leiden and Boston: Brill, 2002.
Reventlow, Henning Graf. *Wächter über Israel: Ezechiel und seine Tradition.* BZAW 82. Berlin: Töpelmann, 1962.
Rudnig, Thilo A. *Heilig und Profan: Redaktionskritische Studien zu Ez 40–48.* BZAW 287. Berlin and New York: de Gruyter, 2000.
Smith-Christopher, Daniel. *A Biblical Theology of Exile.* OBT. Minneapolis: Fortress, 2002.
Stevenson, Kalinda Rose. *The Vision of Transformation: The Territorial Rhetoric of Ezekiel 40–48.* SBLDS 154. Atlanta: Scholars Press, 1996.
Strong, John T. "Ezekiel's Oracles against the Nations within the Context of His Message." Ph.D. diss., Union Theological Seminary in Virginia, 1993.
Tuell, Steven Shawn. *The Law of the Temple in Ezekiel 40–48.* HSM 49. Atlanta: Scholars Press, 1992.
VanGemeren, Willem Arie. "The Exegesis of Ezekiel's 'Chariot' Chapters in Twelfth-Century Hebrew Commentaries." Ph.D. diss., University of Wisconsin, Madison, 1974.
Wong, Ka Leung. *The Idea of Retribution in the Book of Ezekiel.* VTSup 87. Leiden and Boston: Brill, 2001.

III. Articles

Allen, Leslie. "The Structuring of Ezekiel's Revisionist History Lesson (Ezekiel 20:3–31)." *CBQ* 54 (1992): 448–62.

Biggs, Charles R. "The Role of Nasi in the Programme for Restoration in Ezekiel 40–48." *Colloq* 16 (1983): 46–57.

Block, Daniel I. "Divine Abandonment: Ezekiel's Adaptation of an Ancient Near Eastern Motif." Pages 15–42 in *The Book of Ezekiel: Theological and Anthropological Perspectives*. Edited by M. S. Odell and J. T. Strong. SBLSymS 9. Atlanta: Society of Biblical Literature, 2000.

Bodi, Daniel. "Le prophète critique la monarchie: Le terme *nāśî'* chez Ézéchiel." Pages 249–57 in *Prophètes et rois: Bible et Proche-Orient*. Edited by André Lemaire. LD. Paris: Cerf, 2001.

Bowen, Nancy R. "The Daughters of Your People: Female Prophets in Ezekiel 13:17–23." *JBL* 118 (1999): 417–33.

Callender, Dexter E., Jr. "The Primal Human in Ezekiel and the Image of God." Pages 175–93 in *The Book of Ezekiel: Theological and Anthropological Perspectives*. Edited by M. S. Odell and J. T. Strong. SBLSymS 9. Atlanta: Society of Biblical Literature, 2000.

Carley, Keith W. "Ezekiel's Formula of Desolation: Harsh Justice for the Land/Earth." Pages 143–57 in *The Earth Story in the Psalms and the Prophets*. Edited by N. C. Habel. Earth Bible 4. Sheffield: Sheffield Academic Press; Cleveland: Pilgrim, 2001.

Cook, Stephen L. "Creation Archetypes and Mythologems in Ezekiel: Significance and Theological Ramifications." Pages 123–46 in *Society of Biblical Literature Seminar Papers, 1999*. SBLSP 38. Atlanta: Scholars Press, 1999.

———. "Innerbiblical Interpretation in Ezekiel 44 and the History of Israel's Priesthood." *JBL* 114 (1995): 193–208.

Davis, Ellen F. "'And Pharaoh Will Change His Mind . . . ' (Ezekiel 32:31): Dismantling Mythical Discourse." Pages 224–39 in *Theological Exegesis: Essays in Honor of Brevard S. Childs*. Edited by C. R. Seitz and K. Greene-McCreight. Grand Rapids: Eerdmans, 1999.

Day, Peggy L. "Adulterous Jerusalem's Imagined Demise: Death of a Metaphor in Ezekiel XVI." *VT* 50 (2000): 285–309.

———. "The Bitch Had It Coming to Her: Rhetoric and Interpretation in Ezekiel 16." *BibInt* 8 (2000): 231–54.

Dempsey, Carol J. "The 'Whore' of Ezekiel 16: The Impact and Ramifications of Gender-Specific Metaphors in Light of Biblical Law and Divine Judgment." Pages 57–78 in *Gender and Law in the Hebrew Bible and the Ancient Near East*. Edited by V. H. Matthews, B. M. Levinson, and T. Frymer-Kensky. JSOTSup 262. Sheffield: Sheffield Academic Press, 1998.

Duke, Rodney K. "Punishment or Restoration? Another Look at the Levites of Ezekiel 44:6–16." *JSOT* 40 (1988): 61–81.

Eslinger, Lyle M. "Ezekiel 20 and the Metaphor of Historical Teleology: Concepts of Biblical History." *JSOT* 81 (1998): 93–125.

Greenberg, Moshe. "The Design and Themes of Ezekiel's Program of Restoration." *Int* 38 (1984): 181–208.

———. "Notes on the Influence of Tradition on Ezekiel." *JANESCU* 22 (1993): 29–37.

Haran, Menahem. "The Law-Code of Ezekiel XL–XLVIII and Its Relation to the Priestly School." *HUCA* 50 (1979): 45–71.

Kohn, Risa Levitt. "Ezekiel at the Turn of the Century." *Currents in Biblical Research* 2 (2003): 9–31.

Kutsko, John F. "Ezekiel's Anthropology and Its Ethical Implications." Pages 119–42 in *The Book of Ezekiel: Theological and Anthropological Perspectives*. Edited by M. S. Odell and J. T. Strong. SBLSymS 9. Atlanta: Society of Biblical Literature, 2000.

Lapsley, Jacqueline E. "Shame and Self-Knowledge: The Positive Role of Shame in Ezekiel's View of the Moral Self." Pages 143–74 in *The Book of Ezekiel: Theological and Anthropological Perspectives*. Edited by M. S. Odell and J. T. Strong. SBLSymS 9. Atlanta: Society of Biblical Literature, 2000.

Launderville, Dale. "Ezekiel's Cherub: A Promising Symbol or a Dangerous Idol?" *CBQ* 65 (2003): 165–83.

McConville, J. Gordon. "Priests and Levites in Ezekiel: A Crux in the Interpretation of Israel's History." *TynBul* 34 (1983): 3–31.

McKeating, Henry. "Ezekiel the 'Prophet Like Moses'?" *JSOT* 61 (1994): 97–109.

Mein, Andrew. "Ezekiel as a Priest in Exile." Pages 199–213 in *The Elusive Prophet: The Prophet as a Historical Person, Literary Character, and Anonymous Artist*. Edited by J. C. de Moor. OtSt 45. Leiden and Boston: Brill, 2001.

Miller, James E. "The Mælæk of Tyre (Ezekiel 28,11–19)." *ZAW* 105 (1993): 497–501.

———. "The Thirtieth Year of Ezekiel 1:1." *RB* 99 (1992): 499–503.

Monloubou, Louis. "La signification du culte selon Ézéchiel." Pages 322–29 in *Ezekiel and His Book: Textual and Literary Criticism and Their Interrelation*. Edited by J. Lust. BETL 74. Louvain: Louvain University Press/Peeters, 1986.

Niditch, Susan. "Ezekiel 40–48 in a Visionary Context." *CBQ* 48 (1986): 208–24.

Odell, Margaret S. "Ezekiel Saw What He Said He Saw: Genres, Forms, and the Vision of Ezekiel 1." Pages 162–76 in *The Changing Face of Form Criticism for the Twenty-first Century*. Edited by M. A. Sweeney and E. Ben Zvi. Grand Rapids: Eerdmans, 2003.

———. "The Inversion of Shame and Forgiveness in Ezekiel 16:59–63." *JSOT* 56 (1992): 101–12.

———. "You Are What You Eat: Ezekiel and the Scroll." *JBL* 117 (1998): 229–48.

Patton, Corrine L. "'I Myself Gave Them Laws That Were Not Good': Ezekiel 20 and the Exodus Traditions." *JSOT* 69 (1996): 73–90.

———. "'Should Our Sister Be Treated Like a Whore?' A Response to Feminist Critiques of Ezekiel 23." Pages 221–38 in *The Book of Ezekiel: Theological and Anthropological Perspectives*. Edited by M. S. Odell and J. T. Strong. SBLSymS 9. Atlanta: Society of Biblical Literature, 2000.

Pons, Jacques. "Le vocabulaire d'Ézéchiel 20: Le prophète s'oppose à la vision deutéronomiste de l'histoire." Pages 214–33 in *Ezekiel and His Book: Textual and Literary Criticism and their Interrelation*. Edited by J. Lust. BETL 74. Louvain: Louvain University Press/Peeters, 1986.

Schwartz, Baruch J. "Ezekiel's Dim View of Israel's Restoration." Pages 43–67 in *The Book of Ezekiel: Theological and Anthropological Perspectives*. Edited by M. S. Odell and J. T. Strong. SBLSymS 9. Atlanta: Society of Biblical Literature, 2000.

Shields, Mary E. "Multiple Exposures: Body Rhetoric and Gender Characterization in Ezekiel 16." *JFSR* 14 (1998): 5–18.

Ska, Jean Louis. "La sortie d'Egypte (Ex 7–14) dans le récit sacerdotal (Pg) et la tradition prophétique." *Bib* 60 (1979): 191–215.
Smith-Christopher, Daniel L. "Ezekiel on Fanon's Couch: A Postcolonialist Dialogue with David Halperin's Seeking Ezekiel." Pages 108–44 in *Peace and Justice Shall Embrace: Power and Theopolitics in the Bible. Essays in Honor of Millard Lind.* Edited by T. Grimsrud and L. L. Johns. Telford, Pa.: Pandora, 1999.
Stevenson, Kalinda Rose. "If Earth Could Speak: The Case of the Mountains against YHWH in Ezekiel 6:35–36." Pages 158–71 in *The Earth Story in the Psalms and the Prophets.* Edited by N. C. Habel. Earth Bible 4. Sheffield: Sheffield Academic Press; Cleveland: Pilgrim, 2001.
Strong, John T. "God's *Kābôd:* The Presence of Yahweh in the Book of Ezekiel." Pages 69–95 in *The Book of Ezekiel: Theological and Anthropological Perspectives.* Edited by M. S. Odell and J. T. Strong. SBLSymS 9. Atlanta: Society of Biblical Literature, 2000.
Sweeny, Marvin A. "Ezekiel: Zadokite Priest and Visionary Prophet of the Exile." Pages 728–51 in *Society of Biblical Literature Seminar Papers, 2000.* SBLSP 39. Atlanta: Society of Biblical Literature, 2000.
Tuell, Steven Shawn. "Divine Presence and Absence in Ezekiel's Prophecy." Pages 97–116 in *The Book of Ezekiel: Theological and Anthropological Perspectives.* Edited by M. S. Odell and J. T. Strong. SBLSymS 9. Atlanta: Society of Biblical Literature, 2000.
Uffenheimer, Benjamin. "Theodicy and Ethics in the Prophecy of Ezekiel." Pages 200–227 in *Justice and Righteousness: Biblical Themes and Their Influence.* Edited by H. G. Reventlow and Y. Hoffman. JSOTSup 137. Sheffield: JSOT Press, 1992.
van Dijk-Hemmes, Fokkelien. "The Metaphorization of Woman in Prophetic Speech: An Analysis of Ezekiel XXIII." *VT* 43 (1993): 162–70.
Wiesel, Elie. "Ezekiel." Pages 167–86 in *Congregation: Contemporary Writers Read the Jewish Bible.* Edited by D. Rosenberg. San Diego: Harcourt Brace Jovanovich, 1987.
Wilson, Robert R. "The Death of the King of Tyre: The Editorial History of Ezekiel 28." Pages 211–18 in *Love and Death in the Ancient Near East: Essays in Honor of Marvin H. Pope.* Edited by J. H. Marks and R. M. Good. Guilford, Conn.: Four Quarters, 1987.
———. "Prophecy in Crisis: The Call of Ezekiel." *Int* 38 (1984): 117–30.
Zimmerli, Walther. "'Leben' und 'Tod' im Buche des Propheten Ezechiel." *TZ* 13 (1957): 494–508.
———. "The Special Form- and Traditio-Historical Character of Ezekiel's Prophecy." *VT* 15 (1965): 515–27.

Index of Modern Authors

Abba, Raymond 54 n. 37, 85 n. 39
Ackroyd, Peter R. 48 n. 19
Aichele, George 171 n. 4
Albertz, Rainer 86 n. 41
Albright, W. F. 179 n.1
Alexander, Philip S. 129 n. 5
Allan, Nigel 86 n. 39
Allen, Leslie C. 31 n. 10, 32 n. 18, 37 n. 27, 54 n. 38, 161 n. 8, 255, 257
Andersen, Frances I. 66 n. 20
Anderson, Bernard W. 91 n. 2, 167 n. 61
Anderson, Gary A. 71 n. 36
Auerbach, Elias 47 n. 17

Bakhtin, Mikhail M. 205, 252
Barnett, Richard D. 180 nn. 2–3, 186 n. 19, 193 n. 48
Barr, James 173
Barstad, Hans M. 116 n. 37
Bateson, Gregory 123
Beardslee, William A. 218 n. 94
Bechtel, Lyn M. 113 n. 23, 114
Bell, Catherine M. 76 n. 14
Bellis, Alice O. 73 n. 2, 74 n. 8, 77 n. 16
Benjamin, Don C. 77 n. 18
Berlin, Adele 74 n. 5
Berlinerblau, Jacques 16 n. 40
Berquist, Jon L. 45 n. 10, 48, 83
Berry, George R. 61 n. 1
Berry, Thomas 124 n. 79, 125 n. 82
Bewer, Julius A. 61 n. 1
Biggs, Charles R. 79 n. 23, 257
Blenkinsopp, Joseph 77 n. 18, 82 n. 29, 83 n. 31, 84 n. 34, 86 nn. 39 & 41, 142 nn. 4 & 6, 143, 157, 255
Bloch-Smith, Elizabeth 180 nn. 2 & 4
Block, Daniel I. 22, 52 nn. 29–30, 53 n. 33, 63 n. 11, 86 n. 40, 111 n. 15, 116, 191 n. 35, 193 n. 48, 196 n. 57, 203 n. 28, 209–10, 211 n. 72, 214 nn. 79 & 83, 219 nn. 96–97, 220, 221 n. 101, 222, 229 n. 3, 255, 257
Bodi, Daniel 79 n. 23, 170 n. 1, 255, 257
Bowen, Nancy R. 75 n. 10, 257
Brooks Thistlethwaite, Susan 154
Brueggemann, Walter 117–19, 124 n. 77, 241, 246
Burden, Terry 160 n. 8, 162 n. 28
Businck, T. A. 179 n. 1, 186 n. 21

Callender, Dexter E., Jr. 174 n. 15, 183 n. 11, 185 n. 18, 191 n. 35, 192 n. 39, 195 n. 56, 257
Capps, Donald 114, 122 n. 67
Carley, Keith W. v, ix, 2 n. 4, 10, 17, 19–20, 75 n. 12, 109, 111 n. 13, 138, 142 n. 4, 147 n. 27, 228, 235, 245–47, 248, 250, 255, 257
Carroll, Robert P. 106, 108, 116, 122 n. 66, 143, 149, 246
Catling, H. W. 180 n. 4
Childs, Brevard S. 151 n. 45
Clements, Ronald 143 n. 9, 156, 255
Clifford, Richard J. 91 nn. 2–3, 96 n. 11, 103 n. 23
Cody, Aelred 44 n. 4, 45 n. 8, 47 n. 18,

Cody, Aelred (*continued*)
  65 n. 16, 76 n. 15, 77 n. 18, 84 n. 35, 85 n. 39
Collins, John J. 91 n. 2, 124 n. 76
Collon, Dominique 180 n. 2, 191 n. 35
Cook, Stephen L. v, vi, ix, 1, 10, 17 n. 40, 21, 43 n. 1, 77 n. 18, 86 nn. 39 & 41, 92, 177 n. 21, 179, 228, 234 n. 8, 237–39, 249–50, 254, 257
Cooke, G. A. 61 n. 1, 255
Coppes, Leonard J. 114 n. 24
Craigie, Peter 145 n. 18
Cross, Frank Moore 170 n. 2, 255

Dallett, Janet O. 181 n. 5, 184 n. 14
Darr, Katheryn Pfisterer vi, vii, ix, 21–22, 86 n. 40, 199, 204 n. 32, 209 n. 64, 210 n. 66, 214 n. 85, 228, 239, 248, 252–54, 255
Davies, Andrew 112 n. 17, 123–24
Davis, Ellen F. 35 n. 25, 73 n. 3, 74 n. 6, 83 n. 32, 88 n. 45, 167 n. 62, 193 n. 47, 216, 255, 257
Day, John 77 n. 18
Day, Peggy L. 145–47, 250, 257
Dempsey, Carol J. 110, 122 n. 70, 144, 257
Dillard, Annie 124 n. 80
Douglas, G. C. M. 167 n. 58
Douglas, Mary 92 n. 5
Duguid, Iain M. v, ix, 18, 43, 53 n. 35, 52 n. 28, 56 n. 45, 59 n. 52, 62, 65 n. 15, 66 nn. 19 & 21–22, 67 n. 26, 68 n. 27, 70 nn. 34–35, 75 nn. 9–10, 79 n. 23, 81 n. 27, 85 n. 39, 87 n. 43, 92 n. 6, 107 n. 32, 108 n. 34, 230, 232, 242–43, 244, 255, 256
Duke, Rodney K. 62 n. 8, 86 n. 40, 257
Dundes, Alan 201 n. 12, 202 n. 19, 203 n. 27

Eichrodt, Walther 134 n. 14, 135 n. 17, 255
Eisler, Riane 7 n. 18, 109 n. 4, 110, 245
Eissfeldt, Otto 202 n. 23
Eliade, Mircea 75 n. 8, 192 n. 40

Eslinger, Lyle 161 n. 8, 257
Exum, J. Cheryl 142 n. 6

Fechter, Friedrich v, ix, 9, 10, 18, 27, 31 n. 14, 38 n. 30, 228–30, 242, 243, 244, 252, 253
Fensham, Frank Charles 49 n. 24
Fewell, Danna Nolan 171 n. 4
Finnegan, Ruth 201, 207 n. 47
Fishbane, Michael 32 n. 18, 68 nn. 29–30, 159 n. 2
Fleming, Daniel E. 77 n. 16
Fontaine, Carole R. 200 nn. 8 & 10, 202, 204 n. 31, 207 nn. 49–50, 208 nn. 52–53 & 61, 211, 217 n. 92
Freedman, David Noel xi, 66 n. 20, 124 n. 76, 179 n. 1, 185 n. 18, 190 n. 32, 191 n. 33
Friebel, Kelvin G. 73 n. 3, 256
Frye, Northrop 106 n. 28
Frymer-Kensky, Tikva S. 144 n. 13, 152 n. 49, 257

Galambush, Julie v, x, 10, 17, 19, 91, 119 n. 56, 120, 130–31, 136–37, 234–35, 245, 246, 247, 256
Gammie, John G. 76 n. 14
Gardner, Jason 124 nn. 78 & 80
Genette, Gérard 171
Georgi, Dieter 121
Gerstenberger, Erhard S. 31 n. 11, 109 n. 4
Gese, Hartmut 12 n. 27, 85 n. 38, 256
Goetze, Albrecht 212 nn. 75–77
Goldstein, Joshua S. 152–53
Goodwin, Paul D. 202 n. 21, 208 n. 56
Gordon, Pamela 142 n. 6, 147
Gorman, Frank H. 76 n. 14
Gottwald, Norman K. 3 n. 6
Gowan, Donald E. 112, 113, 117, 118
Grabbe, Lester L. 41 n. 38, 44 n. 4, 46 n. 15, 65 n. 16, 73 n. 2, 74 n. 8, 77 nn. 16 & 18, 116 n. 37
Graffy, Adrian 199 n. 2, 221
Green, Anthony 179 n. 1, 192 n. 39
Greenberg, Moshe 11 n. 24, 14, 52 n. 31,

53 n. 33, 62, 63 n. 11, 64 n. 13, 66 nn. 18–19 & 22, 73 n. 3, 78 n. 20, 87 n. 43, 142, 143, 144, 145 nn. 16–17, 159, 160 n. 8, 162 n. 24, 163 n. 32, 164 n. 40, 185 n. 18, 187 n. 25, 188, 190 n. 32, 191 n. 33, 194 n. 50, 219 n. 96, 229 n. 2, 241, 242, 243, 255, 257
Gunkel, Hermann   179 n. 1, 191 n. 37
Gunn, David M.   74 n. 5, 116 n. 38
Gunneweg, Antonius H. J.   86 n. 39

Habel, Norman C.   vi, x, 10, 20, 92, 100, 109 nn. 2–3, 125 n. 82, 127, 128 n. 2, 130 n. 6, 133 nn. 12–13, 135 n. 15, 136, 138 n. 21, 228, 235, 236, 247–48, 257, 259
Habermas, Jürgen   8
Halpern, Baruch   82 n. 28, 124 n. 76
Hals, Ronald M.   219 n. 98, 255
Hamerton-Kelly, Robert G.   137 n. 20
Hanks, William E.   201 n. 15
Hanson, Paul D.   43 n. 3, 77 n. 18, 79 n. 22, 86 n. 41, 255
Haran, Menahem   63 n. 9, 64 n. 12, 68–69 n. 30, 74 n. 4, 80 n. 26, 258
Harris, Robert A.   61 n. 1
Haught, John F.   123
Hederman, Mark Patrick   122 n. 67
Heider, George   163 n. 33
Heschel, Abraham J.   142
Hoonacker, Albin van   54 n. 37
Hooper, Charlotte   156 n. 57
Hoppe, Leslie J.   81 n. 27, 255
Huffmon, Herbert B.   77 n. 16

Jameson, Frederic   92 n. 5, 106 n. 28, 107
Japhet, Sara   151
Jenson, Philip Peter   13 n. 33, 76 n. 14
Joyce, Paul   66 n. 18, 82 n. 30, 163 n. 29, 214 n. 86, 256
Jung, Carl G.   180–84, 188 n. 26, 191, 192 n. 40, 194, 249

Kaiser, Otto   150, 151 n. 45

Kaufmann, Yehezkel   62, 67 n. 24, 166 n. 55, 229 n. 2, 243
Kedar-Kopfstein, B.   118 n. 48
Keel, Othmar   185 n. 17, 186 nn. 19 & 22, 192 n. 40
Kellermann, D.   119
King, Philip J.   179 n. 1, 186 n. 21
Kirshenblatt-Gimblett, Barbara   208
Klein, Ralph   143 n. 9, 145, 156, 256
Knight, Douglas A.   170 n. 2
Knohl, Israel   11 n. 26, 12 n. 31, 186 nn. 20–21, 187 nn. 23–24 & 26, 189 n. 28, 190, 249
Knoppers, Gary N.   77 n. 18
Kohn, Risa Levitt   vi, x, 20, 62 nn. 4–5, 63 n. 10, 159, 161 n. 15, 162 nn. 26–27, 164 n. 36, 167 n. 63, 168 n. 64, 228, 234 n. 7, 237, 251–52, 256, 258
Konkel, Michael   177 n. 21, 256
Kraus, Hans-Joachim   214 n. 79
Krüger, Thomas   31 nn. 9 & 16, 256
Kuhrt, Amélie   77 n. 16, 112 n. 19
Kutsko, John F.   viii, 40 n. 37, 69 n. 32, 82 n. 28, 172, 173, 183 n. 11, 190 nn. 30–31, 256, 258

Lapsley, Jacqueline E.   82 n. 28, 113 n. 23, 256, 258
Launderville, Dale   184, 191 n. 35, 192 n. 39, 195, 196 n. 57, 258
Leithart, Peter J.   77 n. 18
Levenson, Jon D.   16 n. 38, 20 n. 41, 62 n. 6, 79 n. 23, 85 n. 39, 91 n. 3, 103 n. 23, 166 nn. 51 & 53, 167 nn. 56–57 & 59, 256
Levine, L.   129 n. 5
Levinson, Bernard M.   66 n. 17, 144 n. 13, 152 n. 49, 257
Lewis, Theodore J.   53 n. 34
Lieb, Michael   122
Littlewood, Roland   149 n. 37
Lohfink, Norbert   13 n. 32
Longman, Tremper, III   74 n. 5
Lust, Johan   85 n. 36, 161 n. 8, 258

Machinist, Peter   196 n. 58

Magdalene, F. Rachel   147, 154
Mallowan, Max E. L.   180 n. 3, 193 n. 48
Mannheim, Bruce   207 n. 46
Matthews, Victor H.   77 n. 18, 144 n. 13, 152 n. 49, 257
Matties, Gordon H.   82 n. 28, 199 n. 2, 219 nn. 95–97, 223, 256
Mayer, Werner R.   175 n. 16
McBride, S. Dean   77 n. 18, 79 n. 22, 86 n. 41
McConville, J. Gordon   56 n. 46, 85 n. 39, 258
McFague, Sallie   120
McKeating, Henry   166 n. 51, 167 nn. 57 & 60, 258
McNutt, Paula M.   77 nn. 17–18
Mein, Andrew   73 n. 4, 82 n. 28, 84 n. 34, 256, 258
Mendenhall, George E.   3 n. 6
Mettinger, Tryggve N. D.   179 n. 1, 185 n. 17, 186 n. 21, 187 nn. 23 & 26, 195 n. 56
Meyers, Carol L.   79 n. 22, 179 n. 1
Michaels, Walter B.   106, 107 nn. 29–31
Mieder, Wolfgang   201 nn. 12 & 14, 208 n. 53
Miles, Jack   112, 113 n. 21, 114 n. 29, 246, 250
Milgrom, Jacob   11 n. 26, 45 n. 7, 54 n. 36, 186 n. 20, 189 n. 28
Millar, William R.   86 n. 39
Miller, James E.   63 n. 11, 85 n. 36, 180 n. 4, 185 n. 18, 191 nn. 33–35, 192 n. 39, 194 n. 53, 258
Miller, Patrick D.   13 n. 32, 14 nn. 33 & 35, 77 n. 18, 79 n. 22, 86 n. 41
Moltmann, Jürgen   123 n. 74
Monloubou, Louis   85 n. 36, 258
Moore, Michael S.   77 n. 18
Murray, D. F.   199 n. 2

Nathanson, Donald L.   114, 246
Nelson, Richard D.   45 n. 9, 46 nn. 11 & 13–14, 47 n. 16, 77 n. 18, 78 n. 21
Nichols, Terence L.   2 n. 3, 3 n. 7
Niditch, Susan   16 n. 39, 56 n. 47, 177 n. 22, 178, 258

Nurmela, Risto   32 n. 17, 38 n. 31, 86 n. 39

O'Brien, Julia M.   51 n. 26, 65 n. 16, 86 n. 39
O'Connor, Kathleen M.   73 n. 2
O'Connor, Michael P.   57 n. 49, 179 n. 1, 190 n. 32, 191 n. 33, 203 n. 28, 208 n. 57
O'Day, Gail R.   171 n. 4
Odell, Margaret S.   viii, 52 n. 32, 55, 56 n. 44, 67 n. 25, 73 nn. 3–4, 82 n. 28, 85 n. 37, 86 n. 42, 113 n. 23, 114 nn. 25 & 30, 144 n. 12, 148, 174 n. 15, 189 nn. 28–29, 246, 257, 258, 259
Ohnesorge, Stefan   30 n. 9
Olyan, Saul M.   10–11 n. 23, 11 nn. 25–26, 12 n. 31, 14 n. 33, 71 n. 36, 76 n. 14, 79 n. 22
O'Murchu, Diarmuid   123

Pagán, Samuel   48 n. 20
Page, Hugh Rowland, Jr.   191 n. 38, 192 n. 41, 193, 194 n. 54, 195
Page, Ruth   123
Pardes, Ilana   145
Parsons, Stephen   122, 235
Patton, Corrine L.   v, x, 1, 19, 43 n. 1, 68 n. 27, 73, 81 n. 27, 144, 148, 166, 229 n. 3, 230–32, 243–45, 258
Peacocke, Arthur R.   2 n. 4, 110 n. 5, 125 n. 83
Petersen, David L.   vi, x, 21, 128, 129 n. 3, 169, 228, 236 n. 9, 237, 247, 248–49, 250
Phillips, Gary A.   171 n. 4
Plöger, J. G.   99 n. 16
Polk, Timothy   54 n. 37, 203 n. 24, 214 n. 81, 220 n. 100
Pons, Jacques   160 n. 8, 258
Pritchard, James   150
Propp, William H. C.   124 n. 76, 161 nn. 12, 14, & 16, 166 n. 49

Rad, Gerhard von   175
Rahner, Karl   21, 196–97, 250

INDEX OF MODERN AUTHORS

Rasmussen, Larry L.   122, 123 n. 71
Raymond, Joseph   207 n. 51, 208 nn. 53 & 60
Renz, Thomas   73 n. 3, 74 n. 5, 87 n. 44, 88 n. 46, 202 n. 23, 256
Reventlow, Henning G.   52 n. 30, 82 n. 28, 256, 259
Richardson, M. E. J.   111 n. 15
Robertson, Edward   44 n. 5
Rofé, Alexander   160 n. 6
Rooke, Deborah W.   77 n. 18
Rossing, Barbara R.   121
Rudnig, Thilo Alexander   79 n. 23, 86 n. 41, 177 n. 21, 256

Sabourin, Leopold   75 n. 8, 76 n. 15
Scarry, Elaine   99
Schaper, Joachim   86 n. 39
Scharper, Stephen B.   121 n. 62
Schmidt, Ludwig   33 n. 19
Schwartz, Baruch J.   v, x, 11 n. 26, 18–19, 61, 67 n. 25, 69 n. 31, 71 n. 36, 168 n. 65, 229 n. 3, 232–34, 242, 243, 244, 258
Seitel, Peter   201, 202 n. 18, 204, 205, 206 nn. 42–45, 207 n. 46, 210 nn. 68–69, 214 n. 87, 219
Setel, T. Drorah   142, 144
Sharlach, Lisa   150
Shields, Mary E.   145 n. 20, 258
Ska, Jean L.   161 n. 16, 166 n. 54, 259
Skjelsbek, Inger   149
Smith, Cyril Stanley   2, 8, 9
Smith, Mark S.   192 nn. 41–42, 193 nn. 43 & 45
Smith-Christopher, Daniel L.   vi, x, 9, 20, 112 n. 19, 141, 148 n. 34, 157 n. 60, 228, 236–37, 246, 250–51, 254, 256, 259
Soskice, Janet Martin   202 n. 17
Sperling, S. David   129 n. 5
Stager, Lawrence E.   179 n. 1, 186 n. 21
Stevenson, Kalinda R.   54 n. 39, 55 n. 40, 58 n. 50, 73 n. 3, 80 n. 25, 86 n. 40, 88 n. 45, 92 n. 6, 107 n. 32, 135, 176, 177 n. 21, 256, 259
Stiebert, Johanna   113 n. 23, 114 n. 25, 141, 142 n. 1, 143 n. 9, 156, 157 n. 59
Stone, Michael E.   77 n. 18
Strong, John T.   viii, 67 n. 25, 82 n. 28, 113 n. 23, 144 n. 12, 172, 173, 174 n. 15, 189 nn. 28–29, 256, 257, 258, 259
Sweeny, Marvin A.   259
Swimme, Brian   125 n. 81

Taylor, Archer   201, 207 n. 48, 208 n. 58
Tedlock, Dennis   207 n. 46
Thomas, Lewis   124 n. 78
Tucker, Gene M.   102 n. 22
Tuell, Steven S.   vi, x, 11 n. 25, 12 nn. 27–28, 22, 28 n. 2, 37 n. 27, 62 n. 8, 65 n. 16, 79 n. 23, 85 n. 39, 96 n. 11, 177 n. 21, 189 n. 29, 241, 256, 259

Uffenheimer, Benjamin   82 n. 28, 259

van Dam, Cornelis   44 nn. 5–6, 66 n. 17
Van Dijk-Hemmes, Fokkelien   144, 259
Van Seters, John   160 n. 6, 174, 248
Vanderhooft, David   151–52
VanGemeren, Willem Arie   61 n. 1, 256
Vawter, Bruce   81 n. 27, 255
Viviano, Pauline   73 n. 2
Vogt, Ernst   31 n. 15

Wagner, S.   68 n. 30
Wallace, Howard N.   96 n. 12
Wallace, Mark I.   123
Waltke, Bruce K.   57 n. 49, 203 n. 28, 208 n. 57
Washington, Harold C.   142 n. 6, 147, 152
Weber, Max   76 n. 15
Weems, Renita   142, 144, 146 n. 23, 155 n. 53, 156
Weinfeld, Moshe   68 nn. 29–30, 162 n. 23
Wellhausen, Julius   43, 62
Wenzel, Joseph W.   202 n. 21, 208 n. 56
Westermann, Claus   119 n. 55, 170, 174
Wevers, John W.   191 n. 36, 255

White, Lynn, Jr. 121 n. 62
Wiesel, Elie 214 n. 88, 259
Wiggermann, F. A. M. 179 n. 1, 183 n. 12, 192 n. 39
Wilber, Ken 2, 8, 109, 110 nn. 5 & 8, 180 n. 5
Williamson, Hugh G. M. 47 n. 18, 49 nn. 23–24
Wilson, Robert R. 75 n. 8, 81 n. 27, 161 n. 10, 165 n. 48, 183 n. 10, 217, 259
Wolff, Hans W. 68 n. 30
Wong, Ka Leung 111 n. 14, 256
Wood, William P. 189 n. 29

Yadin, Yigael 150 n. 39, 151 nn. 42–43
Yee, Gale A. 146, 148–49

Zalewski, Marysia 150 n. 37
Zimmerli, Walther 12 n. 27, 33 n. 21, 35, 52 n. 29, 55 n. 42, 61 n. 1, 66 n. 18, 73 n. 1, 111, 113, 115 n. 32, 116, 117, 119 nn. 54 & 58, 134 n. 14, 135 n. 17, 160 n. 8, 161 n. 10, 175 n. 17, 176 n. 18, 191 nn. 36–37, 200 n. 5, 202 n. 23, 214 nn. 79–80, 82, & 84, 241, 242, 255, 259

Index of Primary Sources

Hebrew Bible

Genesis
1	104 n. 24, 117, 128, 129, 169, 170, 173, 174, 237, 248, 249
1–3	174 n. 15, 178, 237
1–11	56
1:1	173
1:2	173
1:6–8	185
1:7–8	237
1:20	249
1:21	173, 249
1:24	249
1:26	173
1:27	173
1:28	121 n. 62, 172, 173
1:30	249
2	170, 171, 173, 174, 175, 248, 249
2–3	170, 173, 174, 175
2:3	173
2:4	173
2:7	171, 173, 249
2:9	121 n. 65, 174
2:9–17	174
2:10–14	96, 174
2:11–12	174
2:19	94, 249
3	171, 172, 250
3:24	121 n. 65, 174, 180, 185
8:21	112
9:10	249
9:12	249
9:15	249
9:16	249
15:1	252
17:8	164 n. 45
17:12–13	178
25:22	252
26:33	164 n. 37
28:4	164 n. 45
32:33	164 n. 37
36:7	164 n. 45
37:1	164 n. 45
37:20	94 n. 9
37:33	94 n. 9
47:26	164 n. 37
48:15	164 n. 37
49	177

Exodus
2:25	161 n. 14
3:8	161 n. 18
3:17	161 n. 18
6:2	165 n. 47
6:2–9	161 n. 16
6:3	161 n. 14
6:4	164 n. 45
6:6	161 n. 16, 164 n. 38
6:6–7	165 n. 47
6:7	161 n. 16
6:8	161 n. 12
7:1	166 n. 52
7:1–5	166 n. 54
7:3	166 n. 54
10:6	164 n. 37
12:12	166 n. 50
12:42	161 n. 16

Exodus (*continued*)

12:43	31 n. 13	5:15	163 n. 34
13:2	163 n. 33	5:21	163 n. 34
13:12	163 n. 33	6:3	33 n. 21, 185
13:15	163 n. 33	6:4	33 n. 20
16	189	8	37, 167
18:15	84	8:15–34	31, 229
19:6	13	8:17	29 n. 6
20:4–5	213	8:33	30 n. 7
21:28	184	8:35	30 n. 7
24:9–10	78, 244	9	167
25:8	187	9:11	29 n. 6
25:20	191	10:1–3	38 n. 33
25:22	186	10:10–11	48, 68 n. 30
26:31	185	10:11	45, 68
26:33	13	10:12	12
27:9–19	13	11:10	249
28	167	11:46	69 n. 30, 249
28:1	12	13:59	69 n. 30
29	37, 56 n. 46, 167	15:31	70, 188
29:1–37	31, 229	16	29
29:9	166 n. 55	16:2	186
29:39	33 n. 21	16:18–19	30
29:40	166 n. 55	16:27	29 n. 6
29:42–43	33 n. 21	16:27–28	29
29:45–46	187	17:3–9	39 n. 36
31:13	162 nn. 25–27, 190	18–20	52, 188, 254
31:17	162 n. 26	18:4	162 n. 23
32:11	162 n. 21	18:5	162 nn. 23–24, 165
32:32	68 n. 28	18:7–8	188
33:1	161 n. 13	18:11	188
33:11	164 n. 43	18:19	188
34:6–7	213	18:20	188
34:19	163 n. 33	18:21	164 n. 39
36:35	185	18:25	100, 189, 190
37:9	191	18:26	162 n. 23
38:21	38	18:28	100, 189
39:27–29	33 n. 21	19	16
40:34	187	19:2	16, 190
		19:3	162 n. 25
		19:9–18	16
Leviticus		19:13	188
1:5	11	19:16	188
1:11	11	19:30	162 n. 25, 187, 188
4:5–7	188	19:33–36	16
4:12	29 n. 6	19:37	162 n. 23
4:21	29 n. 6	20:3	165 n. 46, 187

20:7	190	4:28	38
20:8	162 n. 27	4:33	38
20:9	188	5:3	188, 190
20:22	162 n. 23	5:6	163 n. 34
20:23	163 n. 31	5:27	163 n. 34
20:24	161 n. 18	7:89	167
20:26	190	9:15	183 n. 11
21	45	11:15	191 n. 33
21:1–4	33, 61 n. 3	12:6–8	67 n. 24
21:5	55	13	161 n. 17
21:6	45	13–14	162 n. 28
21:8	12 n. 30, 162 n. 27, 190	13:27	161 n. 18
21:11	61 n. 3	14:18	213 n. 78
22:32	12 n. 30, 162 nn. 21 & 27, 165 n. 46, 190	14:30	161 n. 12, 162 n. 28
		16	12 n. 31, 33, 37
23:22	16	16:3	12
24:17–22	16	16:5, 7	11 n. 26
25–26	129, 247	16:8–10	13 n. 31
25:10	16	16:14	161 n. 18
25:17	188	16:38	190 n. 30
25:18	162 n. 23	17:13	190 n. 30
25:23	190	18	11 n. 26, 32, 34, 37, 242
25:23–24	16	18:1–7	15
25:36	188	18:3–4	54
25:42	16	18:7	12 n. 30
26	237	18:15	163 n. 33
26:2	162 n. 25, 187, 188	19	31 n. 13
26:3	163 n. 31	19:10–22	61 n. 3
26:6	94	19:11	33
26:11	187	19:13	188
26:12	130	22:30	164 n. 37
26:14–22	93	23:5	75 n. 8
26:14–39	101	23:12	75 n. 8
26:15	162 n. 23	23:16	75 n. 8
26:34	101	25:10–13	12 n. 29
26:43	162 n. 23	25:12	164 n. 38
26:45	162 n. 22	26:11	213
27:32	164 n. 44	27–36	167 n. 57
		27:12–13	167
Numbers		27:21	231 n. 5
3–4	12 n. 29	28	167 n. 57
3:12	163 n. 33	29	167 n. 57
3:28	13	31:16	163 n. 34
3:32	12 n. 29	32	167 n. 57
4:4	13	33:50–56	167 n. 57
4:26	13	34:1–15	167 n. 57

Numbers (*continued*)		17:11	69 n. 30
35	167 n. 57	17:18	233 n. 6
35:34	189, 190	18:1–8	11
36	167 n. 57	18:10	164 n. 39
		18:15–22	67 n. 24
Deuteronomy		18:18	166
1:8	161 nn. 12–13	19:13	163 n. 30
1:33	161 n. 17	19:21	163 n. 30
4:1	162 n. 23	20:19–20	97 n. 14
4:5	162 n. 23	21:5	45 n. 8
4:14	162 n. 23	24:8	45, 68, 69 n. 30
4:27	163 n. 32, 252	24:16	213, 220, 253
4:28	164 n. 41	25:12	163 n. 30
4:34	164 n. 42	26:8	164 n. 42
4:37	161 n. 11	26:9	161 n. 18
5:1	162 n. 23	26:15	161 n. 18
5:9	213	26:19	13
5:15	164 n. 42	27:3	161 n. 18
5:24	191 n. 33	28	237
5:30	163 n. 31	28:9	13
6:3	161 n. 18	28:36	164 n. 41
6:6	163 n. 29	28:49	184
6:24–25	162 n. 24	28:63	112
7:6	13, 161 n. 11	28:64	164 n. 41
7:7	161 n. 11	29:16	162 n. 19, 164 n. 41
7:9–10	213	29:27	162 n. 20
7:16	163 n. 30	30:2	163 n. 29
8:6	163 n. 31	30:14	163 n. 29
9	162 n. 21	30:15	162 n. 24
9:19	162 n. 20	30:19	162 n. 24
10:1–5	186 n. 21	31:9–13	233 n. 6
10:12	163 n. 31	31:10–13	68 n. 30
10:15	161 n. 11	31:20	161 n. 18
11:9	161 n. 18	32:49–52	167
11:32	162 n. 23	33	177
12:1	162 n. 23	33:8–10	44
12:2	164 n. 35	33:10	44, 68, 69 n. 30, 233
12:3	97	34	167 n. 60
12:5	161 n. 9	34:4	161 n. 13
12:15	39 n. 36	34:10	164 n. 43
12:30	161 n. 9	34:10–12	67 n. 24
13:9	163 n. 30		
14:2	13, 161 n. 11	**Joshua**	
14:21	13	5:6	161 n. 18
16:21	97	7:22–26	213
17:8–13	45 n. 8, 230	9:27	47

13–19	118, 177	6:35	185
13–21	55	8:7	186 n. 21, 191
24:14	166 n. 50	8:10–11	78
24:23	163 n. 29	8:48	163 n. 29
		11:5	162 n. 19
Judges		11:7	162 n. 19
9:8–15	97 n. 13	14:23	164 n. 35
		21	119
1 Samuel		22	231 n. 5
2:27–36	38, 46 n. 13	22:8	252
8	5	22:15–23	75 n. 8
8:7	5		
8:10–18	5	**2 Kings**	
8:14	119	2:22	104
8:20	164 n. 40	11	46 n. 12
10:5–6	75 n. 8	11:4–19	47, 53
14:3	38	14	97 n. 13
14:18–19	44	14:6	213
18:6	153	16:4	164 n. 35
22:16–19	213	16:10–16	46 n. 12
22:20	38 n. 32	17:10	164 n. 35
23:6	44	17:25	94 n. 9
23:9–12	44	19:15	186 n. 22
24:14	208 n. 56	19:18	164 n. 41
30:7–8	44	21:12	213
30:25	63 n. 9	22	231 n. 5
		22:13	213
2 Samuel		22:18	252
7	44, 231 n. 5	23:8	46 n. 14
7:2–3	44	23:9	46 n. 14
8:17	38	23:13	162 n. 19
15:24–25	38	23:24	162 n. 19
15:24–29	38	23:25	163 n. 29, 213
20:26	46	23:26	213
		24:3–4	213
1 Kings		24:14–16	47 n. 17
1:7–8	46	25:9	47
2:26	46	25:11	47
2:27	46 n. 13	25:12	116
2:35	46	25:18–21	47
3:8	161 n. 11		
3:10	112	**1 Chronicles**	
4:2	46	5:27–34	12
4:5	46	5:29–34	38
6:29	185	6:35–38	38
6:32	185	24:1–4	38

1 Chronicles (*continued*)
  24:2 — 38 n. 33
  24:4 — 38 n. 34

2 Chronicles
  4:1 — 57
  12:14 — 252
  14:3 — 252
  15:12 — 252
  18:7 — 252
  28:15 — 151
  36:20–21 — 48 n. 20
  36:21 — 101

Ezra
  2:36–39 — 47 n. 17
  2:40 — 47 n. 17
  2:63 — 44
  3:1–6 — 58
  3:2 — 49, 50
  3:8 — 50, 51
  3:10 — 49, 51
  7:6 — 48, 69
  7:10 — 48, 50
  7:12 — 49 n. 23
  8:15–20 — 51
  9–10 — 50
  9:1 — 50, 51
  10:5 — 51
  10:10 — 77 n. 19

Nehemiah
  2:16 — 50
  3:1 — 50
  12:44 — 51
  13:4–8 — 50
  13:23–28 — 50
  13:28–29 — 50

Job
  10:1 — 114 n. 24
  12:17 — 152
  12:19 — 152
  23:13–14 — 213
  38 — 195
  38–39 — 118, 128
  38:25–27 — 103
  39 — 131
  41 — 94 n. 8

Psalms
  1:1–3 — 97
  18:9 — 183 n. 11
  19:2 — 237
  22 — 114 n. 30
  24:1 — 132 n. 11
  26:6 — 14
  29:10 — 185
  82 — 195
  96:12 — 97
  104 — 103, 170
  104:4 — 183 n. 11
  109:13–15 — 213 n. 78
  136:12 — 164 n. 42
  137:4 — 211
  148:9 — 97
  148:10 — 94
  150:1 — 237

Proverbs
  2:1–8 — 209
  3:18 — 97
  8:22–31 — 118
  15:1 — 201
  22:6 — 209
  30:30 — 93

Ecclesiastes
  7:14 — 220
  10:10 — 200 n. 7

Isaiah
  5:1–2 — 95
  6 — 10, 70, 75, 81
  6:1 — 186 n. 22
  6:2 — 186
  6:3 — 132, 186 n. 22
  11:11 — 160 n. 5
  14 — 195
  14:12 — 250
  19:16 — 153
  20:1–6 — 150, 251

INDEX OF PRIMARY SOURCES 273

20:3	151	13:27	162 n. 19
28:7	78	14:1–6	103
28:7–10	75 n. 8	14:18	77 n. 19
37:1–4	204, 206	16:14–15	160 n. 5
37:3	206	16:18	162 n. 19
37:16	186 n. 22	17:7–8	97
37:19	164 n. 41	18:14	103
40:6	186	18:18	45, 51, 68, 71, 77 n. 19
41:17–20	103	21:5	162 n. 20
42	175	29:8	48
43:20	103	29:15	48
44:23	97	31:29	200 nn. 5 & 7, 203 n. 28
45:4	196 n. 58	32:21	164 n. 42
47	151	32:31	162 n. 20
47:3	151	32:34	162 n. 19
54:4	112	33:5	162 n. 20
54:7–8	112	33:18, 21, 22	11
55:12	97	36:7	162 n. 20
56:1–8	40	36:29	115 n. 36
57:3–10	40	39:10	116
60:13	187 n. 24	41:5	243
65:7	213 n. 78	42:18	162 n. 20
66:1	187 n. 24	44:6	162 n. 20
66:22	175	50:37	153
		51:30	153

Jeremiah

1:1	46 n. 14	**Lamentations**	
2:20	164 n. 35	1:8	152
2:21	95, 103	3:18	64
3:6	164 n. 35	3:54	64
4:1	162 n. 19	5:7	200 n. 6
4:7	184		
4:11–28	139	**Ezekiel**	
4:23–28	100	1	86, 92, 182, 183, 237, 238
4:28	103	1–5	55–56
5:6	103	1–24	99
6:17	66 n. 20	1–39	27, 242
7:20	97, 162 n. 20	1:1	61 n. 1, 63 n. 11
7:30	162 n. 19	1:1–3	49
9:9	103	1:2–3	47, 61, 84, 230
12:4	100, 103, 138	1:3	27, 34, 61 n. 1
12:8–9	103	1:4	183 n. 11
12:9	94	1:5–14	179
12:11	100, 103, 138	1:9	179
13:22	144	1:10	234
13:26	144	1:12	179

Ezekiel (continued)			
1:13	183	6	99, 100, 248
1:14	179	6:1–14	134, 136
1:17	179	6:5	100
1:18	188	6:7	136
1:19	179	6:9	113, 114
1:21	179	6:10	136
1:22–26	185	6:13	136, 164 nn. 35–36
1:23	237	6:14	99, 111, 136, 138
1:24	179	7	99, 100, 245
1:25–26	237	7:2	99, 130
1:26–28	173	7:2–4	101
1:27	183 n. 11	7:3	100
1:28	15	7:4	163 n. 30
1:28–2:5	87	7:7	100
2:1–3:11	166 n. 54	7:8	162 n. 20
2:3	217	7:9	99, 163 n. 30
2:4	166 n. 54	7:11	80
2:5	166, 217, 228	7:13	93 n. 7
2:5–6	251	7:20	80
2:6	95	7:23	130
2:7	217	7:26	27–28, 51, 68, 71, 77 n. 19, 79, 244
2:10	85	8	86
2:10–3:1	166	8–11	52 n. 28, 86, 87, 196, 249
3:6	32, 229	8:1	48, 81, 196, 231, 232
3:10–11	75	8:1–11:25	183
3:16	52	8:2	183 n. 11
3:16–21	52, 217, 230	8:3	196
3:17	237	8:6	188
3:17–21	66, 79	8:8	146
3:22–27	248	8:12	6, 64, 211
3:23	15	8:16	80
4–24	233	8:18	163 n. 30
4:2	234	9	111, 187, 254
4:4–8	85	9–10	182–90, 197, 238
4:9–17	70, 243	9:3	187, 188, 189
4:14	55, 61, 71, 81, 82, 84, 88, 244, 248	9:3–9	215
		9:5–6	216
5:1	55	9:6	187
5:5	129, 247	9:8	85, 216, 248
5:5–6	130	9:9	6, 64, 137, 188, 189
5:11	163 n. 30, 187	9:10	163 n. 30
5:13	162 n. 20	10	92, 183, 237, 238
5:15	162 n. 20	10:1	185, 189
5:16–17	92, 93, 131	10:2	183, 185
5:17	92, 94, 235	10:3	185, 189

INDEX OF PRIMARY SOURCES

10:4	187, 188	14:1	48, 81, 231, 232
10:6	185	14:6	164 n. 38, 222
10:6–7	183	14:12	100
10:7	184, 249	14:12–15	100
10:12	188	14:12–23	100, 235, 248
10:14	184, 234	14:13	100, 163 n. 34
10:15	179, 185	14:13–14	137
10:17	188	14:13–16	93
10:18–19	188	14:14	82
10:20–22	179	14:15	92, 100, 131
10:22	184	14:21	92, 94, 100, 131
11:1–13	115, 199 n. 1	14:21–23	115
11:4	232	15	95 n. 10
11:12	163 n. 31	15:4–8	139
11:13	215 n. 89, 248	15:6–8	134, 136
11:14–17	199 n. 1	15:8	163 n. 34
11:14–21	117	16	10, 81, 95, 129, 141, 146, 148, 216, 237, 250, 251
11:15	105, 106	16:2–5	132
11:16	164 n. 38, 188	16:3–4	175
11:17	105, 163 n. 32, 164 n. 38	16:4–6	145
11:19	120	16:19	164 n. 36
11:19–20	222	16:37	154, 251
11:21	105	16:37–38	250
11:22	185, 185	16:37–39	20, 141–57, 142
11:22–23	188	16:38	147 n. 26
12:2–3	251	16:40	147
12:5	146	16:44	208 n. 56
12:7	146	16:59–63	113
12:15	163 n. 32	16:61	113
12:19	132	16:62–63	113
12:19–20	137	16:63	113, 114, 115 n. 31
12:20	130, 138	17	95, 234, 245
12:21–25	199 n. 1	17:11–21	79
12:22	199 n. 4	17:13	234
12:23	164 n. 38	17:20	163 n. 34
12:26–28	199 n. 1	17:22	96
12:28	164 n. 38	17:22–24	117, 174
13	75	17:24	96
13:3–16	79	18	21, 52, 82, 111, 199–223, 239, 252
13:4	93	18:1	199
13:6	116 n. 39	18:1–4	199, 202 n. 20, 206, 207–10, 221, 253
13:7	75		
13:9	75	18:1–20	199 n. 2, 221
13:13	162 n. 20	18:1–32	199 n. 1
13:22	116 n. 39		
13:23	75		

Ezekiel (*continued*)
18:2	199, 202, 203, 208, 209, 220, 254
18:2–3	52
18:2–4	211, 213, 216, 217, 218
18:3	199
18:3–4	210
18:4	199, 213, 219, 221
18:5	162 n. 24
18:5–9	219, 220, 254
18:6–20	210
18:9	219
18:10–13	188, 219, 254
18:11	188
18:11–13	220
18:12	188
18:13	188, 219
18:14–17	219, 254
18:15–17	220
18:17	220
18:18	220
18:19	216, 220, 254
18:20	220, 221
18:21–24	221
18:21–32	220, 221
18:23	221, 222
18:24	163 n. 34
18:25	211, 216, 221
18:25–28	222
18:28	211
18:30–32	222
18:31	222
18:32	222
19	116, 234, 235, 238
19:1	85
19:3	234
19:5	116, 119
19:6	234
19:6–7	137
19:10–14	95, 245
19:12	98
19:13	131
19:14	85
20	20, 30, 66, 67, 82, 83 n. 31, 159–68, 175, 251, 254
20:1	48, 64 n. 13, 81, 231, 232, 252
20:1–44	251
20:3	165
20:4	52, 53, 66
20:5	161 n. 14, 165 n. 47, 166 n. 49
20:5–9	160, 161 n. 16
20:6	130, 161 n. 17, 165 n. 47
20:7	166
20:8	162 n. 20
20:9	115 n. 32, 165 n. 47
20:9–10	165 n. 47
20:10–32	160
20:12	16, 48 n. 20, 162 nn. 26–27, 190
20:13	48 n. 20
20:14	115 n. 32
20:16	48 n. 20
20:18	163 n. 31
20:18–20	166, 215, 253
20:20	162 n. 26
20:20–21	48 n. 20
20:21	162 n. 20
20:22	115 n. 32
20:23	252
20:24	48 n. 20
20:25	112, 252
20:27–29	215, 254
20:28	161 n. 12
20:30	254
20:31	254
20:32	64 n. 13, 97, 130
20:32–44	31 n. 9, 117, 199 n. 1
20:33–38	15
20:34–35	160
20:36	160
20:38	160
20:40	31 n. 9
20:40–41	30, 65
20:40–44	129
20:41	31 n. 9, 164 n. 36
20:42	31 n. 9
20:43	113, 114
20:44	115 n. 32
21:1–2	85
21:1–5	98 n. 15, 133–34, 247
21:2	133
21:3–4	139

INDEX OF PRIMARY SOURCES

21:4	134	27:21	234
21:5	217, 247	27:26	194
21:6–7	85	28	172, 174, 183 n. 10, 237, 238, 247, 248, 250
21:6–13	134		
21:7–8	99	28:1–10	172, 195
21:8	111, 122, 137	28:2	195
21:13–22	174	28:8	131, 132
21:27	234	28:10	32
21:36–37	139	28:11	85, 196
22	66, 75, 188	28:11–19	173, 190–97
22:1–2	85	28:12	191, 193, 194, 196
22:2	52, 53, 66	28:12–19	238
22:2–12	188	28:13	173, 174, 185, 191, 250
22:4	130	28:14	174, 191
22:5	188	28:15	173
22:6–7	188	28:15–16	194
22:6–12	219	28:16	174, 191, 193, 195
22:8	162 n. 25	28:16–19	195
22:9	188	28:17	191, 195
22:10	188	28:18	183 n. 10, 191, 195
22:12	188	28:24	95
22:15	163 n. 32	28:25	166 n. 49
22:20	162 n. 20	29	194
22:23–28	244	29:3	173
22:24–31	28	29:3–9	93
22:25	28 n. 2, 93	29:4	194
22:26	27, 28, 34 n. 22, 48 n. 20, 52, 57, 67, 68 n. 30, 70, 79, 162 n. 25, 233	29:5	131
		29:9	111
		29:12	163 n. 32
22:27	16, 93	29:16	116 n. 39
22:28	75	29:17	63 n. 11
22:31	139	30:8	139
23	10, 66, 81, 141, 148	30:12	132
23:25	162 n. 20	30:16	139
23:36	53, 66, 85	30:23	163 n. 32
23:38	162 n. 25	30:26	163 n. 32
23:39	187	31	95, 174, 245
24:2	85	31:4	173
24:15–17	138	31:6	93
24:18–24	85	31:7	96
25–48	101, 245	31:8	96
25:7	132	31:9	180
25:14	162 n. 20	31:11	234
26:19	132	31:13	93
27	194	31:15	132
27:1	85	31:18	32

Ezekiel (*continued*)

32	194	36:5	190
32:1–16	93, 191 n. 34	36:8	176
32:2	85, 194, 234	36:8–9	118
32:13	132	36:8–11	139
32:13–15	138	36:8–12	101
32:15	132	36:8–15	101 n. 20
32:18	85	36:9–11	173
32:19–32	32	36:10	176
32:25	131, 132	36:11	118, 172, 173
33–39	233	36:13–14	235
33:2–7	79	36:14	101 n. 20
33:7–20	66	36:16–21	189
33:10	64, 117, 223	36:16–38	117
33:10–20	199 n. 1	36:17	17
33:15	162 n. 24	36:19	163 n. 32
33:17	6, 211	36:21	115
33:23–29	199 n. 1	36:22	139, 164 n. 38
33:24	105, 115, 166 n. 49	36:22–32	115 n. 32
33:25	164 n. 38	36:22–38	101
33:25–26	189	36:25	81
33:27	94, 106	36:26	15, 175, 248
33:27–28	115	36:26–27	120
33:28–29	138	36:27	163 n. 31
33:30–33	83	36:27–28	15
33:32	217	36:29–30	118, 139
33:33	228	36:30	176
34	93, 94, 117, 120	36:31	113, 114
34:1–31	234	36:33	81
34:2–3	80 n. 24	36:33–36	119
34:4	79	36:33–38	117 n. 44
34:5	92	36:34–35	118, 173
34:8	92	36:34–36	102
34:17	234	36:35	103, 118, 176
34:25	92, 94, 101, 131, 245	36:36	102
34:25–27	115	36:37–38	234
34:25–29	94	36:38	176
34:25–31	115, 117, 118	37	248
34:28	93, 118	37:1–8	173
34:30	115 n. 30	37:1–12	120
35:1–9	138	37:1–14	117, 133, 175, 254
35:10	187	37:2	61, 61 n. 3
35:12	93	37:5	175
35:14–15	138	37:8	173
36	118, 120	37:11	6, 64, 115, 117
36–37	40 n. 37, 173	37:11–13	199 n. 1
		37:16	85

37:20	85	40:45	12 n. 27, 36
37:24	177, 190	40:45–46	28 n. 3, 35, 39, 244
37:25	166 n. 49, 177	40:46	11, 35 n. 23, 36, 80
37:26–28	65	40:47–49	35 n. 23
37:27	187	40:48	14
37:27–28	115 n. 30, 117	41:1–4	35 n. 23
37:28	16, 187, 190	41:2, 3	14
38:11	102 n. 21	41:3–4	56 n. 45, 81
38:12	129 n. 5	41:4	35 n. 23
38:16	190	41:8	14
38:18	162 n. 20	41:16–20	185
38:20	93	41:18	180
38:22	98	41:25	185
39:6	139	42:13	53, 80
39:12	190	42:13–14	28 n. 3, 35
39:14–16	190	42:14	13, 33, 53, 184 n. 16, 190 n. 30
39:16	119		
39:17	94, 245	42:20	13, 53
39:17–20	131	43	29, 31, 37, 229
39:25	112, 246	43:1–5	14
39:25–29	113	43:4–7	129
39:26	113	43:7	13, 53, 187
39:29	175	43:7–8	53
40–42	56	43:8	80
40–43	176	43:9	16, 188, 190
40–48	13, 16 n. 39, 18, 20 n. 41, 27, 28, 40 n. 37, 41, 53, 56, 57 n. 48, 58, 65, 78, 79, 80, 85, 86, 87 n. 44, 91, 102 n. 21, 107, 117, 121, 166, 167, 169, 176 n. 19, 177, 178, 184, 229, 237, 242, 243, 249, 252	43:10	70, 166 n. 55, 232
		43:10–12	75
		43:11	54, 58, 70 n. 35
		43:11–12	71, 78, 85, 87
		43:12	176, 177, 184, 233
		43:13–27	57
		43:18–21	243
40:1	247	43:18–24	30
40:1–37	35 n. 23	43:18–27	28, 29–31, 34, 56, 228, 229
40:2	129, 167		
40:5–16	14	43:19	29, 30
40:22	14, 184 n. 16	43:19–21	29
40:26	14	43:20	29
40:28–37	13	43:21	29
40:28–41:26	56	43:22	29
40:31	14, 184 n. 16	43:23	30, 234
40:34	184 n. 16	43:23–24	30
40:37	184 n. 16	43:24	29, 30
40:38–43	13, 35 n. 23	43:25	29, 30, 234
40:38–46	35 n. 23	43:25–27	29, 30
40:44–46	12, 35 n. 23	43:27	30

Ezekiel (*continued*)
44	33 n. 19, 34, 36, 37, 43, 57, 58, 74, 78, 86 n. 40, 87, 229, 230, 242
44–48	85
44:1–2	121
44:1–3	13, 14, 31
44:2	13
44:3	80, 177
44:4–5	87
44:4–31	28, 31–34, 228, 229
44:5	54, 71, 75, 78
44:6–8	32, 34, 53
44:6–9	31
44:6–31	31
44:6–46:18	31
44:7	54, 242
44:7–8	177
44:7–9	32
44:9	13, 32, 120
44:9–10	80
44:9–16	12, 32
44:9–27	34
44:9–31	232
44:10	36, 176
44:10–16	35, 37, 39, 229
44:10–27	62
44:11	11, 54, 77, 176
44:12	32, 57
44:12–13	176
44:13	12, 35, 176, 229, 242
44:14	12 n. 27, 54, 176, 177
44:15	39, 57
44:15–16	11, 15, 56, 57, 80
44:17	34
44:17–19	33
44:17–27	57
44:17–31	33, 40
44:18	33, 34
44:19	13, 34, 184 n. 16, 190 n. 30
44:20	55
44:20–22	34
44:22	17, 84
44:23	34, 48, 57
44:23–24	33
44:24	162 n. 25
44:25	34
44:25–26	33
44:26–27	33
44:28	33, 34, 37 n. 27, 39
44:29	34
44:30	34, 37 n. 27
44:31	34
45–46	58
45:1	37 nn. 27–28
45:1–5	176
45:1–6	167 n. 57
45:1–8	13, 28 n. 3, 37, 39, 54
45:2	37 n. 27, 54, 176
45:3	37 n. 27
45:3–4	54, 78
45:4	39 n. 35
45:5	39, 54, 78
45:6	37 n. 27
45:7	37 n. 27, 53
45:7–8	80
45:7–9	119
45:8	37 n. 27
45:8–9	16
45:9	37 n. 27
45:15	234
45:16	80
45:18–25	28 n. 3, 58, 167 n. 57
46:1–12	80
46:1–15	167 n. 57
46:1–18	177
46:2	13
46:3	13, 184 n. 16
46:9	177
46:16–18	119, 167 n. 57
46:18	16
46:19–24	28 n. 3, 37, 39
46:19–47:12	31
46:20	53, 190 n. 30
47	96, 103, 245, 247, 249
47–48	118, 246
47:1–12	96, 104, 119, 121, 130, 139, 174
47:1–48:35	13
47:9	93, 104, 249
47:10	104
47:11	104
47:13–20	167 n. 57
47:13–48:29	54, 167 n. 57
47:13–48:35	104

47:14	55, 177	**Joel**	
47:22	177, 246	3:16	171
47:22–23	119, 177		
48:1–29	119	**Jonah**	
48:6–15	28 n. 3	1:1	252
48:8–14	176	3:1	252
48:8–15	37, 40, 41		
48:9	37 n. 28	**Micah**	
48:9–14	39	2:2	119
48:10–12	37 n. 27, 54, 78, 87	3:1–4	4
48:11	176	3:11	51 n. 27, 68 n. 30
48:11–12	80	7:14–15	160 n. 5
48:12	39 n. 35		
48:13–14	54, 78, 167 n. 57	**Nahum**	
48:15	176 n. 19	2:6	191
48:17	54	3	145
48:21–22	53, 80, 177	3:5	144, 152
48:30–35	102 n. 21, 176		
48:35	27, 59, 115 n. 30, 126 n. 84, 176 n. 19	**Haggai**	
		2:11ff.	69 n. 30
Hosea		**Zechariah**	
1–3	75	3	50, 57
2	145, 146, 147, 150	3:7	50
2:12	144, 154	4:2	188
2:17	160 n. 5	4:5	188
2:20	94	4:10	188
2:20–24	118	6:1–8	188
4	77 n. 19	7	49 n. 25
4:6	51 n. 27, 68 n. 30	14:2	154
5:8	66 n. 20		
5:10	119	**Malachi**	
8:1	66 n. 20	1–2	68
8:12	68 n. 30, 233 n. 6	1:6–2:9	50
9:8	66 n. 20	1:7–10	50, 58, 67
10:12	252	2:1–9	11
14:3	65 n. 14	2:6–7	50
		2:7	68 n. 28

New Testament

Matthew		**Romans**	
6:11	125	1:18–20	250
Luke		**Revelation**	
11:3	125	1:6	121

Revelation (*continued*)

5:10	121	21:22	121
20:6	121	21:27	121 n. 64
21:8	121 n. 64	22:1–2	121
21:9–27	121	22:2	121 n. 65
		22:11	121 n. 64
		22:15	121 n. 64

OTHER ANCIENT TEXTS

Ugaritic Texts

KTU 1.2.III.1–24	193	*KTU* 1.6.I.66–67	193 n. 45
KTU 1.2.III.13	193	*KTU* 1.23	194
KTU 1.6.I	192	*KTU* 1.24	193
KTU 1.6.I.47–54	193		
KTU 1.6.I.65	195	**Talmudic Texts**	
		b. Yoma 21b	44 n. 6
		b. Yoma 86b	65 n. 14

Subject Index

Aaron 11, 12, 33 n. 19, 38, 40, 56 n. 46, 78, 161 n. 11, 165, 166 n. 52, 244
   Aaronides 11, 12
Abiathar 38, 44, 46
abomination 53, 80, 89, 161, 162, 176 n. 19, 189, 215, 221
adultery 20, 142–48, 153, 155, 250
allusion 162 n. 28, 168, 170, 171–72, 174–75, 248, 252
   intertexuality 170–73, 210, 228, 248
altar 40, 44–46, 49–50, 56–58, 64, 70, 80, 100, 134, 167, 176, 185, 229, 232, 243
   consecration of 30–31, 229
animals 17, 92–95, 98, 108, 116, 137–38, 234–35
   domesticated 19, 93–95, 100–101, 103, 234
   faces on the cherubim 184, 195
   sacrificial 29, 45, 50, 69, 78, 234
   wild 3 n. 8, 92–96, 98, 100–106, 115–16, 118 n. 31, 131, 137, 139, 234–35, 245
anthropocentrism 17, 20, 99, 103, 118, 120, 128, 135
anthropological analysis 19, 75, 76, 244
anthropomorphism 182, 186–87, 192
archetype 180–82, 191–95, 197, 249
Assyria 86 n. 42, 95–96, 98, 112 n. 19, 143, 148–50, 152–54, 156, 160, 192, 193 n. 48, 245, 251
Athtar 192–95
authority 1, 4–8, 17, 21–22, 37, 83, 92, 95–96, 106, 200, 208–10, 217–18, 228, 235, 237

divine authority 91, 97, 99, 105, 107–8

Baal 192–93
Babylon 15, 20, 47–49, 51, 63, 64–65, 92, 99, 111, 117, 134, 143, 146, 148–56, 170, 175, 182–83, 196, 211, 232, 235, 248, 250–51, 253
blood 52, 99, 129, 131, 137, 142, 145, 147 n. 26, 149, 188, 235, 250
   use in ritual 29–30, 45, 56, 58, 78, 242
boundaries and divisions 1, 9, 45, 54–56, 78 n. 21, 80, 88, 104, 119, 179, 184–85, 246
   of the tribes 55, 56, 181, 234

calendar 78, 87, 167 n. 57, 230
chaos 91, 93–94, 96, 104, 131, 137, 154, 234–35, 245
character analysis 73–74, 78, 81–82, 112, 124 n. 76, 175, 230–32, 243–44
characterization 74–76, 83–89
cherubim 1, 21, 92–93, 174, 179–97, 234, 237–38, 249–50
Chronicler 38, 47, 242
circumcision 32, 40, 48 n. 20, 88, 178, 231
city 20, 102, 121, 129–30, 139, 176 n. 19, 247
   of Jerusalem 47, 52, 74, 79, 83, 87, 130, 182–83, 188, 206, 211, 216, 238
   renamed city 27, 40, 59, 115 n. 30, 176 n. 19

283

urban viewpoint 20, 101–2, 106, 129–31, 139, 247
clothing 33, 40, 50, 53, 142, 145, 151, 184–85, 193 n. 48
  linen 33, 184–85
commissioning of Ezekiel 52–53, 87, 133, 166 n. 54, 182–83, 199, 217, 249, 253
call of Ezekiel 10, 52, 166 n. 54, 228, 237
cosmogony 56, 91, 129, 247
cosmos 10, 15, 17, 20–21, 101, 128–37, 139, 172, 175, 179–80, 184, 186–87, 196, 238, 247, 249
creation
  as a synonym for cosmos 9, 21, 91, 93, 97, 108, 117–18, 120–23, 125, 127, 135–36, 139–40, 178
  creation tradition 21, 41, 88–89, 91, 94, 96, 102–6, 117, 120, 123, 128–29, 132, 169–76, 178, 181, 183 n. 12, 185, 188, 210, 234, 237, 245, 247–49

David 38, 44, 46, 153, 175, 208 n. 56, 231 n. 5
defilement 48, 53, 55, 59, 70, 80–81, 84, 119, 152, 163–64, 176, 189, 243, 254
  contamination 61, 69–70
  impurity 9, 28, 34, 40, 58, 68, 69 n. 30, 70, 82, 115, 187–88, 190
  ritual pollution 100, 189, 249
  unclean 45, 48, 50, 52–53, 55–58, 70, 81, 94, 131, 148, 188, 190, 242–43
D(euteronomist) 21, 67 n. 24, 97, 159 n. 4, 160, 161 n. 10, 162 n. 25, 165–68, 186 n. 21, 234, 237, 251–52
Deuteronomistic History 11 n. 25, 46 n. 13, 76, 155, 210 n. 66, 213, 231, 244, 252
disputation oracle 199, 216, 218, 220–21, 223, 239
divine presence 1, 10, 12, 15, 18, 50, 55, 59, 64, 69–71, 75–76, 78, 80–81, 84, 87–89, 97, 121, 123, 129–30, 132, 161 n. 15, 171, 176, 179, 182–89, 191, 231–32, 243–44, 249

divine abandonment 80, 89, 114 n. 30, 189
drought 99, 100, 103

Earth 6, 7, 10, 19–20, 88, 97, 99, 103, 109–11, 114, 116, 120, 121 n. 62, 123–29, 171, 175, 185–88, 195–96, 235–36, 238, 245–48
ecojustice 109, 118, 127–28, 246–47
Eden 102–3, 118–120, 126, 130, 170, 173, 180, 185, 191, 236, 250
  paradise 102, 170, 172, 174, 180, 237, 249
Egypt 95, 111, 116, 138, 143, 153, 160–62, 164–66, 211, 234–35
elders 27–28, 48, 52, 64 n. 13, 78–79, 81, 84, 161, 165, 196, 200 n. 6, 216, 231–32
elite 17, 20, 73, 83, 84 n. 34, 105, 108, 121, 148
E(lohist) 13, 18, 67 n. 24, 162–64, 167, 175 n. 13
enthronement 10, 91, 108, 185, 187, 190
epistemology 21, 196–97, 238
ethics 16–17, 43, 82, 114–15, 123, 187 n. 23, 223, 244
  morality 5, 16, 43 n. 2, 74, 79, 82–83, 86, 89, 95, 97–98, 101, 112 n. 17, 121 n. 62, 123, 141, 146, 159 n. 2, 163 n. 29, 194–95, 219, 244, 254
exile 15, 18, 21, 27, 32–33, 37–41, 43–49, 51–52, 56–59, 62–65, 67, 70–71, 73, 80–83, 87–89, 91–92, 102–3, 105–8, 115–20, 130–31, 146, 148–49, 152, 154–57, 160, 164 n. 45, 167–68, 182, 189, 196 n. 57, 199, 229–30, 232, 234, 237, 242–43, 245–46, 250–54
exiles 9, 19, 48–49, 58, 65, 70, 73 n. 4, 99, 105–8, 115–17, 119–20, 130, 157, 199, 209, 211, 215–16, 221–23, 228, 235–36, 243–46, 253
exodus 117, 160, 164–66, 168, 251

fall of Jerusalem 9, 18, 20, 27–28, 37, 47, 64, 69, 74, 83, 87, 99, 106, 111, 120,

132–33, 134, 136–67, 155, 166, 183, 200 n. 5, 215, 235, 243–44, 254
famine   92–93, 100, 131, 137, 139, 235
feminist criticism   3, 141, 143, 152, 155, 236, 247
fire   92–93, 98 n. 15, 131, 133–36, 139, 183–85, 190–91, 193–95, 238, 247, 249
first deportation   47, 63–64, 65, 73, 75 n. 11, 211
foreigners   10, 13, 21, 32, 36, 47, 51, 53–54, 93–96, 103, 111, 119–21, 143, 153, 162 n. 22, 177–78, 196, 211, 235, 242, 246
   resident aliens   119, 177–78, 246
fullness   132, 137–38, 247

garden   96, 102, 172, 174, 178, 180
genealogy   18, 36, 38–39, 242
geography   54–55, 88
glory/kabod   12 n. 30, 13, 78, 87, 96–97, 129, 132, 182–83, 185–90, 195, 238
God   3, 5, 9, 11, 13, 21, 34, 41, 44–45, 49–52, 55, 58–59, 67–68, 74–81, 83, 89, 94, 96, 101–3, 105, 107, 109–24, 126, 128–30, 132–34, 135–38, 140, 143–45, 147, 154–57, 160, 163, 165–67, 171, 173–75, 179–81, 183, 185–93, 195–97, 200, 204, 209–23, 231–33, 235–36, 238, 244–49, 251, 253–54
   gods 48, 91, 157, 166 n. 50, 181, 195, 238
   Yahweh   45, 48, 52, 58–59, 83, 111–12, 147, 160–67, 189, 251
grace   31 n. 9, 59, 233, 236–37

hierarchy   1–23, 79–80, 109–10, 116, 124–25, 139, 141, 157, 177–79, 182, 184, 186, 190, 196–97, 210, 228, 235–36, 237–39, 242, 244, 247–50
   cosmic   56, 133, 169, 190, 249. 254
   dominator   109–10, 114, 116, 245
   human/social   7, 33, 35, 39–81, 83–85, 87–88, 92, 141, 149, 169, 231–32
   moral   74, 82–83, 128, 136

   spatial   41, 56, 81, 176–77, 178
holiness   1, 12–16, 21, 33, 35, 53, 57, 76 n. 14, 165, 176, 178, 182, 184, 186–90, 197, 238, 249
Holiness Code   11–13, 15–16, 84, 186 n. 20, 187–90, 249, 254
holy 1, 12–14, 18, 37, 45, 53–59, 69–70, 87, 130, 132, 139, 162 n. 21, 165, 176, 180–90, 223, 229, 238, 242, 249
honor   58, 96, 103, 113 n. 23, 115, 122, 127–28, 132, 150, 152, 189, 235

idealization 15–20, 27, 38, 40, 74, 79, 83, 104, 118, 130, 167, 177, 184, 197, 223, 230–31, 245
identity   18, 32, 73 n. 4, 121 n. 64, 149–50
ideology   14–16, 22, 74, 84, 89, 92, 99–100, 102, 104–8, 136, 149, 153, 155, 157, 167–68, 230–31
idolatry   43, 57, 97, 100, 108, 111, 134, 135, 162–66, 214, 252
imperialism   20, 48, 143, 148–49, 153, 155–57, 211, 236, 250–51

Jeremiah   19, 81 n. 27, 101, 103, 122 n. 66, 136, 141, 143, 155, 157, 164 n. 37, 244, 252
Josiah   46 n. 14, 64, 213, 231 n. 5
Judah   18, 40, 44, 47, 49, 79–80, 91, 98, 114, 116, 134, 147, 151, 172, 182, 188, 200, 211, 213, 215, 234
judges   34, 45, 52, 53, 78, 152
   Ezekiel as judge   53, 66, 85, 161, 164, 242
   God as judge   15, 52, 100, 222

king   46, 51, 53, 79–81, 96, 177, 191 n. 34
   God as king   19, 53, 91, 95–97, 172, 185, 195, 215, 234–35
   prince   28, 37 n. 27, 53, 55, 57, 79, 117, 177
   Tyre's king   172, 190–91, 193–97, 238–39, 250
knowledge, priestly   50, 66, 68, 84, 107, 232

instruction   28–31, 33–34, 44–45, 48, 50–51, 55, 58, 62–63, 65, 67–71, 77–79, 85, 88, 121, 167, 230, 232–33

lamentations   85, 88, 116, 138, 195, 203 n. 26, 217
land   10, 13, 19, 37, 39 n. 35, 41, 48, 50, 53–55, 58, 78, 80–81, 83, 87, 89, 92–109, 111, 114–21, 129–39, 147–48, 160–68, 176–77, 184, 188–90, 194, 196, 234–37, 245–48
　　barren   17, 19–20, 37 n. 27, 94, 101, 103, 104, 106, 131–32, 138–39, 245
　　settled   10, 19–20, 93–95, 101–2, 130–32, 135, 137, 139, 245
law (ordinances, statutes)   3, 44, 48, 50–52, 65–69, 71, 79, 97, 112, 147, 162–63, 165–68, 176, 196, 210, 213, 215, 219, 221–22, 232–33, 252–54
　　Ezekiel's law code   63 n. 9, 81, 87, 219 n. 97, 252
　　Mosaic law   45, 48–49, 67 n. 24, 68, 147, 213
legal traditions   21, 30, 66, 68 n. 30, 79, 145, 166, 219, 230
Levi   11, 36, 39, 44, 50
Levites   11–13, 18, 28, 32, 33 n. 19, 36–40, 43, 46–47, 49–51, 54, 57–58, 62, 78–80, 85–87, 176–77, 229–30, 233, 242
literary analysis   10, 15, 28–29, 74 n. 7, 82, 85, 97, 106–7, 123, 145, 156, 170–72, 178, 203, 205, 217, 228, 230, 241, 248, 254

marriage   57, 78, 113, 143, 149, 193
　　intermarriage   50, 51, 58 n. 51
mediation (intermediary)   18, 21, 33–35, 41, 43–44, 48, 67, 75–76, 78, 82–83, 88–89, 120, 166, 182, 184, 229, 231, 243–44, 254
Mercurius   181–84, 191–93, 195, 238, 249

metaphor   2, 66, 92–94, 96, 98–99, 101, 113, 116, 118 n. 51, 133 n. 12, 134, 141, 143, 147, 150, 154–57, 189, 194, 201–3, 206, 208, 217, 235, 250–51, 253
metonymy   97, 100–101, 134–35, 246, 248
Moses   21, 31, 34–36, 45, 48–49, 56 n. 46, 63, 67 n. 24, 68–69, 81, 84, 161–62, 164–68, 186, 213, 229, 233 n. 6, 244
mountains   31 n. 9, 96–97, 99–100, 103, 108, 118, 129, 131–32, 134–36, 138–39, 165, 167, 180, 185, 191, 219, 245, 247–49

narrator   73–74, 83, 92, 102, 105, 108, 235, 243, 245
new heart   21, 117, 119, 120, 163 n. 29, 175, 177, 222, 248, 254

offerings and sacrifices   11, 15, 28–31, 34–37, 39, 41, 44–47, 49–50, 52–54, 56–59, 64–65, 67–69, 76–78, 80–81, 87–89, 94, 104 n. 25, 131, 164, 167, 185, 188, 193 n. 49, 212, 229–30, 234, 242–43, 249
oracles   18, 44, 46 n. 13, 52, 66, 75–77, 78 n. 20, 79, 86 n. 40, 87, 122 n. 69, 196, 209, 212, 215, 217, 238–39, 248, 253
　　of condemnation   15, 20, 27, 31–32, 43, 63, 66, 74, 75 n. 10, 77, 80, 82, 85, 86, 100, 105–6, 115–16, 127, 133–36, 138–39, 142, 147, 160, 172, 175, 182–84, 189–90, 195, 196, 199, 207–8, 210, 218, 222–23, 236–38, 244, 246–49
　　of restoration   13, 15, 18, 21–21, 30, 40 n. 37, 49–50, 53–54, 58, 62, 64–65, 67–68, 70, 73–74, 77, 79–83, 87–89, 96, 101–3, 107, 114–22, 126, 130, 160, 167, 169, 176–78, 184, 219, 223, 229–30, 238, 245–46, 249

Pentateuch   11, 14, 20–21, 69, 160–163, 168, 174, 186–87, 252
people of the land   28, 116, 177, 246
Persia   49, 156, 183
personification   97–98, 100, 105, 145, 151
pestilence   92–93, 115, 131, 139
plants   92, 95–98, 101, 104, 234, 238, 245
postexilic period   31 n. 9, 32–34, 40, 50–51, 58, 62, 65, 69, 83, 229–30, 233, 242, 246, 252
preexilic period   14, 36, 38–39, 43, 50, 53–54, 63, 65, 68–70, 74, 86, 119, 168, 176, 251
priests   6, 18–19, 27–41, 43–59, 61–71, 73–81, 83–89, 92, 94, 105, 116, 121, 152, 166–68, 170, 174, 176–78, 185–87, 190, 199, 215–16
priestly ranks   11–12, 35–39, 43, 46–47, 56–57
P(riestly Writer)   11–15, 18, 21, 33, 44 n. 4, 46, 62–63, 67 n. 24, 68 n. 30, 69, 71, 84, 159 n. 4, 160–68, 170–74, 178, 186–87, 189, 234, 237, 242, 249, 251–52
profane/unholy/common   13, 18, 28, 33–34, 39–41, 45, 53–55, 57–58
propaganda   14–15, 18, 40, 54, 58
prophet   10, 18–22, 27–28, 32, 40, 44–45, 48–49, 52–53, 55–56, 59, 61–63, 65–67, 71, 73, 75–81, 83–84, 87, 89, 92, 95, 97, 103, 110–11, 116–18, 122, 124, 129, 135, 137–38, 142, 146, 148, 151, 155, 159–61, 165–68, 172, 175, 182–83, 185–86, 191, 196–97, 199, 206, 209–10, 215–18, 222, 227–28, 231–33, 236, 238, 241, 243–44, 246–48, 251–54
prophecy   15, 17–18, 20, 44, 63, 66–67, 74–76, 83, 89, 111, 115–17, 119, 121–24, 159 n. 2, 188, 190, 196, 233, 237, 245, 250
proverbs   21–22, 199–223, 239, 252–54
purity   17, 55–56, 68–70, 78–79, 81, 83–84, 86–87, 94, 131, 187 n. 37, 190, 230, 244
purification   29–30, 33, 36, 48 n. 19, 49, 58–59, 70, 81, 85 n. 37, 119, 188

quaternity   180–82, 194, 249

rape   143, 147–50, 152, 154, 250
rebellion   9, 15, 32, 34, 87, 95, 97–98, 105, 162–65, 195, 237, 251
recognition formula   135–36, 236, 248
returnees   15, 44, 106–8, 115, 160 n. 5, 176
revelatory nature of text   7, 17, 196–97
   prophetic revelation   75, 83, 166, 183, 194, 196, 229, 232–33
rhetorical analysis   10 n. 23, 17, 19–21, 23, 35, 66, 76, 85–86, 105, 116 n. 38, 129, 147, 149, 157, 172, 175–76, 201, 219, 222, 238, 247, 252–53
righteousness   16, 52, 82–83, 89, 111, 137, 146, 213–14, 219–23, 254
ritual/cult   13, 15, 17, 19, 28–35, 37, 39–40, 56, 58, 62, 64–65, 67–68, 76–81, 84–89, 91, 94, 97, 115, 167, 170, 174, 176–78, 186 n. 29, 219, 230–33, 243–44, 154

Sabbath   28, 40, 48 n. 20, 67–68, 88, 162–63, 231
sacred   1, 14–15, 20, 28, 33–34, 40–41, 45, 53–55, 69, 76, 80, 119, 129–30, 132, 139, 165, 166 n. 53, 167, 176, 180–82, 185, 187, 189–91, 249, 254
   sanctification   12 n. 30, 14, 15, 21, 53–54, 57, 67–69, 94, 162, 190
scribes   20–21, 49 n. 23, 61 n. 1, 75, 122 n. 66
servants   18, 35–37, 39 n. 36, 43, 46, 47 n. 17, 54, 77, 88, 96, 98, 185, 231
shame   19, 58, 70, 112–16, 122, 150–54, 156–57, 237, 246
sin   18, 35, 58–59, 67, 70, 75, 79–80, 82–83, 85–87, 99–100, 112, 117, 136–37, 147, 155, 160, 164–65, 172,

185, 188, 194, 200, 207, 209, 212–16, 218–23, 235 238, 244–45, 254
son of man   76, 84, 89, 161, 163
space   19, 34, 54–55, 85, 100, 127, 176, 178, 237
   sacred space   55–56, 76, 80, 249
status   2, 4, 12 n. 27, 18–20, 27, 28 n. 2, 32, 35–39, 43, 47–48, 56, 76, 79–84, 86–89, 92, 96, 101–2, 105–8, 121, 150, 168, 177–78, 193, 207–8, 231–32
stripping as punishment 20, 142, 144–55, 176, 237, 250–51
   nakedness 142, 145–46, 148, 150–52
symbolism   21, 66, 80, 83–84, 91–93, 95–97, 99, 102, 108, 119, 129, 134, 138, 150, 153–54, 176, 179–82, 184–85, 187, 189–90, 205, 234–36, 238, 245

tabernacle   12–14, 38, 45, 56 n. 46, 166–67
temple 11–16, 18–19, 27, 29, 34–35, 37, 44–59, 62–64, 67, 69–71, 74, 77–81, 83–84, 86–89, 94, 96–97, 103–5, 108, 116, 119, 121, 130, 166–68, 170, 172, 176–80, 182–90, 194, 211, 213, 229–33, 235–36, 238, 242–43, 246, 249, 252
   courts 11–14, 53, 56–58, 80, 86, 121
   entrances and exits   14, 54, 58, 70 n. 35, 78, 179 n. 1, 184 n. 16
   gates   13–14, 53, 58, 121, 176, 184 n. 16
   holy of holies   36, 57 n. 48, 81, 184 n. 16, 187, 230, 244
   sanctuary   11, 13–14, 18, 29, 33, 37 n. 27, 39–40, 45–47, 53, 57–58, 64, 77, 117, 120, 129, 132, 176, 178, 185, 187–89, 232, 242, 249
throne, divine   121, 179, 182–86, 189, 190, 238, 249
torah 11–12, 20–23, 31 n. 12, 33–34, 45, 48, 49 n. 25, 50–52, 58, 65–70, 78, 88, 159–60, 167–68, 176–78, 186, 230, 232–34, 247, 242–44, 249–52
trees   95–98, 101, 103–5, 107–8, 119, 121, 130, 133–34, 164, 174, 180, 182–85, 192, 245, 247, 249
   cosmic tree   174, 180, 182–83
   forest   98 n. 15, 133–36, 247–48

uncircumcised   13, 53–54, 119, 177, 229
Urim and Thummim   44, 65, 231–32, 244

victim   100–101, 103, 137–40, 149–50, 209–10, 235, 246, 251
vine   95–96, 98, 106, 134, 234, 245
vision report   10, 15, 18, 21, 28, 50, 53–54, 57–58, 62–63, 71, 74, 77–81, 83–84, 86–88, 91, 96, 102, 104, 115, 118–21, 132, 160, 166–67, 175, 177–78, 182–83, 190, 223, 228, 230–31, 242, 247, 249, 254
voice   20, 22, 84, 106, 110, 125, 128, 133, 137–38, 140, 236, 245, 247–48

watchman/sentinel   40, 52, 56 n. 44, 66, 79, 230
weather   92, 98, 245
wife
   city as God's wife   10, 113, 143, 156
   of Ezekiel   84–85, 138
wilderness   38 n. 33, 92–93, 102–3, 111, 119 n. 48, 131–32, 160, 162–64, 166, 215, 251, 253
wildness 17, 19, 98, 102–8, 131–32, 234, 238

Yahwist (J)   67 n. 24, 161 n. 18, 163 n. 33, 164 n. 37, 174, 196 n. 58, 237, 249, 252

Zadok   11–12, 33 n. 19, 38–40, 46
Zadokites   1, 10, 12, 15, 17–18, 35–37, 39 n. 35, 43, 46–47, 54, 56–58, 62, 74, 78–79, 84 n. 34, 85–97, 89, 176, 177, 230–32, 242

www.ingramcontent.com/pod-product-compliance
Lightning Source LLC
Chambersburg PA
CBHW020057020526
44112CB00031B/209